LINGUISTIC THEORIES IN DANTE
AND THE HUMANISTS

BRILL'S STUDIES IN INTELLECTUAL HISTORY

VOLUME 38

to my father and in memory of my mother

TABLE OF CONTENTS

ACKNOWLEDGMENTS

This book has been several years in the making, so there were few who shared in its unfolding. I am deeply grateful to my colleague Eugene Hill for his wise counsel and intellectual support from the earliest phases through the completion of this study and to John Monfasani for reading the whole manuscript and for offering very valuable suggestions. I have benefited from discussions with Paul Kristeller, who kept me abreast of relevant literature and generously supplied needed texts. Philippa and George Goold helped to unravel some of the more intricate passages by the humanists. I would like to thank Joan Ferrante, President of the Dante Society of America, and the Society's Council for inviting me to present a segment of the part on Dante to the 1989 Annual Meeting of the Dante Society of America and to Gian Carlo Alessio for asking me to share some of the ideas on the humanists with his students and colleagues at the University of Venice. My appreciation goes also to the Trustees of Mount Holyoke College for their generous support of the project. My deepest graditude is reserved for my wife, Elizabeth, without whose affection and meticulous reading and preparation of the manuscript this book would not have been possible.

BIBLIOGRAPHICAL NOTE

The documentation relating to the Florentine debate of 1435: Biondo's *De Verbis Romanae Locutionis*, Bruni's letter to Biondo, Guarino's *De Lingue Latine Differentiis*, Poggio's *Disceptatio Convivalis III*, Filelfo's letters to Francesco Sforza and Lorenzo de' Medici and Alberti's proem to the third book of the *Famiglia* have been elegantly edited and published by Mirko Tavoni in his recent study, *Latino, grammatica, volgare. Studio di una questione umanistica* (Padua: Antenore, 1984). All of these documents, except for Poggio's and Filelfo's, enjoy modern, revised editions (see Tavoni, pp. 302-304). For this study I have used the documents in Tavoni's edition. Bruni's letter to Biondo, which in Tavoni is entered as *Leonardus Flavio Foroliviensi S.*, is referred to here by its better-known title, Epistola VI, 10, derived from Lorenzo Mehus, who first edited Bruni's letters (*Leonardi Bruni Arretini Epistolarum Libri VIII* [Florence, 1741]).

For the classical works, including Augustine's *De Civitate Dei*, I have used the texts published by the Loeb Classical Library. Alessandro Wesselofsky's *Il Paradiso degli Alberti. Ritrovi e ragionamenti del 1389. Romanzo di Giovanni da Prato* (Bologna, 1867) constitutes an important source of Chapter 7. This work consists of three volumes with the first volume being divided into two parts. Volume I encompasses a lengthy introduction and numerous documents, including invectives by Cino Rinuccini and Domenico da Prato. Volumes II and III deal specifically with the *Paradiso degli Alberti*. These volumes will be referred to as Wesselofsky I/1, I/2, II, and III.

ABBREVIATIONS

Antidotum	Lorenzo Valla, *Antidotum Primum*, ed. A. Wesseling (Amsterdam: Van Gorcum, 1978).
Apologus II	Lorenzo Valla, *Apologus II* in Tavoni, pp. 260-273.
Baron, *Crisis*	Hans Baron, *The Crisis of The Early Italian Renaissance* (Princeton: Princeton U. Press, 1966).
Camporeale, *Valla*	Salvatore I. Camporeale, *Lorenzo Valla. Umanesimo e teologia* (Florence, 1972).
Capitolo	*Capitolo di Nicholò di Francescho Luna della amiciçia* in Gorni, Appendix II/2, pp. 174-178.
Comento	Lorenzo de' Medici, *Comento ad alcuni sonetti d'amore* in *Scritti scelti di Lorenzo de' Medici*, ed. Emilio Bigi (Turin: UTET, 1965), pp. 295-449.
Convivio	Dante, *Convivio*, ed. G. Busnelli and G. Vandelli, 2nd ed., ed. A. E. Quaglio, 2 vols. (Florence: Le Monnier, 1964).
Corti	Maria Corti, *Dante a un nuovo crocevia* (Florence, 1981).
Dardano, "Alberti"	Maurizio Dardano, "L. B. Alberti nella storia della lingua italiana," in *Atti del convegno internazionale indetto nel V centenario di Leon Battista Alberti*, Accademia Nazionale dei Lincei, Quaderno 209 (Rome, 1974), pp. 263-265.
DC III	Poggio Bracciolini, *Tertiae Convivalis Historiae Disceptatio* in Tavoni, pp. 239-259.
Decades	Biondo Flavio, *Historiarum ab Inclinatione Romanorum Decades* (Basle: Froben, 1531).
Dialogus	Leonardo Bruni, *Ad Petrum Paulum Histrum Dialogus* in *Prosatori latini*, pp. 44-99.
Di Capua	Francesco Di Capua, "Insegnamenti retorici medievali e dottrine estetiche moderne nel *De Vulgari Eloquentia* di Dante," in his *Scritti minori* (Rome, 1959), II, 279-288.
DLLD	Guarino Veronese, *De Lingue Latine Differentiis* in Tavoni, pp. 228-238.
Dragonetti	Roger Dragonetti, *Aux frontières du langage poétique*. Romanica Gandensia, 9 (Ghent, 1961).
DVE	Dante, *De Vulgari Eloquentia*, in *Opere minori*, ed. Pier Vincenzo Mengaldo (Milan-Naples: Ricciardi, 1979), II, 3-240.

DVRL	Biondo Flavio, *De Verbis Romanae Locutionis* in Tavoni, pp. 197-215.
ED	*Enciclopedia dantesca*, 6 vols. (Rome, 1970-1978).
EGV	Remigio Sabbadini, *Epistolario di Guarino Veronese*, 3 vols.(Venice, 1915-1919).
Elegantiae	Lorenzo Valla, *Elegantiarum Libri* in *Prosatori latini*, pp. 594-631.
Epistola VI, 10	Leonardo Bruni, *Leonardus Flavio Foroliviensi S.* in Tavoni, pp. 216-221.
Etymologiae	*Isidori Hispalensis Episcopi Etymologiarum sive Originum Libri XX*, ed. W. M. Lindsay (Oxford: Clarendon Press, 1911).
Faithfull	R. Glynn Faithfull, "The Concept of 'Living Language' in Cinquecento Vernacular Philology," *The Modern Language Review*, 48 (1953), 278-292.
Favati	Guido Favati, "Osservazioni sul *De Vulgari Eloquentia*," *Annali della Facoltà di Lettere e Magistero dell'Università di Cagliari*, 29 (1966), 151-211.
FPLM	Francesco Filelfo, *Franciscus Philelphus Laurentio Medici S.P.D.* in Tavoni, pp. 281-296.
FPSS	Francesco Filelfo, *Franciscus Philelfus Sfortiae Secundo Sal.* in Tavoni, pp. 274-280.
Fubini, "La coscienza"	Riccardo Fubini, "La coscienza del latino negli umanistsi," *Studi medievali* 2 (1961), 505-550.
Gorni	Guglielmo Gorni, "Storia del Certame Coronario," *Rinascimento*, 12 (1972), 135-181.
Inferno	Dante, *Inferno*, ed. Giorgio Petrocchi (Milan: Mondadori, 1966).
Invettiva (Domenico)	Domenico da Prato, *Invettiva* in Wesselofsky, I/2, 321-330.
Invettiva (Rinuccini)	Cino Rinuccini, *Invettiva* in Wesselofsky, I/2, 303-316.
Italia Illustrata	Biondo Flavio, *Italia Illustrata* (Basle: Froben, 1531).
Marigo	Dante Alighieri, *De Vulgari Eloquentia. Ridotto a miglior lezione, commentato e tradotto da Aristide Marigo*, ed. Pier Giorgio Ricci, rpt. of 3rd ed. (Florence: Le Monnier, 1968).
Mancini, *Alberti*	Girolamo Mancini, *Vita di L. B. Alberti* (Florence, 1911).
Mazzocco, "Decline"	Angelo Mazzocco, "Decline and Rebirth in Bruni and Biondo," in *Umanesimo a Roma nel Quattrocento*, ed. Paolo Brezzi and Maristella de Panizza Lorch (Rome: Istituto di Studi Romani, 1984), pp. 249-266.
Mengaldo	Pier Vincenzo Mengaldo, "Introduzione e note," in *DVE*.
Mengaldo, *Linguistica*	Pier Vincenzo Mengaldo, *Linguistica e retorica di Dante* (Pisa: Nistri-Lischi, 1978).

Monarchia	Dante, *Monarchia*, in *Opere minori*, ed. Bruno Nardi (Milan-Naples: Ricciardi, 1979), II, 241-503.
Nardi, "Il linguaggio"	Bruno Nardi, "Il linguaggio," in his *Dante e la cultura medievale. Nuovi saggi di filosofia dantesca* (Bari: Laterza, 1949), pp.148-175.
Nogara	Bartolomeo Nogara, *Scritti inediti e rari di Biondo Flavio con introduzione* (Rome, 1927).
Opere volgari	Leon Battista Alberti, *Opere volgari,* ed. Cecil Grayson, 3 vols. (Bari: Laterza, 1960-1973).
Orazione	Cristoforo Landino, *Orazione fatta quando . . . cominciò a leggere i sonetti di Messere Francesco Petrarca in istudio* in *Scritti critici e teorici,* ed. Roberto Cardini (Rome: Bulzoni, 1974), I, 33-40.
Pagliaro	Antonino Pagliaro, "La dottrina linguistica di Dante," *Quaderni di Roma,* 1 (1947), 485-501. Rpt. in his *Nuovi saggi di critica semantica* (Messina-Florence, 1956).
Panvini	Bruno Panvini, "Introduzione" in Dante, *De Vulgari Eloquentia,* ed. B. Panvini (Palermo: Andò, 1968).
Paradiso	Dante, *Paradiso*, ed. Giorgio Petrocchi (Milan: Mondadori, 1967).
Paratore	Ettore Paratore, "Il latino di Dante" in his *Tradizione e struttura in Dante* (Florence: Sansoni, 1968), pp. 136-153.
Politia	Angelo Decembrio, *Politia Literaria* in Tavoni, pp. 226-227.
Proemio	Leon Battista Alberti, Proemio al libro III della *Famiglia* in Tavoni, pp. 222-227.
Prosatori latini	*Prosatori latini del Quattrocento,* ed. Eugenio Garin (Milan-Naples: Ricciardi, 1952).
Protesta	*Protesta* in Gorni, Appendix I, pp. 167-172.
Purgatorio	Dante, *Purgatorio,* ed. Giorgio Petrocchi (Milan: Mondadori, 1967).
Roma Instaurata	Biondo Flavio, *Roma Instaurata* (Basle: Froben, 1531).
Roma Triumphans	Biondo Flavio, *Roma Triumphans* (Basle: Froben, 1531).
Rossi, *Il Quattrocento*	Vittorio Rossi, *Il Quattrocento,* ed. A. Vallone, 9th ed. (Milan: Vallardi, 1973).
Rotta	Paolo Rotta, *La filosofia del linguaggio nella patristica e nella scolastica* (Turin: Fratelli Bocca, 1909).
Solerti	Angelo Solerti, ed., *Le vite di Dante, Petrarca e Boccaccio* (Milan: Vallardi, 1904).
Tavoni	Mirko Tavoni, *Latino, grammatica, volgare. Storia di una questione umanistica* (Padua: Antenore, 1984).
Terracini	Benvenuto Terracini, "Natura ed origine del linguaggio umano nel *De Vulgari Eloquentia*," in his *Pagine e appunti di linguistica storica* (Florence, 1957), pp. 237-246.

Trabalza, *Storia*   Ciro Trabalza, *Storia della grammatica italiana* (Milan: Hoepli, 1908).

Vinay   Gustavo Vinay, "Ricerche sul *De Vulgari Eloquentia*," *Giornale storico della letteratura italiana*, 136 (1959), 236-274 and 367-388.

Vita   Cristoforo Landino, *Vita e costumi di Dante* in *Scritti critici e teorici*, ed. Roberto Cardini (Rome: Bulzoni, 1974), I, 130-140.

Vita di Boccaccio   Leonardo Bruni, *Vita di Boccaccio* in Solerti.

Vita di Dante   Leonardo Bruni, *Vita di Dante* in Solerti.

Vita Nuova   Dante, *Vita Nuova*, ed. Fredi Chiappelli (Milan: Mursia, 1965-1987).

Vitale, *La questione*   Maurizio Vitale, *La question della lingua* (Palermo: Palumbo, 1962).

Wesseling,   Wesseling, "Introduzione" in *Antidotum*.

Wesselofsky I/1, I/2   Alessandro Wesselofsky, ed. *Il Paradiso degli Alberti.*
II, III   *Ritrovi e ragionamenti del 1389. Romanzo di Giovanni da Prato*, 3 vols. (Bologna, 1867).

LINGUISTIC THEORIES IN DANTE
AND THE HUMANISTS

STUDIES OF LANGUAGE AND INTELLECTUAL HISTORY
IN LATE MEDIEVAL AND EARLY RENAISSANCE ITALY

INTRODUCTION

Perhaps no other subject excited the intellectual circles of late medieval and early Renaissance Italy more than that of language. The issue of language, be it the Latin of antiquity or the vernacular of modern Italy, prompted numerous questions. Was Latin an artificial or a natural language? What was the nature of Latin in antiquity? Was the vernacular a derivative of Latin or an ancient language that had coexisted with Latin? Was the vernacular as effective a linguistic medium as Latin? Should one write in Latin or in the vernacular? Much of the polemic on Latin and the vernacular was wrought with political motives and bore the imprint of one's philosophical beliefs and philological orientation. More often than not, the discussion on language led to the practical matter of stylistic and linguistic propriety. Should the modern writer make use of a Latin that subscribed to the rhetorical and syntactical tenets of Cicero or should he rely on a more up-to-date Latin, a Latin that took into consideration the historical reality of contemporary Italy? As to the vernacular, how could one transform this inherently effectual idiom into a linguistic medium that equalled the efficacy of Latin?

The single most important figure to treat the issue of language in late medieval Italy was Dante Alighieri. A shrewd observer of languages, Dante was the first to recognize the utilitarian value and the potential of the vernacular. Latin, he argued, was no longer a viable language in contemporary Italy, for knowledge of Latin was limited entirely to the literati. Those writers, therefore, who wished to communicate with the whole citizenry needed to make use of the vernacular. Moreover, the vernacular had the potential to approximate the linguistic effectiveness and sophistication of Latin. Thus Dante proposes the creation of an elite vernacular, which he characterizes as illustrious. This illustrious vernacular (*vulgare illustre*) would result from an amalgamation of primal terms (the terms it enjoyed in its first developmental stage) and classical rhetorical tenets. Dante's consideration of the interaction

of Latin and the vernacular causes him to examine the origin of
these idioms. The vernacular, according to Dante, is a natural language that is traceable to Babylonian time, whereas Latin is an artificial, secondary language that came into being to remedy the
linguistic confusion brought about by the construction of the
Tower of Babel.

The medieval/Dantean argument on language with its implicit
acknowledgment of a classical bilingualism and its faith in the efficacy of the vernacular stimulated and defined the discussion on
language in early Renaissance Italy. Dante's ideas played an important role in a momentous debate that took place in Florence in
March 1435.[1] Being influenced by Dante, Leonardo Bruni, one of
the participants of this debate, argued that classical Rome possessed two modes of speaking—a literary (=Latin) and a vernacular—and that the vernacular speech was passed on to later ages.
Though inferior to the literary language, the vernacular speech
was nevertheless a viable idiom, for, as demonstrated by Dante, this
speech had the potential of being an effective linguistic medium.

Bruni's assessment of the linguistic state of antiquity was challenged by Biondo Flavio. Ancient Rome, Biondo contended, possessed only one mode of speaking, though the language of antiquity varied in tone and sophistication according to one's social
milieu and level of literary training. As to the vernacular, its origin
was to be traced to the barbaric invasions. Indeed, the vernacular
was a bastard language that had resulted from the fusion of Latin
and Gothic-Vandal usages.

In subsequent writings, Bruni and Biondo went on to refine
their views of the vernacular. In a manner reminiscent of Dante,
but without the Dantean confidence, Bruni argued that the vernacular had the right to coexist with Latin as a literary language.
Likewise, Biondo reaffirmed his earlier theory about the origin of
the vernacular, noting, however, that the disruption of Latin and
the eventual emergence of the vernacular was due not so much to
the Visigoths (as he had assumed during the Florentine debate),
but to the Lombards. Unlike Bruni, Biondo made no case for the
vernacular. Instead he opted for the use of Latin, but of a Latin
that was free of the straitjacket of Ciceronian rhetoric and more
attuned to the needs of the new historical reality.

The views Bruni and Biondo expressed during the Florentine debate fueled much discussion throughout the Quattrocento, being debated by Guarino Guarini, Poggio Bracciolini, and Francesco Filelfo, all of whom sided with Biondo. These same views even served as stimulus for one of Lorenzo Valla's treatises (*Apologus II*). Valla, however, being more concerned in this treatise with vilifying Poggio than with reconstructing the nature of ancient speech, produced an account of the linguistic state of antiquity that is on the whole sophistic and irrelevant to the issues that informed the Florentine debate and its subsequent discussions.

By far a greater contributor to the polemic generated by the Florentine debate was Leon Battista Alberti, who synthesized the theories of Dante, Bruni and Biondo and projected issues that were to flourish in the second half of the fifteenth century. He concurred with Biondo that ancient Rome was monolingual and that the vernacular came into being with the barbaric invasions, but he also espoused Dante and Bruni's faith in the capacity of the vernacular. Use of the vernacular, argued Alberti on the strength of Dante, made it possible to communicate with the whole citizenry. Moreover, the vernacular had great merit if used effectively. However, as proved by the Latin of ancient Rome, for the vernacular to become a sophisticated linguistic medium, it needed to be used continuously and effectively by the contemporary literati.

Alberti's justification of the use of the vernacular was appropriated by Cristoforo Landino and Lorenzo de' Medici. The latter two, however, injected their argument with a strong dose of patriotism. According to them, the Florentine vernacular was the only one worthy of becoming a literary language. They thus longed for the day when this idiom would emerge as the undisputed literary language of Italy. This feat, Lorenzo mused, could be facilitated by the expansion of the Florentine state. Alberti, Landino, and Lorenzo's argument on behalf of the vernacular set in motion an intense debate on the Italian language (*questione della lingua*) that was to endure for all of the sixteenth century and beyond.

Dante and the humanists' views of language have received much attention from contemporary scholarship. In assessing the linguistic theories of Dante, contemporary scholars have been conditioned by medieval or modern modes of inquiry. Thus, Dante is either an empiricist or an abstractionist, a nominalist or an historical linguist. The fact is, however, that, especially in the area of language, Dante defies any labeling. He is at once a practitioner of modern methods of inquiry and an adherer to medieval beliefs of knowledge acquisition. His genius leads him to an investigation of linguistic phenomena that is essentially empirical and observational, but his scholastic training causes him to qualify this investigation with strictly medieval assumptions—the Aristotelian principle of *reductio ad unum*, the traditional notion of *discretio*, etc. To reduce Dante to a definite mode of inquiry, therefore, is to miss the rich interpretative approach peculiar to his assessment of linguistic phenomena. Moreover, such a reduction can lead (as it has in the case of several scholars who have treated these matters) to oversimplification and to a misreading of the Dantean text.

In my study of Dante's philosophy of language, I have refrained from confining him to a particular mode of inquiry. In so far as possible, I have let Dante be Dante. My study, therefore, evolves from a close scrutiny of the Dantean text. I believe that this open-ended approach makes for a novel reading of Dante's literature on language, a reading that, especially in the area of the illustrious vernacular (the centerpiece of Dante's philosophy of language), differs fundamentally from much of the current scholarship on this subject.

The contemporary scholars' interpretation of the linguistic theories of the humanists is also flawed. On the whole, their assessment of the Florentine debate is sporadic and inconclusive. The rich literature prompted by the debate has not been fully examined, and its many documents have not been integrated effectively. The result is that some flaws of this literature, such as the sophistry of Valla's treatise, go unnoticed. More often than not, the issues raised by the debate are treated in isolation. Bruni and Biondo's views of the linguistic state of antiquity, for example, are rarely considered in the context of their extensive literary production. More important still, being bent on seeing humanism as a clear-cut break from the medieval mold, contemporary scholars have glossed over or overlooked altogether Dante's influence on the Florentine debate.

In a recent study, that deals with much of the material I treat, Mirko Tavoni has attempted to resolve the inconsistency and confusion that mar the scholarship of the Florentine debate. Unfortunately, Tavoni's study falls short of its objective, and in some ways, even adds to the confusion that surrounds this debate.

Much of Tavoni's interpretation is based on a few arbitrarily selected statements that are manipulated to convey a linguistic rationale and an historical "reality" incongruous with the objectives of the Florentine debate and the historical imperatives that fostered it. Tavoni's interpretation is hindered further by a misunderstanding of Dante's philosophy of language and its role in the Florentine debate and by his wanting to view the debate from Valla's perspective. As Tavoni himself admits, Valla had no knowledge of the literature generated by the Florentine debate, except for Poggio's treatise. Moreover, Valla's *Apologus II* (the work that addresses the issues raised by the Florentine debate) was written primarily to vilify Poggio rather than to clarify the linguistic state of antiquity. Notwithstanding the obvious unreliability of *Apologus II*, Tavoni chooses to view the Florentine debate from the prism of this work.[2]

My objective is to reconstruct systematically the whole body of literature engendered by the Florentine debate and to assess this literature in the historical context of the Quattrocento and in light of the medieval/Dantean ideology that preceded it and of the long polemic on language (*questione della lingua*) that followed it. Indeed, the scope of my study is twofold: an in-depth examination of the humanists' dispute on the linguistic state of ancient Rome and a full account of the polemic on the nature and the viability of the vernacular that ensued from this dispute. The result of this comprehensive reconstruction is, I believe, a fresh interpretation of the Florentine debate and its subsequent discussions. The treatise of Leon Battista Alberti, for example, the most studied among the documents generated by the Florentine debate, acquires a new meaning in the context of this all-inclusive investigation.

Though my reading of Dante and the humanists' literature on language differs in many ways from that of previous scholarship, it nevertheless benefits significantly from the work of other scholars. Much of my study on Dante, for example, would have been impossible, or at least more limited in scope, had it not been for the provocative essays of such eminent scholars as Gustavo Vinay, Pier Vincenzo Mengaldo, and Ettore Paratore. Likewise my treatment of the humanists profits significantly from the thoughtful and stimulating work of Riccardo Fubini, Cecil Grayson, and Hans Baron. Baron's method, which makes the text with its relevant historical factors the focus of inquiry, has served as guide for my own research and exposition of the argument.[3]

My objective upon undertaking this project was to concentrate on the Florentine debate and the numerous literary and philosophical forces that came to bear on it, including the influence of Dante. The investigation of the Dantean influence, however, soon made it clear that Dante's linguistic theories stood in as much need of reinterpretation as the humanists'. The result was that the investigation of Dante eventually led to a full-fledged account of his philosophy of language, an account that goes far beyond the linguistic matters (the bilingualism of antiquity, the efficacy of the vernacular, the social nature of the natural languages) that were of concern to the humanists. To have included the full account of Dante's philosophy of language in the text of the study of the Florentine debate would have been awkward and disruptive. Consequently, in the part on the Florentine debate (the first part of this monograph), the references to Dante have been limited to those points that are directly related to the linguistic theories of the humanists. An elaboration of these same points together with other important matters of Dante's philosophy of language (the illustrious vernacular, the Adamic language, the artificiality of the *gramatica*) is then included in the second part of the work.

The second part reinforces and clarifies the issues raised in the first. More important still, being attached to a long discussion of the theories and concerns of humanism, the second part enhances, I believe, our understanding of Dante's own ideology. An important aspect of contemporary Dantean scholarship is the argument by some scholars that Dante embodies many of the characteristics peculiar to Renaissance humanism. Dante, therefore, ought to be acknowledged as a proto-humanist.[4] To the extent that most of the Dantean qualities modern scholars consider humanistic are associated with and find their *raison d'être* in Dante's speculation on language, the second part gives us a good vantage point from which to assess the potential and limitations of what contemporary scholarship characterizes as Dantean humanism.[5]

The issues raised by Dante and the humanists which I describe in this study had resonance in much of Europe, especially France and Spain. The European dimension is applicable not only to the reasoning of Dante, who, at least in the *Divine Comedy*, argues from a universal/European perspective, but also to the more limited and nationalistic disputations of the humanists. The arguments of the humanists served as sources of information and examples for analogous discussions throughout Renaissance Europe. Jean Lemaire de Belges (*La concorde des deux langages*), Desiderius Erasmus (*Ciceronianus*), Antonio de Nebrija (prologue to the *Gramática de la lengua castellana*), Joachim Du Bellay (*Deffence et illustration de la langue françoyse*), and Juan de Valdés (*Diálogo de la lengua*), all of whom lived in Italy, felt the impact of the argumentation on language advanced by the Italian humanists.

Indeed, Lemaire and Valdés' belief in the efficacy of their respective vernaculars has its parallel in the Florentines' faith in the Tuscan idiom; Nebrija's speculation on the Latin derivation of Spanish echoes Biondo, Guarino, and Poggio's thinking on this same problem, and his equating of the fortune of a language with the political strength of its country ("siempre la lengua fué compañera del imperio") reflects Lorenzo's coupling of the success of the Florentine idiom with the political expansion of the city of Florence; Du Bellay's defense of the French language against the claims of Latin bears the imprint of the Florentines' defense of the Tuscan vernacular; and Erasmus' criticism of the blind adherence to Ciceronian linguistic norms and his insistence that Latin be updated to meet the needs of contemporary culture conform with Biondo and other humanists' views (Angelo Poliziano's, for example) on these matters.[6]

In reconstructing the linguistic theories of Dante and the humanists, I have tried to recapture as fully as possible the theoretical assumptions that shaped their thinking: philological empiricism, political ideology, philosophical orientation, stylistic imperatives, literary aspirations. Indeed, the primary concern of this work is the

interconnection between language and culture. The work, therefore, goes beyond the strict, technical periphery of linguistic
inquiry, and it becomes a study of intellectual history.

PART ONE

THE FLORENTINE DEBATE OF 1435

CHAPTER ONE

BRUNI AND BIONDO:
DRAMATIS PERSONAE OF THE FLORENTINE DEBATE

In March 1435 during the Pope's stay in Florence, several members of the papal chancellery engaged in a heated debate about the linguistic state of ancient Rome: did classical Rome have one language common to all the people, or, in a manner analogous to contemporary Italy, have two ways of speaking—one limited entirely to the men of letters, the other spoken primarily by the common people? The participants were Biondo Flavio, Antonio Loschi, Poggio Bracciolini, Andrea Fiocchi, Leonardo Bruni, and Cencio Rustici, all distinguished humanists.[1]

An account of the Florentine debate of 1435 was provided by Biondo in a treatise entitled *De Verbis Romanae Locutionis*, which was completed in April of the same year. After a *captatio benevolentiae* intended for his friend Bruni, to whom the treatise is dedicated, Biondo notes that a dispute (*altercatio*) raged among the scholars of his age, a dispute in which he had often taken part, as to whether the ancient Romans used to speak the native and common idiom (*materno vulgato idiomate*) of the contemporary masses or the grammatical usage (*grammaticae artis usu*) known as Latin.[2]

During the March debate, Bruni, supported by Loschi and Rustici, had argued, according to Biondo, that in ancient Rome there had been a mode of speaking, vernacular and plebeian in nature and fundamentally different from the literary language (*a litteris remotum*), which had been adopted by later ages ("ut posteriora habuerunt saecula"). Even the most learned of orators made use of this vernacular when communicating with the common people. After much cogitation, the discourses pronounced in this vernacular were rendered in grammatical Latin so that they could be transmitted to posterity.[3]

Biondo goes on to note that he, together with Poggio and Fiocchi, had challenged Bruni's reasoning by arguing that all ancient Romans spoke Latin, even though the Latin of the learned was far superior to that of the unlearned.[4] Indeed, as demonstrated by Cicero (*Orator* 195), the speech of the masses was fluid and rambling whereas that of the men of letters was well knit and rhythmical. Nevertheless, the language of the masses was still Latin, for it was not void of Latinity as was the case with the contemporary vernacular: "Nec tamen ideo non latinum vel, quale nostra habent tempora vulgare, omni latinitate carens erat . . . ."[5] The difference between the speech of the learned and that of the illiterates was one of tone and artistic elegance rather than substance. The faultless and pure Latin of the men of letters bore the mark of sound literary and theoretical training.[6]

Moreover, in considering elegance of speech, Biondo argues, one should not overlook the role played by the social milieu. For example, in the case of the Italian vernacular of his time, among whose speakers he conceded superiority to the Florentines, those who were born in good homes, who grew up in the city, and who were exposed to civic instruction spoke much better than the urban masses and rural folk. In fact, even though all of these people used the same terms, the former spoke a pleasant and graceful language, the latter an offensive and disorderly one. Likewise in ancient Rome, though all Romans made use of the same Latin terminology, those with a more refined domestic background and sound upbringing possessed a better mode of speaking, even if they lacked literary training.[7] Indeed, as proved by Cicero (*Brutus* 210-211, 213, 258, and 261), certain domestic situations and historical periods were more conducive to graceful speaking than others. Hence, the distinguished Roman orator Curio, who lacked theoretical and literary training, made use of good Latin because of his home rearing: "Litterarum nihil scivisse et latine non pessime locutum Curionem fuisse, usu aliquo factum domestico credidit Cicero."[8] Curio grew up in a home environment that made correct and elegant speaking a way of life. The domestic background was equally influential in the formulation of the speech of ancient women. Cornelia, mother of the Gracchi, and Laelia, daughter of C. Laelius, possessed a graceful manner of speaking because of proper and decorous upbringing.

Literary Latin, then, was not limited to the men of letters, as assumed by Bruni, but it was spoken in all sectors of Roman society, including the home. The language spoken in Roman homes could not have been anything but Latin, if a domestically trained Curio could become the third most distinguished orator of Rome.[9] Social conditions influenced the manner of speaking of an entire era. The Rome of Caesar, for example, enjoyed a remarkable elegance of speech because of the perfect urbanity prevalent at that time.[10] However, whether the classical speech was coarse and rambling because of crude environmental conditions, or graceful and polished because of formal training or urbane living, the fact remained, concludes Biondo, that all ancient Romans spoke Latin: " . . . omnes pariter latinis verbis usos, mulieres et viros, servos et liberos, doctos et litterarum ignaros; cum diversam pro vitae et morum qualitate dicendi facultatem plurimis fuisse concesserim . . . ."[11] As to the wretched contemporary vernacular, it was completely unknown to the ancient Romans: " . . . licet abiectum hoc nostrum vulgare nulla illis [the ancient Romans] ex parte cognitum . . . ."[12]

Returning to Bruni's supposition that the learned men of antiquity spoke a popular speech with the masses which they then rendered into Latin, Biondo contends that such an assumption was not borne out by classical literature. Today, Biondo argues, we speak of translating into Latin the grammatically structured vernacular works of Dante and Boccaccio. Such, however, was not the case in ancient Rome, for none of the scholars of antiquity, who wrote extensively on Roman oratory, ever hints at the existence of a distinct popular speech that was rendered into literary Latin.[13] Very likely when addressing the masses, the orators of antiquity utilized an intermediate speech: " . . . medium quemdam certumque eliciemus in orando servatum a priscis oratoribus dicendi modum."[14] However, though shorn of its rhetorical, lexical, and phonetic refinement, this speech was still essentially Latin.

The ancient masses' ability to understand literary Latin could also be proved by the foreigners residing at the papal court and by the illiterates of contemporary Italy. Though lacking adequate knowledge of Latin, the foreigners inhabiting the papal court understood fully the Latin spoken at the Curia. Likewise, when exposed to discussions in Latin, the illiterates of contemporary Italy understood without much difficulty the gist of what was being said.[15]

That the ancient Romans were monolingual is proven also by the popularity enjoyed throughout Roman history by the orators and the playwrights. This popularity is predicated on the premise that the common people of ancient Rome understood the oratorical discourses and the theatrical performances in their literary form. Indeed, as demonstrated by Cicero (*Orator* 173, and 183; *Brutus* 171-172, and 242), the common people of ancient Rome had not only a general comprehension of literary speech, but also a perception of its nuances and peculiarities. Biondo notes that, according to Cicero, the spectators of the theatre and the audience of the forum and the senate, although ignorant of grammatical rules, metrical laws, and rhetorical precepts, could detect errors in recitation and could distinguish the elegant Latin of the metropolis from the coarse Latin of the countryside.

At this point Biondo becomes aware that his line of reasoning presents somewhat of a dilemma. To say that the uneducated masses of ancient Rome possessed the language—minus its rhetorical, lexical, and phonetic refinement—of the men of letters would be to imply that they had a theoretical understanding of Latin grammar (declensions, conjugations, verb forms, etc). On the other hand, to assume that the common people of antiquity lacked such an understanding would be to negate that monolingualism (*Latinitas*) he had so vigorously defended up to this point. Biondo resolves the issue by arguing that whether or not the common people of ancient Rome had a theoretical understanding of grammar is irrelevant, for the need to express oneself grammatically is innate in human nature ("natura insitum videmus"). There is no individual, however ignorant, who does not make use of grammatical rules. Indeed, as demonstrated by the numerous vernaculars of contemporary Italy, even the most barbarous of languages is endowed with a certain regularity.[16] This being the case, the common people of ancient Rome, though ignorant of grammatical rules, spoke a language that was grammatically structured. To be sure, their speech lacked the syntactical and rhetorical sophistication common to the men of letters; nevertheless, it encompassed much that is fundamental to Latin grammar.

That the speech of the common people of ancient Rome was grammatically structured could be proved analogically by examining the vernacular of the mountainous areas of central Italy. The peasants of this region, as any scholar from northern Italy could easily detect, utilized freely and effectively numerous linguistic characteristics of classical Latin, characteristics that the contemporary scholars could master only after much studying.[17] Important relics of classical Latin could also be found in the vernacular of contemporary Rome, especially in the speech of women, who, by being more culturally isolated than men, were more effective preservers of the linguistic tradition of ancient Rome. These women used correctly important features of Latin grammar, though lacking a theoretical understanding of its key elements: tenses, moods, numbers, and cases.[18]

Unlike Bruni, who attributes the origin of the vernacular to an essentially identical language in antiquity ("vulgare quoddam et plebeium, ut posteriora habuerunt saecula"), Biondo traces it to the barbaric invasions. Relying again on evidence from Cicero (*Brutus* 258), Biondo notes that some corruption of Latinity was already apparent at the time of Caesar, especially among those residents of Rome who were exposed to a crude domestic environment or had spent their lives outside of Rome. However, full scale deterioration of classical Latin began only after the barbaric invasions. Whereas prior to the arrival of the barbarians the corruption of Latinity was limited to a few small elements of Roman society and was apparent primarily in enunciation, after the barbaric invasions it became universal and fundamental, encompassing every segment of Roman society and every aspect of Roman speech. Consequently the vernacular, rather than being a product of antiquity, was a bastard language resulting from the fusion of Latin and Gothic-Vandal usages.[19]

Biondo concludes the treatise by noting that he does not pretend to have exhausted the argument on the linguistic state of antiquity raised the previous March by the members of the papal chancellery. Nevertheless, he hopes to have demonstrated what the language of antiquity was or, at least, to have generated enough interest in the subject so that Bruni himself or other scholars might want to pursue the matter further.[20] The argument generated by the debate of 1435 was in fact continued by Bruni and other distinguished humanists: Alberti, Guarino, Poggio, and Filelfo. Bruni's views were expressed in a letter (Epistola VI, 10) to Biondo written on May 7, 1435.

Bruni opens his letter by stating what he believes is at issue ("Quaestio nostra in eo consistit") between him and Biondo. You think, Bruni tells his fellow humanist, that the ancient Romans spoke one language and that there was no distinction between the vulgar and the literary language. I, on the other hand, maintain that as in our own days so in antiquity (by antiquity Bruni means ancient Rome at the time of Cicero and Terence) the vulgar speech was distinct from the literary.[21]

Bruni challenges what he considers to be Biondo's first and most important point: the assertion that the common people of ancient Rome understood, in their literary form, the theatrical performances and the orations delivered in the senate and the assemblies. The audience of the senate, Bruni maintains, was literate and therefore capable of understanding literary Latin. In the assemblies where the public was mixed, only the learned members of the audience grasped the full meaning of the orators' speeches. The common people, on the other hand, had a limited comprehension of those speeches much like the modern populace's understanding of the Mass.[22] Moreover, one should not overlook the fact, Bruni adds, that the written version of the orations delivered in the assemblies differed from their spoken form. This is not to say that the orators wrote down something other than what they had expressed in their oral deliveries, but that what they had said orally was rendered in a more elegant and embellished way so that matters, which in the assembly were perhaps (*forsan*) expressed in plain words to enhance the understanding of the audience, could afterward be read from a more concise and polished text. This practice was common among the Latins as well as the Greeks.[23]

As to Biondo's assumption that the masses of antiquity understood the literary Latin of the theatrical works of classical Rome, Bruni argues that what attracted the masses to the theater was not understanding of the texts of the playwrights, but the scenic apparatus (dramatic spectacles, flute playing, miming).[24] That the masses were attracted solely by the theatrical spectacles was corroborated by Plautus and Terence's emphasis on acting (*acta*) rather than recitation (*recitata*). And what is acting, Bruni muses, if

not representation and communication through body move-
ments?[25] Relying on Terence's text (*Hecyra* 14-19), Bruni notes
that the actors themselves were incapable of understanding the
writings of the playwrights unless the playwrights had first instructed them. If the master actors did not understand the text of
the dramatic works they were performing, the masses who came to
these performances must have understood even less: "Si igitur
magistri ipsi agendi non intelligebant, multo minus turba et multitudo."[26]

Biondo had argued that the ability to express oneself grammatically is innate to human nature; consequently all Romans both
literate and illiterate could speak grammatically. Bruni retorts that
such an argument is absurd at best. Do you, Flavio, and your sup-
porters, Bruni asks sarcastically, actually believe that the wetnurses,
the lowly women, and similar people of antiquity were so endowed
by nature that they could acquire without formal education the
linguistic complexities of literary Latin, complexities that the
modern scholars can master only through rigorous training and
intense application?[27] The Latin language differs from the vernacular in many ways: termination, inflexion, signification, construction, accent, etc.[28] To say, therefore, that the common people
of antiquity spoke literary Latin, Bruni goes on to argue, is to imply that they could inflect effectively difficult words such as *su-
pellex*, that they were aware of gender variations such as *dom-
inabus/dominis* and *filiabus/filiis*, that they understood the tense
forms of verbs such as *fero* and that they knew the proper stress of
a *sinápis* and *políxena*.[29]

The literary language and the vernacular differed not only
syntactically, but also lexically. According to Cicero (*Orator* 153),
Duellius was called *Bellius* by the common people: "*Duellium . . .
vulgo Bellum* appellatum fuisse Cicero tradit."[30] Likewise Varro
relates (*De Re Rustica* I, 2, 14) that the illiterates said *vellatura*
and *vella* and the literates *vectura* and *villa*. Bruni, therefore,
concludes that the common people used one type of speech, the
literate another: "Alius ergo vulgi sermo, alius literatorum."[31]

As to Biondo's contention that the social milieu played an important role in refining the speech of the unlearned, Bruni concurs
with his fellow humanist that the social milieu contributes to the
refinement of the speech of the illiterates, but he disagrees with

him that this refinement implies the acquisition of grammatical principles. Learned fathers, slaves, even mothers, Bruni argues, if they are well-bred, can aid the eloquence of their children.[32] Just how significant the influence of the social milieu was in antiquity could be proved analogically by well-bred women of contemporary Rome, who spoke an elegant, if not literate, language. Indeed, the language of these women, as demonstrated by an aristocratic woman he had himself observed, possesses a certain vernacular charm.[33] Given their elegant mode of speaking, contemporary Roman women contributed significantly to the linguistic eloquence of their offspring. In a similar way, the mothers and nurses of antiquity must have contributed to the linguistic refinement of their children's speech. This is not to say, however, that they instructed their children in grammatical matters (inflexion, *variatio*, termination in the literary fashion), but that they instilled in them a pure, polished form of speech. Indeed, the vernacular too has the potential of an excellence all its own as demonstrated by Dante and others who use it free of faults.[34]

Being convinced that the social milieu in and of itself could not convey the principles of grammar, Bruni disputes Biondo's assertion that the literary Latin of aristocratic Roman women, such as Laelia and Cornelia, and of distinguished orators, such as Curio, was strictly the result of a cultivated home environment. Laelia and Cornelia, according to Bruni, were literate and even Curio should be considered literate, notwithstanding his lack of literary training. Curio wrote down his orations and dialogues, and anyone who commits his thoughts to writing is perforce literate, for how can we call illiterate one who expresses himself in a literate form?[35]

Bruni's letter addresses only some of the issues raised by Biondo, and it does so in an inconclusive and amateurish manner. For example, he misinterprets a reference in Terence's *Hecyra* (14-19) as meaning linguistic instruction rather than memorization of lines, as is the intent of Terence. He thus concludes that the actors lacked understanding of the dramatic works they performed. The Ciceronian observation (*Orator* 153) regarding the evolution of *Duellius* into *Bellius* is taken to mean that *Bellius* was a popular term, limited entirely to the common people. The very distinction between the speech of the masses and that of the learned is justified on the basis of a few lexical terms taken at random from Cicero and Varro.

Much of Bruni's argument is intended to discredit Biondo's assertion that the common people of antiquity understood the literary language of the theatrical performances and the Latin of the orations delivered in the senate and the assemblies. He thus glosses over the more important issues raised by Biondo's treatise. For example, he dismisses with a simple sarcastic remark Biondo's belief in the intrinsic regularity of languages and in the ability of all people, even the most illiterate, to speak grammatically. Bruni all but overlooks Biondo's fundamental point that the difference between the speech of the masses and that of the learned is one of tone rather than substance. He insists that knowledge of Latin among the unlearned is totally inadmissible. He thus argues that Curio (whom Biondo, following Cicero, recognizes as being knowledgeable of Latin though lacking in literary training) was in fact learned, because he committed his thoughts to writing ("Qui . . . cogitationes suas litteris mandarit . . .").[36]

Being challenged, it seems, by Biondo's effective argument that the learned men of antiquity did not address the masses in a popular idiom which they then rendered into Latin, Bruni in his letter to Biondo moderates somewhat what must have been (as we learn from Biondo) his earlier view on this matter. He now argues that the speeches delivered to the masses were redone in a refined language, which was nevertheless essentially the language used at the time of their delivery.

A close reading of Bruni's letter reveals that his argument is colored by the modern bilingualism of Latin and vernacular, which he sees as a direct result of an analogous linguistic state in antiquity. In fact, his insistence that the masses of antiquity could not possibly partake of the grammatical complexities of Latin, because Latin and the vernacular are substantially different from one another, betrays an adherence to the linguistic reality of contemporary Italy. Even his assertion (in the last part of the letter) that as in contemporary Rome so in antiquity upper-class women instructed their children in rhetorical embellishment rather than in linguistic sophistication is influenced by the linguistic state of contemporary Italy. As we have seen above,[37] this assertion is prompted by Biondo's argument that in antiquity a cultivated home environment led to the refinement of one's speech. Bruni's interpretation of this factor, however, differs fundamentally from Biondo's. Whereas Biondo, who argues from the classical perspective of linguistic uniformity, sees the home environment as contributing to a more elegant Latin, Bruni, who argues from the modern perspective of bilingualism, sees it as contributing to a more refined vernacular.[38]

It seems that Bruni believes that in antiquity Latin was acquired only through theoretical training; the most one could expect from a cultivated home environment was a more polished vernacular. The common language of the aristocratic circles of antiquity, therefore, like the pure, charming idiom of the upper-class women of contemporary Rome, though more refined than the language of the masses, was still essentially a vernacular.[39] In all fairness to Bruni, we should note that Biondo's treatise is not entirely flawless. As Fubini notes,[40] Biondo gives too much emphasis to social factors—that is to say, he sees languages as primarily the product of social forces. Nevertheless, Biondo demonstrates sounder scholarship and better critical judgment than Bruni. As we will see later, the theories Biondo advances in this treatise (the vernacular's derivation from Latin, the intrinsic regularity of languages, the usefulness of contemporary vernaculars in the study of ancestral languages, etc.) withstand the test of time.

One of the distinguishing characteristics of late-medieval culture is a belief in ancient bilingualism. Antiquity, according to the scholars of the late Middle Ages, possessed two parallel, independent linguistic entities: Latin and the vernacular. Latin, an artificial, secondary language, was solely the language of the learned, whereas the vernacular, a natural, fluid language, was essentially the language of the masses. One of the key exponents of ancient bilingualism in the Middle Ages is Dante Alighieri.

In the opening remarks of his treatise, Biondo notes that the Florentine debate of 1435 took place in the context of an ongoing polemic (*magna altercatio*) on whether the common people of antiquity spoke literary Latin or a vernacular language similar to that of contemporary Italy. I believe that the ongoing polemic Biondo refers to here is an offshoot of the medieval/Dantean notion of ancient bilingualism. Indeed, a close reading of Bruni's letter reveals a strong adherence to the linguistic notions of Dante. To appreciate fully, therefore, the historical and cultural implications of the Florentine debate, we must consider it in light of Dante's linguistic theories.

CHAPTER TWO

DANTE'S LINGUISTIC THEORIES:
ELIXIR VITAE OF THE FLORENTINE DEBATE

Dante's concern for linguistic matters is apparent throughout much of his literary production (*Vita Nuova*, XXV; *Inferno*, XXXI, 67-68; *Purgatorio*, VII, 16-17; *Paradiso*, XXVI, 124-142, etc.) However, the Dantean works that have the greatest bearing on the Florentine debate are the first treatise of the *Convivio* and the first book of the *De Vulgari Eloquentia*.

In the first treatise of the *Convivio*, which serves as the proem of the work, Dante notes that the *Convivio* will consist of fourteen treatises with each treatise encompassing a canzone and a commentary.[1] Both the canzones and the commentaries will be in the vernacular. Dante adds that current scholarly practice would have dictated that the commentaries be written in Latin (I, ix, 10-11). Nevertheless, he has opted for the vernacular for three important reasons: a more effective interpretation of the content of the canzones, a larger readership, and a love for the vulgar tongue (I, v, 2-3).

A commentary in Latin, Dante notes, would have been incongruous with the essence of the canzones, for Latin is a language totally different from the vernacular: "Onde è manifesto che lo latino non è conoscente de lo volgare" (I, vi, 8-9). To be sure, a commentary in Latin would have enjoyed an international readership. However, those readers, such as the Germans and the English, who are not knowledgeable of the Italian vernacular, would have understood the content, but not the artistic beauty of his poems. As for the literati of Italy, they would have grasped the full value of the canzones, but the Italian literati were too few in number and his objective was to reach the largest readership possible (I, vii-viii). This goal could be achieved only by writing the commentaries in the vernacular: " . . . lo latino averebbe a pochi dato lo suo beneficio, ma lo volgare servirà veramente a molti" (I, ix, 4).

The use of the vernacular was due also to a love for the Italian vernacular language. By writing the commentaries in the vernacular rather than in Latin, Dante could demonstrate that the Italian vernacular had the ability to express effectively and gracefully lofty and new matters: "Chè per questo comento la gran bontade del volgare di sì si vedrà; però che si vedrà la sua vertù, si com'è per esso altissimi e novissimi concetti convenevolemente, sufficientemente e acconciamente . . . manifestare" (I, x, 12). Dante argues that the potential to express lofty matters in a cogent and elegant fashion had always been implicit in the Italian vernacular: " . . . in quanto quello elli di bontade avea in podere . . . " (I, x, 9); however, this potential had not been fully realized. His commentary will remedy this deficiency: " . . . io lo fo avere in atto e palese ne la sua propria operazione . . . " (I, x, 9). Indeed, Dante foretells of a day when, on the strength of his commentary, the Italian vernacular would emerge as a respected language, serving as a viable linguistic instrument for the many who have no knowledge of Latin: "Questo sarà quello pane orzato del quale si satolleranno migliaia, e a me ne soperchieranno le sporte piene. Questo sarà luce nuova, sole nuovo, lo quale surgerà là dove l'usato tramonterà, e darà lume a coloro che sono in tenebre e in oscuritade per lo usato sole che a loro non luce" (I, xiii, 12).

Thus Dante chides those individuals who considered the Italian vernacular linguistically inferior to other vulgar tongues, especially the language of *oc* (I, x, 11). The contemporary argument that the Provençal is superior to the Italian vernacular, Dante argues, is as absurd as the ancient contention—a contention censured by Cicero—that the Greek language was more praiseworthy than Latin: "Contra questi cotali grida Tullio nel principio d'un suo libro che si chiama Libro di Fine de' Beni, però che al suo tempo biasimavano lo latino romano e commendavano la gramatica greca per simiglianti cagioni che questi fanno vile lo parlare italico e prezioso quello di Provenza" (I, xi, 14).[2] That the Italian vernacular can be as effective a linguistic instrument as the Provençal is attested to by the works produced by the great vernacular writers of Italy: " . . . guardi che opere ne fanno li buoni artefici . . . " (I, xi, 13).

Dante goes on to argue that it is natural that he should love the vernacular, for as his native language, the vernacular is the most familiar to him and, therefore, the most loved by him. Indeed, the vernacular contributed to his very being in that it was the linguistic means that brought his parents together: "Questo mio volgare fu congiugnitore de li miei generanti, che con esso parlavano" (I, xiii, 4). Moreover, the vernacular made him good, that is to say, made him cultured. In fact, the vernacular launched him on the road to intellectual pursuit and made it possible for him to learn Latin: "Ancora, questo mio volgare fu introduttore di me ne la via di scienza, che è ultima perfezione, in quanto con esso io entrai ne lo latino e con esso mi fu mostrato . . . E così è palese, e per me conosciuto, esso essere stato a me grandissimmo benefattore" (I, xiii, 5).

However, for all its merits, the vernacular was inferior to Latin. At best the vernacular could approximate the linguistic efficiency of Latin (" . . . quasi come per esso latino, manifestare . . . ", I, x, 12) but never equal it, for, as anyone who knows both Latin and the vulgar tongue can attest, Latin has an expressive range far superior to that of the vernacular: " . . . lo latino molte cose manifesta concepute ne la mente che lo volgare far non può . . . " (I, v, 12). The superiority of Latin is due to the fact that Latin is an artificial, conventional language whereas the vernacular is a natural, fluid one: " . . . lo volgare seguita uso, e lo latino arte . . . " (I, v, 14). Hence "lo latino è perpetuo e non corruttibile, e lo volgare è non stabile e corruttibile" (I, v, 7). Dante goes on to note that an examination of the Latin of the dramatic works of antiquity and of the vernacular spoken in the Italian cities would clearly show that Latin has remained remarkably constant whereas the vernacular has changed significantly: "Onde vedemo ne le scritture antiche de le comedie e tragedie latine, che non si possono transmutare, quello medesimo che oggi avemo; che non avviene del volgare, lo quale a piacimento artificiato si transmuta. Onde vedemo ne le cittadi d'Italia, se bene volemo agguardare, da cinquanta anni in qua molti vocaboli essere spenti e nati e variati" (I, v, 8-9). Indeed, so pervasive is the change of the vernacular that should those inhabitants who died a thousand years ago be resuscitated, they would not recognize their ancient vernacular language as their own: "Sì ch'io dico, che se coloro che partiron d'esta vita già sono mille anni tornassero a le loro cittadi, crederebbero la loro cittade essere occupata da gente strana, per la lingua da loro discordante" (I, v, 9-10).[3] Dante concludes this discussion by noting that the mutability of the vernacular will be elaborated in a forthcoming little book entitled *Volgare Eloquenza* (I, v, 10).

In the *De Vulgari Eloquentia* Dante does indeed elaborate on the variable nature of the vernacular. He argues that linguistic mutability is intrinsic in all natural languages. Hence all vulgar tongues are in a constant state of evolution. Languages are mutable, because man's nature, the cause and molder of all linguistic phenomena, is itself very unstable and extremely variable: " . . . homo sit instabilissimum atque variabilissimum animal" (I, ix, 6). Languages change in space as well as in time, but the linguistic change caused by time is by far the more significant.

Dante traces the linguistic instability of the vulgar tongues to the building of the Tower of Babel. Prior to this event mankind spoke a universal, stable language totally immune to man's whims (*a nostro beneplacito*). This language was the language of Adam, which was created concurrently with Adam himself: " . . . illam homini primo concreatam a Deo" (I, ix, 6). Man's presumptuousness displayed in the construction of the Tower of Babel caused the disintegration of this primal language, and this disintegration gave origin to a diversity of languages which in Europe manifested itself as a threefold idiom (*ydioma tripharium*), encompassing the "Germanic," "Romance," and "Byzantine" languages. These European languages evolved into further linguistic forms. Hence, the Romance idiom developed into an *ydioma tripharium*: the languages of *oc*, *oil*, and *sì*. And the languages of *oc*, *oil*, and *sì* themselves ramified into different linguistic entities. The language of *sì*, for example, evolved into fourteen major vernaculars with each vernacular having numerous linguistic derivatives of its own: "Quare adminus xiiii vulgaribus sola videtur Ytalia variari. Que adhuc omnia vulgaria in sese variantur . . ." (I, x, 7).

This constant and inevitable diversification of the natural tongues led to the creation of a secondary language (*locutio secundaria*), which Dante classifies as *gramatica*, (I, i, 3-4). The *gramatica* is an artificial language (*potius artificialis*) regulated by

CHAPTER THREE

DANTE, BRUNI AND THE BEGINNING OF THE *QUESTIONE DELLA LINGUA*

As we turn again to Bruni, we see a remarkable affinity between his linguistic theories and those of Dante.[1] Seizing, apparently, on Dante's notion of bilingualism, Bruni argues that, as in modern times so in classical Rome, there existed two linguistic entities: Latin and the vernacular. Hence, whereas Dante had spoken of a *locutio naturalis* vs. a *locutio artificialis*, Bruni speaks of a *vulgi sermo* vs. a *litteratorum sermo*. As in Dante so in Bruni, these linguistic entities are totally independent of one another. "Onde è manifesto che lo latino non è conoscente de lo volgare," Dante had said; "Atque latina lingua a vulgari in multis differt," says Bruni. Indeed, Bruni's very assumption that the Roman and Greek intelligentsia spoke a vernacular form of speech with the masses, which they then rendered into a literary language, echoes Dante's notion in the *De Vulgari Eloquentia* of a stable, universal *gramatica*, which was limited primarily to the literati of ancient Rome and Greece.[2] Even Bruni's conception of an archetypal vernacular, traceable to classical antiquity ("vulgare quoddam et plebeium, ut posteriora habuerunt saecula"), appears to be borrowed from the Dantean notion of the origin and evolution of the Romance idioms. This reliance on Dante's linguistic theories led Bruni to what Remigio Sabbadini has classified as "il suo famoso e frivolo giudizio."[3]

The question now arises: how could Bruni, one of the towering figures of Italian humanism, produce such a "frivolo giudizio"? Or to put it differently, how could Bruni, at the height of Humanism, still accept Dante's notion of bilingualism? Due to a misunderstanding of a key passage by the distinguished German linguist Hugo Schuchardt, scholars have attributed Bruni's misconception of the nature of classical Latin to a nominalistic interpretation of linguistic phenomena. According to these scholars,

Bruni and his fellow humanists, lacking a clear perception of what was meant by language, had no clear understanding of the linguistic state of ancient Rome.[4] Following this line of reasoning, Vittorio Rossi notes, "Risolvere poi se codesto grado fosse tale che si dovesse ammettere l'esistenza di due lingue non si poteva senza che fosse ben definito il concetto di lingua; problema che i quattrocentisti non si proposero."[5]

That Bruni's account of the nature of classical Latin is methodologically deficient there can be no doubt. As we have seen above, his description of the linguistic state of antiquity is incoherent and fragmentary with too much weight given to a few isolated examples from classical literature. In fact, his letter to Biondo lacks the scholarly rigor one finds in his other works, especially his *Historiae Florentini Populi*. Sabbadini states: "Il Bruni non ragiona, ma parla per impressione."[6] This deficiency, however, is not due to a nominalistic orientation but to a lack of interest in the subject matter under discussion. A close reading of Bruni's letter to Biondo and of the literature generated by the Florentine debate reveals that what interested Bruni throughout the debate was not so much the linguistic state of antiquity but the integrity and nobility of the vernacular. This interest is especially strong in the concluding remarks of his letter, where, echoing Dante's *Convivio* (I, x, 9-13; xiii, 12), Bruni argues that the vernacular has the potential of an excellence all its own.

By vernacular Bruni meant, of course, the Florentine vernacular. In his *Laudatio Florentinae Urbis*, he had noted that the Florentine vernacular was the purest and the most cultivated in Italy; it thus served as an example for those Italians who wanted to speak well and faultlessly.[7] Hence, Bruni's primary objective throughout the debate is to enhance the prestige of the Florentine vernacular. By subscribing to Dante's notion of classical bilingualism, he was able to contribute much to this prestige. In fact, as has been observed by Hans Baron, the notion of two parallel independent linguistic entities made it possible for Bruni to trace the vernacular to classical times. This classical origin gave the vernacular greater respectability. Baron writes:

One wonders whether the pattern of Bruni's thought on the issue of
language might not have run parallel with a somewhat kindred theory
on the origin of knighthood (*militia*) that he had set forth in 1421. In
the treatise *De Militia*, he had tried to prove that knighthood (*militia*)
was not simply a product of medieval developments, but had its roots
in ancient Rome. Here, where we have fuller information on Bruni's
reasoning, thanks to the treatise *De Militia*, we see that his tracing of
a medieval development to ancient origins was intended to enhance its
prestige. Is it not very probable that Bruni's intention was the same
when in later years he thought he could trace the Volgare to Roman
roots?[8]

That Bruni should have displayed such an enthusiasm for the
Florentine vernacular is logical enough, for Bruni was Florence's
major apologist in the early Quattrocento. Prior to the Florentine
debate, he had glorified Florence's three crowns: Dante, Petrarch
and Boccaccio (*Ad Petrum Paulum Histrum Dialogus*); he had
praised Florence's supremacy within the community of Italian
states (*Laudatio Florentinae Urbis*); and he had celebrated
Florence's accomplishments in the Middle Ages (*Historiae
Florentini Populi*).[9] Moreover, the debate took place in an atmo-
sphere charged with great pride in the Florentine vernacular.[10]

Bruni's defense of the vernacular as an effective linguistic
instrument is continued in his *Vita di Dante*. The *Vita di Dante*
(1436), coming only a few months after the letter to Biondo, must
have been prompted to a large degree by the Florentine debate.[11]
Having realized the futility of his argument on classical
bilingualism, Bruni now concentrates on what really had
concerned him throughout the debate: the capacities of the
Florentine vernacular. In the *Vita di Dante*, the disputation over
the *sermo vulgi* vs. *sermo litteratorum* gives way to the argument as
to whether one should write in Latin (*istile litterato*) or in vernacular (*istile vulgare*). Bruni notes:

> Il nome del poeta significa eccellente ed ammirabile stile in versi . . .
> chi compone opere in versi, ed è sommo ed eccellentissimo nel
> comporre tali opere, si chiama poeta. Or questa è la verità certa e
> assoluta del nome e dell'effetto de' poeti; lo scrivere in istile litterato

o vulgare non ha a fare al fatto, nè altra differenza è se non come scrivere in greco od in latino. Ciascuna lingua ha sua perfezione e suo suono e suo parlare limato e scientifico.[12]

Bruni contends in this passage that it makes no difference whether one uses Latin or the vernacular, because the vernacular has the potential to equal Latin. In fact, every language has its own perfection, its own euphony, its own refinement and *parlare scientifico*.[13] Consequently every language has the ability to express in a graceful and elegant fashion any conceivable intellectual subject. Following, it seems, Dante's reasoning, Bruni argues that the choice of writing in Latin or in the vernacular is to be viewed in light of ancient Rome's choice of using Greek or Latin. Just as in antiquity, Greek was not to be regarded as more useful than Latin, so in modern times, Latin is not to be considered more functional than the vernacular. What determines the excellence of one's work is not whether it is written in Latin or in the vernacular, but whether it possesses substance and artistic elegance.

In Bruni's letter to Biondo, then, and in his *Vita di Dante*, we have a reaffirmation of Dante's belief in the proficiency of the vernacular. But, whereas for Dante this proficiency was in a state of becoming—Dante had spoken of a "sole nuovo, lo quale surgerà la dove l'usato tramonterà" (*Convivio*, I, xiii, 12)—for Bruni it is a fait accompli. That it is a fait accompli is confirmed (as Bruni had noted in the letter to Biondo) by the writings of Dante and others (*apud Dantem et alios*) who have used the vernacular effectively. Indeed, in the *Vita di Dante*, Bruni elaborates on the *apud Dantem et alios* of the letter to Biondo by acknowledging specific writers and by emphasizing the monumental contribution of Dante himself. Dante, according to Bruni, had been preceded by several vernacular writers (Guinizzelli, Guittone, Bonagiunta, Guido da Messina), but he had surpassed them all in elegance of expression and in profundity of thought. Such was Dante's excellence in the area of poetry that no one would ever surpass him.[14]

Bruni's objective in this polemic is not to dethrone Latin, but to establish the right of the verncular to coexist with Latin as a literary language. In his *Vita di Petrarca*, while comparing Dante with

Petrarch he clearly regards Latin and the vernacular as two alternate modes of expression:

> Due parti sono nella lingua latina, cioè prosa e versi; nell'una e
> nell'altra è superiore il Petrarca, perocchè in prosa lungamente è più
> eccellente, e nel verso ancora è più sublime e più ornato che non è il
> verso di Dante, sicchè in tutta la lingua latina Dante per certo non è
> pari al Petrarca. Nel dire volgare, il Petrarca in canzone è pari a Dante;
> in sonetti il vantaggia: confesso niente di manco che Dante nell'opera
> sua principale vantaggia ogni opera del Petrarca. E però, conchiudendo,
> ciascuno ha sua eccellenza in parte, ed in parte è superato.[15]

The vernacular should certainly be employed by those writers, such as Dante, who use it effectively and who have a greater command of the vernacular than of Latin:

> . . . pur, chi mi domandasse per chè cagione Dante piuttosto elesse
> scrivere in vulgare che in latino e litterato stilo, risponderei quello che
> è la verità, cioè che Dante conosceva se medesimo molto più atto a
> queto stilo volgare ed in rima, che a quello latino e litterato. E certo
> molte cose sono dette da lui leggiadramente in questa rima volgare, che
> nè arebbe potuto, nè averebbe saputo dire in lingua latina ed in versi
> eroici. La prova sono l'*Egloghe* da lui fatte in versi esametri, le quali,
> posto sieno belle, niente di manco molte ne abbiamo vedute vantag-
> giatamente scritte. E a dire il vero, la virtù di questo nostro poeta fu
> nella rima volgare, nella quale è eccellentissimo sopra ogni altro; ma
> in versi latini, o in prosa, non aggiugne appena a quelli che
> mezzanamente hanno scritto.[16]

In insisting that Dante wrote in the vernacular because of necessity and in claiming that in his vernacular writings Dante achieves an artistic elegance that would have eluded him had he written in Latin, Bruni underscores the need for using the vernacular. Writers must be free to express themselves in the language in which they are most competent lest society be deprived of such monumental works as Dante's *Divine Comedy*.

Could the vernacular be equally effective in poetry and in prose? By couching the argument over the capabilities of the vernacular in a study such as the *Vita di Dante*, which is, among other things, a definition and celebration of poetry, and by citing as exemplary vernacular writers, literary figures who were primarily poets (Guinizzelli, Guittone, Guido da Messina, and Dante), Bruni seems to imply that the vernacular is most effective as a vehicle for poetry.[17] To be sure, his *Vita di Dante*, as a biographical account and literary history, is itself an affirmation of the capabilities of the vernacular in prose form. However, in the *Vita di Dante* Bruni is forced to admit that these matters can be expressed only with difficulty in the vernacular: " . . . con tutto che queste sono cose che mal si possono dire in volgare idioma, pur m'ingegnerò di darle ad intendere . . . ."[18]

Bruni's lack of confidence in vernacular prose writing may be due to the fact that vernacular prose writing was less acceptable in early fifteenth-century Italy than vernacular poetic writing. As has been noted by Paul Oskar Kristeller, early fifteenth-century Italy enjoyed a vernacular poetic language common to the whole peninsula. Vernacular prose writing, on the other hand, was still limited primarily to Tuscany. A common vernacular prose language developed in Italy only in the second half of the fifteenth century.[19] Bruni's lack of confidence in vernacular prose writing may have been compounded by his strong concern for stylistic elegance. Indeed, as is apparent in his theoretical works (*De Studiis et Litteris, De Interpretatione Recta, Epistola* VII, 4), Bruni considered stylistic refinement a fundamental feature of scholarly writing. This refinement was possible within the realm of vernacular poetry in view of the rhythmic and metric laws peculiar to poetic compositions in general. However, lack of orthographic and grammatical manuals—there was as yet no grammar of the vernacular—rendered vernacular prose writing fluid and irregular. Thus, Bruni must have concluded that vernacular prose writing was unsuitable for stylistic elegance and therefore ought to be avoided in the composition of scholarly works.[20]

Notwithstanding Bruni's reaffirmation of Dante's faith in the proficiency of the vernacular, much of his argument on the defense of the vernacular is characterized by a certain hesitancy. His argument certainly lacks the conviction we have noticed in Dante.[21] Unlike Dante, he limits the vernacular to poetic writing.[22] It seems as though Bruni is torn between his allegiance to classicism and his love for the Florentine vernacular. Nevertheless, by arguing that the vernacular was potentially equal to Latin and, therefore, had the right to coexist as a literary language, and by inferring that this right should be reserved solely to the Florentine vernacular, Bruni set in motion a controversy that was to bedevil scholars for centuries. This controversy is, of course, the *questione della lingua.*[23]

In a provocatively bold assessment of Bruni's theory of the vernacular, Hans Baron argues that Bruni's acknowledgment of the vernacular as a sophisticated, refined language capable of treating any subject whatever attributes to the vernacular an expressive power and therefore a legitimacy that had gone unnoticed in the Trecento:

> That much had never been claimed for the Volgare during the Trecento, nor had the Volgare ever been seen in so broad an historical perspective. Dante himself, despite all his praise of the Volgare as the "new sun" for those to whom the old sun of the Latin could give no light, had in the medieval manner placed Latin as "*lingua grammaticalis et artificialis*" on an entirely different and higher level than the "*linguae naturales vulgares.*" He had not doubted that "the Latin makes many intellectual conceptions possible which the Volgare cannot formulate . . . , its efficacy is greater than that of the Volgare." It is true that Boccaccio in his *Vita di Dante,* in words which on the surface look rather similar to Bruni's expression, had stated that Dante had "shown effectively" that "any lofty matter can be treated in Volgare poetry" (*con essa* [i.e., *la poesia volgare*] *ogni alta materia potersi trattare*) and that Dante consequently had elevated the Volgare and brought it into esteem among Italians just as Homer and Virgil had done with their own languages among the Greeks and Latins. But the treatment of every "*alta materia*" of which Boccaccio spoke, referred to Dante's poetry, especially in the *Divina Commedia,* and to nothing else.[24]

Baron adds that this accomplishment by Bruni was rendered possible to a large degree by the views of traditionalists, such as Giovanni da Prato. In fact, Bruni's theory of the vernacular is a redefinition of the views generated by the "traditionalist school" (Giovanni da Prato, Cino Rinuccini, Domenico da Prato):

> It was, indeed, not until a few years before the composition of Bruni's *Vita di Dante* that Giovanni da Prato . . . judged that in the Florentine idiom of his period "one can express, argue, and debate every abstract and profound thought . . . with the most perfect lucidity." Bruni, then, took up a line of reasoning already in the air among his contemporaries, but redefined more sharply the crucial claim that the Volgare was not only a vehicle for great poetry, but had "its own refinement and *parlare scientifico*."[25]

I believe that my study on Bruni's linguistic theories proves that his notions of the capability of the vernacular were neither as novel nor as sweeping as has been suggested by Baron. In fact, his views on the potential of the vernacular coincide with those of Boccaccio and Dante. Like Boccaccio, Bruni believed that the vernacular was especially suited for poetic writing. Like Dante, he recognized an effective, expressive power in the vernacular. Nevertheless, he felt, like Dante, that Latin still remained a more efficient linguistic instrument than the vernacular, especially when dealing with abstract reasoning. To be sure, unlike Dante, Bruni makes no explicit claim for the linguistic superiority of Latin. However, to have done so at the height of humanism would have been redundant. Bruni's very hesitancy in the defense and use of the vernacular is a good indication, it seems to me, of his belief in the linguistic superiority of Latin.

As to the impact on Bruni of the traditionalists' views, most likely the traditionalists heightened Bruni's consciousness of the efficacy of the vernacular. Ultimately, however, his notions of the capabilities of the vernacular resulted from a close analysis of Dante's linguistic theories. That Bruni followed Dante's line of reasoning in his formulation of the theory of the vernacular is attested to, as I have demonstrated above, by the striking relationship between Dante and Bruni's linguistic theories. Bruni's notions of

the capabilities of the vernacular, therefore, are a reaffirmation of
Dante's linguistic theories rather than a redefinition of views
generated by the "traditionalist school." Moreover, a close
scrutiny of the traditionalists' assessment of the vernacular indicates that these writers were themselves influenced by the linguistic
theories of Dante.[26]

relics of antiqutiy, are living proof of Latin's evolution into the Italian vernacular.[18]

Biondo's assessment of the nature of classical Latin and the origin of the vernacular was aided also by a judicious use of classical sources. Hence a close reading of the rhetoricians of antiquity, especially Cicero, led him to reject Bruni's assertion that the learned men of antiquity had communicated with the masses in a vernacular form of speech which they then translated into Latin. The practice of this form of translation, Biondo reminds Bruni, is not borne out by the rhetoricians of ancient Rome.[19]

Given his belief in a correlation between the development of Italian society and that of the Italian vernacular along with his intention to reclassicize contemporary society, did Biondo also plan to reclassicize the Italian vernacular? Biondo never addresses this issue. We can assume, however, that he would have considered a reclassicizing of the Italian vernacular a highly problematic matter. Biondo seems to have believed that the effectiveness of the Italian vernacular was predicated on its grammatical and lexical remoteness from Latin.[20] The crude vernaculars of central Italy, therefore, possessed numerous relics of classical Latin precisely because they had not yet evolved into full-fledged linguistic entities. Thus a reclassicizing of the Italian vernacular would actually lessen its effectiveness. Indeed, if implemented fully, such a reclassicizing would lead to the very annihilation of the Italian vernacular, because it would reestablish the monolingual state of classical times. Hence, Biondo turns his attention to the modernizing of classical Latin rather than to the reclassicizing of the Italian vernacular.

Biondo's theory on the modernization of classical Latin is developed in the preface to the third decade of his *Historiarum ab Inclinatione Romanorum Decades*.[21] Biondo notes in this preface that after struggling with the reconstruction of the history of "medieval" Italy, whose composition had been hampered by the scarcity and unreliability of sources, he had hoped that the writing of the history of modern Italy (the third decade encompasses the history of Italy from 1412 to 1441) would be a simple matter. Instead he discovered that the reconstruction of the history of this period posed a different but equally formidable problem. Indeed, the historian writing the history of this period was faced with the difficult task of achieving linguistic and stylistic propriety.

Biondo goes on to note that his fellow historians, while writing
the history of contemporary Italy, made use of the Latin terminology and the elevated style of the great historians of ancient
Rome: Livy, Caesar, Sallust, Tacitus, Suetonius, and Justin. Such an
approach, Biondo argues, was incongruous at best, for Italy had
undergone numerous and fundamental cultural changes since antiquity: "His namque posterioribus historiarum nostrarum annis,
maxima est facta provinciarum et Italiae urbium publice adminis-
trandarum, ac privatim vivendi, sed maxime gerendi belli rationis
mutatio."[22] For example, the recruitment and the battle arrays of
the troops were no longer consistent with those of antiquity. There
were no levies or swearing-in ceremonies and no organizing of the
recruits into legions, cohorts and maniples. The camps were not
fortified with fences and trenches. The modern fighting itself was
dramatically different from that of antiquity. Whereas the ancient
battles had consisted of fierce and valiant struggles between large
and highly disciplined armies, those of contemporary Italy were
child-like engagements among small groups of men, who were always ready to retreat and disperse. When large armies did engage
in battle, there was rarely any display of the ancient valor. Indeed,
these battles were a travesty of their ancient counterparts, in that
they resulted in numerous prisoners and practically no casual-
ties.[23]

Contemporary Italy had also witnessed significant changes in
place names. The changes in place names presented an even
greater difficulty for the writer of modern history than the cultural
changes, for most localities in Italy had changed name repeatedly
since antiquity and each new denomination had come to refer to
an area different in size from the one indicated by the previous
name. For example, present-day Lombardy, which, according to
Biondo, was often referred to as *Gallia* by contemporary historians, had been known as Insubria and Cenomania in pre-Roman
times—Insubria identified the province of contemporary Milan,
and Cenomania that of present-day Brescia. After Rome expanded
its hegemony in northern Italy, both of these communities, together with the surrounding territories north of the Po river, became known at times as Cisalpine Gaul and at others as
Transpadane Italy. The Roman church identified the eastern segment of Transpadane Italy as Istria. In modern times much of

what the church had called Istria was indicated either as the March of Treviso or as Lombardy.

Given these numerous changes, Biondo concludes that the style and much of the terminology of the classical historians were no longer relevant to the writing of the history of contemporary Italy: "Ideoque qui priscis scriptoribus in promptu et tamquam ex quotidiano loquendi usu facillimi erant, modos dicendi a nobis magna ex parte servari non expediat."[24] Indeed, to describe the modern battles in the elevated style of the classical writers was misleading because such descriptions gave the impression that the modern battles were fought with the heroism and effectiveness of the ancient ones.[25] Likewise, to identify the cannon with terms such as *balista* or *catapulta* (a practice followed by many contemporary historians) was to fail to convey the destructive force of this recently invented weapon. The cannon, one of the few effective weapons of modern warfare, was far more destructive than any of the ancient weapons.

If the mode of expression of the classical historians was no longer relevant to the writing of modern history, reliance on circumlocutions and on the exclusive usage of modern terminology was also ineffectual, for such an approach would lead to a highly deficient style. Biondo resolves this dilemma by choosing a middle course. He thus makes use of classical terminology whenever describing devices or methods, such as plutei, testudines, the erection of towers, etc., that had direct parallels in classical life. He also uses classical terminology in the identification of geographic localities, such as the rivers of Lombardy, which had retained their classical names. When confronted with new means of warfare, however, with new topographical names and with new cultural characteristics, he latinizes the vernacular term rather than adapting an analogous classical one. He thus identifies the cannon as *bombarda* rather than *balista* or *catapulta*. Likewise the galleon is denoted as *galeonus*, the feudatory as *feudatarius*, Lombardy as *Lombardia*, etc. The coining of new terms is predicated at all times on the principle of usage.

As to the form, Biondo shuns the elevated style of the classical authors and makes use instead of a narrative mode that most accurately reflects the new historical reality. More importantly, however, in recording the history of modern Italy, Biondo avoids the stock, battle-scene descriptions common to the historical writings of his contemporaries. The numerous battle scenes that crowd the

third decade are realistic renditions of the historical episodes described, based, for the most part, on information conveyed to
Biondo by firsthand witnesses.[26]

Biondo's modernization of classical Latin was due, to a large
extent, to his sense of historical perspective. The fall of Rome had
engendered a new historical era; the modern scholar, therefore,
should make use of a Latin that reflected accurately the reality of
this new era. Moreover, in coining new terms Biondo was following a procedure that was supported by the stylistic theories of
classical rhetoricians. For example, Horace and Quintilian, both of
whom were familiar to Biondo, found the formulation of new
words acceptable if carried out sparingly. Horace writes: "Licuit
semperque licebit signatum praesente nota producere nomen."[27]
Similarly Quintilian tolerates the adoption of Greek words to express things for which there are no Latin equivalents: ". . . con-
fessis quoque Graecis utimur verbis, ubi nostra desunt . . . ."[28]
Quintilian recommends that usage be the guiding principle in the
coining of new terms: "Consuetudo vero certissima loquendi
magistra, utendumque plane sermone ut nummo, cui publica
forma est."[29] Biondo clearly heeds this recommendation.

Does Biondo's use of Latin rather than the vernacular in the
third decade indicate a typically humanist prejudice against the
vernacular, as many students of Quattrocento Italy have argued?[30]
After all, if he had relied on the vernacular, he would have avoided
the linguistic and stylistic improprities caused by the use of Latin.
The vernacular, a product like contemporary Italian life itself, of
numerous socio-cultural disruptions, would have been much more
suited than Latin to convey the new historical reality of Italy.
There can be no doubt that Biondo, an ardent classicist, was favorably disposed toward Latin. Nevertheless, it is most unlikely that
he ever contemplated the outright rejection of the vernacular. He
was too pragmatic a thinker not to appreciate the usefulness and
the viability of this new linguistic medium. It is true, as some students of Biondo have noted,[31] that he showed little interest in the
Florentine vernacular and the rich vernacular literature of
Duecento and Trecento Florence,[32] but this lack of interest is not
to be taken as a condemnation of the vernacular and vernacular
literature in general. Biondo's lack of interest in Florentine vernacular culture seems to stem from a personal resentment against

the contemporary Florentines' claim that theirs was the only worthwhile vernacular culture in Italy.[33] Biondo's disregard for Dante and other pre-Petrarchan Florentine vernacular writers is due also to the belief that all literature produced prior to Petrarch had little literary value.[34]

Biondo does demonstrate an appreciation for the usefulness and the viability of the vernacular. In an interesting passage of the *Italia Illustrata*, while speaking of the Venetian writer and admiral Pietro Loredano, he says the following:

> Petrum Lauredanum rebus bello gestis clarissimum, quem Veneti alterum Claudium Marcellum in sua patria appellare possunt, hoc in loco a nobis poni mirabuntur qui meminerint eum latinas litteras grammaticales penitus ignorasse. Sed eius ingenium non duximus merita fraudandum laude, quod omnia quae per aetatem suam mari gesta sunt, quorum ipse magna pars fuit, et maris portuositatis navigandique rationem vulgari scrito copiosissime prosecutus est. [35]

The implicit message of this statement is that what renders a work valuable is not the language used, but the content. Thus Pietro Loredano, a distinguished military leader and author of an important work on the naval exploits of Venice and its maritime science, deserves to be acknowledged as one of the most illustrious sons of Venice. He deserves this accolade in spite of his ignorance of Latin and his use of the vernacular. The above statement also seems to suggest that the vernacular has the potential to express effectively difficult topics and concepts, such as maritime science and the naval battles of Venice.[36]

I believe that Biondo's use of Latin in the third decade as well as in his other works is due to practical reasons rather than to a disdain for the vernacular. Biondo was born at Forlì in Romagna. Thus his vernacular, as attested to by two letters to Francesco Sforza (his only specimens in the vernacular),[37] was marred by the stylistic infelicities and grammatical improprieties peculiar to the dialect of that region. Had he, therefore, chosen to write his learned works in the vernacular, he would have encountered insurmountable linguistic difficulties. Furthermore, he would have earned the scornful criticism of the Florentines, who, as we have seen in the case of Bruni, considered the Florentine vernacular the only viable vernacular in Italy. The fact that Biondo's vernacular production is limited to the two letters to Francesco Sforza, who was like Biondo from Romagna, is itself an indication of his insecurity as a vernacular writer.

Another reason for Biondo's choice of Latin over the vernacular must have been the prestige that Latin enjoyed. Latin functioned as the lingua franca of Europe; consequently it made sense for Biondo, who considered himself a writer of international stature,[38] to make use of this language. By using Latin, Biondo assured himself of the readership of the entire scholarly community of Europe.

The issue of Latin vs. the vernacular as it relates to Biondo and other humanists was understood fully long ago by no less a connoisseur of the Renaissance than Jacob Burckhardt:

> Whether Italian was also more suitable for the narrative of events long past, for historical research, is a question which for that period admits more than one answer. Latin was at that time the lingua franca of instructed people, not only in an international sense, as a means of intercourse between Englishmen, Frenchmen, and Italians, but also in an interprovincial sense. The Lombard, the Venetian, and the Neapolitan modes of writing, though long modeled on the Tuscan and bearing only slight traces of the dialect, were still not recognized by the Florentines. This was of less consequence for local contemporary histories, which were sure of readers at the place where they were written, than for the histories of the past, for which a larger public was desired. In these the local interests of the people had to be sacrificed to the general interests of the learned. How far would the influence of a man such as, e.g., Flavio Biondo have reached had he written his great monuments of learning in the dialect of Romagna? They would have sunk into certain neglect, if only through the contempt of the Florentines, whereas written in Latin they exercised the profoundest influence on the whole European world of learning. And even the Florentines of the fifteenth century wrote Latin, not only because their minds were imbued with humanism, but in order to be more widely read.[39]

In assessing Biondo's interpretation of the nature of classical Latin and of its evolution into the vernacular, one notes that his explanation of these linguistic phenomena is somewhat deficient.

In fact, his study of the linguistic state of classical Rome is based entirely on lexical, phonetic and rhetorical elements with practically no consideration given to morphology and syntax, which constitute the core of a language. When speaking of the objectives of his polemic with Bruni he notes: ". . . sed memineris velim verborum non characterum, locutionis non compositionis, corticis non medullae artis disputationem a me institutam esse."[40] However, classical Latin, as Quintilian, among others, attests, varied not only lexically, phonetically, and rhetorically, but also morphologically and syntactically. Hence, classical Rome, though basically monolingual, had a greater linguistic variety than Biondo recognizes. This variety was especially strong in the spoken language, which, as the title of his treatise indicates (*De Verbis Romanae Locutionis*), must have been Biondo's major concern.

Biondo also judges the nature of classical Latin solely in terms of social differences (*urbanitas* vs. *rusticitas*), disregarding almost completely the changes of speech due to time and space. Not realizing that classical Latin varied horizontally and chronologically, that is to say, it varied from region to region and from one epoch to another, he was unable to assess the influence that the pre-Roman languages (*substrata*) exercized upon the vulgarization of Latin.[41] He thus concludes that this vulgarization was entirely the result of the social catastrophe brought about by the barbarians, especially the Lombards. The truth is, however, that the vulgarization of classical Latin was initiated long before the arrival of the barbarians. In fact, as early as Cicero's time, classical Latin was marred by numerous barbarisms and solecisms which resulted from Latin's interaction with the indigenous languages of the conquered nations. The barbaric invasions, then, precipitated rather than originated the transformation of classical Latin.[42]

In all fairness to Biondo, it should be noted that to have gained a more accurate understanding of the nature of classical Latin and of its evolution into the vernacular, he would have had to undertake a systematic and careful examination of the documentary and historical evidence of antiquity and the Middle Ages, paying particular attention to the linguistic irregularities of classical literature and to the vernacular fragments embedded in medieval Latin documents. But such an undertaking was beyond Biondo's reach and scope. His sole objective during the Florentine debate was to prove the monolingual state of classical Rome and thus to argue that the

vernacular was not an ancient language, as Dante and Bruni believed it to be, but a modern one which had resulted from the deterioration of Latin. In this he succeeded fully.

Notwithstanding his flaws in the assessment of the nature of
classical Latin and the origin of the vernacular, Biondo must be
acknowledged as a major contributor to historical linguistics. By
perceiving a strong correlation between language and society, by
seeing in the barbaric invasions a crucial cause of the vulgarization of classical Latin, by insisting on the monolingual state of
ancient Rome and on the vernacular's derivation from Latin, and
by recognizing the natural regularity of languages and the usefulness of contemporary dialects in the study of ancestral languages, Biondo anticipated much of what was to be fundamental
to nineteenth-century Romance philology.[43]

CHAPTER FIVE

THE RAMIFICATIONS OF THE FLORENTINE DEBATE:
THE CONTRIBUTION OF GUARINO, POGGIO, AND FILELFO

The Florentine debate engendered an enduring and, at times, fierce polemic among the humanists of Quattrocento Italy. The argument about whether in antiquity all Romans spoke Latin or whether, in a manner analogous to contemporary Italy, there were two modes of speaking, Latin and the vernacular, found fertile ground in the circle of Guarino Veronese at Ferrara. From the *Politia Literaria* of Angelo Decembrio,[1] a student of Guarino, we learn that Prince Leonello d'Este as well as classicists such as Feltrino Boiardo, Niccolò Pirondoli, and Decembrio himself shared Bruni's belief in ancient bilingualism. The argument, Decembrio notes, that Latin was the sole language of the cities of ancient Italy and that it was natural to the ancient Italians is untenable. In antiquity there were schools and teachers; consequently, one must assume that Latin was learned rather than acquired instinctively in one's own domestic setting.[2] It is hard to believe, Decembrio argues, that the ancients could absorb intuitively a language as difficult as Latin, which in his own time could be mastered only with much effort and diligence.[3] Such an argument by a member of his circle prompted Guarino in August 1449 to write a letter to Leonello in which he challenges the notion of classical bilingualism. Guarino's letter reveals a significant conceptual affinity with Biondo's *De Verbis Romanae Locutionis*.[4]

I

The objective of his letter, Guarino tells Leonello, is to explore what one means when one says that the ancients spoke Latin. Does one mean that they made use of a vernacular language similar to the one spoken by the contemporary masses or that they spoke the literal (*litteralis*) language of the present day scholars, which is correctly identified with the Greek term *grammatica* ("quam graeco vocabulo recte grammaticam appellamus")?[5] Guarino notes that most contemporary scholars believed that Latin was the sole language of ancient Rome; some, however, rejected such a notion, since they found it inconceivable that the populace of antiquity could master as complex a language as Latin.[6] To doubt the universality of Latin in antiquity, Guarino goes on to note, is not all that outlandish when one considers the dramatic changes undergone by Latin. In defending the monolingualism of ancient Rome, therefore, he would reconstruct the historical development of Latin through the ages.

Guarino prefaces this reconstruction with a definition of *Latinitas*. Antiquity recognized two types of *Latinitas*: one void of method and rules and spoken by the entire population, which was nevertheless still Latin ("tamen ipsa litteralis esset") and another, refined with study and art ("qua studio et arte comparata"), which came into being later and which was limited solely to the men of letters.[7] Relying on the *Rhetorica ad Herennium* (IV, 17) and on Isidore (*Etymologiae* I, xxxii, 1-2) Guarino notes that this second type of *Latinitas* is achieved by cleansing the Latin language of its solecisms and barbarisms, which resulted from Latin's contact with the indigenous languages of the conquered nations.

Turning to the reconstruction of the development of the Latin language, Guarino argues that Latin underwent four important stages of development. The first stage took place during the era that extends from Janus to Faunus, prior to the arrival in Italy of Nicostrata, who, it is believed, first introduced writing into Italy: " . . . quae prius litterarum notitiam ad nostrates detulisse fertur."[8] The Latin of this stage, which was disseminated by the Auruncians, the Sicanians, and the Pelasgians, ancient inhabitants of Italy, was totally unstructured and very coarse, much like the language of a child (*velut infans*). Nevertheless, though simple and archaic, because of the primitiveness of the age in which it was produced, the language of the first stage was still Latin in nature: "Quae verba, licet tunc vulgaria ut illius aetatis essent, tamen litteralem gerere formam nemo negaverit."[9]

Latin's second stage of development took place during the reign of King Latinus, son of Faunus. Though more refined than the Latin of the previous stage, this Latin was still badly constructed, being similar to the language of a stuttering girl (*balbutiens puella*). It was spoken by the subjects of King Latinus, that is to say, by the inhabitants of Latium and most of Etruria. It is believed that the laws of the twelve tables were written in this language and that this same language was used by Meneneus Agrippa to address the plebe on Monte Sacro.[10] The language spoken in the second stage, then, was also Latin, but a Latin void of grammatical regulation and dependent more on usage than on art: "Hos grammaticam idest litteralem, non grammatice, locutos contenderim, ut qui consuetudine magis quam ratione et artificio ducti eorum sensa enuntiarent."[11]

The Latin of the third stage was refined, elegant and fully developed. Indeed, a more appropriate name for the Latin of this stage would be Roman, that is to say, robust: "Successit tertia iam formosa iam adulta iam concinna, quam recte romanam, idest robustam, appellaverim."[12] Many a Roman writer—Ennius, Ovid, Virgil, Cato, but especially Cicero—achieved fame by writing in this Latin.

The fourth stage is characterized by a mixed language, which one might more appropriately call a corrupting language (*corruptela linguae*).[13] This corruption was brought about by the many barbarians who poured into Italy at various times. They stained the splendor and sweetness of the Roman language and fouled it like dregs.[14]

Guarino's reconstruction of the development of the Latin language is derived from Isidore.[15] Guarino, however, elaborates extensively on the succinct, sober text of Isidore. He gives his reconstruction a true historical flavor replete with dramatic episodes and important personages. Born at a mythical time in Italy as a whole, Latin achieves adolescence in Latium and part of Etruria, and adulthood in Rome. Purely a spoken language in its earliest stage, it later developed a written form, which became progressively more refined and sophisticated, achieving full fruition in the literary monuments of Republican and Imperial Rome. The onslaught of the barbaric invasions caused it to lose its integrity and to disintegrate.

The reconstruction of the development of the Latin language corroborates and illuminates the two types of *Latinitas* Guarino defines at the outset of this reconstruction. At the very beginning there was an unregulated language which was spoken by all. Starting with the advent of writing, however, there emerged also a normalized language, which, in the third stage at least, evolved into a more restricted, literary language free of solecisms and barbarisms. Guarino's history of the Latin language subscribes closely to the classical notion of the cycles of human development. As the terms *velut infans, balbutiens puella, adulta lingua* and *corruptela linguae* indicate, the Latin language is seen passing through stages of ascent and decline.

Guarino goes on to note that, given the organic development of Latin in the context of the social life of antiquity, Latin was the sole language of the ancients. In fact, all Romans, including the illiterates, understood and spoke Latin which was as natural to them as roaring is to the lion.[16] That all Romans understood Latin is proven by the numerous Latin orations delivered to the common people of ancient Rome. To substantiate this point, Guarino analyzes a list of Tironian notes recently uncovered by Poggio during the Council of Constance. Guarino argues that these notes are written in Latin, that is to say in a language similar to the one spoken by the learned men of his time and different from the contemporary vernacular (*a consuetudine vulgari diversus*).[17] To the extent that these notes recorded speeches delivered at assemblies of common people and soldiers, they demonstrate that the listeners of these speeches understood perfectly (*ad unguem*) the Latin used in them.[18] Indeed, the ancient Romans understood all forms of Latin, including the literary Latin of the dramatic performances, as attested to by the reaction of the spectators, who laughed, cried and sighed, and by the internal evidence of the dramatic works of Plautus and Terence, which exhort the audience to applaud, to be entertained, and to be instructed.

When he says, Guarino notes, that all Romans spoke Latin, he means the women as well. If the women had been incapable of understanding literary Latin, why, he asks sarcastically, would Cicero write so many letters to his wife and daughter?

That Latin was the sole language of ancient Rome and that it was spoken by all Romans, not just in Rome but in its provinces as well, could be proved analogically by examining the state of the Greek language in the contemporary Byzantine world. The Greek spoken in contemporary Constantinople demonstrated that the regulation of the Greek language ("Graecam litteralem esse affirmaverim")[19] derived from usage (*consuetudo*) rather than grammatical training (*grammaticorum ratio*).[20]

Guarino relates that while a student of Manuel Chrysolaras in Constantinople he had had an opportunity to observe first-hand children, women, even peasants speaking a flawless Greek worthy of the great writers of classical Greece. All of these people had acquired their Greek language instinctively in their domestic environment: " . . . tantum poterat absorpta a parentibus et conterraneis per usum forma loquendi absque norma."[21] Regulation, then, was inherent to the Greek language, which was acquired instinctively by all those who lived in the Greek-speaking world.

Guarino reasons that the same modus operandi must have been at work in the Latin-speaking world of antiquity. The Latin language, as the daughter of Greek,[22] must have enjoyed the same linguistic effectiveness and monolingualism common to the Greek language of the Byzantine world. Indeed, the numerous relics of classical Latin preserved in the languages of the former Roman colonies attest to the linguistic effectiveness and widespread use of Latin in antiquity. He cites some examples from Spanish, which he himself had experienced, and which he believes bore a remarkable Latin character.[23]

Guarino concludes his treatise by noting that the monolingualism of ancient Rome was affirmed further by the total absence of vernacular writing in antiquity. Of the numerous literary works of ancient Rome, none was written in the vernacular. If there are no traces of a vernacular writing in antiquity, it is because the vernacular was not part of the linguistic patrimony of the ancients.

As I have noted above, Guarino's letter reveals a strong affinity with Biondo's *De Verbis Romanae Locutionis*.[24] Guarino's objective, like that of Biondo, is to prove the monolingualism of antiquity. To achieve this objective, he relies, like Biondo, on both classical and contemporary sources. He concludes, like Biondo, that all Romans, including women, understood and spoke Latin. He thus concurs with Biondo that the vernacular was a derivative of Latin brought about by the barbaric invasions. That in antiquity there was no vernacular could be proven, Guarino argues on the strength of Biondo, by the lack of internal evidence in the literature of the ancients. Guarino, however, elaborates significantly on some aspects of Biondo's work. For one thing, he uses more sources than Biondo. Whereas Biondo relies primarily on Cicero's *Brutus* and *Orator*, Guarino makes effective use of a variety of classical and early medieval authors with emphasis on Cicero and Isidore.

Guarino justifies analogically, like Biondo, the monolingualism of antiquity, but whereas Biondo relies on evidence from the Italian region (the women of Rome, the peasants of central Italy), Guarino goes outside of Italy to the languages of Constantinople and Spain. The example of the Greek language, which had undergone the same historical trajectory as Latin and which, like Latin, was an inflected language, gives a special plausibility to Guarino's argument. Equally important is the example of Spanish. In making use of this language, Guarino not only justifies the universality and effectiveness of Latin throughout the ancient Roman world, but he also suggests obliquely that Spanish is a derivative of Latin.

Perhaps Guarino's most significant addition to Biondo's thesis is his elaborate account of the evolution (*mutatio*) of Latin. He goes far beyond Biondo's brief reference to the fall of the Latin language and reconstructs the whole development of Latin from what he believes is its origin in the age of Janus to its fall in the era of the barbaric invasions. Why does he undertake such a detailed reconstruction? Guarino himself tells us that the scope of this reconstruction is to prove more effectively the monolingualism of antiquity.[25] I would suggest, however, that the primary objective of this reconstruction is to discredit the medieval/Dantean theory on the origin of Latin and the vernacular, which must have been as prevalent during the debate of Ferrara as it had been during that of Florence. Otherwise why should he have found it necessary to trace the Latin language back to the mythical age of Janus? The monolingualism of antiquity could have been proven rather effectively, as Guarino himself demonstrates, with evidence drawn from classical and contemporary sources.

Dante had spoken of an Italian vernacular, attributable to the Babylonian Confusion, whose intrinsic mutability had led to the formulation of Latin, a language unchangeable in time and space.[26] Guarino counters that the vernacular was a derivative of Latin and that Latin was a natural rather than an artificial language, traceable to the age of Janus. The language of the ancient Romans, therefore, had always been Latin (*litteralis*) even in its earliest stage. As an antecedent of the vernacular, Latin was fundamentally different from its barbarous derivative: " . . . latina lingua litteralis, non ut haec materna vel haec barbaries, erat."[27] More importantly, however, as a natural language, Latin was inborn to the inhabitants of the Latin-speaking world. It thus was acquired instinctively ("absorpta a parentibus et conterraneis per usum absque norma") rather than through theoretical training.[28] Theoretical training, Guarino seems to suggest, was applicable only to that *Latinitas* which was refined with art and study and which found its best expression in the literary works of the great Roman writers.[29] In recognizing two types of *Latinitas*, an unregulated one which all Romans possessed instinctively and a regulated one which was solely the patrimony of men of letters, Guarino reveals a rather accurate perception of the variance between the Latin of the learned and that of the unlearned. He thus improves on Biondo's more general interpretation of a *Latinitas* characterized by a difference in tone and artistic elegance.

An interesting aspect of Guarino's letter is his contempt for the vernacular. Guarino reveals none of the sympathy for and pragmatism toward the vernacular we have seen in Biondo.[30] Indeed, the vernacular for Guarino is not a language at all, but a linguistic malady that forever corrupts the purity and integrity of the Latin language.[31]

II

Another important contributor to the polemic generated by the
Florentine debate is Poggio Bracciolini, who, as we have seen
above, took part in the original debate and sided with Biondo.
Poggio's thesis is expounded in the *Disceptatio Convivalis III*,
written about 1450. As Poggio himself tells us, the objective of
this work is to challenge Bruni's badly stated argument in his letter to Biondo that the ancients possessed two modes of speaking,
one for the men of letters and another for the masses.[32]

In disputing Bruni's thesis, Poggio concentrates on what he believes are the key points of his Florentine friend's letter: namely
Bruni's belief that the ancient masses' understanding of literary
Latin was analogous to the contemporary populace's understanding of the Gospel and the Solemn Mass; his assertion that the
Latin discourses delivered in the senate and in the courts were addressed to literate audiences and that in the assemblies where the
audience consisted of both literates and illiterates only the former
understood fully the meaning of the Latin orations; his argument
that the written form of the ancient orations was different from
and more refined than its oral equivalent; his contention that the
populace of antiquity could not possibly make effective use of the
inflection of cases; and his affirmation that what attracted the
masses to the theater was not recitation but scenic apparatus.[33]

Poggio dismisses outright Bruni's first point. Bruni's simile of
the Gospel and the Solemn Mass, he argues, is useless at best, for
the language of the Gospel and the Mass was not all that different
from the vernacular. Moreover, the populace came to have an understanding of the Gospel through constant exposure and through
interpretation by the clergy. Such was not the case with the Latin
literature of antiquity (orations, speeches, court opinions, poetry),
which not only lacked the familiarity enjoyed by the Gospel of his
day, but which, unlike the Gospel, dealt with a variety of subjects.

In disputing the remaining points of Bruni's letter, Poggio relies on a wealth of information gathered from numerous classical
sources.[34] Thus evidence from Cicero serves to undermine Bruni's
belief that the audience of the senate and the courts was learned.
Such a belief, Poggio maintains, is untenable, for as we learn from

Cicero (*Brutus* 210-213 and 259) the very officials (senators, judges) who presided in these chambers were often unlearned. Information from Quintilian and Cicero leads to the rejection of Bruni's contention that the populace was incapable of understanding the Latin orations delivered in the assemblies. Quintilian (*Institutio* V, 14, 29) and Cicero (*De Oratore* II, 159), Poggio argues, speak of adjusting one's discourse to the taste and interest of the populace. It is most unlikely that they would have contemplated such an adjustment, if the populace had been incapable of understanding Latin. A key passage by Varro is used to dismiss Bruni's argument that the common people of antiquity were incapable of making effective use of the Latin inflection. According to Poggio, Varro relates (*De Lingua Latina* VIII, 6-7) that even the newly acquired slaves were conversant in the Latin declensions. If the slaves had mastered Latin inflection, why should one doubt that the Roman citizenry could do the same? Reliance on Donatus and Cicero makes it possible to negate Bruni's assertion that the common people of antiquity came to the theater solely because of the scenic apparatus. Poggio contends that Donatus (*Commentum. Eunuchus*, Praef., 1,7) states unequivocally that the classical theater emphasized recitation rather than representation, as Bruni believed,[35] and that Cicero affirms (*Orator* 173 and 213-214) that the common people attending the theater appreciated the peculiarities (long and short sound, high and low pitch) of the Latin language and were often moved to applaud and hiss. Such an appreciation and behavior, Poggio concludes, are explicable only if the people understood the dramatic works in the literary mode.

As to Bruni's assumption that the written form of the ancient orations was different from and more refined than its oral equivalent, Poggio notes that he agrees with Bruni that the written orations were more refined than their oral equivalent: "Nam quod limatius asserit orationes scriptas quam dictas fuisse, ego idem sentio . . . ."[36] However, the greater refinement of the written orations does not imply that they were delivered in a language other than Latin: ". . . sed tamen latine dictas asserat necesse est."[37] That the ancient orations were delivered in Latin rather than in a vernacular form of speech and that the common people of an-

tiquity understood the Latin of the literary works was proved further by Juvenal, who states (VII, 82-86) that the populace rushed
to hear the sweetness of Statius' verses. The populace must have
heard Statius' verses in Latin, Poggio reasons, for so inherent a
poetic characteristic as sweetness is lost in translation, as Virgil's
translation into the Italian vernacular makes amply clear.[38]

To reinforce his argument against the bilingualism of Bruni,
Poggio resorts to analogical reasoning. Bruni had argued that it
was impossible for the ancient masses to master as difficult a language as Latin. Poggio retorts that the ancient masses' ability to
master Latin could be proven analogically by the children of
contemporary backward societies, who, through usage, learned
harsh and convoluted languages that scholars, such as himself,
could acquire only with great difficulty. Much the same phenomenon was apparent also among the many unlearned foreigners at the Roman Curia, who through constant exposure to Latin
came to understand it and speak it relatively well.[39] Moreover, the
monolingualism of ancient Rome was proven by the very name of
Latin. Just as the contemporary languages—French, Spanish,
German, Italian—are named after the people who speak them—
the French, the Spaniards, the Germans, the Italians—so Latin
derived its name from the Latins, that is to say, from the inhabitants of Latium who included the Romans.[40] The fact that the language of the Latins was called Latin proved that Latin was the
only language of these people: "Hanc unicam fuisse ipsa ratione
constat."[41] If in ancient Latium there had been a language other
than Latin, it would have been called by a different name, just as
in his own time Latin was identified as *grammatica* to distinguish
it from the vernacular.[42]

Continuing with his analogical reasoning, Poggio notes that the
monolingualism of antiquity was further affirmed by the numerous Latinisms prevalent in the vernacular of Rome and in those of
Spain and Romania, former colonies of the Roman empire. When
one considers the magnitude of the ancient metropolis, the many
barbarians who invaded it and the many foreigners who settled
there, it is extraordinary, Poggio marvels, that Rome's contemporary vernacular should have retained so much of the ancient lan-

guage. The large number of Latinisms prevalent in the Spanish and Romanian vernaculars was even more astonishing, for these countries were far away from Rome, the source of the Latin language, and had undergone a greater devastation than Rome itself. The numerous Latinisms apparent in these vernaculars demonstrated that Latin was strongly entrenched in the Roman world and that it was common to every segment of Roman society.[43]

In relying on the contemporary vernaculars to prove the monolingualism of antiquity, Poggio follows a procedure used by Biondo and Guarino; but whereas Biondo limits himself to the Italian vernacular and Guarino considers the Italian and Spanish vernaculars, Poggio expands his fellow humanists' linguistic horizons to also include Romanian.[44] In arguing that the Roman, Spanish, and Romanian vernaculars bore characteristics of classical Latin, Poggio suggests obliquely that these vernaculars are derivatives of Latin.[45]

Bruni had suggested that Latin was an artificial language learned through formal training; Poggio counters that Latin was a living language which was acquired in one's domestic setting since infancy.[46] Indeed, Latin was as natural for the ancient Romans as the vernacular was for the contemporary Italians.[47]

To prove the naturalness of Latin, Poggio turns to Quintilian. Speaking of the art of Latin eloquence (*latini eloquii scientia*), Quintilian (*Institutio* I, i, 4-6), according to Poggio, recommended that the nurses and those entrusted with rearing children speak accurately so that young Romans could learn from infancy the art of correct speaking and the rudiments of eloquence. Poggio contends that such a remark by Quintilian would have been ludicrous if Latin were learned at school rather than at home: "Quod consilium supervacaneum esset, si lingua latina tunc in scholis a praeceptoribus tradita extitisset, et non domestica loquela communi ab ipsa infantia suscepta."[48]

Linguistic unity, however, did not imply linguistic uniformity. Relying again on Quintilian (*Institutio* I, vi, 27), Poggio argues that, though all Romans spoke Latin, not all of them spoke grammatical Latin: "Quibus constat verbis omnes latine, sed non omnes grammatice loqui solitos . . . ."[49] The learned spoke more correctly than the unlearned: " . . . emendatius docti loqueban-

tur."[50] In fact, although the speech of the learned shared the same
linguistic base of the speech of the unlearned, it differed from the
latter in elocution and embellishment.[51] As in the case of the
contemporary vernacular, Poggio reasons, so in that of classical
Latin, the learned and unlearned speakers of these languages
shared the same linguistic terms, but the learned made more
effective use of these terms.[52]

At this point, bearing in mind, it seems, the heatedly disputed
issue among his contemporaries as to whether Latin was acquired
instinctively or learned in school,[53] Poggio asks: if Latin was a
natural language spoken by all, why did the ancient Romans invest
so much effort and time in teaching it to their children? In other
words, why was formal training in Latin necessary? Poggio resolves this issue by arguing that the objective of formal training
was not the learning of Latin per se, but the acquisition of its linguistic purity. Throughout its long history Rome had subdued
many nations, in and out of Italy, who spoke languages dramatically different from Latin. Many people from the conquered nations settled in Rome and learned to speak Latin. While appropriating Latin they polluted it with modes of speaking of their
own.[54] Consequently those Romans who wished to speak well
needed to cleanse their language of foreign usages. Formal training rendered this cleansing possible.[55] Just how important linguistic purity was in antiquity, Poggio argues, was stated by none other
than Cicero, who noted that only those people who spoke the
purest of Latin were successful in the area of eloquence.[56]

Poggio's *Disceptatio Convivalis III* makes a fundamental contribution to the polemic generated by the Florentine debate in that
it proves unequivocally that Latin was the sole language of ancient
Rome, being spoken by everyone in every social circumstance.[57]
More importantly, however, Poggio's treatise elucidates the thesis
advanced by Bruni. By arguing that the Latin orations were delivered in Latin rather than (as he claims Bruni thought) in a vernacular form of speech which was later transmitted into Latin, and
by insisting that Latin was the sole language of antiquity and that
it was a natural language that was acquired in one's domestic setting rather than (as again he alleges Bruni believed) through for-

mal training, Poggio leaves no doubt that Bruni subscribed to the notion of classical bilingualism.

Poggio's success in proving the monolingualism of antiquity is due to an extensive use of classical sources.[58] Overall Poggio uses his sources effectively, demonstrating good judgment and critical penetration. However, he commits a major faux pax. He misinterprets the already-cited passage by Quintilian (*Institutio* I, vi, 27) on the importance of usage in the ancient speech. To the extent that this misinterpretation of Quintilian constitutes a major flaw of Poggio's treatise, a flaw that has been denounced by contemporary scholars as well as by Lorenzo Valla, Poggio's arch-rival, it behooves us at this point to explore why and how Poggio misreads this passage by Quintilian.

Poggio's statement regarding *Institutio* I, vi, 27 reads as follows:

> Idem in primo sui operis libro, cum de grammatica disputat: "Quid" inquit "de aliis dicam, cum *senatus senatus senatui*, an *senatus senati senato*, faciat, incertum sit? Quare mihi non invenuste dici videtur aliud esse latine, aliud grammatice loqui". Quibus constat verbis omnes latine, sed non omnes grammatice loqui solitos, cum latinam linguam omnibus tribuat, grammaticam, hoc est loquendi doctrinam, literarum peritis. Latine igitur omnes, sed emendatius docti loquebantur, a quibus *senatum* quartae declinationis dici affirmat, ab indoctis secundae. Docti enim ratione iudicabant quod alii usu assequebantur, nulla suorum verborum ratione habita.[59]

Poggio, then, interprets *Institutio* I, vi, 27 to mean that, although all Romans spoke Latin, only the learned spoke grammatical Latin and that whereas the speech of the learned was determined by theory (*ratio*), that of the unlearned was determined by usage (*consuetudo*). That the mode of speaking of the learned was more correct than that of the unlearned is attested to by their using the fourth rather than the second declension when inflecting the term *senatus*.

The fact is, however, that in *Institutio* I, vi, 27 Quintilian makes no mention of the usage of the fourth vs. the second declention when inflecting the term *senatus*. Rather he speaks of the confusion among contemporary Romans over the genitive *senatus/se-nati*. Nor does Quintilian's passage explore the language of the learned vis-à-vis the speech of the unlearned, as suggested by Poggio. The primary objective of this passage, as well as of the entire first book of the *Institutio*, is proper speaking in general.

According to Quintilian, those Romans aspiring to acquire a correct, elegant Latin must subscribe to usage (*consuetudo*), which he equates with *latine loqui*, rather than analogy (*analogia*), which he associates with *grammatice loqui*. Analogy cannot serve as a guide to good speaking because it cannot be applied universally since it is often inconsistent with itself (*Institutio* I, vi, 12). Moreover, analogy, by fostering a mode of speaking patterned on the established linguistic terminology of the past, leads to a trite and archaic language. One should always pursue the correct form and resist the tendency to change; but to cling to forms long obsolete and extinct is sheer impertinence and pretentious pedantry (*Institutio* I, vi, 20). After all, what is ancient speech but ancient usage of speaking: "Et sane quid est aliud vetus sermo quam vetus loquendi consuetudo?" (*Institutio* I, vi, 43). Indeed, analogy is nothing more than the offspring of usage (*Institutio* I, vi, 16). Usage, then, is the surest guide in speaking: "Consuetudo vero certissima loquendi magistra . . . " (*Institutio* I, vi, 3). However, by usage Quintilian means not the mode of speaking of the masses, but the agreed practice of the educated men (*Institutio* I, vi, 5). This being the case, Quintilian's *latine loqui* implies linguistic propriety rather than prosaic speaking, as assumed by Poggio. On the other hand, Quintilian's *grammatice loqui* does not mean grammatical accuracy, as argued by Poggio, but linguistic archaism.

What caused Poggio to misread this passage of the *Institutio*? Though an admirer of Quintilian, in the area of language formation Poggio subscribes to Cicero's purism (*sermo purus et latinus*) rather than to Quintilian's usage (*consuetudo*). To understand Poggio's misreading of *Institutio* I, vi, 27, therefore, we must examine Cicero's notion of linguistic purism. In a key passage of the *Brutus* (258), Cicero argues that excellence in eloquence depended on faultless and pure Latin diction; only those who were so endowed were successful in the area of oratory. Though not universal, pure Latinity was the mark of the age of Gaius Laelius and Scipio the Younger.[60] Everyone in those days (unless one spent time outside of Rome or was exposed to a crude home environment) spoke well and correctly. The pure Latinity of those days, however, had been contaminated by the influx in Rome from different places of many impure speakers. The deterioration of Latin was such that it called for a purge of language and the adaptation of theory (*ratio*) over usage (*consuetudo*), for theory is not subject to change as is the case with usage.[61]

In insisting that the ancient Romans resorted to training to cleanse their language of linguistic impurities and in claiming that such cleansing was advocated by Cicero,[62] Poggio betrays a close adherance to Cicero's conception of linguistic 'purity. In fact, Cicero's rejection of *consuetudo* in favor of *ratio* serves to corroborate Poggio's belief in the qualitative difference between the speech of the learned and that of the unlearned: *Docti enim ratione iudicabant, quod alii usu assequebantur . . . nulla suorum verborum ratione habita.* This strong adherence to Cicero's reasoning causes Poggio to attribute a Ciceronian meaning to *Institutio* I, vi, 27—that is to say, he reads the passage of Quintilian from a Ciceronian perspective. Consequently, Quintilian's *latine loqui*, and *grammatice loqui* which in Quintilian's text stand respectively for linguistic propriety and archaism, in Poggio's reading come to mean the common language of the masses and the refined language of the learned.

III

Francesco Filelfo also made a significant contribution to the polemic generated by the Florentine debate. Filelfo's thesis is expounded in two letters to Francesco Sforza (*Franciscus Philelfus Sphortiae Secundo Sal.*, 1451) and Lorenzo de' Medici (*Franciscus Philelphus Laurentio Medici S.P.D.*, 1473). Like his fellow humanists before him, Filelfo's objective in these letters is to challenge Bruni's notion of classical bilingualism. Filelfo notes that in arguing that Latin was solely the language of the learned and that the masses spoke a vernacular form of speech similar to the vernacular of contemporary Italy ("eadem . . . qua ipsi nunc utimur"), Bruni had missed what is really at issue in the study of the linguistic state of ancient Rome: the difference between learned and common Latin intrinsic to the Latin language itself.[63]

In challenging Bruni's thesis, Filelfo reiterates much that had been said by Biondo, Guarino and Poggio.[64] Like them he maintains that classical Rome was monolingual but that the learned spoke a more refined (*limatior*) Latin.[65] That classical Rome was monolingual could be proved analogically, he argues like Guarino, by the linguistic state of contemporary Constantinople. He concurs with Biondo and Guarino that there had been no vernacular in classical Rome, for there was no proof of it in the rich, extant literature of antiquity, as was the case with the literature of contemporary Italy. Had antiquity produced the type of vernacular works written by a Dante, a Petrarch or a Boccaccio, there would certainly be evidence of it, for such literature cannot be obliterated by time.[66] Following the argument of Guarino, Filelfo contends that the language of the ancient Romans had always been Latin even in its earliest stage. The vernacular of contemporary Italy, therefore, had nothing in common with the archaic speech (*cum vetusto illo sermone*) in use at the time of Cicero.[67] The Italian vernacular, Filelfo argues following Biondo, was caused by the barbaric invasions, which totally corrupted the language and customs of antiquity.[68] As to the linguistic infelicities of Latin prior to the barbaric invasions, Filelfo maintains, like Poggio, that they were due to the linguistic pollution brought about by the many foreigners who settled in ancient Rome.

Filelfo, however, makes a significant contribution to the understanding of the linguistic state of antiquity in that he defines the variance between learned (*Litteratura*) and common (*Latinitas*) Latin. To be sure this variance had been the concern of Biondo, Guarino and Poggio as well; but whereas in these three humanists the examination of the difference between learned and common Latin serves as a means to prove the monolingualism of classical Rome, in Filelfo it becomes an end in itself. Consequently, Filelfo's assessment of *Litteratura* and *Latinitas*, though somewhat flawed, as we will see later, is nevertheless more accurate and extensive than that of his three fellow humanists.

Having dismissed outright the existence of a vernacular in antiquity, Filelfo concentrates on the variance within the Latin language. Were *Litteratura* and *Latinitas* completely similar or totally different from one another?[69] Using the example of ancient Athens, Filelfo concludes that the difference between *Latinitas* and *Litteratura*, though significant, was not a marked one.[70]

Latinitas and *Litteratura* differed in the exposition of the argument, the subject matter, the choice of words, and the inflectional endings and meaning of certain terms. *Litteratura*, which was forever faithful to orthodox significations and inflections,[71] made use of an elevated style rich in archaisms and subtleties.[72] *Latinitas*, on the other hand, which, on the strength of Cicero, Filelfo characterizes as the language of the forum and the people,[73] made use of a direct and linear discourse. *Latinitas* was receptive to common usages;[74] consequently, it was prone to change.[75]

However, the fact that *Latinitas* lacked the stability and sophistication of *Litteratura* did not mean that it was deficient. Relying again on Cicero (*De Oratore*, but especially *Brutus*), Filelfo argues that *Latinitas* was a sound and valuable linguistic medium.[76] As the language of the people, *Latinitas* was much more common than *Litteratura*. Indeed, *Latinitas* was known to both the learned and the unlearned,[77] whereas *Litteratura* was quite rare, being limited almost entirely to the intelligentsia.[78] When viewed within the context of the linguistic state of antiquity, *Latinitas* constituted the koine of classical Rome.[79] It was thus free of both euphemisms and barbarisms.[80]

Latinitas was used not just in speaking, but also in writing. In fact, *Latinitas* was common to that literature and to those documents intended for public consumption. The dramatic literature, for example, which was meant to be understood by the entire Roman society, made use of nothing else but *Latinitas*.[81] The same was true of those documents (ordinances, decrees, laws, contracts, etc.) that needed to be understood by the general public.[82] *Litteratura*, on the other hand, was limited to "elite" literature, such as philosophy and poetry. By virtue of its being highly elaborate and stable, *Litteratura* could serve as a normalizing factor

for *Latinitas*.[83] That being the case no one knowledgeable of
Latinitas had overlooked the importance of *Litteratura*.[84]

By arguing that *Latinitas* was widespread and effective, Filelfo
attributes much more linguistic uniformity and sophistication to
ancient Rome than was the case. The Roman masses were not as
linguistically proficient as he claims. It is true that Cicero (*Brutus*
210-211 and 258), from whom Filelfo derives much of his information, attests to children, women and even distinguished orators
speaking a faultless and elegant Latin which they had acquired at
home and without theoretical training. But here Cicero is referring
to the aristocratic circles of Roman society where proper upbringing contributed significantly to the quality of one's speech. The
speech of the general public, on the other hand, was not that perfect, as even Cicero admits (*Brutus* 258).

This flaw notwithstanding, Filelfo adds significantly to the understanding of the linguistic state of ancient Rome. He elaborates
on Biondo, Guarino, and Poggio's thesis regarding the variance
between the speech of the learned and that of the unlearned, and
he expands this thesis to include the difference between common
and learned literature. The very meaning of the terms *litteralis/
letteratura* undergoes an evolution in Filelfo. Whereas for Guarino *litteralis* denotes both the Latin language and its syntactical
regulation,[85] for Filelfo it comes to have a strictly syntactical,
conceptual meaning—that is to say, it comes to denote the
linguistically and conceptually sophisticated literature of the
learned. Moreover, by arguing that *Litteratura* was endowed with a
certain regularity and that *Latinitas* possessed an intrinsic
mutability, Filelfo advances theories that were to be fundamental
to future classical philologists.

CHAPTER SIX

THE FLORENTINE DEBATE
AND THE UNIQUE POSITION OF VALLA

In a unique way Lorenzo Valla also contributed to the polemic generated by the Florentine debate. Valla's contribution appears in *Apologus II*, written at the beginning of 1453.[1] *Apologus II* is in a dialogue form, with Valla, Poggio, and Guarino as its major dramatis personae. The objective of this work, Valla tells us, is to contradict Poggio's criticism in the *Disceptatio Convivalis* of Bruni's letter to Biondo. Of the several treatises dealing with the controversy generated by the Florentine debate, Valla's has been the most widely acclaimed by contemporary scholarship. *Apologus II* has been seen as a novel and provocative treatise, which not only modifies Poggio's notions about the linguistic state of antiquity, but which also clarifies and illuminates the many issues raised by the Florentine debate. Fubini, for example, notes that Valla provides a fresh examination of concepts and terms.[2] Similarly Salvatore Camporeale maintains that in *Apologus II* Valla challenges effectively the notion of Bruni, Biondo, and Poggio that the ancient *latina lingua* and *grammatica* were one and the same.[3] He thus easily dismisses Poggio's argument that the masses of ancient Rome understood fully the speech of the learned.[4] Poggio, according to Camporeale, had spoken of a linguistic uniformity in classical Rome; Valla, on the other hand, correctly recognizes a qualitative difference between the speech of the learned (*litteratus sermo*) and that of the unlearned (*vulgaris sermo*). Valla, Camporeale adds, traces the contemporary vernacular to the ancient *vulgaris sermo*. The acknowledgment of a genetic relationship between the *vulgaris sermo* of antiquity and the vernacular of modern time renders Valla less negative toward the *vulgaris sermo* than is the case with other humanists, such as Biondo.[5]

Silvia Rizzo also provides a glowing appraisal of Valla's *Apologus II*.[6] Valla, according to Rizzo, sides with Bruni in that, like Bruni, he traces the contemporary vernacular to classical antiquity rather than to the barbaric invasions.[7] However, he differs significantly from Bruni, because while Bruni denies that the language spoken by the ancient Romans was Latin, Valla contends that Latin was spoken not only by the ancient but also by the contemporary Romans.[8]

Valla's *Apologus II* is neither as novel nor as central to the issues raised by the Florentine debate as these scholars claim. Indeed, a close reading of the work reveals that much of Valla's argument is peripheral to the Florentine debate. Unlike the treatises of Biondo, Bruni, Guarino, Poggio, and Filelfo, *Apologus II* results not so much from a genuine interest in the linguistic state of antiquity, but from a need to vilify Poggio's personal life and scholarship.[9] In fact, *Apologus II* is part of an on-going polemic between Poggio and Valla. Begun in February 1452 with the publication of Poggio's *Oratio I* (=*Invectiva in L. Vallam Prima*),[10] which criticizes some key passages of Valla's *Elegantiae*, this polemic lasted until April 1453. Poggio's *Oratio I* was followed by *Orationes II, III, IV*, and *V*. Valla countered with *Antidotum I, Apologus I* and *II*, and *II Antidotum*.[11]

Highly polemical in tone, *Apologus II* is sophistic, convoluted, and deliberately equivocal. In arguing his point of view, Valla cleverly manipulates Poggio's thesis in the *Disceptatio Convivalis*. Given its ambiguity and its manipulative intent, in studying *Apologus II*, I will first reconstruct its overall meaning, then appraise this meaning in light of the views of Poggio and other contributors to the Florentine debate.

Apologus II opens by referring to the key issue of Poggio's *Disceptatio Convivalis*: did ancient Rome have one language common to all the people or did it have two modes of speaking, one for the learned and another for the unlearned? To the character Poggio, who asks what he thinks of the belief that all the ancient Romans spoke Latin, the character Valla answers that no one denies such a belief. And when Poggio rejoins that such a fact had been denied by Bruni, Valla replies that he does not see where in Bruni's argument such denial is present.[12]

Apologus II goes on to discuss the issue of the vernacular. Poggio notes that in contemporary Rome there was a vernacular and a Latin mode of speaking fundamentally different from one another. To the extent that Bruni believed that the common people of ancient Rome spoke a language similar to the one spoken by their modern counterpart, it followed that, as in contemporary Rome so in antiquity, the common people did not speak Latin.[13] "Quid ergo," Valla retorts scornfully, "hebraice nunc Romani loquuntur?"[14] Poggio elaborates that when Bruni speaks of a vernacular in antiquity, he does not mean a variant of Latin, but a language in its own right. In other words, like the vernacular (*volgare*) of contemporary Rome, the vernacular (*vulgaris sermo*) of ancient Rome was an independent linguistic entity.[15]

Poggio's reference to the vernacular of Rome as a linguistic entity independent of and different from Latin prompts Valla to argue that the Roman vernacular, both ancient and modern, was nothing else but Latin: "Itaque non modo quondam loquebantur, verum etiam nunc vulgo latine Romani loquuntur."[16] Exploiting Poggio's argument in the *Disceptatio Convivalis* that all languages, including Latin, derive their name from the people who speak them,[17] Valla contends that the vernacular of the Romans, who as inhabitants of Latium were Latins, had always been Latin and that in arguing otherwise Poggio was contradicting himself.[18]

The discussion on the nature of the vernacular is followed by a debate on the meaning of *grammatica/grammatice*. Referring to that section of the *Disceptatio Convivalis* that deals with the binomial *latina lingua/grammatica* ("latina lingua, quam grammaticam vocamus"),[19] Valla argues that here Poggio misinterprets the meaning of *grammatica*. *Grammatica* is not one and the same with *latina lingua* as Poggio's *latina lingua, quam grammaticam vocamus* suggests.[20] Moreover, the oneness of *latina lingua* and *grammatica* is denied by Poggio himself when he contends in his interpretation of Quintilian's *aliud esse latine, aliud esse grammatice loqui* that all the Romans spoke *latine loqui*, but that only the learned made use of the *grammatice loqui*, for the *grammatice loqui* is more correct and refined than the *latine loqui*.[21] By arguing that all the Romans spoke Latin, but that only the learned spoke grammatical Latin, Poggio, according to Valla, concurs with Bruni, whose thesis he purports to dispute.[22]

At any rate, Poggio, Valla argues, had misunderstood completely Quintilian's *latine loqui* and *grammatice loqui*. By *grammatice loqui* Quintilian did not mean a mode of speaking that is
more correct (*emendatius*) and more learned (*doctius*) than the
latine loqui. On the contrary, Quintilian considers the *latine loqui*
superior to the *grammatice loqui*, for the *latine loqui* derives from
usage (*consuetudo*), which leads to linguistic propriety and sophistication, whereas the *grammatice loqui* depends on analogy
(*analogia*), which leads to archaism and triteness.[23] This being the
case, the *latine loqui* was very much part of the linguistic patrimony of the orators and the learned in general, who made much
more use of it than the *grammatice loqui*.[24] Moreover, why insist,
as Poggio does, that analogy (=*ratio*) be fundamental to good
speaking when linguistic effectiveness, as demonstrated by all the
contemporary languages, can be achieved just as easily with
usage?[25] Usage, Valla contends on the strength of Quintilian
(*Institutio* I, vi, 3), should be the sole guide in good speaking.

To the extent that Latin was the common language of ancient
Rome, it makes no sense, Valla goes on to argue, to speak of
emendatius when referring to the *grammatice loqui* of the learned.
Emendatius implies that the learned of ancient Rome spoke more
Latin (*latinius*) than other Romans. But the language of a people,
like its currency, is typally the same for all.[26] Consequently the
learned of ancient Rome may have spoken in a more grandilo-
quent (*ornatius, eloquentius*), but not in a more Latin, manner.[27]
Furthermore, in limiting the *grammatice loqui* to the learned,
Poggio contradicts himself in that he denies his own assertion that
grammatice loqui was common to all the Romans.[28]

In an apparent reference to Poggio's reasoning on the naturalness of the Latin language,[29] Valla notes that Poggio's argument
that Latin was acquired through constant exposure in one's domestic setting rather than through formal training in school was
untenable. He notes that, as attested to by the many treatises on *ars
grammatica*, by the numerous references in classical literature to
schools and teachers, and by Quintilian, who makes specific references to the formal training of the Roman children (*Institutio* I, ii,
1; iv, 5), grammatical Latin was in fact learned in school. Furthermore, Poggio himself acknowledges indirectly the formal

training of Latin when he states: "Quod consilium supervacaneum esset, si lingua latina tunc in scholis a preceptoribus tradita extitisset."[30] Valla comments that if there were teachers (*preceptores*), there must have been schools.

Grammatical Latin was much too difficult to be acquired in one's domestic setting and without schooling. Valla contends that the two examples (the learning of harsh, convoluted languages by foreign children and the learning of Latin by the uncultivated foreigners at the Roman Curia)[31] Poggio adduces to justify the viability of grammatical Latin among the common people of ancient Rome are irrelevant and ineffectual. Poggio's reasoning that foreign children experience difficulty when learning their language was fallacious, for he failed to realize that all languages appear difficult to non-speakers.[32] As for the uncultivated foreigners of the Roman Curia, he knew of no one there who spoke suitable Latin.[33]

In disputing this last criticism by the character Valla, the character Poggio notes that formal training played an important role in the language learning of antiquity, but the objective of this training was the acquisition of the rules and causes of the Latin language rather than the learning of the language itself: "Ut discerent lingue, quam norant, rationes et causas."[34] How can one, Valla retorts, speak grammatical Latin and not know its rules and causes! Either the *grammatica* was an art that was learned in school rather than at home, or it was not an art at all.[35] Valla argues that in claiming, on one hand, that the ancient Romans acquired grammatical Latin at home and in maintaining, on the other, that they went to school to learn its rules and causes, Poggio contradicts himself once again. Indeed Poggio's entire argument is riddled with inconsistencies and contradictions.[36] At this point the character Poggio resorts to the banal observation that what he means to say is that the speech of the common people of antiquity was not grammatical, but as if (*tanquam*) grammatical.[37]

Apologus II ends with the character Valla claiming that what is at issue in this whole polemic is the difference between the language of the unlearned and that of the learned.[38] Poggio's own argumentation on this matter indicates that the difference between these two modes of speaking is practically nonexistent. The character Valla notes that, for his part, he will not address this issue, because his sole objective in this discussion is to dispute Poggio's thesis.[39]

An appraisal of Valla's *Apologus II* in the context of Poggio's *Disceptatio Convivalis* and of the other treatises generated by the Florentine debate reveals that Valla grossly misrepresents Poggio's thesis and that he overlooks completely the views of the other contributors to the Florentine debate, including Bruni's, whose argument he claims to defend and clarify.[40] To begin with Valla's first point, his argument that Bruni believed that all Romans spoke Latin but that only the learned spoke grammatical Latin, such an assertion by Valla is denied by Biondo, Poggio, and Filelfo who make amply clear that Bruni subscribed to a classical bilingualism.

As to the character Poggio's affirmation that the language of the masses of antiquity and the idiom of the people of contemporary Rome are one and the same and that this latter language is not Latin but a *volgare*, the fact is that Poggio, in the *Disceptatio Convivalis*, does not speak of such similarity, and he shows no interest in the contemporary vernacular. What concerns Poggio in the *Disceptatio Convivalis* is not the *volgare* of modern times,[41] but the *vulgaris sermo* of antiquity. Indeed, the controversy generated by the Florentine debate deals almost entirely with the ancient *vulgaris sermo*. Where the modern *volgare* is an issue, as in the case of Biondo and Guarino, it is used to deny the ancient bilingualism advocated by Bruni.[42] The observations of the character Poggio, then, regarding the similarity between the linguistic state of ancient and modern Rome and his reference to the modern *volgare* are a fabrication of Valla, and they are intended to provoke the character Valla to defend the Latinity of the contemporary Roman vernacular, a factor of utmost importance to Valla, as we will see later.

Valla manipulates much of the material of the *Disceptatio Convivalis III*. Thus, Poggio's discussion concerning the correlation between the Latin people and the Latin language[43] and his criticism of Bruni's thesis regarding the relationship between the contemporary *volgare* and a corresponding ancient vernacular are misrepresented as meaning that the language of the common people of ancient Rome was and still is Latin: "Nunquid Leonardus sentit ita vulgus olim Rome locutum ut nunc loquitur?"[44]

The discussion of the *grammatica/grammatice* is also manipulative to a large extent. Valla here reprimands Poggio for having misunderstood Quintilian's *latine loqui* and *grammatice loqui* and for having wrongly equated *latina lingua* with *grammatica*. This second mistake, according to Valla, had led Poggio to the erroneous conclusion that the ancient masses were equally conversant in *latina lingua* and *grammatica* and that the *grammatica* was learned at home rather than in school. Moreover, by considering *latina lingua* and *grammatica* as one and the same, Poggio had failed to see the qualitative difference (the variance between the language of the learned and that of the unlearned) implicit in the Latin language.

Valla, of course, is correct in criticizing Poggio's reading of Quintilian's *latine loqui* and *grammatice loqui*, which is colored, as we have seen above,[45] by Ciceronian purism.[46] Valla is incorrect, however, in accusing Poggio of having failed to recognize the qualitative difference implicit in the Latin language and of not having seen the importance of theoretical training in the acquisition of grammar.

The fact is that one of the most important points of Poggio's *Disceptatio Convivalis* is the recognition of a variance between the speech of the learned and that of the unlearned, which he corroborates with the linguistic variance present in the contemporary vernacular.[47] For Poggio, as well as for Biondo and Guarino, these two modes of speaking differed in degree rather than in kind. The learned spoke more correctly (*emendatius*) than the unlearned, but they all shared the same linguistic base. As to Poggio's failure to recognize the theoretical training of grammatical Latin, neither Poggio, Biondo, nor Guarino ever deny the importance of theoretical training in the acquisition of the Latin language, though they may have thought that theoretical training played a lesser role in language acquisition than Valla believed.[48] When they, therefore, argue that Latin was learned at home rather than in school, as does Poggio in the statement cited by Valla,[49] what they mean is not that theoretical training was irrelevant to the acquisition of the Latin language, but that Latin was a natural, rather than an artificial, language which was learned instinctively at home rather than *ab ovo* in school.

Valla's argument regarding the *Disceptatio*'s misrepresentation of the assessment of the nature and acquisition of Latin stems from an ingenious manipulation of Poggio's terms *grammatica/grammatice*.[50] As we have seen earlier, Poggio attributes two meanings to the term *grammatica* and its derivative *grammatice*. *Grammatica* means grammatical Latin (*ars grammatica*) as well as the Latin language itself (*latina lingua*). In the interpretation of Quintilian's *grammatice loqui* it stands for *ars grammatica*, but in the remaining cases, as Poggio himself makes amply clear, it denotes *latina lingua*: "latina lingua, quam grammaticam vocamus;" "quam linguam appelletis latinam, eam quam grammaticam vocamus;" "grammaticam, idest latinam linguam."[51] Valla ignores the binomial *latina lingua/ grammatica* implicit in these statements and interprets them to mean that for Poggio *latine loqui* and *grammatice loqui* are one and the same.

The binomial *latina lingua/grammatica* enjoyed a long history in the culture of Italy and Europe. It was common in the Middle Ages, as Dante demonstrates, and it was very much part of the culture of the fifteenth century, as Poggio and other contributors to the Florentine debate reveal.[52] Valla, possibly the most brilliant philologist of his age, must have been aware of the history of this binomial and of its presence in Poggio. If he chooses to ignore it, it is because by interpreting Poggio's *latina lingua, quam grammaticam vocamus* as indicating a similarity between *latine loqui* and *grammatice loqui* he is able to distort completely Poggio's argument in the *Disceptatio Convivalis III*. In fact, by arguing that for Poggio *latina lingua* and *grammatica* are one and the same, Valla is able to deny Poggio any knowledge of the variance implicit in the Latin language. Moreover, such an argument makes it possible for Valla to overlook Poggio's reasoning on the naturalness of the Latin language. And the overlooking of this reasoning in turn allows him to chide Poggio for having failed to see the value of theoretical training in the learning of grammatical Latin and for having made use of examples (the learning of difficult languages by foreign children and the learning of Latin by the uncultivated foreigners at the Roman Curia) that are ineffectual and irrelevant. Such an exquisite manipulation of Poggio's views does give the impression that the *Disceptatio* is highly inconsistent and hopelessly contradictory, as Valla claims, and that *Apologus II* provides an original and revisionist interpretation of the Florentine debate, as the students of this work have argued.

In his desire to prove Poggio inconsistent, Valla falls into some inconsistencies of his own. While arguing that the contemporary Roman vernacular was not a *volgare* in the modern sense of the term and that grammatical Latin was acquired in school, this language being much too difficult to be learned at home, Valla states that the ancient children learned grammatical Latin much more quickly and with much less effort than their modern counterparts. In fact, a couple of years after they first began to form words correctly (*nullo instante, intra biennium*), the children of antiquity mastered a linguistic expertise that contemporary students of Latin could acquire only after many years of assiduous studying. This difficulty on the part of the moderns could not be due to their being intellectually inferior to the ancients, for the moderns equalled the ancients in many ways. That the moderns found it difficult to acquire Latin could be proved by the illiterates of contemporary Italy, who were unable to master Latin terms and expressions they heard incessantly. The people of contemporary Rome, for example, badly mangled commonly used Latin terms and names: *domina covata* for *Domine quo vadis?*; *arocielo* for *Ara Celi*; *arcanoè* for *Arcus Nerve*, etc. One could conclude, therefore, that the speech of the contemporary masses had little in common with Latin ("nullum litterati soni verbum in ore est vulgi").[53] In noting that the children of antiquity learned Latin with ease and that the speech of the contemporary masses had little in common with Latin, Valla contradicts himself, in that he comes very close to concurring with Poggio's view that Latin was a natural idiom which was acquired instinctively at home and that the contemporary vernacular (the vernacular of Rome included) was a language in its own right.

Some of Valla's observations are downright sophistic and ludicrous. His rationalization, for example, that it is accurate to say that the literates of antiquity spoke more ornately (*ornatius*) and more eloquently (*eloquentius*), but inaccurate to argue that they spoke more correctly (*emendatius*), for to say that they spoke more correctly is to imply that they spoke more Latin (*latinius*), is pure sophism. Such reasoning does not square with linguistic logic or with the logic of the great rhetoricians of antiquity, such as Cicero, who believed that Latin could be spoken *emendatius*. The character Poggio is made to utter banal statements, as when he says that the speech of the common people of antiquity was not grammatical, but as if (*tanquam*) grammatical. It is most unlikely that the historical Poggio would have resorted to such a banality.

Given these many flaws, *Apologus II* cannot be considered a fundamental contribution to the Florentine debate, as contemporary scholarship argues. The primary objective of *Apologus II* is to polemicize and trivialize Poggio's reasoning in the *Disceptatio Convivalis*. The strong polemical intent of *Apologus II* is revealed by Valla himself when he notes that his purpose in this work is to dispute Poggio's thesis rather than to explore the qualitative difference implicit in the Latin language. It is true, as most students of this work have noted, that the highly polemical tone of *Apologus II* is due to its having been written at a time when this type of polemicizing was de rigueur,[54] and to its having to combat equally vitriolic and acrimonious tracts by Poggio, but these peculiar historical circumstances do not lessen its flaws and its overall irrelevancy to the Florentine debate.

Though inconsequential in terms of the Florentine debate, *Apologus II* is quite revealing of Valla's scholarly aspirations and of Roman humanism in general.[55] As we have noted earlier, an important aspect of *Apologus II* is Valla's insistence on the Latinity of the contemporary Roman idiom. The contemporary Roman idiom was not a *volgare*, that is to say, it was not a linguistic entity independent of and different from Latin, but a corrupt form of Latin ("et si non adeo ut nunc depravato"), which was nevertheless still Latin ("verum etiam nunc vulgo latine Romani loquuntur"). The insistence on the Latinity of the contemporary Roman idiom was coupled with a belief in the Roman nature (*Romanitas*) of Latin. Unlike Guarino, who argued that Latin was born in the Italian peninsula as a whole and that it achieved its adolescence in Latium and Etruria and its maturity in Rome,[56] Valla argues that Latin was strictly a Roman phenomenon—Latin was formulated in Rome and from Rome it spread to the rest of Italy supplanting the numerous Italian idioms of pre-Roman time. To the extent that Latin was solely the product of Rome, it could be identified as Roman (*romana lingua*). Indeed Valla uses *romana lingua* synonomously with *latina lingua*.[57]

The argument over the Latinity of the contemporary Roman idiom and the Roman nature of classical Latin is not limited to *Apologus II*, but is apparent in much of the literature generated by the Poggio-Valla polemic. In *Oratio I*, for example, Poggio chides Valla for having used *romana lingua* in his *Elegantiae*. Where does one read, Poggio argues, that *romana lingua* can take the place of *latina lingua*? The ancient Romans spoke a Latin and not a Roman language. *Romana lingua* stands for the vernacular of contemporary Rome, which is far removed from Latin (*procul a latina*). Hence *romana lingua* is limited to Rome just as the Florentine vernacular is limited to Florence, the Perugino to Perugia, etc.[58]

Countering this criticism by Poggio, Valla notes in *Antidotum I* that it is absurd to say that only the language of contemporary Rome can be identified as Roman.[59] Now as in antiquity, the language of Rome has always been both Latin and Roman: Latin because it was the language of the Latins from whom the Romans sprang; Roman because it was propagated by and received its dignity from Rome. As is the case with the Florentine of Florence and with other vernaculars of Italy, a language must adopt the name of the city that molds it.[60] The contemporary Roman idiom was still Latin, though a highly degenerated form of Latin. To argue otherwise is to imply that the ancient language of Rome had been supplanted by a new one that had come from who knows where.[61]

In Valla's insistence on the appropriateness of the term *romana lingua* when referring to the contemporary Roman idiom and the Latin of antiquity and in Poggio's denial of such appropriateness, we have more than a dispute on semantics. This discussion is representative of a larger debate among Quattrocento humanists as to whether Rome or Florence was the worthier inheritor and propagator of classical culture. For the Florentine humanists, including Poggio,[62] modern Rome was but a pale image of its ancient counterpart. The grandeur and the civilizing role peculiar to the ancient metropolis had been inherited by contemporary Florence, which the Florentine humanists acclaimed as the new Rome. In the *Laudatio Florentinae Urbis*, Quattrocento Florence's major apol-

ogy, Bruni argues that from a small Roman colony at the time of
Sulla, Florence had risen in his own time to a major metropolis
whose wealth, architectual splendor, political genius, military
prowess and cultural sophistication were unmatched not only in
Tuscany, but in the whole Italian peninsula. Indeed, Florence was
the center and the major propagator of the *studia humanitatis*.
Even the Florentine vernacular was the most expressive and elegant in Italy. It thus served as a model for Italians everywhere.[63]

The Florentines' claim to cultural superiority was disputed by
pro-Roman humanists, such as Valla and Biondo,[64] who considered Rome the sole inheritor and propagator of classical civilization. As a Roman extremely proud of his city,[65] Valla was especially irritated by the Florentines' characterization of Florence as
the new Rome. We gain a glimpse of this irritation in a letter to
Pier Candido Decembrio (1437). Referring to Bruni's *Laudatio
Florentinae Urbis*, Valla laments in this letter that Bruni had had
the audacity to claim that Florence was the inheritor of ancient
Rome and that the Florentines derived from the most illustrious of
Romans, as if Rome itself had ceased to exist and the contemporary Romans were not the descendants of their ancient counterparts.[66] The fact is that the Florentines descended from the worst
of Romans. He thus asks Decembrio to dispute vigorously and effectively Bruni's outrageous claim.[67]

Poggio and Valla's dispute over the Latinity of the contemporary Roman idiom and the distinct Roman character of ancient
Latin bears the imprint of the ongoing debate on Florence and
Rome's relationship to classical antiquity. In maintaining that the
contemporary Roman idiom was void of Latinity and in arguing
that this idiom was a *volgare* restricted to the city of Rome, Poggio
aims at depriving Valla of that cultural continuum so vital to his
Romanism. Like the Florentine *volgare* (a reference which, no
doubt, is intended to evoke the superiority of the Florentine vernacular over the Roman), the contemporary Roman idiom was a
language in its own right. By the same token, in denying classical
Latin a peculiar Roman stamp ("Latine tunc homines loquebantur, non romane"), Poggio nullifies Valla's claim that Latin was
the sole patrimony of contemporary Rome. Latin belonged to all
("sed in usu est et in precio apud multos").[68] On the other hand,

in Romanizing Latin (now as in antiquity Latin had always been Roman because it was formulated in Rome and it was from Rome that it spread to the rest of the world) and in denying a scission in the language of Rome (it is true that the language of ancient Rome had undergone a profound deterioration, but this deterioration did not make the idiom of contemporary Rome a language different from and independent of Latin), Valla establishes contemporary Rome as the sole repository of classical culture. He thus denies the Florentine humanists that classical inheritance so central to their Florentinity.

Valla's insistence on the cultural continuum of Rome may have also been due to the superiority of the vernacular culture of contemporary Florence vis-à-vis its Roman counterpart.[69] In fact, the acceptance of a scission in the socio-linguistic fabric of Rome would have meant recognizing a vernacular Roman culture, and the recognition of a vernacular Roman culture would have meant competing with the far superior vernacular culture of Florence.[70] It is no accident, it seems to me, that in *Apologus II*, as well as in his other works dealing with language, Valla says precious little about the origin and nature of vernacular language and culture.[71]

To conclude, then, *Apologus II* is inconsequential in terms of the Florentine debate, but it is quite instructive as to Valla's scholarly aspirations. Moreover, *Apologus II* sheds light on Roman humanism and its Florentine counterpart. Indeed, the polemic between the Florentine and pro-Roman humanists alluded to in this work informs much of the intellectual life of Florence and Rome in the Quattrocento and defines significantly their cultural orientations.

CHAPTER SEVEN

THE FLORENTINE DEBATE, ALBERTI, AND THE REAFFIRMATION OF THE *QUESTIONE DELLA LINGUA*

Apart from Biondo and Bruni, no humanist made a greater contribution to the issues raised by the Florentine debate than Leon Battista Alberti. Alberti's contribution appears in the proem (written in early 1437) of the third book of the *Famiglia*. This proem synthesizes much of the literature on linguistic theories produced prior to 1437, and it projects issues that were to flourish in the second half of the Quattrocento. Indeed, Alberti's proem heralds a new era in the area of language studies and vernacular culture. Because of its projection of future linguistic and cultural trends, I have decided to study Alberti's treatise last, even though it is chronologically closer to the Florentine debate than the treatises of Guarino, Poggio, Filelfo, and Valla, having been written only about a year after Biondo's *De Verbis Romanae Locutionis* and Bruni's letter to Biondo.

The proem of the third book of the *Famiglia* has been studied by several distinguished scholars. Much of this scholarship is valuable and provocative, but it fails to integrate effectively Alberti's proem in the linguistic rationale of the humanists and the Dantean vernacular tradition. My objective is to provide a fresh interpretation of this important document by exploring its numerous literary underpinnings and its far-reaching implications in the cultural life of late Quattrocento Italy.[1]

In considering the influence of Alberti in the Quattrocento, I will examine closely Cristoforo Landino and Lorenzo de' Medici's treatises on language as well as two other relatively unknown works—the *Protesta*, possibly by Alberti himself, and the *Capitolo* by a certain Niccolò di Francesco della Luna. All of these works are fundamental to the vernacular tradition of the Quattrocento. The treatises of Landino and Lorenzo have not received the attention they merit. More important still, they have not been integrated in the Dantean vernacular tradition with which they are inextricably connected. As for the other two works, they have been overlooked altogether by contemporary scholarship.[2]

Being addressed to Francesco d'Altobianco Alberti, a relative of Leon Battista, the proem of the *Famiglia* consists basically of three parts. After a reference to Antonio Alberti, uncle of Francesco d'Altobianco, and to Antonio's country house (*que' vostri bellissimi orti*) known as Villa del Paradiso in Pian di Ripoli,[3] part one goes on to discuss the fall of the Roman language and empire and the origin of the vernacular. Part two treats the linguistic state of antiquity, noting that classical Roman society was monolingual, and part three tackles the defense of the vernacular, arguing that the vernacular is an effective linguistic medium.

In part one, Alberti reminds Francesco how (as he had learned from his own father Lorenzo) Francesco's uncle Antonio Alberti used to stroll with his scholarly friends through the lovely gardens of his villa and ponder whether the demise of the Roman empire or the disappearance of the Latin language had been a greater loss for Italy.[4] Alberti adds that his father Lorenzo was of the opinion that the demise of the Roman empire, though regrettable, was less of a loss for Italy than the disappearance of the Latin language, because the Latin language served as a vehicle for classical civilization.

That Italy should have lost the empire is clear enough, Alberti goes on to argue, for it is logical that the peoples subdued by Rome wanted to free themselves of Roman domination. Italy's loss of the Latin language, however, was more problematic and lamentable, for this loss was not due to rejection but to the cultural barbarization that followed the demise of the empire.[5] This barbarization came into being because of the many barbarians who invaded Italy. The barbaric invasions led to the corruption and eventual disappearance of the Latin language, which could have been preserved only through use and which in ancient times was common to all.[6]

Alberti's allusion to classical monolingualism and his argument that the vernacular was brought about by the barbaric invasions, which led to the disintegration of Latin, are derived from Biondo.[7] Alberti, however, provides an assessment of the birth of the vernacular that is more descriptive and less contemptuous of the bar-

barians than Biondo's. The corruption of Latin and the eventual
emergence of the vernacular came into being through a prolonged
process ("di dì in dì insalvatichì e viziossi") and resulted from a
need for both the conquered and the conquerors to communicate
with one another.[8]
Having concluded that classical Rome was monolingual and
that the vernacular was a derivative of Latin, Alberti, in part two of
the proem, disputes Bruni's Dantean theory that the vernacular
was traceable to classical times and that Latin was an artificial language restricted to the learned rather than a natural one common
to all. In an obvious reference to Bruni and his followers, Alberti
notes:

> Nè a me qui pare da udire coloro, e' quali di tanta perdita
> maravigliandosi, affermano in que' tempi e prima sempre in Italia
> essere stata questa una qual oggi adoperiamo lingua commune, e
> dicono non poter credere che in que' tempi le femmine sapessero
> quante cose oggi sono in quella lingua latina molto a' bene dottissimi
> difficile e oscure, e per questo concludono la lingua in quale scrissero
> e' dotti essere una quasi arte e invenzione scolastica più tosto intesa
> che saputa da' molti.[9]

The statements "e' quali . . . affermano in que' tempi e prima
sempre in Italia essere stata questa una qual oggi adoperiamo lingua commune;" "dicono non poter credere che in que' tempi le
femmine sapessero quante cose oggi sono in quella lingua latina
molto a' bene dottissimi difficile e oscure;" and "più tosto intesa
che saputa da' molti" leave no doubt that here Alberti is thinking
of Bruni. In fact, these statements echo respectively Bruni's "Ego
autem, ut nunc est, sic etiam tunc distinctam fuisse vulgarem linguam a litterata existimo;" "tu ne quaeso, Flavi . . . vel alii, qui tecum sentiunt, animum inducere potestis ut credatis nutrices et
mulierculas et huiusmodi turbam ita tunc nasci, ut quae nos tot
magistris, tanto usu vix tenemus, illi nullis magistris assequerentur;" and "Intelligunt enim homines, licet inlitterati sint, nec tamen ipsi ita loquuntur nec illo modo loqui scirent, licet intelligant,
propterea quod longe facilius est intelligere alienum sermonem
quam proferre."[10] Moreover, the statement "e per questo con-

cludono la lingua in quale scrissero e' dotti essere una quasi arte e invenzione scolastica"[11] makes amply clear that Bruni subscribed to Dante's notion of classical bilingualism, a fact Bruni is trying to conceal in his letter to Biondo.[12] Indeed, this statement recalls Dante's "però che lo volgare seguita uso, e lo latino arte" (*Convivio* I, v, 14) and "Hinc moti sunt inventores gramatice facultatis" (*DVE* I, ix, 11).

In disputing Bruni's notion of bilingualism, Alberti argues that the monolingualism of classical Rome was proved by numerous Latin letters written to children and wives, by the excellent Latin spoken by some Roman women, and by the fact that some orators spoke an impeccable Latin, even though they lacked literary training. These arguments had already been used by Biondo, and they were to recur in Guarino and Poggio. Alberti, however, emphasizes the benefit derived from the use of Latin in classical society. The ancient Romans wrote in Latin because they wanted to be understood by all: "E con che ragione arebbono gli antichi scrittori cerco con sì lunga fatica essere utili a tutti e' suoi cittadini scrivendo in lingua da pochi conosciuta?"[13]

The allusion to the benefit to be derived from the use of Latin leads Alberti into the third part of the proem and the defense of the vernacular. Whereas parts one and two are rooted in the controversy generated by the Florentine debate, part three is entrenched in the Dantean vernacular tradition. That the proem of the third book of the *Famiglia* is linked to this tradition is made evident by the reference in the opening remarks of the proem to the intellectual gatherings that took place in Antonio Alberti's Villa del Paradiso.[14] As we will see later, these gatherings represent an important moment in the evolution of the Dantean vernacular tradition. What, then, was this tradition and how did it influence the third part of Alberti's proem?

The Dantean vernacular tradition received its impetus from Dante himself, who argued that the vernacular was a viable linguistic medium, capable of expressing lofty and new matters.[15] This tradition was kept alive by Boccaccio, and it achieved full fruition in the late Trecento with Salutati and his circle. Perhaps no other generation of Florentines has been more favorably disposed toward Dante than Salutati's. For Salutati and his generation, Dante was a paradigm of stylistic and linguistic elegance and a

fountainhead of philosophical and theological teachings. By
writing the *Divine Comedy* in the Florentine vernacular, Dante had
enhanced this vernacular's expressive range. This increased
linguistic sophistication had given the Florentine vernacular much
prestige among contemporary Italians. It behooved Florentines
everywhere, therefore, to glorify and emulate this most noble and
distinguished of countrymen.[16]

We gain an insight into this veneration of Dante and vernacular
culture from the historical novel the *Paradiso degli Alberti*.
Written by Giovanni da Prato in the 1420's, the *Paradiso degli
Alberti* commemorates the intellectual gatherings that took place
in Antonio Alberti's Villa del Paradiso in 1389—those same intellectual gatherings referred to by Alberti at the beginning of his
proem.[17] The *Paradiso degli Alberti* is a melange of Boccaccio-
like storytelling and of discussions on political, philosophical, and
historical matters. The society of the *Paradiso degli Alberti* consists of numerous historical figures, including Salutati who towers
over the rest.

The primary objective of the *Paradiso degli Alberti* is the glorification and enhancement of the Dantean vernacular tradition.
Thus, in what is an echo of Dante's own defense of the vernacular,
Luigi Marsili, one of the interlocutors of the novel, remarks that
the Florentine vernacular is a sophisticated linguistic medium capable of dealing with any abstract and profound thought: " . . . e
omai chiaro veggio e conosco che l'edioma fiorentino è si rili-
mato e copioso che ogni astratta e profonda matera si puote
chiarissimamente con esso dire, ragionarne e disputarne."[18] The
very use of the Florentine vernacular in the *Paradiso degli Alberti*
betrays the need to further enhance and ennoble this idiom.[19]
Dante himself and his masterpiece the *Divine Comedy* are the
subject of much praise and emulation in Giovanni's novel.[20]

The reverence for the Dantean vernacular tradition came under
attack about 1400 when an uncompromising classicism emerged
in Florence. For Leonardo Bruni and Niccolò Niccoli, the leaders
of this classicist school, the reverence for the Dantean vernacular
tradition was both threatening and antiquated. In the *Liber I* of
Bruni's *Ad Petrum Paulum Histrum Dialogus* (1401-1407),[21] one
of the best examples of the controversy between the vernacular
school and Latin humanism, Niccoli reminds Salutati that Dante,

Petrarch and Boccaccio (whom Salutati regards as the equal of the best of Latin authors) had produced a literature that was plebeian at best. In fact, Dante was totally void of Latinity, being ignorant of both the Latin language and Latin civilization. How can one who could not even speak Latin be called a poet?[22] Dante's Latin was so deficient that he should be removed from the rank of the learned and be confined instead to the realm of wool-workers, bakers, and such-like people. Indeed, Dante's writing was fit only for the plebe.[23] Niccoli levels much the same denunciation at Petrarch and Boccaccio.

Criticism of the Dantean vernacular tradition was quite common among the humanists. It was prevalent, as we have seen above, in Guarino's circle at Ferrara, and it was implicit in much of Valla's writing on language. But it was one thing to criticize the Dantean vernacular tradition in mid-Quattrocento Ferrara and Rome, where there was no vernacular culture to speak of; it was quite another to do so in early-Quattrocento Florence where the Dantean vernacular tradition was very much part of the intellectual life of the city. Given the entrenchment of this tradition in the intellectual life of Florence, the criticism of Niccoli and Bruni was bound to be resented. We have proof of this resentment in two invectives by Cino Rinuccini and Domenico da Prato, both consummate traditionalists.[24]

In his invective written in the early Quattrocento,[25] Rinuccini reproaches the militant classicists for having unjustly accused Boccaccio of being ignorant of Latin and for having ridiculed Petrarch's *De Viribus Illustribus* as a text fit for Lenten sermons. What was worse, Rinuccini adds, these babblers (*garulli*) had dared to vilify Dante Alighieri, whom they accused of being a poet for cobblers. Contrary to these babblers' view, Dante was the most distinguished of poets who had treated the whole spectrum of the human condition with so much conciseness and grace that his poem seemed to be the product of a divine intellect.[26] Indeed, Dante excels Virgil in both style and content. What renders Dante's accomplishment the more remarkable is that he achieved this feat in the vernacular, which is much less expressive than Latin: " . . . essendo ancora la gramatica sanza comparazione più copiosa che 'l vulgare."[27] Paraphrasing Dante himself (*Convivio* I, ix, 4), Rinuccini notes that this illustrious poet wrote in the vernacular rather than in Latin because by writing in the vernacular he could be more useful to his fellow countrymen: " . . gli umani fatti [Dante] dipigne in vulgare più tosto per fare più utile a' suo' cittadini che non farebbe in gramatica."[28]

Equally fierce is Domenico da Prato's invective, which appears to have been written around 1420.[29] According to Domenico, the classicists had the audacity to claim that Petrarch's lyrics were nothing more than useless poetic tidbits and that Dante, by writing the *Divine Comedy* in the vernacular, had produced a work of such low esteem that its leaves were fit for the paper bags of the apothecaries and fish mongers.[30] The fact is that the vernacular used by Dante was more authentic and praiseworthy than the Latin and Greek used by the classicists. Nor was the scorn of these backbiters, Domenico adds, limited to Dante. Infatuated with antiquity, they rejected everything modern and considered only Latinate works worth reading: "Ma essi susurroni nella loro vanità persistendo, per questo medesimo modo non solo Dante, ma tutti li moderni eloquenti dispregiano . . . et nullo libro per buono che sia gli piace, nè degnerebbe di leggere, non essendo scritto di lettera antica . . . ."[31] In an obvious reference to Niccoli, who clung to the uncompromising classicism we have seen earlier and who continued to criticize the works of the vernacular writers, but who failed to produce any writing of his own,[32] Domenico notes that the critics of vernacular literature were sterile braggarts (*appuntatori sterili*) who invested their energy in worthless etymologizing.[33] Given their inability to be creative, these critics should stop censuring the creativity of the vernacular writers and praise them instead for their noble works.[34]

The controversy between the vernacular school and Latin humanism was resolved by Bruni, who after a period of militant classicism, came to share the traditionalists' reverence for Dante and his vernacular culture. As noted earlier,[35] in the letter to Biondo and in the *Vita di Dante* which were written late in his scholarly career, Bruni concludes that the vernacular, when used effectively, has an excellence all its own and that Dante was a formidable poet who treated with precision and elegance a variety of subject matters. In fact, Bruni's appraisal of Dante closely parallels Rinuccini's assessment of the illustrious poet.[36]

To return to Alberti, his reference at the beginning of the proem to the intellectual gatherings that took place in the Villa degli Alberti leaves no doubt, it seems to me, that the proem is linked to the Dantean vernacular tradition. Indeed, the third part of Alberti's proem bears a strong imprint of this tradition and the controversy that it engendered. In fact, here Alberti concurs with Dante and Rinuccini that Latin is much richer and more ornate than the vernacular: "Ben confesso quella antiqua latina lingua essere copiosa molto e ornatissima . . . ."[37] Nevertheless, he believes, like Dante and Giovanni da Prato, that the vernacular is an effective linguistic medium that can approximate the expressive range of Latin: " . . . costui in questa oggi commune [the vernacular] troverebbe non meno ornamenti che in quella [Latin] . . . ."[38] He thus argues, like Bruni, that the Tuscan vernacular should not be rejected outright, for this vernacular has great merit if used effectively.[39] Following Dante, it seems, Alberti notes that by making use of the vernacular instead of Latin he is able to benefit many rather than to please just a few, for knowledge of Latin among his contemporaries was very limited indeed: " . . . scrivendo in modo che ciascuno m'intenda, prima cerco giovare a molti che piacere a pochi, chè sai quanto siano pochissimi a questi dì e' litterati."[40]

In the third part of the proem, Alberti also joins the polemic against Niccoli's uncompromising classicism initiated by the traditionalists.[41] In a manner reminiscent of Domenico da Prato's criticism of Niccoli, he argues that he cannot tolerate those people who scorn the vernacular, the only language they know, and praise Latin, a language they do not understand.[42] Indeed, these self-serving faultfinders say nothing in Latin and use the vernacular only to censure those who write valuable works in this language: " . . . questi biasimatori in quella antica sanno se non tacere, e in questa moderna sanno se non biasimare chi non tace."[43] The criticism of these faultfinders would be more tolerable if they were themselves active and praiseworthy writers.[44] For his part, he will be unperturbed by this criticism and continue to write in the vernacular, because only by so doing will he be able to be useful to the whole citizenry.[45]

Alberti goes on to note that, besides benefitting one's countrymen, writing in the vernacular strengthens the vernacular itself. He makes the bold suggestion that the vernacular could acquire the dignity of Latin if used effectively and continuously by scholars such as himself: " . . . simile [to Latin] certo sarà la nostra [the vernacular] s'e' dotti la vorranno molto con suo studio e vigilie essere elimata e polita."[46] Indeed, Latin came to gain worldwide authority only because it was used by many learned writers: "E sia quanto dicono quella antica apresso di tutte le genti piena d'autorità, solo perchè in essa molti dotti scrissero . . . ."[47]

Notwithstanding its affinity to the Dantean vernacular tradition, Alberti's proem differs from this tradition in some significant ways. A terribly pragmatic thinker who was born and spent the greater part of his life outside of Florence (Genoa, Venice, Padua, Bologna, Rome),[48] Alberti was free of the *campanilismo* and of the fierce Florentine Republicanism (*Florentinitas*) common to the other adherents to the Dantean vernacular tradition. His defense of the vernacular is based on practical, rather than on historical or patriotic, grounds. Contemporary writers, Alberti seems to argue, must make use of the vernacular not because they need to ennoble the literary tradition of Dante (as Domenico da Prato maintains), but because they need to contribute to the common good. The vernacular itself is accepted as an unquestioned fact. Its use is predicated on its being a viable linguistic medium rather than on its having resulted from an illustrious literary tradition. He thus lacks the awe for Dante peculiar to Rinuccini and Giovanni da Prato. For Alberti, Dante and his followers are a source of information rather than an object of emulation. Indeed, a certain pan-Italian tone pervades Alberti's assessment of the vernacular—the issue of the vernacular is viewed in Italian rather than in Florentine terms.[49] If there is any allegiance to Florence, it is directed primarily to the Alberti family: "Io non aspetto d'essere commendato se non della volontà qual me muove a quanto in me sia ingegno, opera e industria porgermi utile a' nostri Alberti."[50]

Like Bruni, Alberti believes in the coexistence of Latin and the vernacular. Unlike Bruni, however, he affirms this coexistence in both words and deeds. Whereas Bruni uses the vernacular sparingly, limiting it to trifling matters,[51] Alberti employs it extensively, treating moral and technical matters in both verse and prose. In fact, in the area of vernacular writing, Alberti is free of

Bruni's hesitancy and ambivalance. Alberti's faith in the capability of the vernacular equals Dante's.

To summarize Alberti's proem, then, Latin was a natural rather than an artificial language, and it was common to the whole population of ancient Rome. Its use was disrupted by the barbaric invasions. To the extent that the integrity and function of a language are preserved through usage, by causing Latin to fall out of use, the barbaric invasions had induced its corruption and eliminated its viability. It behooved contemporary writers, therefore, to employ the vernacular, the only language commonly used in modern time.

Alberti's call for the use of the vernacular was sensible enough, but apparently it was not heeded by his contemporaries. In the *Theogenius'* dedication to Leonello d'Este, written in 1442, a few years after the proem to the *Famiglia,* he laments that he had been criticized by many for not having written this work in Latin: " . . . molti m'ascriveno a biasimo, e dicono che io offesi la maiestà litteraria non scrivendo materia sì elegante in lingua più tosto latina."[52] Faith in the capabilities of the vernacular and the realization that such faith was not shared by other scholars must have spurred Alberti to persist in the defense of this idiom. Proof of this persistence are a Certame Coronario and a vernacular grammar, known as *La grammatichetta vaticana.*[53]

On October 22, 1441, in cooperation with Piero de' Medici, Alberti organized a poetic contest which he identified with the Latinized term Certame Coronario.[54] The poems to be entered in this contest were to be in the vernacular and were to deal with the theme of true friendship. Apparently the Certame drew many contestants (*molti dicitori*), including Francesco d'Altobianco Alberti, the dedicatee, as we have seen above, of the proem.[55] In deference to Pope Eugene IV, who was still residing in Florence, it was decided that the contest would be judged by ten of his secretaries (*dieci segretarii*), four of whom at least (Biondo, Poggio, Andrea Fiocchi and Cencio Rustici) had taken part in the Florentine debate of 1435.[56]

As we learn from a document (*Capitolo*) of a certain Niccolò di Francesco della Luna, which was to serve as a prose prologue to the collection of poems presented at the Certame Coronario,[57] the objective of the Certame was to glorify and enrich the Florentine

vernacular. Luna argues that, by treating the noble theme of
friendship in the vernacular, the contestants of the Certame would
be able to give the Florentine vernacular a dignity (*degnità*) and a
richness (*ubertà*) no one else had ever given it before.[58] It is
hoped, Luna adds, that, because of the Certame Coronario, the
Florentine vernacular, which in the past had been obscured by the
linguistic hegemony of Latin (*pella latina era obscurata*),[59] would
rise again, achieving so great an expressive range that it would
surpass all other Italian tongues.[60]

The winner of the contest was to be honored with a silver laurel
crown. No one, however, was so honored, because the judges failed
to agree on a clear winner.[61] The crown was, therefore, donated to
the church of Santa Maria del Fiore where the Certame took place.
The failure on the part of the papal secretaries to choose a winner
profoundly irritated the numerous dignitaries and the many
Florentine people who gathered to witness the Certame.[62]

It seems that Alberti was also irritated by the negative outcome
of the Certame. We gain a clue to this irritation from an anony-
mous text known as the *Protesta*, which may have been written by
Alberti himself.[63] The objective of the *Protesta* is to chastise the
papal secretaries for having failed to choose a winner.[64] Writing on
behalf of the Florentine people, the author of the *Protesta* notes
that the papal secretaries had reneged on their agreement with
Leon Battista Alberti to award the laurel crown to a meritorious
contestant.[65] By so doing, they had failed to endorse what had
been an extremely successful public enterprise.[66] Moreover, by re-
fusing to award the laurel crown, they had failed to give due
recognition to the diligence and ingenuity of the contestants,[67]
some of whom, as acknowledged by the papal secretaries themselves, were talented enough to rival the great Tuscan poets of the
past.[68]

The author of the *Protesta* seems to think that the Certame had
failed because the papal secretaries were envious of the fame and
dignity that would have accrued to Florence had they sanctioned
the vernacular compositions submitted by the contestants.[69] The
failure of the Certame was also due, according to the author of the
Protesta, to the papal secretaries' disdain for the vernacular, which
they considered far inferior to Latin: "Solo tra voi sentiamo essere
chi vitupera quessta principiata nosstra laude, e dicie essere cosa

indegna che uno vulgare chon uno nobilissimo literatissimo con-
tenda, e per questo in prima doversi vietare questj ciertamj."[70]
Consequently, they believed that the vernacular was incapable of
treating important literary and philosophical matters. The fact is,
the author of the *Protesta* goes on to argue, that important philosophical and literary subjects could indeed be expressed in the
vernacular, as proven by the poems submitted to the Certame,
which had treated successfully the moral concept of friendship.
Moreover, important matters, such as the concept of friendship,
which contribute to the common good of the republic, need not be
expressed in Latin.[71] As to the vernacular's inferiority to Latin, the
author of the *Protesta* contends that it is true that the vernacular
lacks the sophistication of Latin, but the vernacular is in a state of
becoming and all developing languages are perforce linguistically
deficient. The deficiency of the vernacular, however, should not
keep it from being used as a viable linguistic medium. Just as the
early poets of ancient Rome were not prevented from writing their
valuable works in a then-unpolished Latin, so the talented poets of
contemporary Florence should not be prevented from expressing
themselves in a still-uncultivated vernacular.[72] Languages become
polished and graceful through usage.

The *Protesta* reiterates the issue of Latin vs. the vernacular present in the proem of the *Famiglia*. That such an issue should have
played a role in the deliberations of the Certame is logical enough,
for most of the judges of the Certame (Biondo, Poggio, Rustici,
Aurispa, Fiocchi) were consummate classicists.[73] As in the case of
the proem, the *Protesta* justifies the use of the vernacular by relying on the historical parallel of Latin. Just as the ancient Romans
made use of an imperfect Latin, so the contemporary Florentines
should be allowed to make use of an imperfect vernacular.
However, the *Protesta*, even more than the proem, challenges the
humanists' notion that linked learning with Latin. Important
philosophical concepts such as friendship need not be expressed
in Latin.

An interesting feature of the *Protesta*, which is absent in the
proem, is the cultural politics that inform the discussion on Latin
vs. the vernacular. As we learn from Luna, and to a lesser degree
from the *Protesta* itself,[74] the proponents of the Certame were
concerned not only with the viability and propagation of the ver-

nacular, but also with the glorification and diffusion of Florentine culture, which they saw as inextricably connected with the vernacular itself. The strong political intent of the Certame must have been resented by the papal secretaries judging this contest, especially the non-Florentines (Biondo, Rustici, Aurispa), who bore a strong allegiance to Rome and the classical world.[75] Thus their refusal to sanction the Certame must have been due not only to the belief that the vernacular is inferior to Latin, but also to the realization that the objective of the Certame was to promote the cultural hegemony of Florence.

The disappointing outcome of the Certame did not dissuade Alberti from continuing to argue the case of the vernacular. About three years after the Certame (ca. 1443), Alberti composed the first grammar of the Italian vernacular. The primary objective of this grammar is to demonstrate that the vernacular possesses a regularity parallel to that of Latin. It thus partakes of Latin excellence. The stimulus for this work must have come from Biondo, who had argued that all languages, including the vernacular, are endowed with an intrinsic regularity.[76] In formulating the Italian grammar, Alberti relies strongly on the Latin model.[77] This approach is in keeping with his view of vernacular culture in general. His vernacular prose, for example, borrows heavily from Latin.[78]

Alberti's tenets of the vernacular achieve full fruition in the circle of Lorenzo de' Medici, fueling much of the debate on the question of the Italian language (*questione della lingua*) that took place at the court of this illustrous ruler. Direct inheritor and conduit of Alberti's views of the vernacular in Lorenzo's age is Cristoforo Landino, friend and admirer of Alberti, who contributed to the implementation of the Certame Coronario.[79] Landino produced a rather significant body of vernacular literature; much of it is related to the debate on language ongoing at the time.[80] The documents of Landino most closely connected with Alberti's thinking on the question of the vernacular are the oration delivered upon undertaking the teaching of Petrarch's poetry at the Florentine University (*Orazione fatta . . . quando cominciò a leggere i sonetti di Messere Francesco Petrarca in istudio,* ca. 1467) and the preface to his commentary on the *Divine Comedy* (*Vita e costumi di Dante,* 1481).

While disputing the argument by some distinguished citizens of Florence (*alcuni prestantissimi cittadini*) who maintained that the Tuscan idiom lacked the efficacy of its classical counterparts,[81] Landino argues that it is natural that the Tuscan language should be less effective that the classical ones, for the Tuscan language was in a state of development and all languages are somewhat crude in their developmental stage. Such was certainly the case with Greek and Latin. The elegance of Greek, for example, was not inborn in the language. Rather it came into being through continuous and ingenious use by numerous illustrious writers, who, having to express ever-evolving modes of thought, developed a language that met the needs of the emerging ideology:

> Forse el naturale suo dono e ingenita eleganzia? Nollo creda alcuno. Che addunque? Una copia quasi infinita di scrittori, e' quali al naturale ingegno agiugnendo industriosa arte e lungo studio, poterono a tanta sublimità condurla . . . e' quali volendo ogni dì nuove cose in quella esprimere nuovi vocaboli fabricavono.[82]

The same phenomenon was at work in the formulation of the Latin language, though the eloquence of Latin was aided also by the ever-expanding prestige and power of the Roman empire: "Così ogni dì più crescendo la riputazione e grandeza dello 'mperio, crebbe la eloquenzia."[83] When viewed in the historical context of Greek and Latin, the Florentine idiom did not fare all that badly. In fact, the beginning of the Florentine idiom had not been less distinguished than that of the classical languages: " . . . il nostro patrio sermone non avere avuto più debole principio che gl'altri . . . ."[84] Like the languages of antiquity, the Florentine idiom had enjoyed several illustrious writers who had contributed significantly to its richness and gracefulness.

The most distinguished vernacular writer of Tuscany was Dante, who first demonstrated what an effective linguistic medium the Florentine idiom was: "Lui primo dimostrò quanto fussi idoneo il fiorentino idioma . . . ."[85] He took a coarse, untried language and transformed it into an efficient, elegant linguistic instrument, just short of being perfect.[86] His success was due to his having appropriated the literary tenets and the rhetorical canons of antiquity.

Dante's accomplishment was extraordinary even by Homer and Virgil's standards, because these classical authors built on the linguistic feats of many who preceded them; Dante, on the other hand, created his elegant language ab ovo, since prior to him there had been no noteworthy vernacular writing:

> Trovò Omero la lingua greca molto già abondante ed esculta da Orfeo e da Museo e da altri poeti più vetusti di lui; trovò la latina Virgilio già elimata ed essornata e da Ennio e da Lucrezio, da Plauto e da Terenzio e altri poeti vetusti amplificata; ma innanzi a Dante in lingua toscana nessuno avea trovato alcuna leggiadria nè indotto eleganzia o lume alcuno . . . .[87]

Another important contributor to the Tuscan vernacular was Petrarch. Such was the excellence of Petrarch's poetry that it matched, and in some cases even surpassed, that of the poets of antiquity: "El quale nelle sue canzone e sonetti non dubiterò non solo agguagliarlo a' primi lirici ed elegiaci greci e latini poeti, ma a molti preporlo."[88] A distinguishing feature of his poetry was its richness of subject matter, a richness that gave the Tuscan vernacular an expressive range that had been thought impossible prior to Petrarch.[89] Boccaccio had also contributed to the refinement and enrichment of Florentine eloquence ("dette grande aiuto alla fiorentina eloquenzia"),[90] but since he was less of an artist than Petrarch, his contribution was inferior to that of his fellow Tuscan.

Landino adds that his own century had produced several vernacular writers, the most noteworthy being Bruni, Matteo Palmieri, Buonaccorso da Montemagno, Leonardo Dati, but especially Alberti: "Ma uomo che più industria abbi messo in ampliare questa lingua che Batista Alberti certo credo che nessuno si truovi."[91] Alberti surpassed all vernacular writers in the area of prose: " . . . e in orazione soluta e prosa ha avanzato e vinto tutti e' superiori . . . ."[92] As in the case of Dante, Alberti's success was due to his having appropriated the literary tenets of ancient Rome: "Legete . . . e' libri suoi e molti e di varie cose composti, attendete con quanta industria ogni eleganzia, composizione e dignità che appresso a' Latini si truova si sia ingegnato a noi transferire."[93]

The vernacular of these writers demonstrates that, if used effectively, the Florentine idiom is capable of great expressive power. Consequently, the linguistic deficiency attributed to it by some distinguished citizens (*alcuni prestantissimi cittadini*) of Florence is due not to the Florentine idiom itself, but to the writers who make use of it: "E certo, se e' considerassino diligentemente non solo quello che insino a ora di lei si vede, ma e quello che in essa ancora imperfetto e quasi rozo si potrebbe elimare e con molto ornato ripulire, intenderebbe non la natura d'essa lingua ma la negligenzia di chi l'usa essere in colpa."[94] Indeed, if the Florentine idiom had not made the kind of progress that one would have expected, it is because it lacked learned writers: " . . . e per niente altro essere rimaso indrieto se non per carestia di dotti scrittori!"[95] Landino notes that, in his day, many made use of the Florentine idiom, but only very few of them, the most noteworthy being Lorenzo de' Medici,[96] were truly great vernacular writers.[97]

Given the Florentine vernacular's potential of becoming a great language, it behooved patriotic, talented Florentine writers to make use of their idiom, so that Florence, which already surpassed all the regions of Italy in many other areas of human activity, would surpass them in the area of language as well.[98] Moreover, by so doing, they would benefit the common good of the fatherland: " . . . possiate alla vostra republica in molti e vari casi sovvenire."[99] Indeed, nothing contributes more to the well-being of a free society than high-principled eloquence.[100]

As we learn from the great vernacular writers (Dante, Alberti, etc.), Landino argues, to be successful in the Tuscan language, one must be knowledgeable of Latin: " . . . è necessario essere latino chi vuole essere buono toscano."[101] Since the Tuscan language has not as yet attained the gracefulness and the rhetorical sophistication achieved by classical Latin, the vernacular writers must imitate (*imitare*) their Latin counterparts.[102] Just as Latin became abundant by adopting many new modes of speech from Greek, so the already rich Tuscan language would become even richer by appropriating many new modes of speech from Latin: "Ognuno intende come la latina lingua diventò abondante dirivando molti vocaboli greci in quella, così è necessario che la nostra di ricca venga ricchissima, se ogni dì più transferiremo in quella nuovi vocaboli tolti da' Romani e faremoli triti appresso de' nostri."[103]

A comparison between Alberti and Landino reveals that the latter reiterates much of the argumentation of the former. Like Alberti, Landino makes use of the historical parallel of Latin and reaffirms the efficacy of the vernacular and the importance of the vernacular's reliance on Latin, but he elaborates significantly on these concepts. Whereas Alberti only alludes to the historical parallel of Latin, Landino provides an extensive account of this parallel replete with important historical figures from both the Roman and Greek worlds and tempered with a quasi-scientific analysis of the socio-literary factors that contribute to the formulation and refinement of a language. The excellence of a language, according to Landino, flows from its ever-rigorous utilization by distinguished writers, and it can be aided by political forces, such as the hegemonic power of the Roman state. Similarly, whereas in Alberti, the vernacular's reliance on Latin is a given, in Landino it evolves into a cultural axiom, being exemplified by all the leading vernacular writers, including Alberti, who is a great vernacular writer precisely because of his effective and successful appropriation of the linguistic and rhetorical attainments of classical Latin ("ogni . . . composizione e dignità che appresso a' Latini si truova si sia ingegnato a noi transferire").

Furthermore, Landino reintroduces the patriotic motive which, as we have seen above, is central to the adherents to the Dantean vernacular tradition, but which is all but absent in Alberti. Landino provides a glorification of the three crowns of Florence (Dante, Petrarch and Boccaccio) reminiscent of a Rinuccini and a Domenico da Prato but free of their exaggeration and emotionalism. His praise of the three Florentine writers is based, for the most part, on concrete historical evidence and is tempered by a savvy assessment of the literature of antiquity. Landino's ultimate objective is the cultural supremacy of Florence ("come in molte altre cose tutte le italiche terre avanza, così in questa ottenga il principato"), which he sees as the historical equivalent of the cultural supremacy of ancient Rome. Just as a relatively crude Roman society went on to become the undisputed cultural leader of Italy and the world by adopting the attainments of the more refined civilization of Greece, so a relatively uncultivated Florentine society will eventually emerge as the supreme cultural leader of Italy by appropriating the accomplishments of the richer civilization of ancient Rome.[104]

Alberti and Landino's train of thought on the vernacular was continued by Lorenzo de' Medici, who, as we learn from Landino himself, was one of his closest and worthiest disciples.[105] In his commentary accompanying his collected sonnets (*Comento ad alcuni sonetti d'amore*, ca. 1476), his most important document on the question of the vernacular,[106] Lorenzo argues that four qualities (*condizioni*) give dignity and perfection to a language: the natural ability to effectively express one's feelings and thoughts; the ability to excel other languages in sweetness and harmony; the ability to produce a distinguished literature (a literature that treats the important, useful subjects of metaphysics, theology, and natural and moral philosophy); and the ability to evolve from a provincial to a universal language.

The first and possibly the second of these qualities (the second quality is conditioned in part by the variability of human taste) are inherent in a language and constitute its true worth; the other two are accidental and are due to fortune and to the writers who make use of it rather than to the language itself.[107] Thus, the dignity that accrues to a language because of the quality of its literature is due to the subject matter and not to the language, for the subject matter is the end and the language the means: " . . . è necessario confessare che più presto sia degno il subietto che la lingua, perchè il subietto è fine e la lingua mezzo."[108] As a means to an end, that is to say, as an instrument employed to convey a message ("la lingua abbi fatto l'ufficio d'istrumento"), a language can be good or bad, depending on whether the subject matter expressed is itself worthy or unworthy.[109] Likewise, the dignity that flows to a language because of its universality is also accidental, being due almost exclusively to good fortune: " . . . e questo [the universality of a language] si può più presto chiamare felicità e prosperità di fortuna che vera laude della lingua . . . ."[110] Elaborating on Landino's notion of the correlation between the linguistic expansion of Latin and the political growth of ancient Rome,[111] Lorenzo notes that the Latin language, the most universal of all ancient languages, had certainly been blessed with such fortune. In fact, the universality of Latin was due not to its natural capacity to effectively express feelings and thoughts (the Greek language was more expressive than Latin),[112] but to the expansion of the Roman state. The expanding Roman empire not only introduced the Latin language to the whole world, but made its adoption by the conquered nations almost necessary: "Questa tale dignità d'essere prezzata per successo prospero della fortuna è molto appropriata alla lingua latina, perchè la propagazione dell'imperio romano non l'ha fatta solamente comune per tutto il mondo, ma quasi necessaria."[113]

Lorenzo notes that the Florentine vernacular was fully endowed with those qualities—expressive range and gracefulness—which are inherent in a language. That the Florentine vernacular was so endowed was made amply clear by the language of Dante, Petrarch and Boccaccio. The reader of the *Comedy* would note with what ease Dante expresses many theological and philosophical matters, and how effectively he exploits the low, medium, and high styles. Indeed, unlike his Greek and Latin counterparts who limit themselves to one of these stylistic modes, Dante coalesces all three styles into an harmonious whole (*in uno solo*).[114] The dignified, sweet, and refined poetry of Petrarch is also indicative of the efficacy of the Florentine vernacular.[115] Likewise the eloquence of Boccaccio's *Decameron* with its richness of subject matter, a richness that encompasses the whole spectrum of the human condition, leaves no doubt that no other language has a greater range of expression than the Florentine vernacular:

> Chi ha letto il Boccaccio, uomo dottissimo e facundissimo, facilmente giudicherà singulare e sola al mondo non solamente la invenzione, ma la copia ed eloquenzia sua. E, considerando l'opera sua del *Decameron* , per la diversità della materia ora grave, ora mediocre ed ora bassa . . . ed avendo ad esprimere tutte le nature e passioni degli uomini che si truovono al mondo, sanza controversia giudicherà nessuna lingua meglio che la nostra essere atta ad esprimere.[116]

Besides these three writers, the capabilities of the Florentine vernacular were also attested to by several other writers, especially Guido Cavalcanti, who succeeded in blending dignity of thought with sweetness of style: " . . . abbi insieme congiunto la gravità e la dolcezza . . . ."[117] The existing literature in the Florentine vernacular proves, concludes Lorenzo echoing Landino, that what has been lacking is not an effective language but capable writers who make effective use of the present language: "E però concluderemo più tosto essere mancati alla lingua uomini che la esercitino che la lingua agli uomini . . . ."[118]

Lorenzo adds that the Florentine had fulfilled also the third quality that brings dignity and perfection to a language: the ability to produce a distinguished literature. Certainly in Dante's *Comedy*, the Florentine vernacular had a work that treated important and useful matters. Just how important and useful was this work was attested to by the fact that it had been commentated by very learned and famous people and that it was being cited repeatedly by holy and excellent men.

Like Landino and the author of the *Protesta*, Lorenzo contends that, notwithstanding the feats accomplished so far, the Florentine vernacular still had room for growth. It had reached its adolescence, and, as it evolved toward its youth and adulthood, it would become ever more refined and perfect. Echoing Luna and Landino, Lorenzo notes that he hopes that the future development of the Florentine vernacular will be aided by the growth of the Florentine state.[119]

Lorenzo concludes that to the extent that the Florentine vernacular was fully endowed with those qualities inherent in a language, writers such as himself should be allowed to make use of their native Florentine, especially because by so doing they assented to a modus operandi common to such great languages as Hebrew, Greek, and Latin, all of which had been native and natural in their own time: " . . . che di quelle laudi, che sono proprie della lingua, la nostra ne è assai bene copiosa . . . E per queste medesime ragioni nessuno mi può riprendere se io ho scritto in quella lingua nella quale io sono nato e nutrito, massime perchè la ebrea e la greca e la latina erano nel tempo loro tutte lingue materne e naturali . . . ."[120]

Lorenzo establishes once and for all the right of the vernacular to coexist with Latin. It is true, as we have seen earlier, that other distinguished Florentines from Bruni to Alberti down to Landino had argued effectively in favor of this coexistence, but none had been as forthright and convincing as Lorenzo. In fact, Lorenzo shows none of the hesitancy with regard to the use of the vernacu-

lar characteristic of Bruni. Furthermore, by insisting, contrary to
Bruni, that Boccaccio's *Decameron* is an important exemplar of
the capacities of the Florentine vernacular, he proves obliquely
that this vernacular is effective in both prose and poetry rather
than just poetry, as Bruni believed.[121] Unlike Alberti, who continues to view the vernacular as inferior to Latin and who, therefore,
justifies its use on a purely practical ground—one must use the
vernacular because Latin is no longer the common language of
Italy[122]—Lorenzo sees the vernacular on an equal footing with
Latin and justifies its use on the basis of its merits. One must use
the vernacular, Lorenzo argues, because, as demonstrated by
Dante, Petrarch, Boccaccio and others, this idiom is as linguistically and literarily effective as Latin. The distinguished vernacular writers of Florence, especially Dante, had produced works
that rivaled the best of the ancient classics. To be sure, the
vernacular literature of Florence as a whole had not achieved the
splendor and volume of the literature of ancient Rome, but
continued use of the Florentine vernacular by capable writers
coupled with a hoped-for expansion of the Florentine state would
certainly raise the vernacular literature to the level of its ancient
counterpart. Lorenzo's very favorable appraisal of the Florentine
vernacular and literature causes him to deviate from his mentor
Landino. Whereas Landino argues that to be an effective
vernacular writer one needs to imitate and appropriate the classical
authors of ancient Rome, Lorenzo minimizes the importance of
the classical models and emphasizes instead the example of the
great vernacular writers of Florence.[123]

Lorenzo's success in his defense of the vernacular is due to a
cool analysis of the linguistic, literary, and historical factors that
informed the polemic of Latin vs. the vernacular. For the humanists, Latin was a quasi-sacred language that not only expressed effectively any subject whatsoever, but also gave dignity and
splendor to whatever it treated. Valla, for example, sees Latin as
food for the soul (*animi cibus*), as a civilizing force that was
readily embraced by the conquered nations.[124] Lorenzo divests
Latin of its reverence and mystique and reduces it to a mere
linguistic instrument. Languages, according to Lorenzo, are means
to an end. As such they will prosper or fail depending on whether
they are used by capable writers and blessed by fortuitous socio-

political circumstances. Consequently, the enormous accomplishments of Latin (its heightened efficacy, its splendid literature) were due not to any intrinsic quality of Latin itself but to its having been the official language of a powerful and highly civilized people. The very universality of Latin, which most humanists attributed to a mystical-like quality of the language itself, Lorenzo attributes to political realities—the world-wide expansion of Latin was rendered almost necessary (*quasi necessaria*) by the hegemonic power of ancient Rome. Given the fact that the success of Latin was due to external forces, other languages, endowed like Latin with the two basic linguistic qualities of expressive power and gracefulness, could duplicate the accomplishments of this classical language if blessed with analogous historical circumstances. Indeed, Lorenzo believes that such a duplication is being realized in modern Florence, where distinguished writers equal to the greatest of classical authors and propitious social and political factors were transforming the Florentine idiom from the language of Florence to the language of all of Italy.

Another important point made by Lorenzo, which, however, has more bearing on the Florentine debate of 1435 than on the polemic of Latin vs. the vernacular, is his reference to the naturalness of the Latin language. The fact that Lorenzo finds it necessary to emphasize that Latin together with Hebrew and Greek is a natural language seems to indicate that the Dantean issue of *lingua artificialis* vs. *lingua naturalis* disputed during the Florentine debate had lingered on to his own day.[125] In arguing that Latin was a natural language, Lorenzo reinforces considerably Biondo's assertion on the naturalness of Latin.[126]

The Florentine political expansion augured by Lorenzo, an expansion that should have aided the propagation of the Florentine vernacular in Italy, did not materialize. Nevertheless, due to the effective defense of the vernacular by the Alberti-Lorenzo school, to a need for a universal vernacular language, and to an ever-growing reverence for the great vernacular writers of Tuscany, the Tuscan vernacular did in fact expand in the second half of the fifteenth century. It became well-established in the flourishing courts of Ferrara and Naples where distinguished writers, such as Boiardo and Sannazzaro, wrote their masterpieces in a vernacular that was fundamentally Tuscan. The expansion of the Tuscan vernacular continued unabatedly in the sixteenth century. "In the sixteenth century," Paul Oskar Kristeller writes, "the Tuscan language . . . became the literary language used in all of Italy and for all forms of literature."[127]

To be sure there were dissenting voices that continued to champion the use of Latin. One such dissenter was Romolo Amaseo who, in November 1527 during the meeting in Bologna of Pope Clement VII and Emperor Charles V, delivered two orations on the need to retain the Latin language (*De Latinae Linguae Usu Retinendo*). The dissenters, however, were in a minority, and they subscribed to the dream of the *renovatio Romae* which had been central to the school of Biondo and Valla, but which became progressively more unrealizable, being destroyed altogether by the Sack of Rome. What concerned the intellectuals of the sixteenth century was not whether to write in Latin or in the vernacular, but what the nature of the vernacular should be. Having concluded that the vernacular was a viable linguistic medium, they were now faced with the vexing question (*questione della lingua*) of whether to use a courtly, pan-Italian idiom, or a strictly Tuscan language. And if they made use of the Tuscan language, whether to rely on the living language of contemporary Florence or on the literary usage of the distinguished Tuscan writers of the fourteenth century. Trissino and Castiglione argued for a universal language of literature that would encompass the best linguistic characteristics of Italy and would be representative of all its regions. Machiavelli, on the other hand, fostered the adoption of the current Florentine usage whereas Bembo championed the lofty language of the great writers of the Trecento.[128] These three approaches with some variants dominated the *questione della lingua* in the sixteenth century and beyond.[129]

Given their concern, as it were, with the creation of a viable and praiseworthy literary language, the contributors to the *questione della lingua* tended to disregard the scientific aspects of language formation (its etymology, its phonological phenomena, etc.) and concentrated instead on the expressive ability of a language (its rhetorical sophisitication, its artistic achievements). They thus lionized Bruni and Alberti's argumentation on the dignity and efficacy of the vernacular and overlooked the more scientific speculation of the school of Biondo. Bruni's fragmentary and inconclusive letter to Biondo, for example, was hailed as a valuable indicator of the origin of the vernacular, whereas Biondo's more substantial and historically accurate treatise (*De Verbis Romanae Locutionis*) was all but forgotten.[130] The efforts of Biondo and his followers, however, were not in vain. Their discoveries—the monolingualism of ancient Rome, the naturalness of Latin, the "Romance" vernaculars' derivation from Latin, etc.—became fully integrated in the culture of sixteenth-century Italy, being exploited by the more scientifically oriented scholars of the Cinquecento (Tolomei, Cittadini, Varchi)[131] and achieving full fruition, as noted above,[132] in the investigations of the Romance philologists of the nineteenth century.

Begun as a dispute on the linguistic state of ancient Rome, the Florentine debate eventually evolved into a polemic on the viability and nature of the vernacular. To the extent that both the understanding of the linguistic state of antiquity and the acceptability of the vernacular as the language of Italy constituted two of the burning issues of the Italian Renaissance, the Florentine debate represents one of the most important events in the cultural history of Renaissance Italy.[133]

PART TWO

DANTE'S THEORIES OF LANGUAGE AND STYLE

CHAPTER EIGHT

DANTE'S NOTION OF THE ILLUSTRIOUS VERNACULAR:
A REAPPRAISAL

Perhaps no other facet of Dante's scholarship has been the subject of greater controversy than his notion of the illustrious vernacular (*vulgare illustre*).[1] Developed in the *De Vulgari Eloquentia* I, ix-xix and II, iv-vii, Dante's notion of the illustrious vernacular has been on the whole misinterpreted or, at least, not fully explored. The objective of this study is to reappraise this important aspect of Dante's thought by considering it in light of past and present scholarship. The study, therefore, will consist of three sections: section one synthesizes the most representative works on the illustrious vernacular from the Cinquecento to the present; section two provides my own interpretation of the illustrious vernacular; and section three assesses my findings vis-à-vis those of the scholars studied in section one.

I

Giangiorgio Trissino, the scholar who first introduced the *De Vulgari Eloquentia* to the intellectual circles of Cinquecento Italy (1513?),[2] saw the illustrious vernacular as a composite language containing the best linguistic elements of all the vernaculars of Italy. Thus to those scholars who challenged the feasibility of his thesis on a national Italian language, he noted: "Ma sia come si voglia, tutte queste difficultà sono spianate, e dichiarate da Dante nel libro della Volgare Eloquenzia, nel quale insegna a scegliere da tutte le lingue d'Italia una lingua illustre e cortigiana, la quale nomina lingua volgare italiana."[3]

The assumption that by illustrious vernacular Dante implied the synthesis of the best linguistic features of Italy was rejected outright by Niccolò Machiavelli (1514). In a fictitious discussion with Dante he maintains that the standard language of Italy was fundamentally Florentine. Indeed, Dante's own *Divine Comedy* was written in Florentine notwithstanding the presence of some loan-words from other Italian vernaculars. A few borrowed words, Machiavelli argues, have little bearing on the nature of a language: "E tu che hai messo ne' tuoi scritti venti legioni di vocaboli fiorentini e usi i casi, i tempi e i modi e le desinenze fiorentine, vuoi che li vocaboli adventizii faccino mutar la lingua?"[4] Rather than being influenced by extraneous vernaculars, the Florentine vernacular of Dante together with the vernaculars of other distinguished Florentine writers had themselves influenced the vernaculars of other regions of Italy, giving rise eventually to a standard Italian language: "Ma quello che inganna molti circa i vocaboli comuni è che, tu e gli altri che hanno scritto essendo stati celebrati e letti in varii luoghi, molti vocaboli nostri sono stati imparati da molti forestieri e osservati da loro, tal che de proprii nostri son diventati comuni."[5] Hence "la lingua in che essi oggi scrivono è la vostra, e per conseguenza vostra; e la vostra non è comune con la loro."[6]

As the *questione della lingua* intensified during the Cinquecento so did the polemic on the precise meaning of the illustrious vernacular.[7] The proponents of the Tuscan school of the *questione della lingua* went so far as to question the very authenticity of the *De Vulgari Eloquentia*. Claudio Tolomei (1528) notes: ". . . e finite le vivande, di uno in un altro ragionamento trascorrendosi, accadde parlar di quel libro di Dante della Volgare eloquenza. Del quale assai distesamente ragionandosi, e per esser di simile ingegno, qual fu Dante, e per la vaghezza del soggetto suo, e ancora perchè egli non è ancora troppo divulgato, fu chi tra loro stimasse non esser cotal libro di Dante opera."[8] Benedetto Varchi (1570) found the *De Vulgari Eloquentia* so faulty that he considered it unworthy not just of Dante, but of any cultured individual: ". . . è indegno non di Dante, d'ogni persona ancorachè mezzanamente letterata."[9]

With the resurgence of the *questione della lingua* in the nineteenth century, Dante's notion of the illustrious vernacular became once again the object of great controversy. As in the Cinquecento, scholars continued to be baffled by the meaning of the illustrious vernacular. Antonio Cesari (1808) writes: ". . . e al tutto a leggere quell'opera, ci bisogna venire a queste due cose; a dir che fu uno

stordito [i.e. Dante], uno sciocco e vano scrittore, l'altra che a se
medesimo col fatto e con l'opera contradisse."[10] The linguistic
implications of the illustrious vernacular puzzled Alessandro Manzoni (1868) as well, a strong adherent to the Tuscan school of the
questione della lingua.

Manzoni resolves the issue by declaring the *De Vulgari Eloquentia* void of any theory on language:

> Riguardo alla *questione della lingua* italiana quel libro è fuor de'
> concerti, poichè in esso non si tratta di lingua nè punto nè poco . . .
> Dante era tanto lontano dal pensare a una lingua italiana nel comporre
> il libro in questione, che alla cosa proposta in quello non dà mai il
> nome di lingua . . . Se Dante non diede al volgare illustre il nome di
> lingua, fu perchè, con le qualità che gli attribuisce, e con le condizioni
> che gl'impone nessun uomo d'un buon senso ordinario non che un
> uomo come lui avrebbe voluto applicargli un tal nome.[11]

Thus, according to Manzoni, the objective of the *De Vulgari
Eloquentia* was not the Italian language but the "linguaggio della
poesia, anzi di un genere particolare di poesia."[12]

Manzoni's claim that the *De Vulgari Eloquentia* was void of
any linguistic theory, prompted Francesco D'Ovidio (1873) to argue that, though in the second book of his work Dante concentrates primarily on style and *ars poetica*, in the first book he does
in fact speak of language: "Che se nel libro secondo parla Dante
più di stile e d'arte poetica che di lingua, nel libro primo però è
evidente che egli vuol proprio parlar di lingua . . . ."[13] However,
like many of his predecessors, D'Ovidio chides Dante for having
failed to see the strong connection between the illustrious vernacular and the Tuscan dialect: "Sennonchè, io cerco di mostrare
come Dante, pur intuendo assai felicemente quanto di letterario vi
dovess'esser nella lingua colta, non riuscisse dall'altro lato a ben
misurare quanto ella dovesse al dialetto, in particolare al toscano."[14] Hence D'Ovidio concludes that the illustrious vernacular is a pure abstraction: ". . . siamo sempre a una pura astrazione, cioè a un certo *ideale* o *genio* linguistico nazionale; a
quella certa fisionomia comune di tutti i volgari italiani, la quale fa

sì che essi si ragruppino sotto una sola classe e denominazione, *volgare italiano*, ma che poi non esiste in sè e per sè."[15]

Pio Rajna (1906) also saw the illustrious vernacular as an abstraction: "La lingua a cui Dante, scartati i volgari singoli, assegna il primato, è un'astrazione."[16] In fact, this language is arrived at through an a priori reasoning: "Quel linguaggio eccellentissimo . . . sarebbe rivelato da un ragionamento aprioristico, fondato sul concetto di genere e di specie e sopra altre astrattezze."[17] Taking a position quite at variance with Rajna, Bruno Nardi (1921) considers the illustrious vernacular real, being intermixed with the existing dialects: "Il volgare illustre . . . è il sustrato comune che affratella fra loro tutti i dialetti d'Italia, ed esiste già in atto, commisto con essi."[18] It thus waits to be uncovered and utilized for the expression of the noblest of sentiments: "Il volgare illustre esiste di già, e attende che lo si scopra e lo si adopri da tutti, per esprimere i sentimenti più alti e più nobili che sbocciano dall'anima italiana."[19]

With the publication of Aristide Marigo's translation with commentary of the *De Vulgari Eloquentia* in 1938, the scholarship on this Dantean work and its centerpiece, the illustrious vernacular, reaches a new plateau. Like his mentor, Pio Rajna, Marigo considers the illustrious vernacular an abstraction: "Certo egli [Dante] si muove nella sfera dell'astrazione . . . Il volgare illustre appare appunto al Poeta come l'*Unum simplicissimum*, contenente il principio di perfezione formale, misura e regola dei *multa vulgaria* che sono dello stesso genere . . . ."[20] Indeed, Dante, according to Marigo, goes so far as to compare the illustrious vernacular with God himself and this comparison, undoubtedly, makes of the illustrious vernacular an abstract phenomenon:

> . . . giunge tanto oltre da paragonarlo con Dio stesso . . . in quanto contiene in sè tutte le forme degli esseri inferiori [i.e. the *multa vulgaria*], ciascuna delle quali ridà, più o meno, il profumo della sua essenza creatrice . . ., secondo la maggiore o minore nobiltà che le spetta nell'ordine dell'universo . . . L'immagine della mitica pantera profumata e il paragone con Dio ci prevengono dall'inanità di ogni sforzo per fissare l'esistenza concreta del volgare illustre con indagine empirica.[21]

Dante's notion of the illustrious vernacular depends then entirely on metaphysical principles and deductive reasoning: "Dante, che non è glottologo e rifugge dal nudo empirismo che non gli dà l'essenza delle cose, ricorre per dimostrarlo ai princìpi della metafisica ed al ragionamento deduttivo."[22]

Marigo goes on to note that for Dante the illustrious vernacular exists potentially in all the Italian cities, and it is the sole property of the distinguished writers of Italy (*doctores illustres*) who realize it through a sort of artistic sublimation: " . . . in tutte [the Italian cities] il volgare illustre trovasi in potenza, da cui l'hanno tratto fuori, attuandolo col loro magistero in una specie di sublimazione d'arte (*magistratu sublimatum*), gli scrittori più eccellenti d'Italia, maestri d'eloquenza (*doctores eloquentes*)."[23] Dante's notion of the illustrious vernacular, therefore, must be explained in light of this potentiality: ". . . coi concetti di potenza-atto e materia-forma si spiega il pensiero di Dante . . . ."[24] Indeed, for Dante the illustrious vernacular is present in the language and literature of the populace, but it becomes a reality only in the elite literature of the excellent writers.[25]

As Ruggero Ruggeri has noted, Marigo's commentary of the *De Vulgari Eloquentia* is excessively detailed and at times ponderous: "Se un punto si può muovere al suo commento, è quello di essere eccessivamente minuzioso, qualche volta faticoso e prolisso."[26] Nevertheless, because of its magnitude and its generally provocative exegesis, Marigo's work gave a new impetus to the study of the *De Vulgari Eloquentia*, adding much fuel to the polemic on the illustrious vernacular.

Unlike their predecessors in the sixteenth and nineteenth centuries, whose study of the illustrious vernacular was prompted primarily by the *questione della lingua*, contemporary scholars have approached this Dantean concept without any utilitarian motives. The illustrious vernacular is an important cultural phenomenon that deserves to be studied for its own sake. Overall, contemporary scholars have come to regard the illustrious vernacular either as an abstraction or as a concrete linguistic entity. The subscribers to the theory of an abstract language see the illustrious vernacular as the product of a deductive method of investigation, closely adhering to the linguistic and rhetorical doctrines of the Middle Ages, whereas the proponents of the theory of a concrete language see it as the fruit of an inductive method of research, heralding the theories of modern historical linguistics. Of the numerous studies written after the publication of Marigo's work, the most representative are the ones by Antonino Pagliaro, Gustavo Vinay, and Pier Vincenzo Mengaldo.[27]

Pagliaro has made the strongest case for the concreteness and, therefore, the modernity of the illustrious vernacular. Pagliaro notes:

> A Dante non bastava formulare l'essenza dell'italianità linguistica in astratto, piuttosto, tal postulazione era in funzione di una ricerca concreta di una *lingua comune*, che potesse assurgere ad espressione di arte. Era questo il fine ultimo della sua indagine, la legittimazione di una *lingua comune*, di un *volgare italiano* comune, non beninteso, come lingua per tutti gli usi, ma lingua di elezione . . . . [28]

Hence the illustrious vernacular or *lingua comune*, as Pagliaro calls it, is rendered feasible by the existence of certain fundamental characteristics, *primissima signa*, inherent in all the dialects: "In quanto italiani parlanti, noi abbiamo delle caratteristiche fondamentali comuni, alla stregua delle quali bisogna giudicare tutte le diversità dialettali."[29] For Dante, Pagliaro adds, the *primissima signa* were the *genus*, that is to say the *lingua comune*, whereas the dialects were the *species*. If the raison d'etre of the *lingua comune* depends on the *primissima signa*, then it follows that this *lingua comune* can be realized only by rediscovering the *primissima signa* and by utilizing those linguistic elements that are compatible with these *signa*:

> Se . . . l'italianità linguistica ha la sua essenza e la sua misura in alcuni caratteri fondamentali, "primissima signa", il volgare illustre, cioè la lingua comune, non può aversi se non attraverso lo scoprimento di questi caratteri e il riferimento ad essi di ogni particolare uso dialettale; accettazione, quindi, di ciò che si conforma ad essi ed eliminazione del deviato e del difforme. [30]

To the extent that the *primissima signa* constitute the *genus* and the *genus* is one and the same with the *lingua comune, lingua comune* means nothing less than a return to the primal state of the Italian idiom. That, argues Pagliaro, is precisely what Dante is trying to do: "Ed è appunto su questa via che Dante cerca d'individuare il volgare illustre, cioè la *lingua comune* nel suo primo momento formativo."[31]

Dante's *lingua comune*, according to Pagliaro, is conceptualized not in a vacuum, but in the context of the ethnico-geographic unity of the Italian people: "Egli considera questa unità [i.e. *lingua comune*] come inerente alla stessa unità di popolo, la quale si attua nei costumi, negli istituti, in tutti gli aspetti della vita."[32] An illustrious vernacular thus conceived is endowed with an extraordinary modernity: "Orbene, questa concezione è di una modernità che sorprende."[33] Indeed, implicit in this view of the illustrious vernacular are three very modern notions, namely: ". . . la nozione del divenire delle forme espressive in rapporto con il trasformarsi degli uomini e delle società umane, la nozione di comunione linguistica in rapporto con la varietà dei dialetti e delle parlate locali, la nozione, infine, di *lingua comune* come opera cosciente di elezione."[34]

Unlike Pagliaro who argues that the illustrious vernacular is a concrete linguistic entity whose conceptualization is predicated on some very modern notions, Vinay maintains that the illustrious vernacular is neither concrete nor modern: ". . . 'corte' è per lui [Dante] innanzitutto un concetto metastorico come metastorico è quello del volgare illustre, il quale . . . è già in certo modo una realtà prima di qualsiasi scelta storica."[35] Hence, Dante perceives the illustrious vernacular as a pure abstraction: ". . . dice il Marigo, Dante considera il volgare illustre 'metafisicamente,' come se altrove la sua teoria si impostasse storicamente. La verità è che Dante non ha mai giustificato o spiegato il volgare illustre in altro modo . . . ."[36]

Vinay disputes much of Marigo's thesis, being especially critical of Marigo's assumption that the illustrious vernacular is an artistic sublimation:

> L'interpretazione del Marigo riposa sul presupposto che tutto . . . si spieghi con i concetti di potenza-atto, materia-forma. Egli supera così effettivamente la tesi secondo cui "il volgare illustre è la lingua depurata di tutti i municipalismi e regionalismi," ma tradisce per un altro

senso il pensiero di Dante che di potenza e di atto non parla e non parla soprattutto di "sublimazione" ad opera dei poeti. [37]

To say that the illustrious vernacular is an artistic sublimation, Vinay adds, is to imply that the illustrious vernacular is strictly a literary language; it thus can be realized solely by the writers of Italy. However, such is not the intention of Dante. Indeed, for Dante the illustrious vernacular is the appanage of all the people of Italy:

> Non si tratta cioè di una potenza che altri deve tradurre in atto per noi e che accogliamo in qualche modo per imitazione, ma che attuiamo noi stessi spontaneamente nell'esplicare su piani successivi la nostra attività. È chiaro che non tutti sapranno essere italiani, come non tutti sanno essere cittadini e neppure uomini: è questione di attitudini, di intelligenza, di cultura, ma questo non cambia nulla al fatto che il volgare illustre non è *ex origine* una lingua letteraria.[38]

Moreover, if we accept Marigo's theory of sublimation, Vinay goes on to note, how can we then justify Dante's assertion in Chapter XVIII of Book I that if there were an Italian court, all its members would speak the illustrious vernacular? It is absurd to think that a functionary of an hypothetical Italian court could speak the type of illustrious vernacular envisioned by Marigo:

> ... se il volgare illustre è la lingua dell'alto stile, come è ammissibile, verbigrazia, che un funzionario della corte italiana [se ci fosse] parli volgare illustre che è la lingua propria esclusivamente della canzone, dell'epistola e della concione d'apparato? È un mettere il carro davanti ai buoi perchè, *hic et nunc*, il volgare illustre non è ancora la lingua di uno stile. [39]

The functionaries of the Italian courts, then, would be capable, according to Vinay, of speaking the illustrious vernacular, because the illustrious vernacular is inherent in all the people of Italy.

Also inherent in the people of Italy is the potential of an Italian court (*DVE* I, XVIII, 5), which would evolve automatically should Italy be endowed with a king: "In Italia non esiste l''aula' nè

quindi una 'curia' fisicamente unita: esistono tuttavia degli uomini che, qualora l'Italia avesse un re, ne costituirebbero, diciamo
così, automaticamente, la curia."[40] In the absence of a king, this
court is rendered feasible by the *lumen rationis*:

> Una curia dunque esiste "corporaliter" ma è un "corpus" disperso per-
> chè manca un re. Ma un "corpus" disperso non è neanche un "corpus"
> se non c'è un ente che lo unifichi: l'ente non è il principe "corpora-
> liter" inesistente: che cosa sarà dunque? Un ente non fisico ma che
> possa, spiritualmente, considerarsi sostitutivo del principe. Ed ecco
> Dante invocare il *"lumen rationis"* che non sarà dunque la ragione, ma
> quel particolare momento della ragione che, quando il principe c'è, è
> incarnato da lui. [41]

Vinay concludes that when viewed in its totality, Dante's reasoning
on the illustrious vernacular reveals a serious paradox. In fact, in
the first book of the *De Vulgari Eloquentia* (xvi-xix), Dante
equates the illustrious vernacular with the vernacular of Italy
(*vulgare latium*), a language common to all the people of Italy; in
the second book (i, 1; ii, 1; iii; iv, 1, 6-7; vii) he establishes it as the
language of literature and of only the highest form of literature,
the canzone. Hence "Dante, in tutto il *De Vulgari Eloquentia*, ha
inseguito due cose distinte senza accorgersene, o accorgendosene
senza riuscire a conciliarle."[42] This paradox made it impossible
for Dante to complete the *De Vulgari Eloquentia*. Furthermore,
had he continued his treatise, the difficulties caused by this paradox (language of a people vs. language of a style) would have
been compounded by other equally insoluble problems:

> Se Dante avesse voluto continuare, un altro nodo sarebbe del resto
> venuto al pettine col quarto del *Convivio*. Se la corte del rè è la sede
> per eccellenza del volgare illustre, di quale lingua sarà sede la corte
> dell'imperatore? O che la "reductio ad unum" deve fermarsi ai confini
> dell'Italia o della Francia o della Germania? E come immaginare una
> lingua "imperiale" diversa dal latino? Ma il latino non è una lingua
> artificiale? E perchè le lingue naturali non devono superare l'ambito
> di un regno? Dante era troppo logico per non rendersi conto di queste
> difficoltà e non rinunciare al sistema, come di fatto ha rinunciato. [43]

The most recent, extensive studies on the illustrious vernacular have been written by Mengaldo, who refutes the thesis advanced by Pagliaro and others that the illustrious vernacular is a concrete, linguistic entity genetically related to the numerous Italian vernaculars from which it is formulated. He argues that a genetic relationship between the illustrious vernacular and the vernaculars of Italy is totally foreign to Dante's reasoning. Had Dante believed in such a relationship, he would have elaborated on the linguistic kinship that would necessarily bind the illustrious vernacular to the regional tongues: ". . . Dante non si preoccupa affatto di chiarire, come noi ci aspetteremmo, il rapporto genetico che necessariamente lega un volgare letterariamente eloborato alla sua base municipale, ed il concetto del primo come raffinamento e sublimazione della seconda gli è, contrariamente a quanto hanno pensato alcuni interpreti, del tutto estraneo."[44] Far from establishing a kinship between the illustrious vernacular and the regional vernaculars, Dante "fa sì che fra la massa dei dialetti respinti nel loro particolarismo municipale e quel volgare illustre non esista comunicazions, sì che di esso viene taciuta la genesi concreta."[45]

The illustrious vernacular is not something that comes into being through an empirical process but something that exists metaphysically: "Il volgare illustre non è infatti per Dante qualcosa che 'diviene,' che nasce e si crea in un processo concreto, ma qualcosa che 'è' metafisicamente."[46] Hence, "il volgare illustre è un dato, non il risultato di un processo."[47] That the illustrious vernacular is a metaphysical entity is confirmed, according to Mengaldo, by the reasoning of Chapter XVI of Book I:

> . . . il ragionamento di *VE* I, xvi, non lascia dubbi in proposito. L'inseguimento della *pantera* , come Dante chiama metaforicamente il volgare i[llustre], attraverso le lingue municipali d'Italia si è risolto in un nulla di fatto: nessuna di esse s'identifica col volgare illustre. Perciò, per afferrarlo concettualmente, occorre procedere *rationabilius*, come dice Dante esplicitamente, sottolineando il passaggio da un procedere empirico a uno astratto e deduttivo, e la propria convinzione che solo quest'ultimo è risolutivo. [48]

In fact, this abstract, deductive method is continued in Chapter XIX, the last chapter of Book I, where Dante equates the illustrious vernacular with the Italian vernacular:

> Il *vulgare* . . . *illustre* . . . è senz'altro identificato col *vulgare latium* (cioè italiano), sulla base di un ragionamento ancora di tipo astratto e deduttivo, per cui, com'è vero che esiste un volgare di Cremona, così via via, ne esiste anche uno proprio della Lombardia, e poi di tutta la parte "sinistra" dell'Italia (*semilatium*) e infine dell'Italia intera . . . . [49]

Mengaldo concurs with many of the arguments advanced by Vinay; however, he disputes Vinay's assumption that the illustrious vernacular is an appanage of all the people of Italy. The illustrious vernacular is the sole property of the *doctores illustres*, Mengaldo argues, who are its only *familares et domestici*. In fact, nowhere in the *De Vulgari Eloquentia* does Dante imply that the illustrious vernacular is written or spoken by anyone other than the *doctores illustres*: ". . . ma in tutto il trattato non c'è una sola riga in cui si dica che di fatto qualcuno di diverso dai *vulgares eloquentes* parla o 'si esprime' in italiano illustre."[50] The fact that Dante attributes to the illustrious vernacular extra-literary criteria does not mean, as is assumed by Vinay, that the usage of the illustrious vernacular extends beyond the literary circle of the *doctores illustres*; it means rather that the illustrious vernacular, as conceptualized by the *doctores illustres*, serves as beacon for an Italian nation *in fieri*:

> Perciò che esso [i.e. the illustrious vernacular] in I xvii-xviii sia qualificato in base a criteri e valori non letterari, ma fondamentalmente sociali e politici . . . non significa che Dante finisca per disconoscere che "di fatto" il volgare illustre è appannaggio dei soli poeti; ma semplicemente che riconosce, come è spesso avvenuto in Italia in seguito, una portata profondamente politica a quell'unificazione linguistica su base letteraria, di anticipo e arra delle strutture giuridiche e politiche di una "nazione" italiana unitaria . . . .[51]

As is apparent from this synthesis, the views held by the scholars who have studied the illustrious vernacular are varied and often contradictory. This fact prompts a number of fundamental questions: is the illustrious vernacular the amalgamation of the best linguistic elements of all the vernaculars of Italy (Trissino) or is it simply an elaboration of the Tuscan/Florentine vernacular (Machiavelli, Tolomei, Varchi, Cesari, D'Ovidio)? Is the illustrious vernacular a concrete, refined language genetically related to the Italian vernaculars (Pagliaro and to a certain degree Nardi) or is it an abstract, metaphysical phenomenon (D'Ovidio, Rajna, Marigo, Vinay, but especially Mengaldo)? Is the illustrious vernacular the product of an inductive, empirical method of investigation (Pagliaro) or is it the result of an a priori reasoning (Rajna, Marigo, Mengaldo)? Is the illustrious vernacular the appanage of an intellectual elite, the *doctores illustres* (Marigo, Mengaldo), or is it the property of all the people of Italy (Vinay)? What precisely are the social and political implications of the illustrious vernacular (Pagliaro, Vinay, Mengaldo)? Does the illustrious vernacular in fact serve as a beacon for an Italian nation *in fieri* (Mengaldo)? And finally, is the conceptualization of the illustrious vernacular really beset with contradictions, contradictions that ultimately caused the discontinuance of the *De Vulgari Eloquentia* (Vinay)? Before I can answer these questions, I must reconstruct as fully as possible what I take to be Dante's notion of the illustrious vernacular.

II

In Chapter IX of Book I of the *De Vulgari Eloquentia* Dante notes that he will investigate the mutability of languages, a phenomenon never studied before: "Nos autem nunc oportet quam habemus rationem periclitari, cum inquirere intendamus de hiis in quibus nullius autoritate fulcimur, hoc est de unius eiusdemque a principio ydiomatis variatione secuta" (I, ix, 1). However, rather than investigating the evolution of all languages he will limit himself, for reasons of familiarity, to his own language, realizing that what is applicable to one language is applicable to all. The language he is going to treat is of a threefold nature encompassing the vernaculars of *oc*, *sì* and *oïl*: "Est igitur super quod gradimur ydioma tractando tripharium . . . nam alii *oc*, alii *sì*, alii vero dicunt *oil*" (I, ix, 2). Notwithstanding its present threefold nature, this language had originally been a single idiom. That it had been a single idiom can be proved by the fact that the vernaculars of *oc*, *oil* and *sì* possess many similar linguistic terms: "Et quod unum fuerit a principio . . . apparet, quia convenimus in vocabulis multis . . ." (I, ix, 2). In fact, the Spaniards,[52] the Frenchmen, and the Italians, the three peoples who speak respectively the languages of *oc*, *oil* and *sì*, call many things by the same names, ". . . multa per eadem vocabula nominare videntur, ut 'Deum,''celum,''amorem,' 'mare,' 'terram,' 'est,' 'vivit,' 'moritur,' 'amat,' alia fere omnia" (I, viii, 5). Why then had this language, which had originally been a single linguistic entity, evolved into three different idioms? And why had these idioms themselves (as demonstrated by the multiplicity of vernaculars that have resulted from the language of *sì* [I, ix, 4-5]) undergone numerous successive stages of transformation?

This mutability had resulted from the confusion caused by the construction of the Tower of Babel, a confusion that meant nothing less than the total oblivion of the primal language of Adam. Since that time languages have been reconstructed according to man's fancy (*a nostro beneplacito*). And because man's nature is very unstable and extremely changeable, languages are themselves unstable and changeable. Indeed, not just languages, but all that which is part of the human condition, such as usages and styles (*mores et habitus*), change in space and in time.[53] The change in time is by far the more pervasive and therefore the more significant. In fact, if we examine closely all of mankind's past and present works, we discover that we differ much more from the inhabitants of antiquity than from those of our own time, including those living far away from us (I, ix, 7). Thus, if the ancient inhabitants of Pavia were to be reborn, they would speak a language substantially different from that of their modern counterparts.[54]

In Chapter X of Book I, in what is obviously a continuation of the argument set forth in Chapter IX, 1-2, Dante notes that he will study the Italian vernacular by describing and comparing its many derivatives: "Nos . . . tractatum nostrum ad vulgare latium retrahentes, et receptas in se variationes dicere nec non illas invicem comparare conemur" (I, x, 3). However, before undertaking this study he gives a brief account of the linguistic geography of Italy. According to Dante, Italy is divided into two major geographic areas, one right and the other left of the Apennines. The area right of the Apennines comprises part of Apulia, Rome, the Duchy of Spoleto, Tuscany, the March of Genoa, plus the islands of Sicily and Sardinia, whereas the area left of the Apennines encompasses the rest of Apulia, the March of Ancona, Romagna, Lombardy, the March of Treviso with Venice, plus the regions of Friuli and Istria. Dante notes that the geography of Italy is characterized by significant linguistic differences. These differences are evident between the major areas right and left of the Apennines as well as among the regions of each one of these areas, among the cities of each region, and, at times, even among the districts of each city. Thus, within the area left of the Apennines the vernacular of Lombardy differs from that of Treviso, and within the region of Lombardy itself the vernacular of Ferrara differs from that of Piacenza (I, x, 4-7).

A certain inconsistency pervades this section (I, ix-x) of the *De Vulgari Eloquentia*. What was intended as a study of the mutability of the *ydioma tripharium* (*oc, oil, sì*) is narrowed down to the description of the Italian vernacular in its multiplicity of forms. No doubt, as has been observed by Marigo, Dante's concentration on the Italian vernacular was due to his greater familiarity with this branch of the *ydioma tripharium*.[55] I would add, however, that this concentration was also due to the belief on the part of Dante that, except for some inflectional variances, no significant lexical and morphological characteristics differentiated the language of *oc, oil* and *sì*.[56] Indeed, he seems to imply that the difference among these three elements of the *ydioma tripharium* is primarily phonetic: "Triphario nunc existente nostro ydiomate . . . secumdum quod trisonum factum est" (I, x, 1).[57] Moreover, one should not overlook the fact that Dante's primary concern in the *De Vulgari Eloquentia* is the creation of an Italian language (*vulgare illustre*). Consequently it is logical that he should concentrate on the Italian vernacular. To the extent that the three branches of the *ydioma tripharium* enjoy lexical and morphological uniformity, Dante may have reasoned that the information gained through the study of one of these branches, that of *sì*, is applicable to the other two, *oc* and *oil* .

Be that as it may, the Italian vernacular, like the *ydioma tripharium* is changeable. It thus has ramified from what was obviously one idiom (*unum ydioma*) to numerous vernaculars.[58] Most importantly, however, like the *ydioma tripharium*, indeed, like all natural languages, the Italian vernacular is a social phenomenon.

Dante's acknowledgment of the natural languages as social phenomena constitutes one of the most important features of the *De Vulgari Eloquentia*. For Dante language is an integral part of man's cultural patrimony. Such is the implication, it seems to me, of sections six and seven of Chapter IX of Book I, where terms such as *omnis nostra loquela, alia que nostra sunt, mores et habitus*, and *alia nostra opera* denote nothing less than man's culture of which language is but one characteristic. In fact, throughout the *De Vulgari Eloquentia, mores, habitus* and *locutio* become code words for the culture of a people.[59] Being an integral part of man's cultural patrimony, the quality of a language is conditioned by the culture of the region in which it comes to fruition. Hence, the idiom of contemporary Rome is very base (*turpissimum*), because the culture in which it has been realized is itself very base: "Dicimus igitur Romanorum non vulgare, sed potius tristiloquium, ytalorum vulgarium omnium esse turpissimum; nec mirum, cum etiam morum habituumque deformitate pre cunctis videantur fetere" (I, xi, 2).

Languages, usages, styles, all that which is produced by man change in space and in time, for man's products are regulated neither by nature nor by a common accord: ". . . qui nec natura nec consortio confirmantur . . ." (I, ix, 10). Rather they are totally dependent on man's fancy: " . . . sed humanis beneplacitis . . . nascuntur," (I, ix, 10). This inevitable mutability of all that is man-made, including languages, led to the creation of the *gramatica*, namely Latin. As an unchangeable lingustic entity, the *gramatica* had served for many centuries as a functional linguistic instrument for the peoples of different ages and different regions.[60] However, in recent times its effectiveness had been hampered by a decline in literacy, that is to say, a decline in the knowledge of Latin language and culture.

Dante's acknowledgement of this decline in literacy is first apparent in the *Vita Nuova*. Speaking of the origin of vernacular love poetry, Dante notes that it was a recent phenomenon: "A cotale cosa dichiarare, secondo che è buono a presente, prima è da intendere, che anticamente non erano dicitori d'amore in lingua volgare, anzi erano dicitori d'amore certi poete in lingua latina . . . E non è molto numero d'anni passati, che appariro prima questi poete volgari" (XXV, 3-4). In fact, vernacular love poetry had been in existence for only a hundred and fifty years: "E segno che sia picciolo tempo, è che se volemo cercare in lingua d' *oco* e in quella di *sì*, noi non troviamo cose dette anzi lo presente tempo per cento e cinquanta anni," (XXV, 4). Prior to this time, love poetry was written solely in Latin: " . . . non volgari ma litterati poete queste cose trattavano" (XXV, 3). The usage of the vernacular was prompted by the illiteracy of the ladies for whom the poetry was composed: "E lo primo, che cominciò a dire sì come poeta volgare, si mosse però che volle fare intendere le sue parole a donna, a la quale era malagevole d'intendere li versi latini" (XXV, 6).

The decline in literacy and the consequent need for a vernacular language are elaborated further in the *Convivio*, where not just the women, but most of contemporary Italian society, are deemed illiterate: ". . . principi, baroni, cavalieri, e molt'altra nobile gente, non solamente maschi ma femmine, che sono molti e molte in questa lingua, volgari e non litterati" (I, ix, 5). In fact, so pervasive was this illiteracy in contemporary Italy that fewer than one in a thousand could be considered truly conversant in Latin (I, ix, 2). Given the deplorable state of Latin in contemporary times, those who wanted to instruct and enlighten society, a moral responsibility of any sage, as Dante himself acknowledges in *Convivio* I, i, 8-9, had to make use of the vernacular. That is the reason, Dante goes on to note, that he had decided to write the commentaries of the *Convivio* in the Italian vernacular. Had he written them in Latin, the moral message implicit in these commentaries would have been beneficial only to a few literati, whereas in the vernacular they will benefit a large number of Italians: ". . . manifestamente si può vedere come lo latino averebbe a pochi dato lo suo beneficio, ma lo volgare servirà veramente a molti" (I, ix, 4). Nor should one doubt the efficacy of the Italian vernacular, for the Italian vernacular has the potential to approximate the linguistic efficiency of Latin. Indeed, the Italian vernacular has the potential to express the most complex and noblest of concepts.[61]

The feasibility and need of an Italian vernacular are acknowledged also in the *De Vulgari Eloquentia*.[62] In the proem Dante notes: ". . . volentes discretionem aliqualiter lucidare illorum qui tanquam ceci ambulante per plateas, plerunque anteriora posteriora putantes, Verbo aspirante de celis locutioni vulgarium gentium prodesse temptabimus . . ." (I, i, 1). However, whereas in the *Convivio* the Italian vernacular is seen as a de facto phenomenon depending primarily on the individual effort of Dante himself,[63] in the *De Vulgari Eloquentia* it is seen as a de jure entity resulting from the collective effort of the distinguished writers of Italy. Furthermore, whereas in the *Convivio* Dante is concerned with the effectiveness of the Italian vernacular in general, in the *De Vulgari Eloquentia* he concentrates on its quintessence, the illustrious vernacular: ". . . decentiorem atque illustrem Ytalie venemur loquelam" (I, xi, 1). What then is the illustrious vernacular and where does one find it?

Dante notes that some of his contemporaries claimed that their regional vernacular was so superior that it deserved to be acknowledged as the illustrious vernacular of Italy. This claim was advanced by the Romans (I, xi, 2) and the Bolognese (I, xv, 2 and 6), but it was especially strong among the Tuscans. Indeed, not just the populace of Tuscany, but even some of its distinguished literary figures believed that their vernacular deserved the accolade of illustrious vernacular: "Post hec veniamus ad Tuscos, qui propter amentiam suam infroniti titulum sibi vulgaris illustris arrogare videntur. Et in hoc non solum plebeia dementat intentio, sed famosos quamplures viros hoc tenuisse comperimus: puta Guittonem Aretinum . . . Bonagiuntam Lucensem, Gallum Pisanum, Minum Mocatum Senesem, Brunectum Florentinum . . ." (I, xiii, 1).

Spurred in part by this claim, Dante sets out to investigate whether in fact there is a regional vernacular that can be classified as the illustrious vernacular of Italy. He begins by eliminating what he considers to be the coarsest and the basest among the Italian vernaculars: ". . . ut nostre venationi pervium callem habere possimus, perplexos frutices atque sentes prius eiciamus de silva" (I, xi, 1). He thus eliminates all rural vernaculars because of their excessive *rusticitas*, all peripheral vernaculars because they had evolved outside of the linguistic mainstream of the Italian people, and the Sardinian vernacular because it is not a language in its own right, but a bad imitation of the *gramatica* (I, xi, 7).

Of the remaining vernaculars, the most prestigious was that of Sicily. The status of this vernacular was due to its having produced a highly refined poetry and to its having given the name Sicilian to Italian poetry in general: ". . . quicquid poetantur Ytali sicilianum vocatur. . ." (I, xii, 2). Excellent poetry had been also produced by some Tuscans—Guido Cavalcanti, Lapo Gianni, Dante himself and Cino da Pistoia (I, xiii, 4)—and by Bolognese, such as Guido Guinizzelli (I, xv, 6).

Dante maintains that the vernacular used by these distinguished poets was elegant, refined, and therefore worthy of being classified as illustrious. Thus speaking of the vernacular of the Sicilian poets, he observes that this vernacular is not at all different from the illustrious vernacular: " . . . nichil differt ab illo quod laudabilissimum est . . ." (I, xii, 6). However, the vernacular utilized by the distinguished poets of Italy was by far more refined than the standard vernaculars of their respective regions. In fact, the language of these poets was a linguistic sublimation of their regional vernaculars. One notes a significant detachment, Dante observes, between the language of these poets ("a proprio divertissent") and the standard vernacular of their regions. Indeed, the quality of the language of these poets was proportionate to its detachment from the standard vernacular of their regions—the greater its detachment, the higher its refinement.

There was then a language with sufficient elegance and refinement to be considered illustrious. But this language was solely the appanage of a few superior poets (Guido delle Colonne, Guinizzelli, Cino da Pistola, etc.) whom Dante classifies as *doctores illustres*. The standard regional vernaculars of Italy were, on the whole, rather base. For example, the Tuscan vernacular was nothing more than a cacophonous language (*turpiloquium*) (I, xiii, 4). An exception was the Bolognese vernacular which had a certain beauty, but its beauty was relative to other regional vernaculars rather than absolute (I, xv, 5-6). Dante, therefore, concludes that none of the Italian vernaculars could be considered illustrious. Nevertheless, to the extent that some vernaculars had produced specimens of illustrious vernacular, it followed that by reason of analogy the illustrious vernacular exists potentially in all the regional vernaculars of Italy. Indeed, the illustrious vernacular, like the panther which can be scented everywhere but can be found nowhere ("redolentem ubique et necubi apparentem" I, xvi, 1), exists in all the Italian vernaculars but can be identified with none of them.[64] Thus, having searched for this panther, i.e. illustrious vernacular, among the Italian vernaculars and having failed to find it, he resumes his search for it by utilizing a sounder method of investigation: ". . . ut ipsam reperire possimus rationabilius investigemus de illa . . ." (I, xvi, 1).

To understand what is at stake here, one must turn to the *Monarchia*. Echoing Aristotelian theories, in the *Monarchia* Dante notes that in every category (*genus*) of things, the best category is that which is the most unified. Thus, unity appears to be the root of good and diversification that of evil.[65] Again, in the *Monarchia*, he observes that all things of the same category may be reduced to one, which constitutes the norm of all the things encompassed by that category.[66]

If all the things of the same category can be reduced to one which serves as gauge of all the things of that category, and if the best category is that which is the most unified, it follows that the illustrious vernacular, which is by nature excellent (*nobilissimum*) and norm of all the vernaculars of Italy, as we will see later, consists in the *reductio ad unum* of all the Italian vernaculars. That is precisely what Dante says in Chapter XVI of Book I, where he resolves the issue of the illustrious vernacular:

> . . . dicimus quod in omni genere rerum unum esse oportet quo generis illius omnia comparentur et ponderentur, et a quo omnium aliorum mensuram accipiamus: sicut in numero cuncta mensurantur uno, et plura vel pauciora dicuntur secundum quod distant ab uno vel ei propinquant, et sicut in coloribus omnes albo mensurantur—nam visibiles magis et minus dicuntur secundum quod accedunt vel recedunt ab albo. Et quemadmodum de hiis dicimus que quantitatem et qualitatem ostendunt, de predicamentorum quolibet, etiam de substantia, posse dici putamus: scilicet ut unumquodque mensurabile sit, secundum quod in genere est, illo quod simplicissimum est in ipso genere. Quapropter in actionibus nostris, quantumcunque dividantur in species, hoc signum inveniri oportet quo et ipse mensurentur.

Nam . . . in quantum ut homines latini agimus, quedam habemus simplicissima signa et morum et habituum et locutionis, quibus latine actiones ponderantur et mensurantur. Que quidem nobilissima sunt earum que Latinorum sunt actiones, hec nullius civitatis Ytalie propria sunt, et in omnibus comunia sunt: inter que nunc potest illud discerni vulgare quod superius venabamur. . . (I, xvi, 2-4).

The illustrious vernacular, then, is a *simplicissimum signum,* that is to say, a *maxime unum signum,*[67] that is found among the *simplicissima signa* of the *actiones* of the Italian people. As *praedicamenta* which diversify into species, these *actiones* are seen as *genera.*[68] Consequently the *simplicissima signa* function as norms of the species of these *actiones* ("quibus Latine actiones ponderantur et mensurantur").[69] The *simplicissima signa* are *nobilissima,* because they are very perfect: ". . . se volemo riguardo avere," says Dante in the *Convivio,* "de la comune consuetudine di parlare, per questo vocabulo 'nobilitade' s'intende perfezione di propria natura in ciascuna cosa" (IV, xvi, 4). As the most perfect manifestations and embodiments of the *genera,* the *simplicissima signa* become synonymous with the *genera* themselves. They are thus common to all the Italian cities but belong to none of them in particular ("hec nullius civitatis Ytalie propria sunt, et in omnibus comunia sunt"), because what prevails in each individual city is not the *genus* (the universal, the national) but the *species* (the particular, the regional). The illustrious vernacular is a *simplicissimum signum,* but what does Dante mean by this *signum*?

In Chapters IX and X of Book I, Dante affirms that the language of *sì* had ramified from a single linguistic entity (*unum ydioma*) to many vernaculars (*multa vulgaria*). The *simplicissimum signum* of Chapter XVI is none other, it seems to me, than the *unum ydioma* of Chapters IX and X. That by *simplicissimum signum* Dante implies this *unum ydioma* is verified by a conceptual and textual correlation between sections six and seven of Chapter IX and sections three and four of Chapter XVI, two key passages on the theory of the vernacular. In fact, in Chapter XVI, Dante recapitulates and elaborates the theories advanced in Chapter IX. He repeats the same terms of Chapter IX—*mores, habitus,* and *locutio*—and reaffirms their cultural value. They are characteristics of the cultural patrimony of the Italian people ("in quantum ut homines latini agimus"). The Italian language is but one feature of this patrimony; consequently it is to be found among the various elements of the culture of Italy ("inter que nunc potest illud discerni vulgare"). However, in Chapter XVI, we have two very important additions—the notion of the *simplicissimum signum* and the characterization in *genera* of man's activities (*actiones*).

From the synthesis of sections six and seven of Chapters IX and sections three and four of Chapter XVI, we deduce that if it is true that human activities are subject to an inevitable mutability because of the unstable and changeable nature of man, it is also true that they are endowed with a *simplicissimum signum*, that is to say, with a *reductio ad unum* of their species. Therefore the linguistic unity of the Italian vernacular, which had been lost because of its ramification into the *multa vulgaria*, can be reacquired by reconstructing the *simplicissimum signum* of these *vulgaria*. This *simplicissimum signum* is the panther for which Dante had searched in vain among the many regional vernaculars of Italy. He had searched for it in vain, because this *simplicissimum signum* is the *genus* of the linguistic patrimony of Italy, whereas the regional vernaculars are its *species*. In conclusion, then, the illustrious vernacular means the reacquisition of the Italian idiom in its first developmental stage. An Italian idiom thus reconstructed serves as norm of all the regional vernaculars of Italy: ". . . quo municipalia vulgaria omnia Latinorum mensurantur et ponderantur et comparantur" (I, xvi, 6).

As source of the linguistic multiplicity of Italy, the illustrious vernacular exists potentially in every Italian city ("quod in qualibet redolet civitate"). Indeed, like God, the most perfect and universal of all substances (*simplicissima substantiarum*), whose influence is greater in some elements of the universe than in others, the illustrious vernacular manifests itself in one city more than in another.[70] We could add, given Dante's classification of the Italian vernaculars in Chapters XI-XV of Book I,[71] that, according to Dante, the illustrious vernacular manifests itself in the vernacular of Bologna more than in that of Florence, in that of Florence more than in that of Rome, and that it is absent from the peripheral vernaculars and the vernacular of Sardinia, since these latter ones have evolved outside of the linguistic mainstream of Italy.

My contention that by illustrious vernacular Dante implies the reacquisition of the Italian idiom in its primal state is reinforced by the reasoning of Chapter XIX, the last of Book I. This chapter is a recapitulation in reverse of the thesis on the ramification of the Italian idiom expounded in Chapters IX and X.[72] Whereas in Chapters IX and X, Dante traces, through successive stages of transformation, the dissolution of the Italian idiom from an *unum ydioma* to a *multa vulgaria*, in Chapter XIX he reconstructs the oneness of the Italian idiom by rising from the most particular linguistic element of the Italian people—that of the city—to the most universal—that of all of Italy.

Thus, taking Lombardy and the area left of the Apennines as examples, Dante reasons that to the extent that there is a vernacular peculiar to Cremona, there must be also one peculiar to all of Lombardy, and if there is one for Lombardy, there is also one for the entire area left of the Apennines and finally one for the whole of Italy. And whereas the first is identified as Cremonese, the second as Lombard, the third as semi-Italian, the fourth, by encompassing the whole of Italy, must be identified as Italian (*latium*).[73] This *vulgare latium* coincides with the illustrious vernacular: "Hoc autem vulgare quod illustre . . . ostensum est, dicimus esse illud quod vulgare latium appellatur" (I, xix, 1). As such, it was used by all the distinguished poets of Italy: "Hoc enim usi sunt doctores illustres qui lingua vulgari poetati sunt in Ytalia, ut Siculi, Apuli, Tusci, Romandioli, Lombardi et utriusque Marchie viri" (I, xix, 1).

The conclusion of Dante's reasoning in Chapter XIX is that there is an illustrious vernacular because there are its *species*, and this illustrious vernacular is the primal *unum ydioma* of the linguistic patrimony of the Italian people. As the *simplicissimum signum* of the *multa vulgaria* of Italy, the illustrious vernacular merits being classified as Italian (*latium*). Moreover, this illustrious vernacular is viable because it is proved as such by the *doctores illustres* of Italy.

There is then an illustrious vernacular that has been used by the *doctores illustres* of Italy, but how is this vernacular formulated? In Chapter IV of Book II, Dante argues that the only language

worthy of the tragic style is the illustrious vernacular: "Si tragice
canenda videntur, tunc assumendum est vulgare illustre . . ." (II,
iv, 6). In the same chapter, while clarifying the meaning of the
tragic style, he notes that the tragic style implies the harmonizing
of profundity of thought with elevation of construction and excellence of vocabulary: "Stilo equidem tragico tunc uti videmur
quando cum gravitate sentente . . . constructionis elatio et excellentia vocabulorum concordat" (II, iv, 7). If elevation of construction (*constructionis elatio*) and excellence of vocabulary
(*excellentia vocabulorum*) are the essential components of the
tragic style, and if the only language worthy of the tragic style is
the illustrious vernacular, it follows that the illustrious vernacular
consists of two key elements: *construtionis elatio* and *excellentia
vocabulorum*.[74] This being the case, to understand the essence of
Dante's illustrious vernacular, we must understand what he means
by *vocabula* and *constructio* and how these two key elements are
integrated with one another.

The meaning of the term *vocabula* in the context of the *De
Vulgari Eloquentia* is somewhat ambivalant. In Chapter VII of
Book II, Dante argues that the *vocabula* of the Italian idiom are
varied and numerous. However, the formulator of the illustrious
vernacular must make use of only the grand words (*grandiosa vocabula*) (II, vii, 1). He thus must submit the numerous linguistic
terms available to him to a rigid selective process, limiting himself
to those terms which are carded (*pexa*) and hirsute (*yrsuta*), for
these alone can be considered grand: ". . . pexa atque yrsuta . . .
illa que vocamus grandiosa . . ." (II, vii, 2).

The formulator of the illustrious vernacular must utilize the
grandiosa vocabula, but what is the meaning of the term *vocabula*? Does the terms *vocabula* have a circumscribed or a broad
meaning? Does it denote the lexical composition of the language
or the language as a whole? I believe that the term *vocabula*, and
more specifically the term *grandiosa vocabula*, implies all those
characteristics—lexicon, morphology, phonetics—that Dante considers fundamental to a natural language (*locutio vulgaris*).[75] That
by *grandiosa vocabula* Dante intends the *locutio vulgaris* in
general rather than its lexical composition is indicated by the type
of terms he adduces as examples of the *vocabula pexa* and *yrsuta*.
These examples include not only nouns but also pronouns (*me, te*,

sè, ì), adjectives (*alleviato, benaventuratissimo*), adverbs (*sì, no, u'*, *inanimatissimamente*), prefixes (*im-possibilità, dis-aventuratissimamente*), compound words (*ben-aventuratissimo, sovra-magnificentissimamente*), verbs (*donare, è*) and inflections of the same verb (*à, ò*).[76] Moreover, while selecting the *grandiosa vocabula*, he pays close attention to their phonetic suitability.[77]

Dante contends that the *grandiosa vocabula* are by their nature very perfect ("que nobilissima sunt" [II, vii, 4]) and that their reconstruction is a difficult task indeed. In fact, only those who are endowed with *discretio* can carry out this task effectively: "Et que iam dicta sunt de fastigiositate vocabulorum ingenue discretioni sufficiant" (II, vii, 7). To the extent that perfection is a pivotal characteristic of the *primissima signa* of the *actiones* of the Italian people[78] and that *discretio* is the single most important factor in the reconstruction of these *signa*, as we will see later, Dante, by referring to the perfection of the *grandiosa vocabula* and by acknowledging the importance of *discretio* in the formulation of these *vocabula*, indicates, it seems to me, that he regards the *grandiosa vocabula* as the primal terminology of the Italian idiom. Collectively the *grandiosa vocabula* constitute the *simplicissimum signum* of the *multa vulgaria* of Italy. To wit they are the raw material of the illustrious venacular.

The meaning of the term *constructio*, the other key component of the illustrious vernacular, is also ambivalent. Indeed, the term *constructio* is one of the most problematic in Dante's lexicon. In a telling statement in the *Convivio,* Dante observes: "O uomini, che vedere non potete la sentenza di questa canzone, non la rifiutate però; ma ponete mente la sua bellezza, ch'è grande sì per construzione, la quale si pertiene a li gramatici, sì per l'ordine del sermone, che si pertiene a li rettorici, sì per lo numero de le sue parti, che si pertiene a li musici" (II, xi, 9-10). On the basis of this statement, it would appear that by *construzione* Dante implies grammar. However, in Chapter VI of Book II of the *De Vulgari Eloquentia*, a key chapter on the nature of *constructio*, Dante sees *constructio* primarily as a rhetorical device. *Constructio*, especially the *excelsa constructio*, the only one worthy of the illustrious vernacular (II, vi, 5-6), must concern itself with stylistic elaboration. It seems, as noted by Francesco Di Capua[79] and reiterated by Aldo Scaglione, that in the *De Vulgari Eloquentia*, Dante substitutes *constructio* for *compositio*. Scaglione notes: "Dante is using *constructio* to mean *compositio*, which indeed was the traditional way of referring to sentence structure. *Compositio*, however, was not part of grammar, as *constructio* was, but of rhetoric . . . ."[80]

Be that as it may, *constructio* plays a vital role in the formulation of the illustrious vernacular in that it weaves into elegant form the *grandiosa vocabula*. For all their perfection, the *grandiosa vocabula* are ultimately only components of the illustrious vernacular: ". . . que nobilissima sunt et membra vulgaris illustris" (II, vii, 4). To be fully effective they must be arranged artistically according to the rhetorical precepts of *constructio*. Whereas the *grandiosa vocabula* are traced to the origin of the Italian idiom, the rhetorical expertise of *constructio* is derived from classical authors. Hence, Dante recommends that the formulators of the illustrious vernacular become totally familiar with the writers of antiquity so that the rhetorical precepts implicit in the works of the ancient authors may be easily assimilated in one's own writings.[81]

To return to the question we raised earlier: how is the illustrious vernacular formulated? The illustrious vernacular, according to Dante, is formulated by reconstructing the *grandiosa vocabula* of the Italian idiom and by molding these *vocabula* according to the rhetorical precepts of *constructio*. A language so constructed would have a regularization lacking in the regional vernaculars. It thus could serve as norm of the *multa vulgaria* of the Italian people (I, xvi, 6).

Elaborating on the normalizing function of the illustrious vernacular, Dante argues that the illustrious vernacular is the paterfamilias of the many Italian idioms. As paterfamilias, the illustrious vernacular purifies and normalizes the linguistic jungle engendered by these idioms. In fact, the formulators (*agricole sui*) of the illustrious vernacular cleanse this linguistic jungle by polishing or eliminating altogether coarse, existing terms, and by creating elegant, new ones.[82] The result of this diligent work, as demonstrated by Cino da Pistoia and Dante himself, is a language that, in contrast to the linguistic morass of the regional vernaculars, is lexically excellent (*egregium*), stylistically refined (*extricatum*), morphologically perfect (*perfectum*), and phonetically urbane (*urbanum*).[83]

Because of its sophistication, the illustrious vernacular can be formulated only by the wisest and the most learned of men (II, i, 5-6). To the extent, however, that the illustrious vernacular implies the rediscovery of the primal language of the Italian idiom, the formulators of the illustrious vernacular must possess not only wisdom and learning, but also *discretio*. As Dante himself notes, *discretio* is "lo più bello ramo che de la radice razionale consurga" (*Convivio*, IV, viii, 1). Indeed, in the *De Vulgari Eloquentia*, *discretio* is seen as a divine gift, enjoyed by a chosen few.[84] *Discretio*, therefore, becomes the single most important factor in the formulation of the illustrious vernacular, for only *discretio* can recapture that linguistic purity which had been lost throughout the course of many centuries. Consequently it is logical that Guido Guinizzelli and the members of his school, Italy's major contributors to the illustrious vernacular, should be endowed with a strong sense of *discretio*: " . . . qui doctores fuerunt illustres et vulgarium discretione repleti" (I, xv, 6).

The argument on the illustrious vernacular is paralleled by an equally important, though not as well developed, argument on *Italianitas*. In Chapter XVIII of Book I, while discussing the nature of the illustrious vernacular, Dante notes that the illustrious vernacular is royal (*aulicum*) because if there were a royal residence in Italy, the illustrious vernacular would reside in that residence. That the illustrious vernacular should reside in the royal dwelling of Italy is logical enough, Dante argues, for this dwelling, by being the home common to the whole kingdom and the revered mistress of every part of the kingdom (*omnium regni partium gubernatrix augusta*), is very becoming to the illustrious vernacular, which is itself the language of all of Italy, and the paterfamilias of all the Italian vernaculars. Indeed, all those elements, which, like the illustrious vernacular, are common to all the regions of Italy and peculiar to none, should inhabit the royal residence of Italy: ". . . quicquid tale est ut omnibus sit comune nec proprium ulli, conveniens est ut in ea conversetur et habitet. . ." (I, xviii, 2).

Dante maintains again in Chapter XVIII that, besides being royal, the illustrious vernacular is also courtly (*curiale*).[85] The illustrious vernacular is courtly because courtliness (*curialitas*) is nothing else than the norm with which one ponders the things to be done. And since such a norm is to be found only in the loftiest of courts, it follows that whatever in our actions is well pondered is courtly: ". . . et quia statera huiusmodi librationis tantum in ex-cellentissimis curiis esse solet, hinc est quod quicquid in actibus nostris bene libratum est, curiale dicatur" (I, xviii, 4). The illustri-ous vernacular, having being pondered in the loftiest of Italian courts, deserves to be called courtly.

Dante goes on to note that it is ludicrous to say that the illus-trious vernacular has been pondered in the loftiest of Italian courts since Italy lacks a court ("curia caremus"). However, this appar-ent illogicality can be explained by the fact that, although Italy lacks a unified court, like the court of the king of Germany, it nevertheless has the members of a court ("membra tamen eius non desunt") (I, xviii, 5). And just as the members of the court of Germany are unified by one prince so those of the court of Italy are united by the grace-given light of reason: " . . . et sicut mem-bra illius [Germany's] uno Principe uniuntur sic membra huius [Italy's] gratioso lumine rationis unita sunt" (I, xviii, 5). The Italians, therefore, though lacking a prince have a court, but the corpus of this court is scattered: ". . . curiam habemus, licet cor-poraliter sit dispersa" (I, xviii, 5).

I believe that implicit in these remarks is the acknowledgement of *Italianitas*, which is arrived at through the same reasoning with which Dante arrives at the notion of the illustrious vernacular. In fact, like the illustrious vernacular, Dante's *Italianitas* is a *simpli-cissimum signum*. But whereas the *simplicissimum signum* of the illustrious vernacular is limited solely to language (*locutio*), that of *Italianitas* encompasses also usages (*mores*) and styles (*habitus*). In other words, *Italianitas* is the *reductio ad unum* of all the ele-ments of Italian culture. That in Chapter XVIII Dante implies such a *reductio* is confirmed by a strong conceptual parallelism be-tween this chapter and Chapter XVI of Book I, where he elaborates on the notion of the *simplicissimum signum*.[86]

In Chapter XVI Dante notes that in every category of things there is a *simplicissimum signum* which serves as norm for the elements of that category: ". . . scilicet ut unumquodque mensu-rabile sit, secundum quod in genere est, illo quod simplicissimum est in ipso genere" (I, xvi, 2). In Chapter XVIII he observes that courtliness (*curialitas*) is nothing else than the norm with which one ponders the things to be done: ". . . curialitas nil aliud est quam librata regula eorum que peragenda sunt" (I, xviii, 4). Hence, courtliness is synonymous with *simplicissimum signum*. However, whereas the *simplicissimum signum* of Chapter XVI is intended as norm of the *species* of one of the *actiones* of the Italian people, the *curialitas* of Chapter XVIII is intended as norm of all of these *actiones*. This *curialitas* is none other, it seems to me, than the aggregation of the *simplicissima signa et morum et habituum et locutionis* of section three of Chapter XVI. As such, this *curialitas* is the most perfect manifestation of *Italianitas*. To the extent that *curialitas* implies the *reductio ad unum* of the characteristics of Italian culture, the illustrious vernacular by being a *reductio ad unum* of the *multa vulgaria* of Italy is itself courtly (*curiale*).[87]

Italianitas, then, coincides with the *curialitas* of the Italian people. Contemporary Italians lack a *curialitas* because they lack a *curia*,[88] and they lack a *curia* because they lack a prince who renders the *curia* possible. Nevertheless, contemporary Italians possess the members of a *curia*, which are scattered throughout Italy. In other words, contemporary Italians, though lacking an actual *curia*, have the potential for such a *curia*. To understand what Dante means by this potentiality, we must go back once again to Chapter XVI of Book I.

In this chapter Dante argues that the illustrious vernacular exists potentially in all the cities of Italy and that it represents only one characteristic of the cultural patrimony of the Italian people. Thus the *simplicissimum signum* denoting the illustrious vernacular is found among the *simplicissima signa* of the other elements of Italian culture.[89] If the illustrious vernacular, a *simplicissimum signum* of the Italian *locutio*, and, therefore, an integral part of the cultural patrimony of the Italian people, exists potentially in all the cities of Italy, it follows that the *simplicissima signa* of the other elements of this cultural patrimony are also potentially present throughout Italy. In fact, Dante says as much when he affirms that the *simplicissima signa* of the elements of the Italian culture are peculiar to no Italian city but are common to all: ". . . hec [simplicissima signa] nullius civitatis Italiae propriae sunt, et in omnibus comunia sunt" (I, xvi, 4).

   I believe that Dante is thinking of the logic of this argument
when in Chapter XVIII he says that Italy is not void of the members of a court ("membra tamen eius non desunt") even though
the corpus of this court is scattered ("licet corporaliter sit dispersa"). He equates the *simplicissima signa* with the *membra*, i.e.,
the formulators of these *signa*. Like the *simplicissima signa*, the
membra are scattered throughout Italy. If Italy had a prince, these
membra would be assembled to form a court (*curia*). Lacking a
prince, they are united by the grace-given light of reason ("membra huius gratioso lumine rationis unita sunt"). In other words, if
Italy had a prince, it would have an actual court, lacking a prince,
it has the potential of a court. This potential is perceived by
human reason, hence the justification for attributing to human reason the power to unite the dispersed members of the Italian court.
Human reason unites the Italian court in that it perceives this
court's potential existence.
   The prince, were Italy to have one, would not himself formulate
the *simplicissima signa* that constitute the Italian *curialitas*. Rather
he would assemble highly learned individuals (*membra*) with expertise in one of the areas of Italian culture, who would, in turn,
formulate the *simplicissimum signum* for their particular area of
expertise in much the same fashion the *doctores illustres* of the
Italian *locutio* formulate the *simplicissimum signum* of the *multa
vulgaria* of Italy. Collectively these intellectuals, who would no
doubt be endowed with *discretio*, would represent the quintessence
of Italian society and provide the balance (*statera*) which Dante
claims is found only in the loftiest of courts (I, xviii, 4). These intellectuals, therefore, would serve as a civilizing and normalizing
force for the regional populations of Italy, just as the illustrious
vernacular serves as a sustaining and regulating factor for the
multa vulgaria of the Italian people. As repositories of the *genera*
rather than the *species* of Italian culture, these individuals would
be worthy inhabitants of the royal palace, which is common home
and revered mistress of the whole kingdom of Italy.
   As we have seen above,[90] Dante saw a strong correlation between
language and culture. In fact, as an integral part of a people's
culture, the language of a people is refined or base depending on
whether the culture of that people is itself sophisticated or coarse.
This being the case, the inhabitants of the royal palace of the

kingdom of Italy, indeed the inhabitants of any royal palace of any country, as the quintessence of the society of that country, must speak a language that is itself quintessential of the country's linguistic patrimony, that is to say, they must speak the illustrious vernacular of their respective country, which they possess by virtue of their high level of culture. This, I believe, is what Dante means in Chapter XVIII, when he says that those who frequent royal palaces always speak the illustrious vernacular: "Et hinc est quod in regiis omnibus conversantes semper illustri vulgari locuntur" (I, xviii, 3).

Dante notes that if Italy had a royal residence, the *doctores illustres* of the Italian *locutio* would reside in that residence. Lacking such a residence, they are forced to wander like strangers and to reside in humble shelters.[91] However, Dante believes that the state of the *doctores illustres* of Italy had not always been this unfortunate, for there had been in Italy a royal palace of the type he describes in Chapter XVIII, which served as worthy residence for the *doctores illustres* of Italy. Dante attributes this distinction to the palace of Emperor Frederick II and his son Manfred. In fact, his account in Chapter XII of Book I of the role and meaning of the reign of these two sovereigns is both an affirmation and a clarification of the theories he expounds in Chapter XVIII. Dante argues that Emperor Frederick II and his worthy son Manfred by living as heroes (*heroico more*) rather than as brutes attracted to their palace the most virtuous and the most gifted of Italian men: "Propter quod corde nobiles atque gratiarum dotati inherere tantorum principum maiestati conati sunt . . ." (I, xii, 4). Hence, whatever eminent Italian minds accomplished at that time first came to fruition at the royal residence of these great sovereigns: ". . . ita ut eorum tempore quicquid excellentes animi Latinorum enitebantur primitus in tantorum coronatorum aula prodibat" (I, xii, 4).

One of the cultural activities that flourished at the court of Frederick II and Manfred was lyric poetry. In fact, Dante considers the court of these two sovereigns the fountainhead of Italian lyric poetry. Consequently he observes that all vernacular poetry produced in Italy since the reign of these monarchs is characterized as Sicilian: " . . . et quia regale solium erat Sicilia, factum est ut quicquid nostri predecessores vulgariter protulerunt, sicilianum

vocetur . . ." (I, xii, 4). This characterization, however, is predicated not on this poetry's use of the regional vernacular of Sicily,
as some critics believe,[92] but on its emulation of the prototypal
poetry of the period of Frederick II and Manfred, who happened
to have their royal residence in Sicily ("quia regale solium erat
Sicilia"). The very palace (*aula*) of Frederick II and Manfred, by
housing the quintessence of Italian society, must have been seen
by Dante as the *omnium regis gubernatrix augusta* of Chapter
XVIII.

III

IS THE ILLUSTRIOUS VERNACULAR THE SYNTHESIS OF THE BEST LINGUISTIC
ELEMENTS OF ALL THE ITALIAN VERNACULARS, OR IS IT SIMPLY AN
ELABORATION OF THE FLORENTINE VERNACULAR?

Having explored the implications of Dante's illustrious vernacular, I would like now to return to the questions I left
unanswered at the end of section one, beginning with the first: is
the illustrious vernacular the synthesis of the best linguistic
elements of all the Italian vernaculars, as is assumed by Trissino,
or is it simply an elaboration of the Florentine vernacular, as is argued by Machiavelli, Tolomei, Varchi, Cesari, and D'Ovidio? The
illustrious vernacular, as understood by Dante, is not a synthesis of
the vernaculars of Italy because what Dante is pursuing in the *De
Vulgari Eloquentia* is not a pan-Italian but a proto-Italian. In
other words, Dante's objective in the *De Vulgari Eloquentia* is not
the amalgamation of the best linguistic elements of the existing
Italian vernaculars, but the rediscovery of the primal linguistic
elements of these vernaculars and the subsequent artistic arrange-
ment of these elements according to classical rhetorical precepts.
Ultimately, however, what Dante considers illustrious vernacular is
nothing else than the elaboration of the Florentine vernacular, as
demonstrated by the lyric poetry of Dante himself. But if it is so,
why did Dante believe that he was formulating a proto-Italian?

The *De Vulgari Eloquentia* was written during the first years of
Dante's exile (1303-1305). This was a period of much personal
suffering for the poet, but it was also a period of great intellectual

growth, especially in the area of languages. "Poi che fu piacere," Dante observes in the *Convivio*, "de li cittadini de la bellissima e famosissima figlia di Roma, Fiorenza, di gittarmi fuori del suo dolce seno . . . per le parti quasi tutte a le quali questa lingua [the Italian language] si stende, peregrino, quasi mendicando, sono andato, mostrando contra mia voglia la piaga de la fortuna . . ." (I, iii, 4).[93] During his wandering throughout much of the Italian peninsula, but especially during his sojourns at Bologna,[94] where students from all parts of Italy gathered, Dante had an opportunity to experience firsthand the numerous Italian vernaculars. To the keen mind and discriminating ear of Dante the many vernaculars of Italy must have appeared to have a common linguistic denominator. Today we know that this common linguistic trait is due primarily to the Latin base of the Italian vernaculars. Dante, however, ignored this important historical fact. He thus attributed the common linguistic denominator of the Italian vernaculars to their being derivatives of a protolanguage, traceable to the Babylonian Confusion. He believed that highly learned and divinely inspired poets (*doctores illustres*) could reconstruct this common linguistic denominator. Indeed, he thought he found confirmation of this theory in the lyric poetry of the Sicilian school of Guido delle Colonne, the Bolognese school of Guido Guinizzelli, and the Tuscan school of Cino da Pistoia and Dante himself.

The poetry of these three schools did in fact enjoy a significant linguistic uniformity. This uniformity, however, was due not to the rediscovery and utilization of a primal linguistic terminology, as Dante assumed, but to the reliance on a strongly Latinized language. Being highly literate, as acknowledged by Dante himself throughout much of the *De Vulgari Eloquentia*,[95] the poets of these three schools made use of a learned terminology that was rooted in the Latin language. It is no accident, therefore, that most of the terms cited by Dante as peculiar to and worthy of the poetry of the *doctores illustres* are Latinisms (*DVE* I, viii, 6; ix, 3; II, vii, 5-6).[96] This linguistic uniformity was reinforced further by an early assimilation of many Tuscan linguistic features into the lyric poetry of the Bolognese school and by the Tuscanization of the poetry of the Sicilian school.[97] Given this linguistic similarity, Dante must have concluded that the poets of these three schools wrote in a language that transcended their respective regional vernaculars. In other words, these poets wrote not in the regional vernaculars of Sicily, Bologna and Tuscany, but in the primal language of Italy.

This was an honest enough mistake on the part of Dante, but a mistake that caused much consternation among the adherents to the Tuscan school of the *questione della lingua*.[98] In questioning the uniqueness and soundness of the Tuscan vernacular, Dante struck at the very foundation of these scholars' argument. Most likely had Dante been a secondary writer, his theories on the illustrious vernacular would have been relegated to the fringe of literary lunacy. Dante, however, was not only a great writer, but the very writer whose language was to constitute the nucleus of the standard Italian that these scholars were trying to formulate— hence the insistence upon finding a logical explanation for Dante's theories. The caustic Machiavelli reminds Dante of the Florentine nature of the illustrious vernacular, whereas Manzoni absolves the great poet altogether by declaring the *De Vulgari Eloquentia* void of any linguistic intent.[99] In the absence of a tenable explanation, these scholars questioned, as did Varchi, the very authenticity of Dante's work.

Is THE ILLUSTRIOUS VERNACULAR A CONCRETE, REFINED LANGUAGE, GENETICALLY RELATED TO THE ITALIAN VERNACULAR, OR IS IT AN ABSTRACT, METAPHYSICAL PHENOMENON?

Contrary to D'Ovidio, Rajna, Vinay, but above all Mengaldo, who argue that the illustrious vernacular is a metaphysical phenomenon, I believe that the illustrious vernacular, as perceived by Dante, is a concrete linguistic entity. In the *Convivio* Dante notes that metaphysics implies "le cose incorruttibili, le quali ebbero da Dio cominciamento di creazione e non averanno fine" (II, xiv, 11). To say, as Mengaldo does, that the illustrious vernacular is "qualcosa che 'è' metafisicamente"[100] is to imply that for Dante the illustrious vernacular is of divine rather than human creation, and that it is unchangeable. However, as Dante makes amply clear in the *De Vulgari Eloquentia*,[101] all post-Babel languages, except for Hebrew, are man-made and, therefore, changeable. But if the illustrious vernacular, as a post-Babel language, is man-made and changeable, it follows, conforming again to Dante's logic in this section of the *Convivio*, that the illustrious vernacular is concrete (*fisico*) rather than metaphysical, for all changeable elements are part of the physical world: "Chè per lo movimento ne lo quale ogni die si rivolve, e fa nova circulazione di punto a punto, significa le cose naturali corruttibili, che cotidianamente compiono loro via, e la loro materia si muta di forma in forma; e di queste tratta la Fisica" (II, xiv, 10).

While disputing the concrete nature of the illustrious vernacular, Mengaldo argues that Dante sees no genetic relationship between the illustrious vernacular and the regional vernaculars, for had he believed in such a relationship, he would have elaborated on the genesis of the illustrious vernacular.[102] It is true that Dante does not give a systematic account (sounds, forms, syntactic combinations, lexicon) of the formulation of the illustrious vernacular. Nevertheless, as noted above,[103] he does provide some general guidelines—the illustrious vernacular is to be formulated by rediscovering the primal terminology (*grandiosa vocabula*) of the Italian idiom and by submitting this terminology to the rhetorical canons of classical scholarship. Moreover, Dante may have felt that a detailed account of the formulation of the illustrious vernacular was superfluous, since this language was to be realized primarily through the God-given gift of *discretio*.

At any rate, the lack of a proper genesis of the illustrious vernacular does not preclude a genetic relationship between it and the regional vernaculars of Italy. The illustrious vernacular, as understood by Dante, is in fact genetically related to the *multa vulgaria* of Italy. This relationship, however, depends not on its having evolved from the *multa vulgaria* of Italy, a theory espoused by several students of the illustrious vernacular and rejected by Mengaldo, but on its having served as the linguistic source from which these *vulgaria* have derived.

Marigo's assertion that the comparison of the illustrious vernacular with God in Chapter XVI of Book I proves without any doubt the abstract nature of the illustrious vernacular is also untenable.[104] The image of God serves to illuminate rather than dematerialize the meaning of the illustrious vernacular. To wit, the illustrious vernacular is comparable to God not because like God it exists outside of the physical world, but because like God it possesses certain characteristics (its role as *simplicissimum signum* of the *multa vulgaria* of Italy, its uneven distribution in these *vulgaria*) that render this comparison feasible.

The very acknowledgment on the part of Dante that there exists an illustrious vernacular formulated by the distinguished poets of Italy and that this vernacular, as demonstrated by the language of the lyric poetry of Cino da Pistoia and Dante himself,[105] is highly refined and very pure attests to his belief in the concreteness of the illustrious vernacular. The notion of the illustrious vernacular as a concrete and man-made language is further confirmed by the telling passage in Chapter XVIII of Book I where Dante describes the diligent work put forth by the formulators of the illustrious vernacular.[106] Had Dante believed in the metaphysical nature of the illustrious vernacular, the selectivity and creativity he claims is exercised by its formulators would have been unnecessary.

Modern historical linguistics has discovered that languages are organic elements which come into being through an evolutionary process and which acquire elegance and sophistication through artistic elaboration. For Dante, however, the illustrious vernacular is realized through a process that is diametrically opposed to the one modern linguistics regards as fundamental to language formation. The illustrious vernacular, according to Dante, is to come into being through an ascending rather than a descending process. The formulators of the illustrious vernacular must move backward rather than forward. They must depart from their respective vernaculars (I, xii, 9; xiv, 3 and 7; xv, 6) and rise to the protolanguage the Italian people enjoyed at the time of the Babylonian Confusion.[107]

The formulation of the illustrious vernacular (the *genus* of the *multa vulgaria* of Italy) through an evolutionary process would have been inconsistent with Dante's reasoning, because evolution implies fragmentation of the *genus*, and the best *genus*, as he had learned from Aristotle,[108] is that which is the most unified. Consequently the modern notion of evolution as an enriching and civilizing factor is anathema to Dante.[109] History itself is seen by Dante not as a logical sequence of well-defined epochs, but as a chaotic becoming which forever worsens every facet of the human condition. In the case of the Italian vernacular, this chaotic becoming had created a linguistic jungle that seriously restricted the ex-

pressive power of the Italian people. It behooved men of good will
and wisdom, therefore, to find a linguistic means that would arrest
and alleviate this malady. The solution lay in the formulation of
the illustrious vernacular, primal language of the Italian people
and norm of the Italian vernaculars.

The question now arises: if for Dante the illustrious vernacular
is a natural and therefore changeable language, as I have demonstrated above, how does one reconcile this mutability of the illustrious vernacular with the normalizing and regulating role Dante
attributes to it throughout much of the first book of the *D e
Vulgari Eloquentia*? The regularity of the illustrious vernacular,
as understood by Dante, is relative rather than absolute. In fact,
even if the *doctores illustres* were to recapture the total purity of
the proto-Italian of Babel time,[110] their language would never
achieve complete regularity and stability because it would remain
a natural language. And regularity and stability, as Dante notes in
conjunction with the formulation of Latin,[111] are characteristics
peculiar only to the artificial languages. Nevertheless, as an artistic
elaboration of the primal terminology of the Italian idiom, the illustrious vernacular possesses a regularization lacking in the regional vernaculars. Consequently it can serve as a normalizing and
regulating element for the *multa vulgaria* of Italy.

Given the intrinsic mutability of the illustrious vernacular, we
can assume that Dante saw the effectiveness and endurance of this
idiom as depending on the diligence and ingenuity of the *doctores
illustres*. Without the continuous, diligent work of the *doctores illustres*, the illustrious vernacular would not only fail to flourish,
but would actually disintegrate.

IS THE ILLUSTRIOUS VERNACULAR THE PRODUCT OF AN EMPIRICAL METHOD OF
INVESTIGATION, OR IS IT THE RESULT OF AN A PRIORI REASONING?

According to Mengaldo, after attempting in Chapters XI-XV of
Book I to formulate the illustrious vernacular empirically, Dante
concludes at the end of Chapter XV that such an approach is
leading him nowhere. He thus abandons his inductive method and
for the remainder of the discussion on the illustrious vernacular—
Chapters XVI-XIX—relies solely on an a priori reasoning. That

Dante undertakes such a change of method, Mengaldo contends
on the strength of Marigo, is attested to unequivocally by the
statement *rationabilius investigemus de illa* at the beginning of
Chapter XVI, which implies nothing less than a switch from an inductive to a deductive method of investigation. The deductive nature of the illustrious vernacular is demonstrated further, Mengaldo maintains, by the reasoning of Chapter XIX which, he
claims, evolves along deductive lines.[112]

I believe that Dante's notion of the illustrious vernacular is arrived at primarily through an inductive method of investigation
and that it is developed in Chapters IX-X and XVI-XIX of Book I
with significant ramifications in Chapters IV-VII of Book II rather
than in Chapters XI-XIX as maintained by Mengaldo. Indeed,
Dante's thesis on the illustrious vernacular encompasses a *destruens* and a *construens* phase. The *destruens* phase, which studies the
disintegration of the *unum ydioma* into the *multa vulgaria*, is
carried out in Chapters IX-X, whereas the *construens* phase, which
examines the reduction of the *multa vulgaria* into the *unum
ydioma*, is implimented in Chapters XVI-XIX. Having justified the
feasibility of the illustrious vernacular, Dante goes on in Chapters
IV-VII of Book II to study its formulation. Chapters XI-XV,
which Mengaldo considers central to the conceptualization of the
illustrious vernacular, are actually a polemic digression as we shall
see later. They thus have little bearing on Dante's thesis.

This being the case, the *rationabilius investigemus de illa* at the
beginning of Chapter XVI denotes a link between the *destruens*
and *construens* phase of Dante's thesis on the illustrious vernacular. That this statement implies such linkage is attested to by the
strong textual and conceptual correlation between Chapters IX-X
and Chapters XVI-XIX.[113] After the futile search and long digression of Chapters XI-XV Dante finds it necessary to undertake a
more rational method of investigation ("rationabilius investigemus de illa") which, however, need not be deductive, as assumed
by Marigo and Mengaldo. In fact, given the nature of the methodology of Chapters IX-X to which it is linked and the reasoning
of Chapters XVI-XIX and Chapters IV-VII of Book II which
follows it, *rationabilius investigemus de illa* implies an empirical
mode of investigation. Dante's conceptualization of the illustrious
vernacular developed in these sections of the *De Vulgari Elo-*

quentia is based almost entirely on practical, observational experience. The original oneness of the *ydioma tripharium*, for example, and the intrinsic mutability of the natural languages are predicated on Dante's observation of humankind's culture in general (I, ix, 7-10) as well as on his examination of the Romance literatures and the Italian vernaculars (I, viii, 6; IX, 2-4; X, 5-9); the viability of the illustrious vernacular depends on his inquiry of the literature of the *doctores illustres* (I, xii, 2 and 6; xiii, 3; xiv, 7; xv, 6; xvii, 3; xviii, 1; xix, 1); the rhetorical canons to be utilized by the formulators of the illustrious vernacular are deduced from a close reading of the major modern and classical writers (II, vi); and the reconstruction of the *grandiosa vocabula* (the raw material of the illustrious vernacular) is based on a scrutiny of the linguistic patrimony of the Italian people (II, vii). Even the reasoning of Chapter XIX, which Mengaldo regards as developing along deductive lines, is, in fact, inductive and therefore supportive of Dante's empirical method. In fact, as demonstrated above,[114] the reasoning of this Chapter evolves from the particular to the general. And any reasoning which evolves from the particular to the general, as attested to by Dante himself,[115] is perforce inductive.

To be sure, while conceptualizing the illustrious vernacular Dante makes use of an important abstract principle: the *unum simplicissimum* of Aristole. But this Aristotelian principle per se does not render Dante's method deductive, because the objective of this principle is to justify the *reductio ad unum* of the *multa vulgaria* of Italy, and this *reductio ad unum* means nothing less than the concrete reconstruction of the primal language of the Italian people. In other words, in the context of Dante's conceptualization of the illustrious vernacular, the *unum simplicissimum* of Aristotle serves as impetus for his empirical inquiry. "Che egli derivi la nozione dell'*unum simplicissimum* dalla filosofia aristotelica," Pagliaro argues, "importa poco, se la sua applicazione alla considerazione della lingua è assolutamente nuova ... È da attribuire a grande merito l'avere Dante portato la nozione astratta contenuta nell'*unum* aristotelico sul piano dell'universalità concreta, storica, in cui la lingua si attua come unità, pur nella varietà delle parlate particolari che ne costituiscono la specie."[116]

For all its reliance on factual evidence, however, Dante's method cannot be considered scientific in the modern sense of the word. He makes no use of quantitative information. His observations are, for the most part, sporadic and undirected, being prompted by intuitive curiosity rather than systematic experimentation.[117]

I have noted that Chapters XI-XV are a polemic digression and that they, therefore, have only a slight bearing on the conceptualization of the illustrious vernacular. I would now like to explore the nature of and reason for this digression. As Dante tells us, the objective of Chapters XI-XV is to investigate whether in contemporary Italy there is a regional vernacular worthy of being considered illustrious. The result of this investigation is a lengthy description of the oral and written features of the major vernaculars of Italy.

The linguistic apparatus of modern Italy, according to Dante, is complex and varied. Some of the vernaculars are extremely smooth, others are extremely harsh. Some are predominantly rustic, others are prevailingly burghal. Others still, though spoken within Italy, are not Italian strictly speaking, because they are polluted with numerous foreign terms. Though the Italian vernaculars are on the whole coarse, one of them at least, that of Bologna, possesses a certain dignity and elegance.

None of the Italian vernculars, Dante goes on to argue, not even the Bolognese, can be considered illustrious, because the illustrious vernacular is a linguistic sublimation that is achieved by rising above one's own regional vernacular ("a proprio divertisse"). Of the numerous Italian poets only a selected few—Guido delle Colonne (Sicilian), Giacomo da Lentini (also Sicilian but mistakenly called Apulian by Dante), Rinaldo d'Aquino (Apulian), Guido Cavalcanti, Lapo Gianni, Dante himself, and Cino da Pistoia (all Tuscan), and Guido Guinizzelli (Bolognese)—had succeeded in mastering the illustrious vernacular. In fact, the Sicilian poets had written in a language that was one and the same with the illustrious vernacular (xii, 6), Rinaldo d'Aquino and Giacomo da Lentini had utilized the most courtly of terms (XII, 8), Cavalcanti, Lapo, Dante, and Cino had understood fully the excellence of the illustrious vernacular (XIII, 4) whereas Guinizzelli, the greatest of the Bolognese poets (*maximus Guido Guinizelli*), had made use of a language that was significantly detached from the vernacular of Bologna (XV, 6).

As for the remaining Italian poets, some, such as Tommaso and Ugolino Bucciola of Faenza and Aldobrandino dei Mezzabati of Padua, wrote in a language that approximates the illustrious vernacular.[118] Others, such as the Sicilian Cielo d'Alcamo and the Mantuan Sordello (XII, 6; XV, 2)[119] utilized a language that was graceful and practical but void of the brilliance and universality of the illustrious vernacular. The majority of the poets of contemporary Italy, however, poets such as the Tuscan Guittone D'Arezzo, Bonagiunta da Lucca, Gallo da Pisa, Mico da Siena, and Brunetto Latini, wrote in a language that was not courtly at all, but strictly provincial: ". . . quorum dicta, si rimari vocaverit, non curialia sed municipalia tantum invenientur" (XIII, 1). Indeed, Guittone d'Arezzo, the best known of this group of poets, never turned his attention to the courtly vernacular: ". . . qui nunquam se ad curiale vulgare direxit . . ." (XIII, 1).

The lengthy discussion of Chapters XI-XV indicates, it seems to me, that in these chapters Dante is concerned with more than the existence of a regional Italian vernacular worthy of being considered illustrious. Had the search for an illustrious regional vernacular been the sole concern of Dante, he would not have undertaken such a detailed examination of the linguistic apparatus of Italy. The absence of a regional vernacular worthy of being considered illustrious could have been proven effectively with a brief statement on the sublime nature of the illustrious vernacular and with a few examples from key representative poets. The whole discussion could have been comprised in a single chapter much like the discussion on the linguistic geography of Italy, which is limited to only a couple of paragraphs (I, x).

If Dante in Chapters XI-XV finds it necessary to undertake a detailed examination (phonetic, morphological) of the major vernaculars of Italy and to support this examination with numerous examples from a variety of vernacular poets (the distinguished Guido Guinizzelli, the controversial Guittone d'Arezzo, the obscure Mico da Siena, etc.), it is because what interests Dante in these chapters is not just language but poetry itself. Indeed, in Chapters XI-XV the appraisal of the linguistic state of Italy is inextricably interwoven with a valuation of contemporary poetry in its diversity of linguistic and stylistic forms. Hence the praise for the language of the *doctores illustres* is extended to their poetry, which is seen as lofty and cosmopolitan. Likewise the negative assessment of the language of Guittone d'Arezzo and his followers is expanded to their poetic production, which is regarded as plebeian and provincial.

That Dante's interest in Chapters XI-XV extends beyond the strictly linguistic sphere and that he sees a strong correlation between language and poetry is proved also by Chapter VI of Book II, which is, in some ways, a reaffirmation of the issues raised in Chapters XI-XV. Dante notes in this chapter that the poetry of the *doctores illustres*, such as Guido delle Colonne, Guinizzelli, Cavalcanti, Cino, and Dante himself,[120] can serve as a perfect example for the lofty construction, the only construction worthy of the canzone. Such merit, however, cannot be attributed to the poetry of Guittone d'Arezzo and his followers because their poetry makes use of plebeian words and constructions: ". . . nunquam in vocabulis atque constructione plebescere desuetos" (II, vi, 8). He therefore advises those too ignorant to recognize truly great poetry to stop extolling Guittone and his followers: "Subsistant igitur ignorantie sectatores Guictonem Aretinum et quosdam alios extollentes . . ." (II, vi, 8).

A distinctive feature of Chapters XI-XV is a profound admiration for the *doctores illustres*, especially Guinizzelli, and a strong disdain for Guittone and his school. It is true that Guittone lacked the sweetness and fluidity of a Guinizzelli. His poetry, however, was not as deficient as Dante claims. In many ways, Guittone's poetry was comparable to that of a Giacomo da Lentini. But if this is so, how does one explain Dante's contempt for Guittone?

Dante's harsh criticism of Guittone is due not so much to Guittone's poetic deficiency as to his cultural preeminence. When the *De Vulgari Eloquentia* was being written, Guittone, though dead for about ten years, continued to exercise considerable influence on the poetic circles of Tuscany. He must have been viewed as a formidable rival by Dante, who, as is apparent from much of the *De Vulgari Eloquentia*, saw himself as the leader of a new school of poetry which was now flourishing in Tuscany. Born in Sicily, according to Dante, and strengthened by Guinizzelli and his school, this poetry was now achieving new heights in Tuscany. Its development, however, was being hampered by those who adhered to the old school of Guittone. Thus Dante must have found it necessary to discredit his predecessor. It was imperative that Guittone be proved to be far inferior to any other distinguished poet of Italy, for only by discrediting Guittone could Dante enhance his own prestige and that of his school. "È chiaro che Guittone," writes Umberto Bosco, "il poeta della precedente generazione per comune giudizio ritenuto il maggiore, doveva essere il bersaglio polemico dei giovani: se non si distruggeva la sua fama, la poesia nuova non aveva modo di farsi valere . . . Tutti sanno infatti come frequentemente Dante miri a quel bersaglio in versi e in prosa . . . ."[121] Chapters XI-XV, then, rather than being a key section on the empirical investigation of the illustrious vernacular, as Mengaldo argues, are actually an important digression on contemporary cultural politics.[122]

Is the Illustrious Vernacular the Appanage
of an Intellectual Elite, or Is It the Property of
All the People of Italy?

While disputing Marigo's assumption that the illustrious vernacular is an artistic sublimation realized solely by the *doctores illustres*, Vinay argues that, rather than being the sole property of a few distinguished writers, the illustrious vernacular is the appanage of all the people of Italy. Such is the implication, Vinay contends, of Chapter XVIII of Book I, where Dante states that were Italy to have a court all its members would speak the illustrious vernacular. It is absurd to think that a common functionary of an hypothetical Italian court, Vinay adds, could speak the refined language of the *doctores illustres*. If the functionaries of an hypothetical Italian court can make use of the illustrious vernacular, it is because the illustrious vernacular is inherent in all the people of Italy. Reacting to this assumption by Vinay, Mengaldo argues that the illustrious vernacular is in fact the sole property of the *doctores illustres*, for nowhere in the *De Vulgari Eloquentia* does Dante indicate that the illustrious vernacular is written or spoken by anyone else other than the *doctores illustres*.[123]

Both scholars are partially right and partially wrong. Vinay is correct in assuming that the illustrious vernacular is not limited to the *doctores illustres*, but he is incorrect in arguing that the illustrious vernacular is common to all the people of Italy. Likewise, Mengaldo is correct in maintaining that the illustrious vernacular is not as widespread as assumed by Vinay, but he is incorrect in limiting the illustrious vernacular solely to the *doctores illustres*. The fact is, as I have shown above,[124] that Dante believed that the illustrious vernacular was peculiar not just to the *doctores illustres*, but to all the people worthy of inhabiting a royal palace. The inhabitants of the royal palace possessed this rare gift by virtue of their high level of culture. Hence, contrary to Mengaldo's opinion, the usage of the illustrious vernacular would extend beyond the circle of the *doctores illustres*. On the other hand, it would not include the whole Italian population, as argued by Vinay. Rather, it would be limited to the illustrious assemblage of the royal court, the quintessence of Italian society. In visualizing a royal court peopled with common functionaires, Vinay appears to have been influenced by the officialdom of modern governments. However, Dante's conception of an hypothetical Italian court was modeled on the court of Frederick II and his son Manfred, which he believed to have consisted of the most virtuous and the most gifted of Italian men.

Does the Illustrious Vernacular in Fact Serve as Beacon for an Italian Nation in Fieri? What Precisely Are the Social and Political Implication of the Illustrious Vernacular?

Does the illustrious vernacular serve as beacon for an Italian nation *in fieri*, as maintained by Mengaldo?[125] In the course of Italian history, literary Italian has in fact functioned as a force in the formulation of *Italianitas*. However, that is not the way Dante views the illustrious vernacular. For Dante the illustrious vernacular is only one of the components of the *curialitas* of the Italian people, which he equates with *Italianitas*.[126] And this Italian *curialitas* can be realized only by an illustrious prince, as he believed had happened in the case of Frederick II.[127] Had Dante been convinced of the illustrious vernacular's ability to mold the *curialitas* of the Italian people in Chapter XVIII of Book I he would have argued that the *doctores illustres*, the formulators of the illustrious vernacular, had the potential to unify the Italian *curia*. Instead he insists that such unification can be brought about only by the prince.[128]

If the unity of the Italian *curia* can be realized only by the prince, how does one explain Dante's suggestion that the Italian *curia* is unified by the grace-given light of reason? To put it differently, what are the implications of the *lumen rationis* in Chapter XVIII of Book I of the *De Vulgari Eloquentia*? Vinay maintains that *lumen rationis* is a substitute for the prince and that it does not imply reason in general but merely the rational powers possessed by the prince.[129] I believe that *lumen rationis* is not a substitute for the prince, for *lumen rationis* does not provide a concrete unity of the Italian *curia* (such unity, Dante believes, is provided by the prince). Rather *lumen rationis* perceives the potential of the Italian *curia*, and therefore is not limited to the prince, but is common to all those rational people who are capable of envisioning this potential existence.

Is the Conceptualization of the Illustrious Vernacular Really Beset with Contradictions—Contradictions that Ultimately Caused the Discontinuance of the *De Vulgari Eloquentia*?

According to Vinay, the conceptualization of the illustrious vernacular is paradoxical because in Book I Dante equates the illustrious vernacular with the *vulgare latium*, the common language of Italy, whereas in Book II he regards the illustrious vernacular as the language of the lofty style of the canzone: ". . . in II, 7 sembra essere presente il concetto di una lingua italiana che comprende ma non si identifica col volgare illustre . . . ."[130] Moreover, by arguing that the illustrious vernacular is the language par excellence of the royal court, Dante, according to Vinay, found himself faced with some insoluble problems: namely should the *reductio ad unum* of the natural languages be limited to a single country—Italy, France, Germany? Why shouldn't the natural languages, like the artifical Latin, extend beyond the border of a single country? In other words, why shouldn't a natural language become the official language of the empire? But if this were to happen, how could one tolerate that anything other than Latin be spoken at the imperial court? Vinay concludes that these contradictions made it impossible for Dante to complete his work.[131]

I do not concur with Vinay that the conceptualization of the illustrious vernacular is paradoxical, because I do not believe that there is any divergence between the illustrious vernacular of Book I and the language of the canzone in Book II. The language of the canzone is one and the same with the illustrious vernacular. Indeed, the illustrious vernacular is considered worthy of the canzone precisely because it is illustrious (*illustre*).

Vinay's error stems from a misunderstanding of the meaning and function of the illustrious vernacular. Because the illustrious vernacular would be the official language of the royal court were Italy to have one and because it is equated with the *vulgare latium* (the Italian vernacular), Vinay concludes that the illustrious vernacular must perforce be the common language of Italy and that, therefore, it is unworthy of the lofty style of the canzone. However, the fact that the illustrious vernacular would be the official language of an Italian court does not make it the common language of Italy, because the officials of the Italian court would speak a distinguished vernacular (i.e., illustrious vernacular) by virtue of their high level of culture. Likewise the fact that the illustrious vernacular is equated with the *vulgare latium* does not mean that by illustrious vernacular Dante has in mind the common lanuage of Italy, because *vulgare latium* for Dante is none other than the *simplicissimum signum* of the linguistic patrimony of Italy.[132]

As to whether Dante was perplexed by the feasibility of the *reductio ad unum* of the natural languages extending beyond the borders of a single country and by the possibility of one of them becoming the official language of the empire, I don't believe that these matters are an issue in the *De Vulgari Eloquentia*. Dante's sole concern in the *De Vulgari Eloquentia* is the *reductio ad unum* of the *multa vulgaria* of Italy. That in the *De Vulgari Eloquentia* Dante is concerned solely with this matter is attested to by his shifting in Chapter IX-X of Book I from a study on the mutability of the *ydioma tripharium* to the description of the Italian vernacular in its multiplicity of forms.[133] This focusing on the formulation of an Italian language is confirmed also by the nationalistic tone of the work. The *De Vulgari Eloquentia* incorporates remarks (the Italian vernacular has a greater affinity with the *gramatica*, the lyric poetry of Italy is more refined and more profound than that of France and Provence, etc.) that demonstrate interest and pride in the Italian language and people. Even the court of Frederick II is viewed primarily in Italian terms.[134] Moreover, it is doubtful that Dante would have ever contemplated the formulation of a supernational natural language that would emerge as the official language of the empire. Communication among the nations of the empire could be carried out effectively in Latin, which was best suited for the empire not only because, like the empire, it was a well established and, when employed properly,[135] a most efficient supernational linguistic entity, but also because, like the empire, it functioned as a *reparatio*.[136] Latin remedied the linguistic fall prompted by the Babylonian Confusion much as the empire rectified the human greed and dissension caused by the original sin. ". . . che a perfezione de l'umana vita," argues Dante in the *Convivio*, "la imperiale autoritade fu trovata, e che ella è regolatrice e rettrice di tutte le nostre operazioni" (IV, ix, 1).

Dante's reasoning in the *De Vulgari Eloquentia*, then, is not beset with contradictions, as assumed by Vinay. Consequently its discontinuance cannot be attributed to internal factors. Rather, it must be sought in causes extrinsic to the work; it must be attributed to stylistic and not linguistic matters, because the remainder of the *De Vulgari Eloquentia*, had Dante completed it, would have dealt with style and not language. I believe that the discontinuance of the *De Vulgari Eloquentia* was caused by a conflict that would have resulted between the stylistic tenets pursued in it and the stylistic norms that were eventually adopted in the *Divine Comedy*. To wit, in the *Divine Comedy* Dante reassesses his notion of style and this reassessment leads to the interruption of the *De Vulgari Eloquentia*. To understand why, therefore, the *De Vulgari Eloquentia* was interrupted, we must reconstruct the stylistic doctrine contemplated in it and see how this doctrine differs from the stylistic makeup of the *Divine Comedy*.

Reconstructing the stylistic principles of the *De Vulgari Eloquentia* is not an easy task, because of the three styles—tragic, comic and elegiac—Dante intended to investigate, only the tragic style is discussed fully. However, in Book II (especially Chapters

IV-VII) there are enough bits of information on the other two styles to permit an adequate reconstruction of what might have been the stylistic doctrine of a fully developed *De Vulgari Eloquentia*.

Following the principle of suitableness (*convenientia*), Dante argues in the *De Vulgari Eloquentia* that the tragic style, as the highest of styles (*summus stilorum*), must make use of the illustrious vernacular, the most refined of vernaculars, and the canzone, the most perfect of poetic compositions (II, iv, 6). Moreover, the tragic style must treat feats of arms, love and virtue, the loftiest of themes (*magnalia*), and must be limited to the *doctores illustres*, the only poets with enough wisdom and technical expertise to bring it to full fruition (II, iv, 8-10). These, then, are the criteria of the tragic style, the highest of styles. But what are the criteria of the comic and elegiac styles, which Dante characterizes as intermediate and low respectively (II, iv, 5-6)? To wit, what would be the vernacular of these styles? What kind of metric schemes would they use? What would be their subject matter?

Other than noting that the comic style uses sometimes the intermediate and sometimes the low vernacular and that the elegiac style relies solely on the low vernacular (II, iv, 6)[137] the *De Vulgari Eloquentia* says precious little about the appropriate language of these styles. However, by investigating Chapters VI and VII of Book II, which, as we have seen,[138] treat respectively the *excelsa constructio* and the *grandiosa vocabula*, the two components of the illustrious vernacular, we can reconstruct rather effectively the type of language Dante deemed applicable to these two styles.

In Chapter VII Dante maintains that the *vocabula* can be classified as puerile (*puerilia*), feminine (*muliebria*), and virile (*virilia*). Of the *vocabula* characterized as virile some are rustic (*silvestria*) and others are urbane (*urbana*), and of the urbane some are carded (*pexa*) and highly smooth (*lubrica*), others are hirsute (*yrsuta*) and bristling (*reburra*). The formulators of the illustrious vernacular, Dante argues, must discard outright the puerile, the feminine and the rustic *vocabula*, because of their simplicity, softness and coarseness, and concentrate instead on the urbane *vocabula*. But among the urbane *vocabula* they must choose only the carded and the hirsute, since the highly smooth and the bristling transgress the boundaries of reasonable smoothness and harshness.

A certain gradation is evident in this assessment of the *vocabula*. Dante seems to suggest that the best *vocabula* are the *pexa* and the *yrsuta*, the second best are the combinations *pexa/lubrica* and *yrsuta/reburra* (i.e. the urbane *vocabula*), whereas the *puerilia*, the *muliebria* and the *silvestria* are the least worthy. Since Dante tells us that the carded and the hirsute *vocabula* are the *grandiosa vocabula* used to form the illustrious vernacular, we can assume, following the principle of *convenientia*, that the urbane *vocabula* would constitute the intermediate vernacular and that the puerile, the feminine, the rustic *vocabula* would make up the low vernacular.

An analogous reasoning prevails in Chapter VI of Book II where Dante explores the lofty construction (*excelsa constructio*). According to Dante there are two types of constructions: the congruous (*congrua*) and the incongruous (*incongrua*). The congruous construction can in turn be divided into the one without flavor (*insipida*) which is used by the ignorant; the one with flavor (*sapida*) which is used by disciplined scholars and teachers; the one with flavor and grace (*sapida et vetusta*) which is used by those who possess some knowledge of rhetoric; and the one with flavor, grace and excellence (*sapida et vetusta etiam excelsa*) which is used by the most illustrious of writers. The formulators of the illustrious vernacular should concern themselves with the *congrua constructio* and only with its highest form—the *excelsa constructio*—which is the only one worthy of the illustrious vernacular.

Like the *vocabula*, the *constructio* is also seen as possessing a gradation. The *excelsa constructio* is the best construction, the *sapida* or *sapida et vetusta* is the second best and the *incongrua* or *insipida* is the worst. If the *excelsa constructio* is perforce the construction of the illustrious vernacular, it follows that the *sapida* or *sapida et vetusta* is the construction of the intermediate vernacular and that the *incongrua* or *insipida constructio* is the construction of the low vernacular. To the extent that the comic style would partake of the intermediate vernacular and that the elegiac style would make use of the low vernacular, we can surmise that the comic style would consist of urbane *vocabula* and *sapida* or *sapida et vetusta constructio* and that the elegiac style would comprise the puerile/feminine/rustic *vocabula* and the *incongrua* or *in-sipida constructio*.

The *De Vulgari Eloquentia* is rather explicit as to the poetic forms to be utilized by the comic and elegiac styles. The comic style makes use of a middle-level poetry, such as the ballad, the sonnet and the canzonet (II, iii, 5-6; iv, 1; viii, 8), whereas the elegiac style would rely on the simplest and crudest (*inlegitmos et inregulares modos*) of poetic compositions (II, iii, 2).[139] But the *De Vulgari Eloquentia* says precious little about the subject matter to be handled by these styles. However, by surveying the rich classical and medieval literature on the *ars poetica* (much of which was known to Dante)[140] and by examining the several poetic specimens provided in Chapters XI-XV of Book I, we can conjecture that the comic style would treat commonplace matters, such as the travails of ordinary people and popular love, whereas the elegiac style would deal with humble everyday things, such as banal love rivalries and plebeian altercations.[141]

To summarize, in the *De Vulgari Eloquentia* Dante envisioned a stylistic doctrine which encompassed three markedly different and non-interchangeable styles.[142] The tragic style would make use of the illustrious vernacular and the canzone and would treat the lofty themes of feats of arms, love and virtue. The comic style would partake of the intermediate vernacular and of a middle-level poetry and would deal with commonplace matters. The elegiac style would utilize the low vernacular and the simplest and crudest of poetic compositions and would discuss humble everyday things. As we turn to the *Divine Comedy*, we note that the rigid stylistic schematization envisioned in the *De Vulgari Eloquentia* is overlooked altogether in the later work. The *Comedy* coalesces the characteristics of all three styles.[143] It thus treats a variety of arguments from the charity of St. Bernard (*Paradiso* XXXI) and the patriotism of Cacciaguida (*Paradiso* XV-XVI) to the indolence of Belacqua (*Purgatorio* IV) and the vainglory of Oderisi (*Purga-*

torio XI-XII) down to the riotuous vulgarity of Vanni Fucci (*Inferno* XXIV-XXV) and the malicious ribaldry of the devils of the fifth bolgia (*Inferno* XXI-XXII).

The richness in subject matter is coupled with a richness in language. Indeed, the *Comedy* makes use not only of the *grandiosa vocabula*, but also of puerile terms (*mamma* and *babbo*) and of those urbane *vocabula* which are excessively soft or harsh (*femmina* and *corpo*). More important, however, the *Comedy* utilizes many terms, such as *introcque* (*Inferno* XX, 130), *accaffi* (*Inferno* XXI, 54), *cuticagna* (*Inferno* XXXII, 97), *istra* (*Inferno* XXVII, 21), *issa* (*Purgatorio* XXIV, 55) and *grattar* (*Paradiso* XVII, 129), which are typical of the crudest of Italian vernaculars.[144]

The versification of the *Comedy* is equally varied. In fact, the *Comedy* encompasses *rime dolci e leggiadre* (*Purgatorio* XXVI, 99) as well as *rime aspre e chiocce* (*Inferno* XXXII, 1), and the *rime aspre e chiocce* are structured according to the criteria of the *excelsa* rather than the *insipida constructio*. Indeed, in the *Divine Comedy* Dante deviates from the principle of *convenientia*. The unlawful love of Paolo and Francesca (*Inferno* V), for example, is couched in civility and is expressed with studied elegance. It is true that in the *Divine Comedy* Dante continues to emulate the tragic style now sublimated in the sweet new style,[145] but the sweet new style represents only a strand in the rich stylistic tapestry of the *Comedy*.

It seems that while writing the *Divine Comedy*, Dante became convinced that great art must treat the whole spectrum of human emotions and must do so by utilizing a whole range of rhetorical and linguistic means. Therefore, the tragic, the intermediate and the low styles rather than being incompatible with one another, as he had assumed in the *De Vulgari Eloquentia*, are now seen as reinforcing one another. Together they give the work of art an energy and a richness that it would otherwise lack were it to rely solely on the tragic style.[146] In view of this reassessment of what constitutes great art, the stylistic schematization envisioned in the *De Vulgari Eloquentia* must have appeared too conventionalized and rarefied to Dante. He thus saw no need to complete the work.

In this chapter I have concentrated on the meaning and ramifications of the illustrious vernacular. The *De Vulgari Eloquentia*, however, encompasses issues other than the illustrious vernacular. Among other important matters treated in the *De Vulgari Eloquentia* are the Adamic language, the origin and justification of the human discourse, the intrinsic mutability of the natural languages and the role of the *gramatica*. All of these issues are reconsidered and elaborated in *Paradiso* XXVI, 124-138, which is the subject of the next chapter.

CHAPTER NINE

"LA LINGUA CH'IO PARLAI FU TUTTA SPENTA": DANTE'S REAPPRAISAL OF THE ADAMIC LANGUAGE (*PARADISO* XXVI, 124-138)

Upon meeting Adam in the eighth heaven of Paradise (*Paradiso* XXVI, 97-142), Dante poses four unspoken questions: What was the date of creation? How long was the period of innocence? What was the nature of the original sin? And what was the character of the primal language? Adam gives brief and somewhat casual answers to the first three questions, but he elaborates on the fourth one:

> La lingua ch'io parlai fu tutta spenta
> innanzi che a l'ovra inconsummabile
> fosse la gente di Nembròt attenta:
> ché nullo effetto mai razïonabile,
> per lo piacere uman che rinovella
> seguendo il cielo, sempre fu durabile.
> Opera naturale è ch'uom favella;
> ma così o così, natura lascia
> poi fare a voi secondo che v'abbella.
> Pria ch'i' scendessi a l'infernale ambascia,
> *I* s'appellava in terra il sommo bene
> onde vien la letizia che mi fascia;
> e *El* si chiamò poi: e ciò convene,
> che l'uso d'i mortali è come fronda
> in ramo, che sen va e altra vene.
> *Paradiso* XXVI, 124-138

These tercets constitute a rectification of an analogous argument in the *De Vulgari Eloquentia*, where Dante contends that the Adamic language is of divine creation and therefore immutable.[1] The objective of this chapter is to examine the rationale that led to this rectification. To the extent, as we will see later, that in the *De Vulgari Eloquentia* Dante recognizes a certain correlation between the immutability of the Adamic language and that of the *gramatica*, this chapter will also explore whether the acknowledgment in *Paradiso* XXVI of the changeable nature of the Adamic language causes Dante to recognize a changeableness in the *gramatica* as well.

In the *De Vulgari Eloquentia*, after arguing that the first speaker was Adam and not Eve and that the first word uttered by Adam was *El*, i.e. God, Dante goes on to note that the Adamic language was created by God simultaneously with Adam himself and that this language was from the outset a fully developed language.[2] Dante maintains that the Adamic language was passed on unchanged to all subsequent generations and that this same language would still be spoken in his own time were it not for the Babylonian Confusion (I, vi, 4-5). Indeed, the construction of the Tower of Babel led to the creation of numerous distinct languages, one for each category of workers. This diversification of the Adamic language eliminated forever the linguistic uniformity and stability mankind had enjoyed up to the Babylonian Confusion (I, vii, 6-7).

The only people to be spared the Babylonian Confusion were the Hebrews, who not only did not take part in the construction of the Tower of Babel, but vehemently disapproved of its undertaking: "Quibus autem sacratum ydioma remansit nec aderant nec exercitium commendabant, sed graviter detestantes stoliditatem operantium deridebant" (I, vii, 8). Consequently the Hebrews, alone among the peoples of the world, were allowed to retain the sacred language of Adam: "Fuit ergo hebraicum ydioma illud quod primi loquentis labia fabricarunt" (I, vi, 7).[3] And this language remained the official language of the Hebrews up to their dispersion: ". . . qui [populus Israel] antiquissima locutione sunt usi usque ad suam dispersionem" (I, vii, 8). That the Hebrews should have retained the language of Adam is clear enough, for it is logical that Christ, who was to spring from their stock, should speak a language not of confusion, but of grace: "Hiis solis [Hebrei] post confusionem remansit, ut Redemptor noster, qui ex illis oriturus erat . . . non lingua confusionis, sed gratie frueretur" (I, vi, 6).

The construction of the Tower of Babel contributed not only to the emergence of many diverse languages, but also to the continuous mutation of these same languages. Thus, whereas prior to Babel there had been one unchangeable language, after Babel there were numerous languages, each of which, except, of course, for Hebrew, was marred by intrinsic mutability. It is logical that languages should be mutable, Dante argues, for after the Babylonian Confusion languages had come to depend entirely on man's discretion: " . . . omnis nostra loquela . . . sit a nostro beneplacito reparata post confusionem illam . . ." (I, ix, 6). And because man is a most inconstant and changeable being, it follows that languages are themselves inconstant and changeable. After all, no effect is stronger than its cause, since nothing can produce that which itself it is not: " . . . nullus effectus superat suam causam . . . quia nil potest efficere quod non est" (I, ix, 6).

The intrinsic mutability of the natural languages led to the creation of a secondary, artificial language: the *gramatica*. Resulting from the common consent of many peoples, the *gramatica* was immune to individual choices; it thus was immutable in time and space: "Hinc moti sunt inventores gramatice facultatis: que quidem gramatica nichil aliud est quam quedam inalterabilis locutionis ydemptitas diversibus temporibus atque locis. Hec cum de comuni consensu multarum gentium fuerit regulata, nulli singulari arbitrio videtur obnoxia, et per consequens nec variabilis esse potest" (I, ix, 11). The *gramatica* had been mastered by the Romans, the Greeks, and a few other peoples, for the rules and the art of this language can be attained only with lengthy and assiduous study: "Est et inde alia locutio secundaria nobis, quam Romani gramaticam vocaverunt. Hanc quidem secumdariam Greci habent et alii, sed non omnes: ad habitum vero huius pauci perveniunt, quia non nisi per spatium temporis et studii assiduitatem regulamur et doctrinamur in illa" (I, i, 3).[4]

As we turn again to the tercets of *Paradiso* XXVI, we note a significant *retractatio* vis-à-vis the thesis of the *De Vulgari Eloquentia*. To be sure *Paradiso* XXVI reaffirms the mutation of the natural languages. As in the *De Vulgari Eloquentia* this mutability is attributed to man's fancy:

> ché nullo effetto mai razïonabile,
> per lo piacere uman che rinovella
> . . . sempre fu durabile.   (127-129)

However, *Paradiso* XXVI denies one of the basic tenets of the *De Vulgari Eloquentia*: the divine creation of the Adamic language. Man's primal language was the product of Adam rather than God, as Adam himself admits: " . . . l'idïoma ch'usai e che fei" (XXVI, 114). This *retractatio* is justified on the ground that God has endowed man with the discursive faculty but not the actual language. The language is an elaboration of man himself:

> Opera naturale è ch'uom favella;
> ma così o così, natura lascia
> poi fare a voi secondo che v'abbella.
> (130-132)

Being man-made, the Adamic language had undergone dramatic changes; it had become unrecognizable by the time Nimrod undertook his nefarious project:

> La lingua ch'io parlai fu tutta spenta
> innanzi che a l'ovra incosummabile
> fosse la gente di Nembròt attenta.
> (124-126)

Just how profound had been the change of the Adamic language could be proved by the transformation of God's name, which was *I* at the time of Adam, but eventually evolved into *El*:

> Pria ch'i' scendessi a l'infernale ambascia,
> *I* s'appellava in terra il sommo bene
>
> . . .
>
> e *El* si chiamò poi . . .
> (133-136)[5]

The primary source of Dante's argument on the Adamic language and the Babylonian Confusion in the *De Vulgari Eloquentia* and

Paradiso XXVI is *Genesis* II, 19-20, 23; X, 8-10, 21-25; and XI. Dante's assessment of these issues, however, depends not so much on the biblical text itself, but on the patristic and scholastic exegeses of this text, with the thesis of the *De Vulgari Eloquentia* relying heavily on the patristic interpretation, especially Augustine's, and that of *Paradiso* XXVI depending on the scholastic explanation, especially Thomas Aquinas'. The thesis of the *Paradiso* is reinforced further by Horace's *Ars Poetica*.

Augustine's most complete account of the primal language and the Tower of Babel appears in the *De Civitate Dei* XVI, iii, iv, xi. Elaborating on *Genesis* X, 21-25 and XI, Augustine argues that the descendents of Heber, i.e. the Hebrews, were the only people to be exempted from the Babylonian Confusion. They thus retained the language that prior to the construction of the Tower of Babel had served as the common and unchangeable speech of all mankind: ". . . quando merito elatioris impietatis gentes linguarum diversitate punitae atque divisae sunt et civitas impiorum confusionis nomen accepit, hoc est, appellata est Babylon, non defuit domus Heber ubi ea quae antea fuit omnium lingua remaneret . . . Et ideo credenda est ipsa [the Hebrew language] fuisse prima illa communis . . ." (XVI, xi). In fact, the Hebrew race was spared the linguistic mutability that marred all post-Babel peoples: " . . . cum aliae gentes plecterentur mutatione linguarum, ad istam [the Hebrew race] non pervenit tale supplicium" (XVI, xi). Augustine speculates that the Hebrews' exemption from the Babylonian Confusion may have been due to their being a godly race: ". . . quoniam de poena venit illa multiplicatio mutatioque linguarum et utique praeter hanc poenam esse debuit populus Dei" (XVI, xi).

A comparison of Dante's account of the Adamic language and the Babylonian Confusion in the *De Vulgari Eloquentia* with that of Augustine in the *De Civitate Dei* reveals a close adherence on the part of Dante to the Augustinian exegesis.[6] Dante believes, like Augustine, that the Hebrews were exempted from the Babylonian Confusion and that they alone, among the peoples of the world, came to inherit the pre-Babel language. Dante also concurs with Augustine on the intrinsic mutability of post-Babel languages. Dante, however, elaborates considerably on the Augustinian exegesis. In fact, he not only accepts as fact Augustine's speculation that the Hebrews may have been exempted from the Babylonian

Confusion, but he actually has the Hebrews scorn and deride the nefarious undertaking of Nimrod and his people. Similarly Augustine's simple reference to the diversification of language acquires a broader and more concrete meaning in Dante—the many languages that resulted from the Babylonian Confusion were predicated on the various activities of the builders of the Tower of Babel. Expanding, it seems, on Augustine's assumption that the pre-Babel language was unchangeable, Dante concludes that the language of the Hebrews was one and the same with Adam's. More important still, Dante innovates on the Augustinian exegesis, indeed on the whole patristic and medieval exegetic tradition, by claiming that the Adamic language was of divine creation.

What prompted Dante to assume that Adam's language was created by God? *Genesis* is rather vague on this point.[7] Some scholars have speculated that this assumption may have derived from the linguistic theories of the classical philosopher Eunomius (335-394), who believed that the human discourse was the product of God.[8] I would argue, however, that the notion of the divine nature of Adam's language in the *De Vulgari Eloquentia* is a pure Dantean invention. Having decided that the Hebrew language was one and the same with the language of Adam and that it was unchangeable, Dante had no choice but to conclude that Adam's language was of divine creation, for, as we will see later, Adam, as a fallen man, could not provide his language with the stability Dante attributes to it.

Be that as it may, Dante's belief in the divine creation of the Adamic language constitutes one of the most remarkable and daring statements of the *De Vulgari Eloquentia*. By claiming that Adam's language was created by God, Dante takes a position that is at variance with contemporary scholarship. As has been argued effectively by Paolo Rotta,[9] scholasticism believed that man was endowed with the potential for a language, but not the language itself. Language per se was an elaboration of man himself. "Significare conceptus suos est homini naturale," notes Thomas Aquinas, "sed determinatio signorum est secundum humanum placitum" (*Summa Theologica* II, ii, q. 85, a, i, ad 3).[10] Thus when Dante in the *Paradiso*, several years after writing the *De Vulgari Eloquentia*, rectifies his theory on the Adamic language, he does so by concurring with the contemporary view of language formation. In fact, the key verses denoting this rectification (*Paradiso* XXVI, 130-132) are an adaptation of the Thomist theory. Why did Dante rectify his theory on the Adamic language? Or to put it differently, why did Dante at the time of the *De Vulgari Eloquentia* argue, relying on patristic exegesis, that the Adamic language was of divine formation and therefore unchangeable, whereas at the writing of *Paradiso* XXVI he maintains, following scholastic theories, that it was man-made and therefore changeable? To answer this question we must explore the notion of *gramatica* in Dante's time as well as Dante's doctrine of creation, both of which are inextricably connected, I believe, with Dante's acceptance and subsequent rejection of the divine nature of Adam's language.

Among contemporary scholars, at least among those scholars who most likely influenced Dante, *gramatica* was seen as a secondary, artificial language created ab ovo to remedy the fluidity and diversity of the natural languages. The languages most often considered as *gramaticae* were Hebrew, Greek, and Latin.[11] These languages were seen as enjoying world preeminence, and they were often characterized as sacred. Brunetto Latini, for example, who surely was no stranger to Dante, notes in his *Tresor* that prior to the Tower of Babel the human race spoke one single language: Hebrew. After the Babylonian Confusion, however, there was a diversity of languages among which prevailed three sacred ones: Hebrew, Greek and Latin: "Et a la verité dire, devant ce que la tour Babel fust faite tout home avoient une meisme parleure naturelement, c'est ebreu; mais puis que la diversités des langues vint entre les homes, sor les autres en furent .iii. *sacrees*, ebrieu, grieu, latin."[12]

The Tuscan versification of Brunetto's *Tresor* reaffirms the world preeminence of Hebrew, Greek and Latin, but denies them their sacredness:

> La parlatura generale sicome si truova, è trina,
> Ebrea, grecha e latina:
> Le subalterne di queste tre sono settantadue.[13]

The author of the versification of the *Tresor* goes on the say that these three languages were due to the linguistic diversity that resulted from the Babylonian Confusion. Indeed, in the Latin world alone—that is to say in that part of the world where Latin functioned as the official, artificial language—there were many diverse idioms with the Italians, the Germans, the English, and the French each speaking a different language:

> Ne la latina parlaura à diversi linguaggi:
> Uno linguaggio ànno l'Italici e un altro i Tedeschi,
> E altro quelli d'Inghilterra e altro i Francieschi,
> E tutti sono della parlaura latina comunemente. [14]

The same linguistic diversity manifested itself among the Hebrews and the Greeks:

> E sì addiviene delli Ebrei e dei Greci, che ànno fra
>   lloro diversità di gente,
> E diversi linguaggi ànno tra lloro
> E perciò sono i Greci e li Ebrei sicome Latini
>   costoro. [15]

Given this linguistic diversity, the ancient sages of the Latin, Greek, and Hebrew worlds found it necessary to formulate the *gramatica*, a pan-linguistic medium that would facilitate communication among the peoples of their respective areas:

> E perciò i Latini antichi e saggi
> Per rechare inn uno diversi linguaggi,
> Chè s'intendesse insieme la gente,
> Trovaro la Gramatica comunemente;
> E così gli Greci e lli Ebrei in loro parlaura
> Trovaro loro gramatica e loro scritura. [16]

The *gramatica* of the Hebrews was formulated first, that of the Greeks was second, and that of the Latins was last:

> Quella delli Hebrei fu la primiera,
> Quella de li Greci fu la secondana,
> Quella de' Latini fu la diretana. [17]

The Hebrews, as attested to by written records, formulated their *gramatica* in Egypt; the Greeks, as proved by ancient histories, found their *gramatica* in Athens; and the Latins, as indicated by the term Latin, achieved their *gramatica* in Rome:

> E li Ebrei, secondo che trovo per scritto,
> Trovarono la loro gramatica in Egitto;
> I Greci, secondo che l'antica storia contiene,
> Trovarono la loro gramatica ind'Athene;
> I Latini, secondo il loro ydioma,
> Trovarono la loro gramatica a Roma. [18]

The artificial, derivative nature of the *gramatica* is acknowledged also by Egidio Romano, another contemporary author well known to Dante. Past philosophers, according to Egidio, having realized that none of the vernacular languages possessed the expressive power to describe effectively the important issues of the human condition, formulated a language of their own, which they called Latin. This language was so accomplished and versatile that it could express any subject matter whatsoever:

> Videntes . . . Philosophi nullum idioma vulgare esse completum et perfectum, per quod perfecte exprimere possent naturam rerum, et mores hominum, et cursus astrorum, et alia de quibus disputare volebant, invenerunt sibi quasi proprium idioma, quod dicitur latinum, vel idioma literale: quod constituerunt adeo latum et copiosum, ut per ipsum possent omnes suos conceptus sufficienter exprimere. [19]

In his assessment of the *gramatica* in the *De Vulgari Eloquentia* Dante concurs with much of contemporary scholarship on this matter.[20] Like the author of the Tuscan versification of the *Tresor* and Egidio, he regards the *gramatica* as an artificial, derivative language which had been formulated by sages (*inventores*) to facilitate communication among the peoples of different regions and different eras. However, he elaborates significantly on the Tuscan versification of the *Tresor* and Egidio by adding that the *gramatica* was reduced to rule by the common consent of many peoples and that this mode of formation rendered it immutable in time and space. Dante also deviates from Brunetto's notion of the sacredness of Hebrew, Greek, and Latin. He attributes this sacredness only to Hebrew, the language of grace (I, vi, 6 and vii, 8), believing, it seems, that Greek and Latin, as man-made languages, cannot be characterized as sacred.[21] In denying Greek and Latin their sacredness, Dante concurs with the author of the versification of the *Tresor*, who, however, regards even Hebrew as an artificial language: "E li Ebrei . . . Trovarono la loro gramatica in Egitto."

Whatever their origin or mode of creation, Dante believes that Hebrew, Greek, and Latin are all immutable. This belief in the immutability of these three languages is at the base, it seems to me, of Dante's reasoning in the *De Vulgari Eloquentia* on the divine creation of the Adamic language. Having decided, on the strength of Augustine, that Hebrew is an immutable language and that it is one and the same with Adam's language, Dante in the *De Vulgari Eloquentia* must have been hard pressed to justify the immutability of the Adamic language. The immutability of the Adamic language could not be attributed to its having been realized through the common consent of many peoples, as he thought was the case with Latin, Greek, and other *gramaticae*, since this language at the time of its formation was spoken solely by Adam and Eve. Nor could the immutability of the Adamic language be ascribed to Adam's nature, because, as a fallen man, Adam was, like his progeny, *instabilissimum atque variabilissimum animal* (I, ix, 6).[22] Consequently he could not give his language stability, because, as argued by Dante himself,[23] nothing can produce that which itself it is not ("quia nil potest efficere quod non est"). Dante, therefore, must have concluded that the immutability of the Adamic language could be justified only by virtue of its being of divine creation. The Adamic language was immutable, because it was created by God simultaneously with Adam himself, and this God-given language was from the outset highly stable and fully developed, being lexically, syntactically and phonetically very sound: ". . . dicimus certam forman locutionis a Deo cum anima prima concreatam fuisse. Dico autem 'formam' et quantum ad rerum vocabula et quantum vocabulorum constructionem et quantum ad constructionis prolationem" (I, vi, 4).[24]

God, then, comes to function as the counterpart of the *inventores* of the *gramatica*. Indeed, Dante seems to recognize a certain relationship between the Adamic language and the *gramaticae* (Greek, Latin, etc.). The *gramaticae* came into being to compensate for the disappearance of the Adamic language. Moreover, the Adamic language, preserved in the Hebrew idiom, came to function as a model for the *gramaticae*. In fact, the *gramatica*, as conceived by Dante, bears all the major attributes of the Adamic language, being, like the Adamic language, stable, cosmopolitan, functional and immune to individual choices.

The same factor—the changeableness of Adam's nature—that, I believe, prompted Dante to view the Adamic language as a sacred language, must also have caused him in *Paradiso* XXVI to doubt this very sacredness. Indeed, as has been observed by Terracini, Dante's assertion in the *De Vulgari Eloquentia* of the divine nature of the Adamic language is tinged with a latent contradiction:

> Quando in I, ix, 6 [Dante] affronta il problema di questa lingua [the natural language] come creazione dell'uomo e quindi variabile per natura, la lingua adamitica perfetta gli si para dinanzi come un'eccezione molesta che egli espone in via puramente parentetica (*preter*, ecc.) quasi avvertendo che fra questa sua concenzione umana del linguaggio, e la teoria della lingua adamitica residuata nell'ebraico vi è una certa latente contraddizione. [25]

Dante's doubtfulness about the divine origin of the Adamic language must have intensified as he became more familiar with the phenomenon of creation. It is no accident, it seems to me, that the rectification on the divine origin of the Adamic language is made after Dante had thought through the phenomenon of creation (*Paradiso* VII, 124-148; XIII, 52-87).

While discussing the phenomenon of creation, Dante argues that all elements created directly by God are eternal: " Ciò che da lei sanza mezzo distilla/non ha poi fine . . ." (*Paradiso* VII, 67-68). According to this theological principle, then, the Adamic language should have lasted forever. Yet in the *De Vulgari Eloquentia* he had noted that this language had ceased to exist with the dispersion of the Hebrews (I, vii, 8). Furthermore, how could Adam, a fallen man, be endowed with the language of grace when in fact, as Dante demonstrates in *Paradiso* VII, 25-30, 34-39, 85-87, he had been deprived of all of his God-given privileges? The idea that Adam, a changeable, imperfect, mortal being, could partake of the language of grace, a stable, perfect and eternal element must have appeared totally untenable to Dante. He thus concludes that the language of Adam is the product of Adam himself. In reaching this conclusion Dante was undoubtedly influenced by the prevailing scholastic view on language formation, which argued, as we have seen above, that God endowed man with the discursive faculty, but not the language itself.

In the final analysis, then, the Adamic language is a natural language much like the Italian vernacular to which it bears a striking resemblance. "Onde vediamo . . . molti vocabuli essere spenti e nati e variati," Dante had said in *Convivio* I, v, 9 with regard to the Italian vernacular; "l'uso d'i mortali è come fronda/in ramo, che sen va e altra vene," he says in *Paradiso* XXVI, 137-138 with respect to the Adamic language. Likewise the "Quapropter audacter testamur quod si vetustissimi Papienses nunc resurgerent, sermone vario vel diverso cum modernis Papiensibus loquerentur" of *De Vulgari Eloquentia* I, ix, 7 finds its parallel in "La lingua ch'io parlai fu tutta spenta" of *Paradiso* XXVI, 124.

That Dante's reasoning on the phenomenon of creation played a vital role in the rectification of the divine formation of the Adamic language is attested to by *Paradiso* XXVI, 127-129:

> ché nullo effetto mai razïonabile,
>   per lo piacere uman che rinovella
>   seguendo il cielo, sempre fu durabile.

This tercet synthesizes Dante's theory on mutability treated in *De Vulgari Eloquentia* I, ix, 6-7 and *Paradiso* VII, 133-141 and XIII, 58-66. In fact, "nullo effetto mai razïonabile/per lo piacere uman che rinovella" conjures up *De Vulgari Eloquentia* I, ix, 6-7 whereas "seguendo il cielo" recalls *Paradiso* VII, 133-141 and XIII, 58-66. The notion of "seguendo il cielo,"—that is to say, the notion of the heavenly spheres' impact on sublunar matters—is absent in the *De Vulgari Eloquentia*, where the phenomenon of mutability is explained primarily in naturalistic terms. Its inclusion here suggests that the rectification of the divine origin of the Adamic language is due, to a large extent, to the theological reasoning on the doctrine of creation.

Whereas the philosophical principle of linguistic mutability is explained through naturalistic and theological tenets, its concrete, historical process is justified on the basis of Horace's doctrine of mutation. Thus paraphrasing Horace's *Ars Poetica* 60-63, Dante argues that it is logical that the language of Adam should have changed so drastically, for "l'uso d'i mortali è come fronda/in ramo, che sen va e altra vene."[26]

Does the mutability of the Adamic language imply that the *gramatica* is also mutable? In other words, given the relationship between the Adamic language and the *gramatica* alluded to before,[27] can we assume that Dante in recognizing the mutability of the Adamic language also came to recognize the mutability of the *gramatica*? In a telling passage of the *Convivio* Dante notes:

> Dico che 'l cielo de la Luna con la Gramatica si somiglia [per due propietadi], per che ad esso si può comparare. Che se la Luna si guarda bene, due cose si veggiono in essa proprie, che non si veggiono ne l'altre stelle: l'una si è l'ombra che è in essa, la quale non è altro che raritade del suo corpo, a la quale non possono terminare li raggi del sole e ripercuotersi così come ne l'altre parti; l'altra si è la variazione de la sua luminositade, che ora luce da uno lato, e ora luce da un altro, secondo che lo sole la vede. E queste due proprietadi hae la Gramatica: chè, per la sua infinitade, li raggi de la ragione in essa non si terminano, in parte spezialmente de li vocabuli; e luce or di qua or di là in tanto quanto certi vocabuli, certe declinazioni, certe costruzioni sono in uso che già non furono, e molte già furono che ancor saranno: sì come dice Orazio nel principio de la Poetria quando dice: "Molti vocabuli rinasceranno che già caddero." *Convivio* II, xiii, 9-10

This passage, which was undoubtedly written after *Convivio* I, v and *De Vulgari Eloquentia* I, ix where Dante defends adamantly the immutability of the *gramatica*, seems to indicate that by the time he made these remarks he had come to regard the *gramatica* as having a certain mutability. In fact, contrary to the position he had taken in *Convivio* I, v, 7 and *De Vulgari Eloquentia* I, ix, 11 where he had argued that Latin is "perpetuo e non corruttibile" and that the *gramatica* "nichil aliud est quam quedam inalterabilis locutionis ydemptitas," he now claims that in the *gramatica* "certi vocabuli, certe declinazioni, certe costruzioni sono in uso che già non furono, e molte già furono che ancor saranno."

This mutability, however, is only apparent, for what Dante is speaking of here is not an unbroken linear development of the *gramatica*, as he does in the case of the Italian vernacular and the Adamic language, but of a periodic variation of some of the *gramatica*'s features. Because of its profundity (*infinitade*), the *gramatica* is not utilized identically by all ages. Similarly, because of changes in stylistic norms, different characteristics of the *gramatica* are used by different ages ("luce or di qua or di là"). Hence linguistic features used by bygone eras are revived in future times. This peculiar use of the *gramatica* accounts for the presence of new words, new declensions and new constructions and for the recurrence of those words, declensions and constructions that had long ceased to exist. What varies, therefore, is not the *gramatica* itself, which remains constant at all times, but the writers' usage of the *gramatica*. This variation differs fundamentally from that of the Italian vernacular and the Adamic language, in both of which change leads to a total and definite transformation of the original linguistic medium.

That Dante in this passage of the *Convivio* is referring to a periodic variation, which takes place independently of the *gramatica*, is rendered clearer by the analogy with the moon. Just as the luminosity of the moon varies from one side of the planet to the other, according to how the sun shines upon it, and this variation has no effect on the nature of the moon itself, so the form of the *gramatica* changes from one era to another, according to the stylistic taste (*la ragione*) of the age in which it is realized, and this change, as in the case of the moon, has no impact on the actual essence of the *gramatica*.

Dante's argument as to the periodic variation of the *gramatica* is further reinforced by the quotation from Horace: ". . . sì come dice Orazio nel principio de la Poetria quando dice: 'Molti vocabuli rinasceranno che già caddero.'" This quotation, which is a translation of "multa [vocabula] renascentur quae iam cecidere . . . " (*Ars Poetica* 70), is misused by Dante. In Horace's work this statement is part of a lengthy passage intended to prove the withering and eventual disappearance of linguistic terms (*vocabula*).[28] Dante, however, uses it to justify the periodic recurrence of certain linguistic features of the *gramatica*. Indeed, he generalizes Horace's statement to encompass all facets of the *gramatica*—words, declensions, constructions—rather than just words (*vocabula*), as is the case with Horace.

Contrary, therefore, to the opinion of those scholars[29] who see in *Convivio* II, xiii, 9-10 the affirmation of the mutability of the *gramatica*, this statement leaves fundamentally unaltered Dante's view of the *gramatica* expressed in *De Vulgari Eloquentia* I, i, 3 and ix, 10. For Dante the *gramatica* remains a secondary, artificial language, unchangeable in time and space.

Not even the *lingua nostra* of *Purgatorio* VII, 16-17 ("O gloria di Latin," disse, "per cui/mostrò ciò che potea la lingua nostra."), which is often cited as attesting to the mutability of Latin (=*gramatica*), can be taken as a revision of Dante's belief in the unchangeableness of the *gramatica*.[30] Charles Singleton, for example, glosses *lingua nostra* as follows: "'Lingua nostra,' as here used by Sordello, embraces Latin and all its Romance derivatives and regards them as one language—to which a patriotic 'nostra' attaches."[31] For Singleton, then, and for those scholars who accept this interpretation, Dante's characterization of Latin as *lingua nostra* is predicated on his acknowledgment of Latin as the mother tongue of the Romance idioms. Hence, Dante, acording to these scholars, saw Latin as a mutable language.

I believe, however, that for Dante Latin was *lingua nostra* because it functioned as the official, artificial language of the Latin world (Italy, Germany, England, France, etc.).[32] Latin, therefore, belonged to all the nations of this world; they possessed it together with their respective natural language (Italian, German, English, French, etc.). If one had asked Dante, "is the empire ours?" his answer, of course, would have been in the affirmative. There is no reason why he should have felt any differently with respect to Latin, which, as we have seen above,[33] he regarded as coincident with the empire. It is marvelous that this supernational language should have achieved its highest poetic expression through Virgil, an Italian (*O gloria di Latin*).[34]

In one of the most engaging studies on Dante's notion of *gramatica* (=Latin), Ettore Paratore argues that Dante regarded Latin as having been originally a living language and source of the Romance idioms: ". . . un latino che fosse originariamente lingua viva e radice dei volgari romanzi."[35] Indeed, according to Paratore, Dante believed that the Latin of medieval time was traceable to the era of Caesar Augustus when Virgil and other distinguished writers molded a lofty, literary language out of vulgar Latin (*latinus vulgaris*). Dante further believed, Paratore contends, that, due to the grammarians of the late empire and the *gramatice positores* of the Middle Ages, the literary Latin of antiquity had become highly regularized and conventional, whereas vulgar Latin had evolved into the Romance idioms. Dante, therefore, understood much better than it may at first appear the historical development of contemporary Latin, which from a quasi-living language in Virgil's time had evolved into a fossalized one in his own day: "Dante quindi finisce per mostrarcisi molto più edotto di quanto non sembri del processo storico che ha portato il latino dalla creazione di Virgilio, ancora intelligibile per i più, alla fossilizzazione degli attuali *gramatice positores* attraverso l'opera dei tardi grammatici antichi."[36]

Since one cannot deny, Paratore adds, that Dante regarded the Romance vernaculars as derivatives of the vulgar Latin of Virgil's time, one can see why in *De Vulgari Eloquentia* I, x, 1-4 Dante argues for a genetic relationship between the highly regularized Medieval Latin and the prevailing Romance idioms:

> E dato che è innegabile postulare che i volgari romanzi derivassero, anche per Dante, dal volgare italico dei tempi di Virgilio, ecco confermato come anche quella costruzione ormai artificiale, quell'estremo precipitato erudito ch'era la *gramatica* estratta dal latino letterario, dovesse conservare quel lontano potere di riscontro coi volgari romanzi cui accenna *DVE*, I, x, 1-4.[37]

Paratore's opinion notwithstanding, at no time does Dante imply that the *gramatica* was to be identified with a vulgar Latin of Virgil's time. Indeed, Dante never exclusively associates the *gramatica* with the Romans, though he may have believed, like the author of the Tuscan versification of the *Tresor*, that it was formulated in Rome.[38]

Dante's thinking about the origin of the *gramatica* is crystal-clear. The Babylonian Confusion caused the disintegration of the primal language, and this disintegration gave origin to a diversity of languages which in Europe manifested itself as a threefold idiom encompassing the Germanic, Romance, and Byzantine languages. These European languages evolved into further linguistic forms of their own. Hence, the Romance idiom developed into the languages of *oc, oil* and *sì* and the languages of *oc, oil* and *sì* themselves ramified into different linguistic entities. The language of *sì*, for example, evolved into fourteen major vernaculars with each one of these vernaculars having numerous derivatives of its own. This constant and inevitable diversification of the natural tongues led to the creation of the *gramatica*, a fixed and unchanging linguistic medium, which was reduced to rule by the common consent of many peoples (*de comuni consensu multarum gentium*).[39]

If Dante, as suggested by Paratore, had believed that the fossilized Latin (=*gramatica*) of his day was traceable to a vulgar Latin of Virgil's time and was antecedent to the Romance idioms, he would have said so. If Dante makes no reference to the classical origin of Latin and if he sees it as a direct result of the constant and inevitable mutation of the natural languages, it is because he believes, like Egidio and the author of the versification of the *Tresor*, that Latin was a secondary, artificial language intended to facilitate communication in time and space. And by space, as the term "consent of many peoples" indicates, he must have meant not just the Romance countries, but all those European countries (England, Germany, etc.) where Latin functioned as the official language of scholarship. The genetic relationship, then, between Latin and the Romance idioms alluded to in *De Vulgari Eloquentia* I, x, 1-4 is not due, as Paratore believes, to their being derivatives of an identical source—vulgar Latin—but to Latin's adaptation of vernacular Romance usages.

Dante's understanding of the historical development (*il processo storico*, in Paratore's words) of Latin was hampered by the fossilized nature of Medieval Latin. As noted by Paratore himself, the *dictatores* of the *gramatica*, following the universally accepted criteria of the *artes dictandi*, had transformed Latin into a uniform and timeless linguistic medium, applicable to any age and any people and foreign to any existing living language: ". . . i maestri delle *artes dictandi*, sulla base del latino letterario formulato dai grandi autori, hanno fissato le strutture di una lingua valida per i dotti fuori di ogni limite di tempo . . . essa non corrispondeva neppure parzialmente a nessuna lingua viva . . "[40] Medieval Latin, then, had the appearance of being a secondary, artificial language; it thus satisfied fully Dante's theory of linguistic *reparatio*.

For Dante to comprehend the historical development of Latin, he would have needed to understand the cultural dynamics of classical and medieval Italy, and to gain such an understanding he would have needed a rigorous method of research; he would have needed the ideological orientation and methodology of a Biondo, the intellectual, who, as we have seen above,[41] first proved that Latin was not an artificial language, but a natural one which had eventually evolved into the Italian vernacular. Dante, however, was not in a position to match Biondo's achievement, notwithstanding his gift for empirical reasoning and his propensity for innovation, for he wrote in an age void of the wealth of historical evidence, the sense of historical perspective, and the philological sophistication that rendered Biondo's discovery possible.

The question still remains: how could Dante in light of Horace's *Ars Poetica* 60-72, which in fact recognizes a mutability of Latin, and in the face of the linguistic divergence between the Latin of the classical authors and that of his contemporaries go on believing that the *gramatica* was immutable? I suspect that these factors did not go unnoticed by Dante and that they may have contributed to the periodic variation he alludes to in *Convivio* II, xiii, 9-10.

To prove the drastic change of the Adamic language Dante notes:

> Pria ch'i' scendessi a l'infernale ambascia,
> *I* s'appellava in terra il sommo bene
>
> . . .
>
> e *El* si chiamò poi . . .
>
> (133-136)

By noting that God's name in Adam's time had been *I* (which *I* had eventually evolved into *El*), Dante in effect refutes his assertion in the *De Vulgari Eloquentia* that Adam's name for God had been *El*.[42] This refutation raises some important questions: why did Dante discard *El* as Adam's name for God? How did he arrive at the term *I*? What is the relationship between *I* and *El*?

In a key study, which is representative of much of the scholarship on this problem, Domenico Guerri maintains:

> Giacchè tutta era spenta la lingua di Adamo prima del misfatto di Babele, il nome che questi pronuncia non può essere un vocabulo di una lingua conosciuta, tolto il solo caso che la "I" fosse, secondo qualche tradizione religiosa, leggendaria o comunque formatasi un nome rivelato: cosa che nessuno ha saputo mostrare che risulti. Neanche apparisce che questo nome sia mai stato indicato come adamitico. Dunque con verosimiglianza Dante lo foggiò da sè e palesemente lo volle semplicissimo, avendolo costituito da una semplice vocale. La scelta della "I" dovette parergli conveniente forse per la figura sottile e il suono esile, qualità che la grammatica del medio evo insistentemente invitava a considerare, ma più pe' simboli, interpretandosi scienza e principio la corrispondente lettera ebraica, che è insieme l'iniziale del nome divino più venerato nella tradizione biblica, Iehovah. S'aggiunga che un grammatico fra i più famosi, Giovanni di Garlandia, il quale rassomiglia le vocali agli elementi, la *a* al fuoco, la *e* all'aria, la *o* all'acqua, la *u* alla terra, trovava alla *i* il suo posto conveniente considerandola *anima mundi, sive divina dispositio ligans elementa naturalia*; e Ubertino da Casale, in un libro ben noto al Poeta, dimostrava che questa lettera, nel nome Iesus, significa la persona divina.[43]

Guerri adds that the choice of *I* was due also to the fact that it denotes unity: "Ma preponderante dovette essere la ragione che la 'I' siccome corrisponde alla cifra latina che significa 'uno' . . . richiamava l'idea dell' 'unità,' convenientissima come attributo di Dio . . . Sicchè la 'I' risultava doppiamente conveniente: e come segno fonico, e come segno numerico."[44]

Guerri's argument resolves only in part the problem of *Paradiso* XXVI, 133-136. He tells us why Dante discarded *El* as

Adam's name for God and why *I* was an appropriate term for God's name. But he does not tell us what the relationship is between *I* and *El*. Why and how did *I* evolve into *El*? To answer this last question we must go back to what I have said about Dante's reasoning on the illustrious vernacular.

According to Dante the Italian language had evolved from a single linguistic entity (*unum ydioma*) sometime after the Babylonian Confusion into numerous vernaculars (*multa vulgaria*) by his own time. This evolution had severely debased the Italian idiom, for, in diversifying into many vernaculars, the Italian idiom had lost its unity, and, as he had learned from Aristotle, the only really excellent elements are those which are the most unified ("illud est optimum quod est maxime unum"). The illustrious vernacular, therefore, a truly excellent linguistic medium, was to be achieved by recapturing the Italian protolanguage of Babylonian time.[45]

I believe that this same reasoning is at the basis of his reconstruction of the protoname of God. *El,* according to the medieval scholarly tradition (Jerome, *Epistola ad Marcellam*, Isidore, *Etymologiae* VII, i, 3; Uguccione da Pisa, *Magnae Derivationes*, etc.), was the first of ten Hebrew names for God.[46] This is the reason, as most commentators have noted, that Dante chose it as Adam's name for God in the *De Vulgari Eloquentia*. However, when, in *Paradiso* XXVI, he concluded that Hebrew was a derivative of Adam's language, he could no longer accept *El* as the Adamic name for God. In fact, *El* together with the other nine Hebrew names, must have been seen by Dante as linguistic dissolutions of a protoname of Adam's time much as the many vernaculars of Italy were regarded as linguistic transformations of an Italian protolanguage of Babylonian time.[47]

What, then, was the protoname for God? Since *El* begins with *e*, Dante must have reasoned that the linguistic base for *El* had to be a term whose phonological development would have caused it to evolve into *e*. In the *Convivio* while discussing the function of the five vowels in the term *auieo*, which vowels, as Dragonetti argues,[48] are arranged in a natural phonological order, Dante notes:

> E chi ben guarda lui [auieo], ne la sua prima voce apertamente vedrà che elli stesso lo dimonstra, che solo di legame di parole è fatto, cioè

di sole cinque vocali, che sono anima e legame d'ogni parole, e composto d'esse per modo volubile, a figurare imagine di legame. Chè, cominciando da l'A, ne l'U quindi si rivolve, e viene diritto per I ne l'E, quindi si rivolve e torna ne l'O. *Convivio* IV, vi, 3-4

According to this statement, then, the *I* evolves into *E* ("viene diritto per *I* ne l'*E*").[49]

Since it is in the nature of *I* to evolve into *E*, Dante must have concluded, by engaging in a bit of what today we might characterize as historical phonology, that the linguistic base for *El* could not be anything else but *I*. This empirical reasoning must have been reinforced by the Aristotelian principle of the *maxime unum* (the slenderness of the *I* conforms fully with this principle) as well as the mystical quality of the letter *I* noted by Guerri.

To conclude, Dante's rectification in *Paradiso* XXVI of his perception of the Adamic language is due to a rethinking of the phenomenon of creation and of the changeable nature of Adam. This rethinking, however, does not alter his view of the *gramatica* expounded in the *De Vulgari Eloquentia*. For ideological and historical reasons Dante continues to view the *gramatica* as an artificial, derivative language unchangeable in time and space.

APPENDICES

THE BINOMIAL *LATINA LINGUA/GRAMMATICA* IN DANTE AND THE HUMANISTS

A vexing problem facing the student of Dante's literature on language and of the documents generated by the Florentine debate is the usage of the binomial *latina lingua/grammatica*. This binomial came into being in the Middle Ages, and it derived from Latin's being viewed as an incorruptable, artificial language intended to remedy the variability of the natural languages. Dante uses both terms interchangeably: "anzi erano dicitori d'Amore certi poeti in lingua latina" (*Vita Nuova* XXV, 3); "lo latino molte cose manifesta concepute nella mente;" "non avrebbe lo latino così servito a molti" (*Convivio* I, v, 12; ix, 2); and "l'uno si è d'uno verbo molto lasciato da l'uso in gramatica" (*Convivio* IV, vi, 3); "gramaticam tanquam simie homines imitantes;" "et in gramatica tredena perficitur in duobus obliquis" (*DVE* I, xi, 7; II, vii, 6).

Often in Dante, *latina lingua/gramatica* is paralleled by the binomial *latinus/litteratus* (*litteralis*). *Litteratus* has both the restricted meaning of Latin (*latinus*) and the broader meaning of speaking, understanding and being conversant in Latin and in Latin culture.[1] The term *litteratus* (*litterato*) is usually used in opposition to *vulgaris* (*volgare*): "non volgari ma litterati poeti queste cose trattavano" (*Vita Nuova*, XXV, 3); "che da litterati e non litterati è inteso;" "che sono molti e molte in questa lingua, volgari e non litterati" (*Convivio* I, vii, 12; ix, 5).

The binomial *latina lingua/grammatica* recurs in Biondo who uses it to clarify the term *grammatica*. As though to divest it of its medieval/Dantean sense of artificiality, Biondo insists that *grammatica* was just another name for Latin: "materno ne et passim . . . aetate nostra vulgato idiomate, an grammaticae artis usu, quod latinum appellamus . . . Romani orare fuerint soliti."[2] The binomial *latinus/litteratus* is also present in Biondo, and it has the same clarifying function of *latina lingua/grammatica*: "Constet vero . . . verba orationum, dum pronuntiarentur, fuisse latina, qualia nunc dicimus litterata."[3]

Bruni is no stranger to the binomial *latina lingua/grammatica*: "Apparò grammatica da grande, e per questa cagione non ebbe mai la lingua latina molto in sua balia."[4] Nevertheless, he makes no use of it in Epistola VI, 10 where, except for a reference to *latina lingua* ("latina lingua a vulgari in multis differt"),[5] he relies entirely on *litteratus* and the more emphatic *latinus ac litteratus*. *Litteratus* in Bruni has the same meaning that it has in Dante and as in Dante is often used in opposition to *vulgaris* (*volgare*): "nec alium vulgarem, alium litteratum;" "tunc distinctam fuisse vulgarem linguam a litterata existimo;" "Haec ne quaeso mulierculae et nutrices et vulgus illiteratum dicent, quae nos litterati vix dicere valemus?"[6] Bruni follows this same procedure in the *Vite di Dante e di Petrarca* where Latin and the *volgare* are an issue: "lo scrivere in istile litterato o vulgare non a fare al fatto;" "Dante piuttosto elesse scrivere in vulgare che in latino e litterato stilo," and "al tempo di Dante lo stile litterato pochi sapevano."[7]

Of course, the binomial *latina lingua/grammatica* and its corresponding *latinus/litteratus* are central to the Poggio-Valla polemic,[8] and they are used extensively by Guarino. Guarino's use of these terms is similar to Biondo's: "cum eos latine locutos dicimus; eane fuerit, quam hac aetate vulgo et ab indoctis usurpari sentimus, an litteralis et a peritis observata, quam graeco vocabulo recte grammaticam appellamus;" "Hos grammaticam idest litteralem, non grammatice, locutos contenderim."[9] Indeed, in the humanists, the binomial *latina lingua/grammatica* usually has a clarifying function, that is to say, it is intended to clarify that *grammatica* stands for *latina lingua* and vice versa.

The binomial *latina lingua/grammatica* is absent in Alberti and his school whose primary objective is the formulation of the vernacular language rather than the reconstruction of the linguistic state of antiquity, the area of investigation connected with this binomial. Alberti and his followers make use exclusively of the term *lingua latina*.

The binomial *latina lingua/grammatica* persists well into the Cinquecento. For example, in Machiavelli's *Mandragola* (Act I, scene iii), we read: " . . . lui è per crederlo facilmente . . . per

essere tu litterato e poterli dire qualche cosa in grammatica."
However, *grammatica* as implying *latina lingua* seems to acquire a
pejorative meaning in the Cinquecento.

INTERCONNECTION BETWEEN *DE VULGARI ELOQUENTIA* I, XI-XV; II, VI AND *PURGATORIO* XXIV, 42-62; XXVI, 92-123: A CLARIFICATION OF THE *DOLCE STIL NOVO*

In discussing *De Vulgari Eloquentia* I, xi-xv and II, vi, I noted that these chapters constitute the first phase of what was to become the polemic on the poetics of the sweet new style (*dolce stil novo*).[1] In fact, one notes a strong conceptual affinity between these chapters and *Purgatorio* XXIV, 49-62 and XXVI, 92-123, the sections where this polemic is developed. Hence the acknowledgment in *De Vulgari Eloquentia* I, xv, 6 of Guinizzelli as the greatest and most proficient of Bolognese poets (*maximus Guido Guinizeli*) is paralleled in *Purgatorio* XXVI, 98 by the recognition of Guinizzelli as the most influential and excellent of poets (*il padre/mio e delli altri miei miglior*), whose poetry will endure forever:

> . . ."Li dolci detti vostri,
> che, quanto durerà l'uso moderno,
> faranno cari ancora i loro incostri."
> XXVI, 112-114

Similarly the assertion in *De Vulgari Eloquentia* II, vi, 8 that there are individuals (*ignorantie sectatores*) who, by being too ignorant to recognize truly great poetry, have judged Guittone as a distinguished poet, is equaled by the claim in *Purgatorio* XXVI, 119-126 that there had been fools (*stolti*) who, by giving heed to rumor rather than truth, had acknowledged Guittone as the best among the poets of the previous generation, superior even to Guinizzelli. As in the *De Vulgari Eloquentia* (I, xiii, 1 and II, vi, 8), so in the *Purgatorio* Dante minimizes the cultural contribution of Guittone and his school:

"O frate, issa, vegg'io" diss'elli "il nodo
che 'l Notaro e Guittone e me ritenne
di qua dal dolce stil novo . . ."
                                    XXIV, 55-57

However, these similarities are coupled with some very significant differences. In *Purgatorio* XXIV, 56, Giacomo da Lentini, who in *De Vulgari Eloquentia* I, xii, 8 is characterized as a distinguished writer who had made use of the most courtly of terms (*vocabula curialiora*), is grouped with Guittone and Bonagiunta, who, according again to Dante's assessment in *De Vulgari Eloquentia* I, xiii, 1 were popular writers, who had utilized provincial rather than courtly terms. Following the logic of the *De Vulgari Eloquentia*, in the *Purgatorio* Giacomo da Lentini should have been associated with Guinizzelli and not Guittone. What is even more surprising, however, is the total absence in the *Purgatorio* of the Sicilian school—Dante considered Giacomo da Lentini Apulian (*DVE* I, xiii, 8). Given the fact that the poets of the Sicilian school had set the norms, according to Dante, for modern Italian poetry (*DVE* I, xii)[2] and that they were fully conversant in the illustrious vernacular, one would have expected that they would have been acknowledged as the founders of the sweet new style. Instead Dante attributes this distinction to Guinizzelli:

. . . il padre
mio e de li altri miei miglior che mai
rime d'amor usar dolci e leggiadre.
                                    XXVI, 97-99

What is the reason for these differences?

In the *De Vulgari Eloquentia* Dante argues that the tragic style, that is to say great lyric poetry, consists in the harmonizing of profundity of thought with splendor of verses, elevation of construction and excellence of vocabulary. The tragic style, therefore, must treat the noble themes of feats of arms, love and virtue (II, iv, 7-8). In the *De Vulgari Eloquentia*, then, great lyric poetry depends equally on form and content, which Dante sees as mutually reinforcing. However, in the *Purgatorio*, while defining the sweet new style, Dante makes content the primary criterion for great lyric poetry. Form, on the other hand, flows from and is conditioned by content:

> . . . "I' mi son un che, quando
> Amor mi spira, noto, e a quel modo
> ch'e' ditta dentro vo significando."
>
> XXIV, 52-54

Moreover, contrary to his position in the *De Vulgari Eloquentia*, where he argues that great poetry must treat the noble themes of feats of arms, love and virtue, he now maintains that the subject matter of the sweet new style must be limited to love and to a unique type of love. The love of the poet of the sweet new style is not sensual nor passionate but pure and spiritual, and it need not be reciprocated by an actual lover. Indeed, as in *Vita Nuova* XVII-XX, from which this love is spun, the poet of the sweet new style is in love with love.[3]

This being the case, it is logical that Guinizzelli be acknowledged as the father of the sweet new style poetry, for, as Dante himself tells us, Guinizzelli is the originator of the type of love poetry emulated by this style:

> Amore e'l cor gentil sono una cosa,
> sì come il saggio [Guinizzelli] in suo dittare pone.
>
> *Vita Nuova* XX, 1-2

Likewise it is logical that the Apulian and Sicilian poets, who wrote a utilitarian and formalistic poetry, be either demoted to the school of Guittone, as is the case with Giacomo da Lentini, or overlooked altogether, as happens with the Sicilian school.

Be that as it may, in *Purgatorio* XXIV, 49-62 and XXVI, 92-123 Dante revises the poetic doctrine of the *De Vulgari Eloquentia*. Great lyric poetry is first and foremost the celebration of virtuous love. Elegance of form (*vulgare illustre*), therefore, and profundity of thought per se do not earn one's acceptance into the pantheon of the poets of the sweet new style.[4] Lyric poetry itself is seen as being less varied in the *Purgatorio*. In the *De Vulgari*

Eloquentia, Dante perceives poetry as being excellent, good, average, poor. In the *Purgatorio* poetry is polarized into bad and excellent—bad poetry is that which is kept short of the sweet new style (*di qua dal dolce stil novo*), excellent poetry is that which has mastered the canons of this style.[5]

APPENDIX THREE

A RECENT CONTRIBUTION TO THE FLORENTINE DEBATE OF 1435: MIRKO TAVONI'S *LATINO, GRAMMATICA, VOLGARE. STORIA DI UNA QUESTIONE UMANISTICA**

As noted above, Mirko Tavoni has written the most comprehensive study on the Florentine debate and the polemic that it engendered. Tavoni's work consists of two parts. Part One provides a study of the humanists who contributed to the debate and is divided into seven chapters which deal respectively with Bruni and Biondo, Bruni and Alberti, Guarino, Poggio, Valla, Filelfo, and Pompilio. Part Two edits the documentation that resulted from the debate. As Tavoni tells us (302-304), in publishing these documents he has emended significantly the *Disceptatio Convivalis* of Poggio and the *Epistolae* of Filelfo, which are adapted from deficient sixteenth-century editions, but has made only minor changes in the remaining documents, all of which enjoy well-grounded modern editions.

Overall, Tavoni's editing of the documentation of the Florentine debate is scholarly and sound. He clearly identifies the many classical sources appearing in this documentation, noting whether the author under scrutiny has adapted them from other contributors to the Florentine debate or whether he has taken them directly from the classical sources. By gathering all of these documents in a single work, Tavoni makes readily available an important body of information that was previously scattered in several different publications. If Tavoni's editing of these documents is solid and useful, his analysis of them (that is to say Part One of his monograph) is marred with significant flaws. The objective of this appendix is to synthesize Tavoni's interpretation of these docu-

---

* Mirko Tavoni, *Latino, grammatica, volgare. Storia di una questione umanistica*. Medioevo e Umanesimo, 53. Padova, Antenore, 1984. Pp. xxiv + 328

ments and qualify this interpretation in terms of my own assessment of the debate.

I

Tavoni opens Part One of his work by studying Bruni and
Biondo, whom he correctly characterizes as the originators
(*capostipiti*) of the Florentine debate. In claiming in the *De Verbis
Romanae Locutionis* that Bruni believed that the ancient Romans
spoke a vernacular form of speech that was transmitted to later
ages, Biondo, according to Tavoni, misinterprets Bruni's position
on the linguistic state of antiquity. In fact, as proved by his letter to
Biondo, Bruni makes no explicit reference to a direct relationship
between the contemporary vernacular and a corresponding ancient
one. For example, the statement *ego autem, ut nunc est, sic etiam
tunc distinctam fuisse vulgarem linguam a literata existimo* at the
beginning of Bruni's letter is not referring to the vernacular per se
but to the total linguistic situation: " . . . *non* è . . . riferito al volgare, ma alla situazione complessiva" (7). As in modern time so in
antiquity, there must have been a clear distinction between literary
language and the common language. Even those statements in
Bruni's letter that appear to imply a correlation between the contemporary vernacular and a corresponding ancient one—the comparison between the aristocratic women of contemporary Rome
and those of antiquity, the reference to the vernacular of Dante, the
observation on the marked difference between Latin and the vernacular ("Latina lingua a vulgari in multis differt")[1]—cannot be
taken as proof of such a correlation, for what Bruni is implying
here is not a corrispondence between an ancient and the modern
vernacular but a parallel identity between two analogous linguistic
situations:

> " . . . il Bruni allude bensì a una parallela identità, o analogia, fra
> volgare antico e volgare moderno . . . All'identità fra l'antica e la
> moderna *litterata lingua* corrisponde un'identità fra l'antica e la moderna
> *vulgaris lingua*. Ma si tratta, nel secondo caso, di una identità definita
> in negativo, l'identità fra due caselle sul cui contenuto il Bruni non dà
> (ne possiede) alcuna informazione, se non quella di affermare che

occupano la stessa posizione in uno schema rimasto identico a se stesso" (7).

Biondo's misinterpretation of Bruni's position is not due to malice, Tavoni argues, but to a methodological approach that differs fundamentally from Bruni's. Whereas Biondo views the linguistic state of antiquity from an historical perspective, Bruni sees it from a grammatical viewpoint. The former, therefore, thinks diachronically, the latter synchronically. Biondo's diachronic mode of thinking causes him to interpret Bruni's inference to a parallel identity between the ancient and modern vernacular as implying that the ancient vernacular had evolved into its modern counterpart: " . . . e di conseguenza credeva di vedere nel pensiero del Bruni l'affermazione che tale idioma esisteva fin dall'antichità" (10).

Biondo's perception of the linguistic state of antiquity is colored by Ciceronian rhetoric, especially the *Brutus*, which he had recently transcribed. The Ciceronian influence prompts Biondo to view the linguistic state of antiquity as characterized by a linguistic stratification (*una gradualità di livelli linguistici*). Indeed, Biondo comes to view the ancient speech in terms of the Ciceronian rhetorical tripartition: the ancient speech was differentiated into common, oratorical and poetic, with the oratorical speech corresponding to the *medius modus*, the idiom Biondo believed was used by the learned when addressing the masses.[2]

Tavoni adds that whereas Biondo's historical orientation causes him to view the ancient speech as stratified and fluid, Bruni's grammatical approach leads him to perceive the ancient idiom as bipolar and static, with the learned speaking a highly grammatical language, and the unlearned a totally agrammatical one. If Biondo's assessment of the linguistic state of ancient Rome was colored by the Ciceronian rhetorical tripartition, that of Bruni was influenced by the Dantean prejudicial identity of Latin with *grammatica*: " . . . si profila nel Bruni quella pregiudiziale identificazione di latino e grammatica (non diversamente che per Dante) che costituisce il nucleo implicito nel suo rifiuto di ammettere che *la litterata lingua* potesse essere padroneggiata dagli *illiterati* . . . " (xii). Indeed, Bruni espouses the Dantean notion in the *Convivio* that the vernacular follows usage and Latin art and

that, therefore, the two are opposed to one another: " . . . resta il
fatto che l'opposizione fra il volgare naturale e il latino artificiale,
fra il volgare che seguita uso e il latino che seguita arte è costitutiva
tanto del *De vulgari eloquentia*, che i nostri umanisti non cono-
scevano, quanto del *Convivio*, che un uomo come il Bruni assai
verosimilmente poteva conoscere" (15-16).

However, Bruni's reference to the linguistic bipolarity of ancient Rome is not to be taken as indicative of a classical bilingualism, for when Bruni speaks of the language of the learned being
significantly different from that of the unlearned, he does not
mean that they were two different languages, but that they were
variants of the same language: " . . . si può . . . vedere . . .
l'attitudine del Bruni a concepire il volgare sì come una parlata diversa, ma una parlata che non è altro che la varietà agrammaticale
del latino . . ." (50). This being the case, a more appropriate term
to describe Bruni's notion of the linguistic state of antiquity would
be "diglossia."[3]

That Bruni is thinking of variants of the same language rather
than of two different languages is attested to by the terminology of
his letter to Biondo. The prevalent terms in this letter are *sermo
vulgaris/lingua vulgaris* and *sermo litteratus/lingua litterata*. The
latter two terms are qualified further with *latine litterateque* and
latine ac litterate of which *litterate*, according to Tavoni, is the key
term. The same type and grouping of terms recurs in Bruni's *Vita
di Dante* (*istile vulgare/istile litterato*) and in Biondo's *De Verbis
Romanae Locutionis* (*vulgare/litteratum*) where Biondo para-
phrases Bruni. The term *latina lingua* and its derivatives are absent
in Bruni. The emphasis on *lingua vulgaris* and *lingua litteralis*
with their derivatives and the absence of *latina lingua* indicates,
Tavoni argues, that what concerns Bruni in his letter to Biondo is
not the contrast between the vernacular and Latin, as it is often believed, but the opposition between the vernacular and learned
speech: "Nel Bruni, come l'opposizione in termini di parlanti è fra
vulgus e *litterati*, così conseguentemente l'opposizione in termini
di forme linguistiche non è fra volgare e latino, come imprecisa-
mente viene spesso riportato, ma fra *sermo vulgi* e *sermo litteratorum* . . ." (29). In other words, what Bruni is talking about here,
according to Tavoni, is a totally unregularized, agrammatical

speech (*sermo vulgaris*) vs. a highly regularized, grammatical one (*sermo litteralis*).

Unlike Bruni, Biondo makes extensive use of the terms *latina lingua* and its derivatives *latinus, latine, latinitas*. Biondo's reliance on the term *latina lingua* is due to his viewing the linguistic state of antiquity in strictly rhetorical terms. To be sure, the term *litteratus* appears in Biondo as well, but in Biondo it is strictly a synonym for *latinus*.

From the Bruni-Biondo polemic Tavoni goes on to explore the relationship between Bruni and Alberti. He begins by challenging Baron's assertion that Alberti's proem is linked to Bruni in that Alberti, according to Baron, continues and elaborates Bruni's reasoning on the capability of the vernacular. Tavoni contends that there is no link whatsoever between Bruni and Alberti, because they differ drammatically in their perception of the vernacular. In fact, Alberti contrasts Bruni's notion of an agrammatical vernacular with the affirmation of a vernacular that is inherently grammatical: "Alla visione bruniana del volgare come idioma per definizione agrammaticale l'Alberti contrappone l'affermazione piena della sua grammaticalità" (49).

Bruni and Alberti's divergent views of the vernacular are due to socio-historical factors. Indeed, their divergence mirrors an analogous cultural divergence present in the Florentine society of the early Quattrocento. Alberti was the representative of the Florentine bourgeoisie. As such, he was disinterested in the lofty vernacular culture of the "Three Crowns" (Dante, Petrarch, and Boccaccio) of the fourteenth century and fostered a more popular culture that made of the vernacular a highly regularized idiom capable of competing with Latin. Bruni, on the other hand, was representative of the Florentine oligarchy. He thus lionized the "Three Crowns" and the culture they exemplified and regarded the vernacular as agrammatical and subordinate to Latin. Unlike Alberti, therefore, who saw the vernacular as competing with Latin, Bruni saw the vernacular as coexisting peacefully with its classical counterpart.

Tavoni adds that the contrast between these two social classes and Bruni and Alberti who represented them is best expressed in the ideology and events that engendered the Certame Coronario. Alberti, according to Tavoni, organized the Certame to counteract Bruni's belief in the linguistic cleavage separating the language of the masses from that of the learned: " . . . questi testi coronari mostrano che il Certame stesso è nato come risposta nei fatti all'idea bruniana della separatezza linguistica fra volgo e letterati" (66). Indeed, the Certame wants to establish a linkage between these two modes of speaking: " . . . il Certame . . . vuole rappresentare un suo superamento nei fatti, un'impresa collettiva che getti effettivamente un ponte sopra questa frattura . . ." (66).

As we learn from the document by Luna[4], Tavoni claims, Alberti and his collaborators tried to make the Certame palatable to the papal secretaries chosen to judge this contest by defending the Tuscan vernacular in humanistic terms. They thus argue that the Tuscan idiom was traceable to Etruscan time, that Latin got its name from Latium, and that the works of the ancient playwrights were understood by the common people of antiquity. The observation on the Etruscan origin of the Tuscan idiom would have been of interest to Bruni, whom Tavoni believes was one of the judges of the Certame (71), whereas the remaining points made by Luna would have appealed to the other humanists judging this contest.

Tavoni claims that the attempt on the part of the organizers of the Certame to win the support of the papal secretaries was to no avail. The Certame failed nevertheless. It failed because the scholars called upon to judge it and the competitors who took part in it constituted two unreconcilable groups which espoused conflicting cultural objectives: "Il collegio dei segretari apostolici giudici del Certame . . . e la lista dei suoi concorrenti, stanno a rappresentarci gruppi inconciliabili . . ." (71).

Tavoni goes on to argue that the conflict that characterizes the exchange between Bruni and both Biondo and Alberti is absent between Bruni and Guarino. The Dantean notion of the artificiality of Latin, Tavoni adds, championed by Bruni in Florence during the debate of 1435 recurs at the court of Leonello at Ferrara during the discussions of the 1440's. But this notion is handled differently at Ferrara. In fact, Biondo and Guarino who dispute this notion in Florence and in Ferrara respectively react in a different manner to this problem. Biondo provides a non-grammatical answer whereas Guarino relies on a strictly grammatical one: " . . . i modi in cui Biondo e Guarino reagiscono, contro un'opinione che è sostanzialmente la stessa nel Bruni e nei ferraresi, sono diversi . . . quella di Biondo è una risposta fondata al di fuori del terreno grammaticale; su un terreno, potremmo dire riassumendo la nostra analisi . . . storico e retorico. Quella di Guarino è invece la risposta di un grammatico . . ." (81).

Building on Bruni's notion of diglossia, Guarino, according to Tavoni, recognizes a *latinitas I* and a *latinitas II* which can be characterized respectively with the terms *forma loquendi* and *norma loquendi*. The *latinitas I/forma loquendi* is peculiar to what Guarino identifies as the first and second ages, and it implies *vox litteralis* ("cum vox tamen ipsa litteralis esset"),[5] that is to say the phonological configuration of the speech: " . . . sosterrò che la *vox litteralis* che qualifica la *latinitas I* è traducibile in termini moderni, credo senza troppa infedeltà, in un concetto che potremmo definire di chiara configurazione fonologica della parola" (82). The *latinitas II/norma loquendi*, on the other hand, which is peculiar to the third age, the adult age, implies linguistic purity and is achieved with *studio et arte*.

Guarino, Tavoni claims, sees the *forma loquendi* of the *latinitas I* as evolving into the *norma loquendi* of *latinitas II*. The most important episode in this historical evolution is the introduction of the *litterae* into Italy by Nicostrata. Nicostrata's introduction of the *litterae*, however, is not to be taken as the invention of writing, but as the foundation of human speech in its viable form: "Tale evento non si riduce affatto all'invenzione della scrittura . . . Al contrario, ancora nel pensiero di Guarino la comparsa delle *litterae* si presenta col carattere, direi demiurgico, della fondazione del linguaggio umano articolato" (83).

Tavoni contends that by distinguishing a *latinitas I/forma loquendi* (which constitutes solely the spoken aspect of the language, but which is still *litteralis* because it encompasses the elements of a speech that is articulated) from a *latinitas II/norma loquendi* (that denotes a syntactically sophisticated and lexically and phonetically refined language that allows one to write and speak grammatically), Guarino improves significantly on his fellow humanists' reasoning on the issue of language. Guarino's discovery is rendered possible by a full understanding of the term *littera* in the context of the grammatical literature of antiquity.

An understanding of the classical *littera* also leads Guarino to conclude that the contemporary vernacular is not *litteralis*.

According to Tavoni, Guarino takes *litteralis* to mean *vox articulata et litterata*, that is to say, the articulation of that which is writable (*scrivibile*) as against *vox confusa et irrationalis*, the uttering of that which is unwritable. This being the case, when Guarino says that the vernacular is not *litteralis*, he means that it is not writable. One might ask, Tavoni speculates, how Guarino in the face of the rich, vernacular literature of fourteenth-century Tuscany could speak of the unwritability of the vernacular. However, Tavoni argues, when Guarino says that the vernacular is not writable, he is not speaking of the Tuscan vernacular. Rather he is thinking of the Italian vernaculars in general, especially of the northern ones with which Guarino was familiar. The multiplicity of dialects with its varied orthography, everchanging phonetics, and reliance on Latin or Tuscan norms characteristic of the linguistic landscape of Italy deprives the Italian vernacular of that *vox articulata et litterata* Guarino considers fundamental to the writability of a language.

From Guarino, Tavoni goes on to analyze Poggio, and he concludes that Poggio adhers closely to Biondo's reasoning. In fact both humanists lack the Dantean notion of linguistic divergence peculiar to Bruni: "L'opposizione categoriale che è costitutiva del discorso del Bruni è assente tanto in Biondo quanto in Poggio. Per ragioni che ignoriamo . . . né l'uno né l'altro sono stati influenzati da questa linea, che per comodità possiamo continuare a chiamare 'dantesca'" (111). They thus interpret Bruni's *sermo litteralis* as meaning Latin and its difference from the *sermo vulgaris* as implying the difference between two different linguistic entities: " . . . il *sermo litteratus* viene tradotto senz'altro in 'latino', la differenza col *sermo vulgaris* viene intesa come una differenza fra due sostanze" (111). In both Biondo and Poggio the argumentation is based on lexical rather than syntactical criteria, as is the case with Bruni. Poggio, however, does not share Biondo's belief that Bruni's *sermo vulgaris* of antiquity is to be identified with the contemporary vernacular.

Biondo had contrasted Bruni's diglossia with a rhetorical tripartition derived from Cicero. Poggio contrasts it with a bipartition —*aliud esse latine, aliud grammatice loqui*—deduced from Quintilian.[6] Poggio's reliance on this bipartition by Quintilian reveals that his argumentation is homologous to Bruni's: " . . . la bipartizione che Poggio ingenuamente desume da Quintiliano vale in sè, e dichiara la sua flagrante omologia . . . con lo schema bruniano" (112). Indeed, for all their arguing, Biondo and Poggio's assessment of the linguistic state of antiquity is not all that different from Bruni's. The disagreement between Biondo and Poggio on one hand and Bruni on the other is due to the nominalistic obfuscation that mars their dispute: " . . . scarsissime sono in realtà le ragioni fattuali del disaccordo, e assolutamente primario è invece l'abbaglio 'nominalistico' in cui essi restarono presi" (109-110). The reason for this *abbaglio nominalistico* is that the interlocutors of the Florentine debate are dealing with a linguistic reality—the nature of the classical *sermo vulgaris*—which they do not understand clearly. Tavoni commends Hugo Schuchardt who, according to him, first acknowledged the nominalistic orientation of the Florentine debate, noting that his own analysis of the debate relies heavily on Schuchardt's line of reasoning: "Trovo assai acuto questo giudizio [Schuchardt's] e da esso mi sono lasciato guidare nell'analisi che segue" (4).

Of the treatises prompted by the Florentine debate, Tavoni finds Valla's *Apologus II* the most useful. Valla's objective in this treatise, Tavoni believes, is to demonstrate how Poggio had misunderstood Bruni's position. In criticizing Poggio, Valla provides a very lucid interpretation of the Florentine debate in general: " . . . Valla scrive . . . una critica lucidissima dell' intera questione come era stata fin qui impostata" (128). Tavoni adds that apparently Valla was only familiar with Poggio's *Disceptatio Convivalis III*; he even lacked direct knowledge of Bruni's letter to Biondo: "L'unico testo che Valla ha sicuramente, e ovviamente, presente è quello di Poggio, mentre dall'*Apologus II* non è dimostrabile nemmeno, a rigore, la conoscenza diretta dell'epistola del Bruni . . . e certamente non quella dei testi di Biondo Flavio, dell'Alberti e di Guarino" (128). Nevertheless, through a savvy usage of Poggio's *Disceptatio*, Valla was able to reconstruct effectively the line of reasoning of Biondo's school and of the position of Bruni during the debate. Tavoni notes that Valla's reconstruction of the Biondo-Bruni exchange parallels closely his own interpretation of this dispute. His analysis of the Florentine debate, therefore, is indebted to Valla's *Apologus II*: " . . . e questa critica [Valla's] si svolge in termini non dissimili da quelli dell'analisi da noi compiuta nel capitolo precedente. Quella analisi deve dunque dichiarare verso il Valla il suo debito" (129).

Valla resolves conclusively, Tavoni contends, Biondo and Poggio's misunderstanding regarding Bruni's notion of the linguistic state of antiquity. Biondo and Poggio had argued that Bruni's terms *litteratus* and *sermo vulgaris* stood respectively for Latin and the vernacular; Valla proves that these two terms denote two linguistic variants within Latin itself rather than two distinct linguistic entities. Valla also rectifies Biondo's misunderstanding regarding the classical *sermo vulgaris* of Bruni. He proves effectively that this *sermo vulgaris* was not to be identified with the modern vernacular, as Biondo believed.

Valla, according to Tavoni, savages Poggio's *Disceptatio Convivalis III*. Valla's success in demolishing Poggio's reasoning in this work is due to Poggio's equation of Latin with *grammatica* ("linguam . . . latinam, eam quam grammaticam vocamus"). Tavoni argues that in this equation of Latin with *grammatica* we have the naïve adherence on the part of Poggio to the medieval notion (by then obsolete and totally irrelevant to the Florentine debate) which made of *grammatica* a simple synonym of Latin: " . . . il . . . degrado del termine *grammatica* a suo banale sinonimo, relitto terminologico defunzionalizzato di una visione medievale del latino quì definitivamente assente dall'universo del discorso" (106-107). Be that as it may, the equation of Latin with *grammatica* places Poggio in an indefensible position. He is forced to contradict himself throughout *Appologus II*, being eventually silenced altogether: " . . . il Valla mette l'interlocutore in una posizione insostenibile . . . Poggio è ridotto al silenzio . . . è costretto a ripiegare, contraddicendosi . . . " (134).

Given Valla's tendency in the *Apologus II* to vilify Poggio and to ridicule his argumentation, his remarks regarding the ease with which the children of antiquity learned grammatical Latin are not to be interpreted (as is often the case with contemporary scholars) as implying that the children of antiquity acquired grammatical Latin without theoretical training.[7] Were Valla to make such an assumption, he would be concurring with Poggio. Rather these remarks are to be taken as a means to ridicule Poggio: "La verità è che il Valla ha voluto essere ancora una volta sarcastico col povero

Poggio, suggerendogli una citazione che non fa al caso . . ."
(138).

Tavoni concludes his study of the Florentine debate with two brief chapters on Filelfo and Paolo Pompilio. According to Tavoni, Filelfo's writings on the linguistic state of antiquity are due to ulterior motives. His letter to Lorenzo de' Medici, for example, is predicated on his trying to secure a teaching position at the University of Florence. Filelfo rehashes many of the arguments advanced by Biondo, Guarino and Poggio. As to Pompilio, his major contribution is to the "realtà empiriche dei volgari" (183). He expands on Biondo and Poggio's theory on the vernacular's derivation from Latin. As a Roman, Pompilio defends the integrity and autochthony of Latin.

II

Tavoni's reading of the documentation generated by the Florentine debate is forced, reductive, and, at times, downright sophistic. His flaws stem in part from a misunderstanding of Dante's linguistic theories. It is true, as Tavoni notes, that Dante believed that "il volgare seguita uso" and "il latino arte," but when Dante says that the vernacular subscribes to usage and Latin to art he does not mean, as Tavoni suggests, that the vernacular is agrammatical and that Latin is grammatical. Rather, Dante's point is that the vernacular is a natural language subject to the whims of man, whereas Latin is an artificial one immune to such whims. For Dante, therefore, the vernacular and Latin are not varieties of the same language, but two distinct languages which are used side by side. Dante, then, saw the linguistic state of classical antiquity as characterized by a bilingualism rather than a diglossia. It is this bilingualism that is espoused by Bruni and that is disputed vigorously by his opponents from Biondo to Filelfo. Thus, rather than being unaffected by Dante's reasoning on languages, *la linea dantesca* in Tavoni's words, the opponents of Bruni were very much aware of this reasoning and of its implications in Bruni's thesis. Indeed, the dispute on the classical bilingualism of antiquity was not new to the Florentine scholarly circles of the early Quattrocento, but, as Tavoni himself admits (3), it predated the debate of 1435.

That Bruni subscribed to the Dantean notion of classical bilingualism and that his opponents had this bilingualism in mind while disputing Bruni's thesis is attested to by the argumentation and terminology of their treatises. All of these documents open with the question: did classical Rome have one language common to all or two languages—one limited entirely to the literates and the other spoken primarily by the illiterates. In other words, was classical Rome monolingual or bilingual? The documents then go on to argue that classical Rome was monolingual and that Bruni was wrong in believing otherwise. The very terminology of these documents (*materna, naturalis, artificialis, invenzione scolastica*, etc.) betrays an awareness of the Dantean/medieval notion of classical bilingualism. For example, while disputing Bruni's belief in the artificiality of Latin, Alberti makes use of a language that echoes Dante's statements on this matter.[8]

If one can speak of a diglossia in the literature of the Florentine debate, this diglossia is to be found in Biondo and his school rather than in Bruni, because it is Biondo and not Bruni who recognizes a variance within the Latin language. Biondo's notion is refined by Guarino and it achieves full fruition in Filelfo's concept of *Litteratura* and *Latinitas*.[9] In fact, Filelfo gives not only the most convincing proof of a classical diglossia, but he also provides the most forceful denial of Bruni's acceptance of such linguistic phenomenon in antiquity. In a key statement overlooked by Tavoni (indeed, Tavoni dismisses Filelfo's treatises as inconsequential), Filelfo maintains that, by arguing that the illiterates were totally ignorant of Latin, Bruni had failed to recognize the two variants, *Latinitas* and *Litteratura*, which characterize the Latin language: "Et fieri nulla ratione potuisse Leonardus ait, ut latinitas hominibus indoctis foret cognita, eandemque putat esse latinitatem ac litteraturam . . . ."[10]

Tavoni's reading of the documentation generated by the Florentine debate is hindered further by his eagerness to attribute theories to the humanists that they could not have known (see especially 39, 84-86, 95), and which, if they had known them, they would have discarded, because these theories address issues that are irrelevant to their concerns. This *modus operandi* leads to a reading of this literature that is fanciful and reductive. In fact, Tavoni's interpretation of these documents is based for the most part on a few arbitrarily selected statements, which are manipulated to convey a linguistic rationale and an historical "reality" incongruous with the objectives of the Florentine debate and the historical imperatives that fostered it. This interpretatative mode influences all of Tavoni's major assumptions.

To begin with his most important assumption: Biondo and his followers misinterpreted Bruni's assessment of the linguistic state of antiquity, for as proven by Valla, Bruni's *sermo vulgaris* is not to be taken as being one and the same with the contemporary *volgare* and his *sermo vulgaris* and *sermo litteralis* do not stand for two distinct linguistic entities. This assumption by Tavoni is untenable, being denied by the textual evidence of the literature of the Florentine debate as well as the interaction between Biondo and Bruni. That Bruni believed in a classical bilingualism and in the ancient origin of the contemporary vernacular is attested to by all the major contributors to the Florentine debate from Alberti to Guarino, down to Filelfo. It is most unlikely that such distinguished humanists would misunderstand so clear-cut an issue as the medieval/Dantean notion of classical bilingualism, particularly in view of the fact that this issue, as we learn from Biondo, had been part of humanistic discussions prior to the Florentine debate. This misunderstanding is especially doubtful in Alberti, who was a friend of Bruni and who wrote his proem only about two years after the debate, and in Poggio, who like Alberti, was close to Bruni and who had taken part in the actual debate of 1435.

The best proof, however, of the accuracy of Biondo's interpretation of Bruni's reasoning is provided by Biondo himself. Modern scholarship is unanimous in attributing to Biondo a high level of integrity and a critical expertise worthy of a modern philologist. Biondo may have been wanting in stylistic refinement, but he was unmatched in the area of historical reconstruction. It is true that by the time of the Florentine debate, Biondo had no major publication to his credit (the *De Verbis Romanae Locutionis* is his first work). Nevertheless, he was by then a forty-three-old scholar, who, as we learn from his letters, had acquired a formidable knowledge of Roman life and history. As is apparent from the tone of the *De Verbis Romanae Locutionis*, one of the objectives of Biondo in this work is to ingratiate himself with Bruni, then the doyen of Italian humanism. In light of his historical perspicacity and his critical acumen, it is highly doubtful that Biondo would have misunderstood Bruni's train of thought. Indeed, given his reverence for Bruni, we can assume that by taking issue with his elder fellow humanist, Biondo must have felt confident that he fully understood Bruni's position. Moreover, if Biondo was in fact guilty of a misunderstanding (*fraintendimento*), as Tavoni contends, a misunderstanding that was eventually adopted by some of the leading humanists of Italy, it is most unlikely that Bruni, seeing himself discredited among his fellow humanists, would have let Biondo's misrepresentation of his thesis go unchallenged. We can assume, given the highly charged intellectual milieu of the time where the least of disagreements could precipitate a bitter polemic,[11] that Bruni would have censured Biondo vigorously had he believed his younger fellow humanist was misconstruing his views. Instead, he countered with a brief, incoherent, ambiguous letter which, far from being a challenge to Biondo's argument, as Tavoni suggests, is in fact a halfhearted reaffirmation of his position during the debate of 1435.

What renders Tavoni's assumptions regarding Biondo's misunderstanding of Bruni's position the more questionable, however, is his reliance on Valla. It is startling that Tavoni should have discarded the views of Biondo, Alberti and Poggio and concentrated instead on Valla, who, as Tavoni himself admits (128), had knowledge only of Poggio's *Disceptatio* and who was motivated primarily by a need to denounce Poggio. As I have argued above,[12] the sole objective of Valla in the *Apologus II* is to vilify Poggio and to enhance the prestige of Rome and its language. To achieve this objective, he engages in an exquisite manipulation of Poggio's reasoning. Tavoni is completely beguiled by the argumentation of Valla. Indeed, he comes to accept the fictional exchange of *Apologus II* as an actual debate in which Valla, according to Tavoni, totally demolishes Poggio (134).

Tavoni's argument that the Florentine debate was marred by a nominalistic mode of interpretation and that this nominalistic approach made it impossible for the humanists to gain an adequate understanding of the *sermo vulgaris* is also questionable. This conclusion by Tavoni is deduced from a misreading of the German philologist Hugo Schuchardt. Tavoni interprets Schuchardt to mean that the humanists' assessment of the linguistic state of antiquity was hindered by a nominalistic interpretation of linguistic phenomena when, in fact, the German scholar is implying that the humanists' problem was due to their arguing about verbal labels instead of historical facts.[13] Moreover, the contributors to the Florentine debate were not interested in the reconstruction of the ancient *sermo vulgaris* and its rapport with the *sermo litteralis*, as Tavoni suggests. The *sermo vulgaris* became an important issue only among the Romance philologists of the nineteenth century. Rather, they were concerned solely with whether or not ancient Rome was bilingual. Their references to the *sermo vulgaris*, therefore, are intended to prove or disprove, as the case may be, the bilingualism of antiquity.

Even the references by Biondo, Guarino, and Poggio to the Latin derivation of the Italian, Spanish, and Romanian vernaculars cannot be taken as an attempt to reconstruct the evolution of the *sermo vulgaris* into the Romance vernaculars. These references are intended to counter Bruni's assertion that the contemporary vernacular was traceable to antiquity. Indeed, Bruni's opponents prove unequivocally that he is speaking of a direct correspondence between an ancient and the modern vernacular rather than of a parallel identity between two analogous linguistic situations, as Tavoni claims. And not just the references to the *sermo vulgaris* but all the data adduced by the opponents of Bruni are intended to disprove the bilingualism of antiquity. Consequently, Biondo's reference to Cicero's rhetorical works (*Brutus, Orator*) cannot be taken to mean, as Tavoni argues, that Biondo's interpretation of the linguistic state of antiquity is fundamentally rhetorical and that he views the ancient speech in terms of the Ciceronian rhetorical tripartition. Rather these references are to be seen as a means to dismiss Bruni's belief in classical bilingualism, which is Biondo's sole concern throughout the debate. To the extent, Biondo argues, that Cicero speaks of an ancient speech that is stratified, we can assume that all Romans spoke Latin, but that the Latin of the unlearned differed in tone and artistic elegance from that of the learned. The same can be said of Biondo's reference to an intermediate mode of speaking (*medius modus*) which Tavoni equates with the Ciceronian oratorical speech, but which in fact has a more generic meaning. As noted by Fubini, Biondo's *medius modus* is to be defined not according to the Ciceronian rhetorical tripartition, but according to the ability to communicate with the masses.[14]

Just as Biondo's reference to Ciceronian rhetoric does not give his interpretation of the linguistic state of antiquity a rhetorical slant, so Bruni's reference to some elements of Latin grammar does not give his assessment of the classical speech a grammatical bent. Bruni's use of grammatical elements is predicated on his belief (a belief colored by the contemporary linguistic reality) that Latin could be acquired only through theoretical training.[15] Contrary to Tavoni's claim, therefore, both Biondo and Bruni subscribed to an historical approach.

The elaborate terminological reconstruction Tavoni adduces to justify his thesis regarding Biondo's misunderstanding of Bruni's position is fruitless. It is true that Bruni makes use almost exclusively of *sermo litteratus/lingua litterata*, rather than *sermo latinus/lingua latina*. But Bruni is no stranger to the latter terms. *Lingua latina*, for example, recurs in the *Vita di Petrarca*[16] as well as in the letter to Biondo: "Atque latina lingua a vulgari in multis differt . . . ."[17] At any rate, the reference to the terms *sermo litteratus/lingua litterata* per se does not imply that with these terms Bruni was alluding to a variant of Latin rather than to Latin itself. As Tavoni admits is the case with Biondo (and, I would add, as is the case with all the contributors to the Florentine debate as well as Dante) Bruni's terms *sermo litteratus/lingua latina* stand respectively for *sermo latinus/lingua latina*.[18]

Tavoni is equally wrong in arguing (as he does in the case of Poggio) that by identifying *latina lingua* with *grammatica*, the opponents of Bruni were naïvely adhering to the already obsolete and totally irrelevant medieval binomial *latina lingua/grammatica*. Far from being obsolete and irrelevant to the dispute of the Florentine debate, the medieval binomial *latina lingua/grammatica* was central to this dispute. That this binomial was very much part of the Florentine debate is attested to by the several references, on the part of Biondo, Guarino, and Poggio, to the synonymousness of *latina lingua* and *grammatica*. The obsolescence and irrelevance of the synonymousness of *latina lingua* and *grammatica* is admissible only if one accepts, as does Tavoni, Valla's misinterpretation of Poggio's use of these terms.[19]

Tavoni's misconstruction of the position of Bruni leads him to misrepresent the position of Guarino as well. Contrary to Tavoni's view, Guarino's assessment of the linguistic state of antiquity is connected to Biondo rather than to Bruni. In fact, the two types of *Latinitas* recognized by Guarino are traceable to the former and not to the latter, for the linguistic variance presupposed by these *Latinitates* is found in Biondo and not in Bruni.[20]

Being bent on relating Guarino to Bruni and to the linguistic bipolarity he believes characterizes Bruni's assessment of the linguistic state of antiquity, Tavoni insists that the *Latinitas* Guarino regards as fluid and popular, the *Latinitas* peculiar to the first two ages, is strictly phonological and void of a written form, whereas the regularized *Latinitas*, the *Latinitas* peculiar to the third age, is highly grammatical and predominantly written. The fact is, however, that Guarino does not attribute to these two forms of *Latinitas* the type of rigid schematization implied by Tavoni. It is true that Guarino saw the *Latinitas* of the first two ages as being limited primarily to speaking and that he regarded the *Latinitas* of the third age as characterized by much writing, but this does not mean that for Guarino the *Latinitas* of the first two ages was void of writing and that, therefore, Nicostrata brought about the foundation of articulated speech rather than the invention of writing, as Tavoni suggests. The *Latinitas* of the first two ages, according to Guarino, did in fact enjoy some writing as he himself attests when he notes that the Latin of this period was used to write the laws of the twelve tables.[21] If in the second age there existed a form of writing and if this writing resulted, as Guarino makes amply clear, from the introduction of the *litterae* into Italy by Nicostrata, then these *litterae* stand for the invention of writing rather than the foundation of human speech, as Tavoni claims. Moreover, the difference between the unregularized *Latinitas* (*latinitas I*) and the regularized one (*latinitas II*) is not as marked as Tavoni contends. Like Biondo, Guarino believed that the speech of antiquity was characterized by a linguistic gradation rather than a linguistic bipolarity.

Much of Tavoni's misconstruction of Guarino's position stems from a misreading of the term *litteralis*, which he interprets as meaning spoken language and articulation of that which is writable, but which in fact stands, at least in the statements cited by Tavoni, for Latin and the Latin language.[22] Thus, Tavoni interprets Guarino's key statement *qua (latinitas) priscos sine ratione sine regulis . . . cum vox tamen ipsa litteralis esset* to mean that the unregulated *Latinitas* was limited entirely to the spoken language, which language, however, could be rendered in a written form because it articulated that which is writable. The fact is that in the context of Guarino's treatise, this statement implies that, though void of method and rules, the unregulated *latinitas* was still Latin (*litteralis*).[23]

The misinterpretation of the term *litteralis* makes it possible for Tavoni to undertake an elaborate, but totally unfounded, discussion of Guarino's view of the contemporary vernacular (*volgare*). According to Tavoni, Guarino considers the vernacular unwritable because it is not *litteralis*, that is to say, it does not articulate that which is writable. This conclusion on the part of Tavoni represents a complete misreading of Guarino's text. Nowhere in his treatise does Guarino demonstrate any interest in the writability of the contemporary vernacular. Indeed, for Guarino the vernacular is not a language at all, but a linguistic malady. It is unthinkable, given Guarino's contempt for the vernacular, that he would entertain the type of linguistic speculations about this idiom suggested by Tavoni.[24] The efficacy of the vernacular did become an issue at Ferrara in the second half of the Quattrocento, and it may have been a concern for Leonello and other pro-vernacular scholars at the time of the writing of the *De Lingue Latine Differentiis*, but it was totally absent in Guarino. As a consummate classicist, Guarino was concerned solely with the linguistic state of antiquity in this treatise, as the title itself indicates.

Tavoni's interpretation of Alberti is also seriously flawed. Alberti was in fact linked to Bruni, as Baron argues. They both believed in the capabilities of the vernacular and its coexistence with Latin, though Bruni was less sanguine about the potential and use of this idiom than Alberti.[25] If their assessment of the vernacular appears to be significantly different to Tavoni (agrammatical in the case of Bruni, grammatical in that of Alberti), it is because he has attributed to Bruni a perception of the vernacular that is inconsistant with the intent of Bruni's documents on this subject. Nowhere does Bruni imply that the vernacular is agrammatical. Indeed, given his argument that this idiom has the potential to equal Latin if used effectively and his high regard for the vernacular of the *Divine Comedy*,[26] it is most unlikely that Bruni would have considered the vernacular agrammatical. Tavoni's misconception of Bruni's assessment of the vernacular stems from his misreading of Bruni's *sermo vulgaris*, which he interprets as meaning a popular agrammatical variant of ancient Latin rather than a linguistic entity in its own right. Tavoni then transfers this agrammaticalness to Bruni's notion of the contemporary vernacular, concluding that Bruni's assessment of this idiom differs fundamentally from Alberti's.

Tavoni's misreading of Bruni's *sermo vulgaris* and of its counterpart the *sermo litteralis*, which he understands to be a highly regularized variant of Latin that was the sole patrimony of the learned, appears to color also his long discussion on the socio-historical factors of early Quattrocento Florence and the linguistic cleavage he believes was engendered by these factors. This discussion is on the whole fanciful, being based for the most part on a forced interpretation of the literature generated by the Certame Coronario.

It is true, as Tavoni contends, that Alberti did not share Bruni's reverence for the "Three Crowns of Florence" and Florentine culture in general and that he exhibited a vernacular language that was more Latinate and practical than Bruni's, but this divergence in and of itself does not establish Alberti as the advocate of a regularized vernacular and Bruni as the promoter of an agrammatical one. Though one can speak of an opposition in the artistic and in the politico-economic spheres of fifteenth-century Florence, one cannot attribute, as does Tavoni (70-71), such opposition to the sphere of the vernacular language. As attested to by all the writers who made use of the vernacular from Dante to Lorenzo de' Medici and including Bruni ("lo scrivere in istile litterato o vulgare non ha a fare al fatto"), the contrast in the area of language was not between a popular and a learned vernacular, but between the vernacular and Latin.

The numerous disparaging remarks leveled at "The Three Crowns" as well as at the participants of the Certame Coronario indicate that the vernacular (be it the highly refined vernacular language of Dante and Petrarch or the less successful vernacular language of the contestants of the Certame Coronario) was seen strictly as a popular language by the non-vernacular writers. Contrary to Tavoni's claim, therefore, Alberti's organization of the Certame was not due to the need to counter a cleavage between a popular and a learned vernacular, but to the urgent need to demonstrate the efficacy of the vernacular. Alberti's enterprise was resented by the judges who were called upon to evaluate the Certame Coronario. Strongly classical in their orientation and for the most part non-Florentines, the judges of the Certame saw in the advocacy of the vernacular a threat to Latin, which they regarded as the only worthy language of literature.[27] The failure of the Certame then was not due to a clash between the bourgeoisie and the oligarchy of Florence, as Tavoni contends, but to the classicists' refusal to sanction the acceptability of the vernacular as a viable literary language. Moreover, how can one speak, as does Tavoni, of the oligarchy jettisoning the Certame, when one of the organizers of this event was Piero de' Medici and when several of the poems submitted for this contest were eventually included in the collection of representative Tuscan poems Lorenzo de' Medici sent to Federigo d'Aragona?[28]

Tavoni's misinterpretation of Alberti's contribution to the Florentine debate evolves from a forced reading of the sources. For example, he argues that Luna defends the Tuscan vernacular in humanistic terms in order to win the support of the papal secretaries. The truth of the matter is, however, that, on the whole, the points made by Luna—the derivation of the name Latin from Latium, the populace's understanding of the dramatic works, etc.— were very much part of the intellectual community of early Quattrocento Florence, being shared by both vernacular and non-vernacular writers.[29]

The issues raised by the literature generated by the Florentine debate—the linguistic state of antiquity and its spinoff, the efficacy of the vernacular as a literary language—are complex and emotional. Tavoni has failed to address these issues effectively. Nevertheless, he has written a highly provocative work which should energize anyone exploring the interaction of Latin and the vernacular in Quattrocento Italy.[30]

NOTES

INTRODUCTION

[1] For an historical reconstruction of this debate, see Nogara, pp. lxxv-lxxix.

[2] For a detailed account of Tavoni's study and its relationship to my assessment of the Florentine debate, see Appendix 3.

[3] Given the strict philological approach of my work and the ambiguous nature of much of the literature studied, in reconstructing the linguistic theories of Dante and the humanists, I have cited extensively from the sources used.

[4] See, among others, Augustin Renaudet, *Dante humaniste* (Paris, 1952).

[5] I do not share fully the notion of a Dantean humanism. I believe that Dante had the potential to be a superb humanist, but this potential was never realized. His many humanistic enterprises were diluted and often stifled by an ever-present scholasticism. Dante lacked the sense of historical perspective and the philological expertise that rendered Renaissance humanism possible.

[6] The influence of fifteenth-century Italian linguistic theories on Renaissance non-Italian literature on language still awaits exploration. Scholars studying this literature have either overlooked altogether the influence of the Italian Renaissance or have limited this influence to the sixteenth century. For example, Pierre Villey (*Les sources italiennes de la "Deffense et illustration de la langue Françoise" de Joachim Du Bellay* [Paris: Champion, 1908]) and Ignacio Navarrete ("Strategies of Appropriation in Speroni and Du Bellay," *Comparative Literature*, 41 [1989], 141-154) see Du Bellay's work as evolving entirely from the theories of Sperone Speroni. Though there can be no doubt that sixteenth-century Italian theorists did stimulate the works of students of language outside of Italy, I would argue nevertheless that the linguistic treatises of non-Italians owe more to the fifteenth than to the sixteenth century, simply because the issues treated by non-Italians (the origin of the vernaculars, the defense of the vernacular languages against the claims of Latin, the political implications of national languages, the updating of Latin, etc.) are closer to those explored by the Italian scholars of the fifteenth century. On the Italian humanists' influence on Nebrija see A. Mazzocco, "Los fundamentos italianos de *la gramática de la lengua castellana* de Nebrija," forthcoming in the *Proceedings of the Congreso Internacional de Historiografía Lingüística*, Nebrija-V Centenario, Universidad de Murcia, Murcia, Spain 1-4 April, 1992, ed. Ricardo Escavy Zamora et al.

CHAPTER ONE

[1] The following are some of the more valuable and comprehensive studies on the Florentine debate of 1435: Mancini, *Alberti*, pp. 192-200; Trabalza, *Storia*, pp. 11-49; Maurizio Vitale, "Le origini del volgare nelle discussioni dei filologi

del '400'," *Lingua nostra*, 14 (1953), 64-60; Hans Wilhelm Klein, *Latein und Volgare in Italien* (Munich, 1957), pp. 50-60; Baron, *Crisis*, pp. 332-353; Cecil Grayson, *A Renaissance Controversy: Latin or Italian?* (Oxford: Oxford University Press, 1960); Fubini, "La coscienza", pp. 505-550; Achille Tartaro, *Il primo Quattrocento toscano* (Bari: Laterza, 1971), pp. 5-11; and Tavoni, pp. 3-193.

    2 "Magna est apud doctos aetatis nostrae homines altercatio, et cui saepenumero interfuerim contentio, materno ne et passim apud rudem indoctamque multitudinem aetate nostra vulgato idiomate, an grammaticae artis usu, quod latinum appellamus, instituto loquendi more Romani orare fuerint soliti." *DVRL*, p. 198.

    3 "Tecum enim . . . Luscus et Cintius sentire videbantur, vulgare quoddam et plebeium, ut posteriora habuerunt saecula, Romanis fuisse loquendi genus a litteris remotum, quo doctissimi etiam oratores apud populum illas dicerent orationes, quas postmodum multa lucubratione in grammaticam latinitatem redactas posteris reliquerunt." *Ibid.*

    4 " . . . ut litterata orationis latinitate, quam Romanis omnibus femellis pariter cum viris unicam fuisse constanter assevero, doctos longe multum indoctam multitudinem praestitisse concedam." *Ibid.*, p. 202.

    5 *Ibid.*, pp. 203-204.

    6 "Pari itidem forma, quam Romani prima loquendi consuetudine communem habuerant dictionem, bonarum artium studiis excolentes nonnulli reddiderunt meliorem." *Ibid.*, p. 204.

    7 " . . . opinor non negabis, in vulgari aetatis nostrae loquendi genere, cuius gloriam inter Italicos apud Florentinos esse concesserim, multo facundiores esse qui honesto nati loco ab urbanis educati parentibus et civilibus innutriti sint officiis, quam ceteram ignavae aut rusticanae multitudinis turbam; cumque eisdem verbis sermonem utrique conficiant, suaviloquentia unum placere multitudini, incondito garritu alterum displicere. Pari modo apud Romanos, etsi latinis omnes verbis, quibus uni utebantur et reliqui, quos tamen parentes educatio consuetudo bona et morum gravitas vita praestantiores reddiderunt, quamquam litteris carerent, oratione etiam praestantiores ac potentiores erant . . . ." *Ibid.*, pp. 206-207.

    8 *Ibid.*, p. 205.

    9 "Si tantam itaque vim domesticus habebat usus, ut sine doctrina, sine litteris non pessime latine loquentem splendidioribus uti verbis et tertium urbis oratorem faceret Curionem, non latinus esse non potuit sermo ille domesticus." *Ibid.*

    10 This observation is deduced from *Brutus* 252, 258, and 261. Biondo misinterprets somewhat these Ciceronian passages, especially "aetatis illius ista fuit laus tamquam innocentiae sic latine loquendi" (*Brutus* 258), which refers to the age of C. Laelius and Scipio the Younger (second century B.C.) rather than to the era of Caesar. Biondo notes: "Restat ut C. Caesaris testimonio innixus Cicero latinitatem Romanis omnibus eam sine litteris fuisse ostendat . . . Cum enim illum omnium fere oratorum latine elocutum elegantissime dixisset, paulo post addidit: 'aetatis illius ista fuit laus, tamquam innocentiae, sic latine loquendi.'" *DVRL*, p. 207. On this see also note 60 to Chap. 5.

    11 *Ibid.*

    12 *Ibid.*, p. 208.

    13 " . . . nulli debet videri dubium quin, si altera lingua, quam si placet velim appelles vulgarem, dictum fuisset, quod postea in hanc latinam numerositatem orationis est positum, M. Cicero, Quintilianus, Q. Asconius Pedianus aliique

plurimi, quibus oratorum quaeque minima referre cura fuit otiumque, hanc etiam
orationis diversitatem aliqualiter innuissent; quod nostra et patrum nostrorum aetatibus a plerisque factatum vidimus, de florentini Dantis Comoediis, de luculentis Bocchacii vulgaribus fabulis vel ut ipse appellat novis, quae cum grammaticis
astricto regulis sermone scripta videmus, in latinitatem dicimus esse conversa."
Ibid., p. 200.

[14] *Ibid.*, p. 208.

[15] *Ibid.*, pp. 209-210. The contemporary illiterates' understanding of Latin
prompts Biondo to speculate that perhaps there existed a strong linguistic affinity between classical Latin and the vernacular of the illiterates of contemporary
Italy: " . . . cumque ab illis sciscitarer quo id evenisset modo, mihi respondisse,
vicinitatem similitudinemque vulgari et latino sermoni permaximam sibi vi-
deri . . . ." *Ibid.*, p. 210.

Biondo's reference earlier to the contemporary vernacular's lack of Latinity
(see p. 14 above) and his assumption here of a strong linguistic relationship between classical Latin and the vernacular have caused Riccardo Fubini to see a vas-
cillation in Biondo's reasoning. Fubini, "La coscienza," p. 532. It should be
noted, however, that when Biondo speaks of a contemporary vernacular void of
Latinity he is referring to such sophisticated idioms as the Florentine vernacular.
He believed that these vernaculars, as proved by Dante and Boccaccio's writings,
had evolved into effective, independent linguistic entities: " . . . quae cum
grammaticis astricto regulis sermone scripta videmus . . . " *DVRL*, p. 200. They
thus had little in common with Latin. On the other hand, when he speaks of a
linguistic affinity between Latin and the vernacular, he is referring to the illiterates and especially to those illiterates living in the isolated communities of central Italy (see note 17 to this chapter). The Latinity of the vernacular of these
people was due to its being a crude language which had not yet evolved into a
full-fledged Italian vernacular. It thus bore the strong imprint of Latin, its ancestral language. This being the case, the reasoning of Biondo is sound and logical.

[16] " . . . quamquam omnibus ubique apud Italos corruptissima etiam vulgaritate
loquentibus idiomatis natura insitum videmus, ut nemo tam rusticus, nemo tam
rudis tamque ingenio hebes sit, qui modo loqui possit, quin aliqua ex parte tempora casus modosque et numeros noverit dicendo variare, prout narrandae rei tem-
pus ratioque videbuntur postulare." *Ibid.*, p. 213.

[17] "Si Pelignos Brutios, si Marsos Aequiculos Campanos Sabinos et vicinas
urbi gentes alias, quae loca inhabitant montana, adiverit Mediolani Brixiae aut in
reliquis Galliae Cisalpinae urbibus civiliter enutritus et apprime doctus, loquentes
rusticos mulieresque audiens communis Romanorum loquela qualis olim fuerit
scire numquam desiderabit: plurima illic, quae longo studio et assidua librorum
revolutione vix discere potuerit, scalpra inter et sarculos et asello bobusque ad-
hortandis deterrendisque frequentari latina sentiet verba." *Ibid.*, p. 212.

[18] "Tempora vero modos numerosque et casus ab arte illas [the contemporary
Roman women] nequaquam nosse non dubito, quas tamen alicubi errantes multa
recte et ordine video proferre." *Ibid.*, p. 213.

[19] "Temporibus vides quae Ciceronis aetatem praecesserant illos qui aut extra
Romam vixerant, aut Romae domesticam habuerant aliquam barbariem, a nitore
locutionis romanae aliqualiter recessisse, et barbarie illa infuscatos fuisse:
postea vero quam urbs a Gothis et Vandalis capta inhabitarique coepta est, non
unus iam aut duo infuscati, sed omnes sermone barbaro inquinati ac penitus sordi

dati fuerunt; sensimque factum est, ut pro romana latinitate adulterinam hanc bar-
barica mixtam loquelam habeamus vulgarem." *Ibid.*, pp. 214-215.

20 *Ibid.*, p. 215.

21 "Quaestio nostra in eo consistit, quod tu apud veteres unum eumdemque
fuisse sermonem omnium putas, nec alium vulgarem, alium litteratum. Ego
autem, ut nunc est, sic etiam tunc distinctam fuisse vulgarem linguam a litterata
existimo." Epistola VI, 10, p. 216.

22 "Praestantes igitur homines oratorem latine litterateque concionantem
praeclare intelligebant, pistores vero et lanistae et huiusmodi turba sic intelligebant oratoris verba ut nunc intelligunt Missarum solemnia." *Ibid.*, p. 217.

23 " . . . oratores ipsos aliter scripsisse orationes suas quam dixerant, quod et
apud Graecos et apud Latinos exploratissimum est, non quod diversum scriberent,
sed quod ornatius et comptius id ipsum quod dixerant litteris mandabant, ut
quaedam in concione dicta verbis forsan vulgatis et apertis et ad intelligentiam
accomodatis, limatius postea contractiusque scripta legantur."*Ibid.*

24 "Tu enim turbam convenisse putas ad carmina poetae intelligenda, ego
autem convenisse puto ad ludos scenicos spectandos." *Ibid.*

25 "Agere vero quid est, nisi repraesentare actuque referre?" *Ibid.*

26 *Ibid.*, p. 218.

27 "Tu ne quaeso, Flavi . . . vel alii, qui tecum sentiunt, animum inducere
potestis ut credatis nutrices et mulierculas et huiusmodi turbam ita tunc nasci, ut
quae nos tot magistris, tanto usu vix tenemus, illi nullis magistris assequerentur . . . ?" *Ibid.*, pp. 218-219.

28 "Atque latina lingua a vulgari in multis differt, plurimum tamen termina-
tione, inflexione, significatione, constructione et accentu, de quibus omnibus
simul dicamus . . . ." *Ibid.*, p. 219.

29 *Ibid.* The choice of *sinápis* and *políxena* must have been due to the difference in stress in their corrisponding vernacular terms *sínape* and *poliscéna*.

30 *Ibid.*, pp. 219-220.

31 *Ibid.*, p. 220.

32 "Fateor: parentes enim litterati, et servi, matres etiam si elegantes sunt,
adiuvare eloquentiam filiorum possunt." *Ibid.*

33 "Haec illa puro nativoque romano proferebat sermone, ita ut admodum sim
equidem delectatus, cum et verba nitorem gravitatemque sententiae et pronuncia-
tio ipsa vernaculam quandam haberet suavitatem." *Ibid.*, p. 221.

34 "Hoc ego modo filiis matres, et nutrices alumnis profuisse ad elegantiam
puto. Non quod casus inflecterent, aut verba variarent ac terminarent litterate, sed
quod purum et nitidum ac minime barbarum sermonem infunderent. Nam et habet
vulgaris sermo commendationem suam, et apud Dantem poetam et alios quosdam
emendate loquentes apparet." *Ibid.*

35 "At Caius Curio 'nichil admodum sciebat literarum', tamen est inter oratores numeratus splendore et copia optimorum verborum. Credo stadia haec
maiora non attigerat; sed idem Curio orationes suas et dialogos scripsit. Qui
autem cogitationes suas litteris mandarit, eum dicemus litteras nescivisse?" *Ibid.*,
p. 220.

36 It seems that in the case of Curio, at least, Bruni associates learnedness
with mastery of grammatical theory rather than cultural sophistication, as is the
case with Biondo.

37 See pp. 19-20.

[38] That Bruni here is thinking in terms of the vernacular rather than Latin, as is assumed by Baron (Baron, *Crisis*, pp. 341-342) among others, is attested to by his insistence that the idiom imparted by the aristocratic women of ancient Rome was void of inflection of cases, *variatio*, and termination in the literary fashion. To the extent that these grammatical principles are fundamental to Latin, as Bruni himself affirms while discussing the difference between Latin and the vernacular (Epistola VI, 10, p. 218-219), their being absent in the language of the aristocratic women of antiquity indicates that these women imparted a vernacular rather than a Latin form of speech. That Bruni here is thinking of the vernacular rather than Latin is reinforced by the *Nam et* (also) in *Nam et habet vulgaris sermo commendationem suam* (Epistola VI, 10, p. 221). *Nam et* establishes a direct link between the *vulgaris sermo* of this sentence and the *purum et nitidum sermonem* that preceeds it: "Non quod casus inflecterent, aut verba variarent ac terminarent litterate, sed quod purum et nitidum ac minime barbarum sermonem infunderent. Nam et habet vulgaris sermo commendationem suam, ut apud Dantem poetam et alios quosdam emendate loquentes apparet." The collective meaning of these two statements is that the aristocratic women of ancient Rome instructed their children with a pure, polished speech, for the vernacular speech, as demonstrated by Dante and others, also *(nam et)* has the potential of being excellent.

[39] A certain ambiguity pervades much of Bruni's letter. It seems as though he is trying to mask his belief in the bilingualism of antiquity, which as Biondo's *De Verbis Romanae Locutionis* indicates, must have been quite explicit during the actual debate. In interpreting this document, I have borne in mind the treatises of Poggio, Filelfo, and Alberti on the linguistic state of antiquity as well as the linguistic theories of Dante all of which, as we will see later, shed much light on Bruni's position during his debate with Biondo.

[40] Fubini, "La coscienza," pp. 533-534.

CHAPTER TWO

[1] Dante left the *Convivio* unfinished, completing only four of the fifteen projected treatises.

[2] This passage has been the object of much speculation among Dante scholars. See, among others, Panvini, pp. 14-15; P.V. Mengaldo, "Gramatica," in *ED*, III, 261; and Cecil Grayson, "'Nobilior Est Vulgaris': Latin and Vernacular in Dante's Thought," *Centenary Essays on Dante*, Oxford Dante Society (Oxford: Clarendon Press, 1965), pp. 58-60. My reading is based on Grayson's lucid and convincing interpretation.

[3] Cf. Corti, pp. 57-58.

[4] On the binomial *latina lingua/grammatica* see Appendix 1. Dante's notion of Latin as an artificial, secondary language has been accepted, with few exceptions, by all the students of the *De Vulgari Eloquentia*. See Silvio Pellegrini, *Saggi di filologia italiana* (Bari: Adriatica, 1962), p. 68, n. 1. For an extensive account of Dante's notion of the *gramatica*, see below pp. 161, 165-169, and 171-176.

[5] On the interrelationship between Latin and the illustrious vernacular, see below p. 132.

⁶ In interpreting this passage, I have followed Grayson's reconstruction in "'Nobilior Est Vulgaris': Latin and Vernacular in Dante's Thought," pp. 51-65. Cf. also Corti, pp. 61-62.

⁷ For a detailed account of Dante's illustrious vernacular and its interpretation in the Cinquecento, see below pp. 108-109 and 124-133.

CHAPER THREE

¹ Bruni was unquestionably familiar with the *Convivio*, as internal evidence in his letter to Biondo and in his *Vita di Dante* indicates. He certainly had secondary knowledge of the central issue of the first book of the *De Vulgari Eloquentia* (*locutio naturalis* vs. *locutio artificialis*), as his letter to Biondo and the reaction to it by his fellow humanists suggest. See especially Alberti's reaction, pp. 84-85 below. But whether or not he was familiar with the *De Vulgari Eloquentia* itself is a moot question, since this Dantean work appears to have been unknown in the Quattrocento. Cf. Mengaldo, *Linguistica*, pp. 22-25. I would argue, however, that most likely Bruni had direct knowledge of the *De Vulgari Eloquentia*. That Bruni may have known this work is attested to by both external and internal evidence. A significant source of external evidence is Boccaccio whose *Vita di Dante* and *Teseide* reveal clearly Boccaccio's own familiarity with the *De Vulgari Eloquentia*. Indeed, this Dantean work informs both Boccaccian writings. Cf. Giorgio Padoan, "Boccaccio," *ED*, I, 645-650. Given Bruni's strong connection with Boccaccio, especially Boccaccio's *Vita di Dante*, which Bruni claims to have revised and supplemented (see note 11 to this chapter), we can speculate that Bruni was spurred to secure the *De Vulgari Eloquentia* as a key Dantean source.

Even more important, however, is the internal evidence present in Bruni's own *Vita di Dante*. Bruni notes in this work that, according to Dante, Italian vernacular poetry came into being 150 years prior to Dante himself and that the major contributors were Guido Guinizzelli, Guittone d'Arezzo, Bonagiunta da Lucca, and Guido da Messina: "Cominciossi a dire in rima, secondo scrive Dante, innanzi a lui anni 150; e furono i principi in Italia Guido Guinezzelli bolognese, e Guittone cavaliere Gaudente d'Arezzo, e Buonagiunta da Lucca, e Guido da Messina, i quali tutti Dante di gran lunga soverchiò . . . . " *Vita di Dante*, p. 106.

I believe that this passage is derived from Dante's *Vita Nuova* and *De Vulgari Eloquentia*. The first segment of this passage, the reference to the origin of vernacular poetry, is taken from *Vita Nuova* XXV,4 whereas the second segment, the allusion to the great vernacular poets prior to Dante, is derived from the *De Vulgari Eloquentia*. That the second part of Bruni's statement is deduced from the *De Vulgari Eloquentia* is attested to by the reference to Guido da Messina, who is cited in the *De Vulgari Eloquentia* I, xii, 2; II, v, 4, vi, 6, but is not mentioned in any other work by Dante, not even *Purgatorio* XXIV, 49-62 and XXVI, 92-126 where Dante redefines vernacular Italian poetry. On this redefinition see Appendix 2. Of course, in considering Bruni's familiarity with the *De Vulgari Eloquentia*, we should not overlook the fact that in the *Vita di Dante* (p. 107) he lists the *De Vulgari Eloquentia* as one of Dante's Latin works: "Scrisse ancora un altro libro intitolato *De vulgari eloquentia*."

² However, Bruni, as R. Glynn Faithfull indicates, does not seem to consider Latin a secondary, derivative language: "What was to a large extent Dante's

viewpoint survived at least until the first half of the fifteenth century. Leonardo Bruni, in his famous letter to Flavio Biondo in 1435, although he does not consider that Latin is *locutio secundaria*, at least believes the two languages [Latin and the vernacular] to have existed side by side from ancient to modern times and considers Italian to be much the same as the *sermo plebeius* of ancient Rome." Faithfull, p. 284.

3 *EGV*, III, 408.

4 This misconception appears to have originated with Girolamo Mignini, "La epistola di Flavio Biondo: *De Locutione Romana*," *Propugnatore*, 3 (1890), 138. The following is Schuchardt's passage in question: "Man kämpfte von beiden Seiten mit viel Worten und wenig Methode. Jede Partei hatte Recht, weil jede Unrecht hatte. Die Einen setzten die Differenz zwischen der Sprachweise der Gebildeten und der der Ungebildeten zu gross, die Anderen zu klein an. Und dieses Auseinandergehen in der Grössenbestimmung beruhte nicht sowohl auf einer Verschiedenheit in der Annahme des Thatsächlichen, als auf einer Verschiedenheit des angewandten Massstabes. Man war nicht einig darüber, was unter Sprache zu verstehen sei und daher nicht einig darüber, ob jene Differenz, die im Grunde von Keinem geläugnet werden konnte, als Differenz zweier Sprachen betrachtet werden müsse. Der ganze Streit war ein nominalistischer, kein realistischer." *Der Vokalismus des Vulgärlateins* (Leipiz, 1866), I, 44-45. The nominalistic orientation of Bruni is deduced primarily from the last sentence of this passage, which is taken to imply that the humanists talked about philosophical nominalism vs. philosophical realism, but which in fact means that the humanists argued over mere verbal labels instead of over historical facts. I would like to thank Professor John Monfasani for having pointed out to me the misappropriation of Schuchardt's passage in the reasoning of Bruni and of the Florentine debate in general.

5 Rossi, *Il Quattrocento*, p. 108.

6 *EGV*, III, 409.

7 "Sola enim hec in tota Italia civitas purissimo ac nitidissimo sermone uti existimatur. Itaque omnes qui bene atque emendate loqui volunt ex hac una urbe sumunt exemplum." *Laudatio Florentinae Urbis* in Hans Baron, *From Petrarch to Leonardo Bruni* (Chicago-London, 1968), p. 263.

8 Baron, *Crisis*, pp. 342-343.

9 By the time the Florentine debate took place, Bruni had completed at least six of the twelve books of the *Historiae*. See *DVRL*, p. 200.

10 Baron, *Crisis*, pp. 334-336.

11 Bruni himself attributes the writing of this work to a need to supplement Boccaccio's *Vita di Dante*, which according to him, had overlooked the most valuable and pertinent features of Dante's life: "Avendo in questi giorni posto fine a un'opera assai lunga, mi venne appetito di volere, per ristoro dello affaticato ingegno, leggere alcuna cosa volgare . . . Cercando adunque con questo proposito, mi venne alle mani un'operetta del Boccaccio intitolata *Della Vita, costumi e studi del chiarissimo poeta Dante*, la quale opera, benchè da me altra volta fusse stata diligentissimamente letta, pur al presente esaminata di nuovo, mi parve che il nostro Boccaccio, dolcissimo e soavissimo uomo, così scrivesse la vita e i costumi di tanto sublime Poeta, come se a scrivere avesse il *Filocolo*, o il *Filostrato*, o la *Fiammetta*. Perocchè tutto d'amore e di sospiri e di cocenti lagrime è pieno; come se l'uomo nascesse in questo mondo solamente per ritrovarsi in quelle dieci giornate amorose, le quali da donne innamorate e da gio-

vani leggiadri raccontate furono nelle Cento Novelle. E tanto s'infiamma in queste parti d'amore, che le gravi e sustanziali parti della vita di Dante lascia addietro e trapassa con silenzio, ricordando le cose leggieri e tacendo le gravi. Io adunque mi posi in cuore per mio spasso scrivere di nuovo la vita di Dante con maggior notizia delle cose estimabili. Ne questo faccio per derogare al Boccaccio; ma perchè lo scriver mio sia quasi in supplimento allo scrivere di lui." *Vita di Dante,* pp. 97-98. Notwithstanding this statement of purpose by Bruni, his overriding concern in this work, as it will become apparent in this chapter, is to establish the legitimacy of the vernacular.

12 *Ibid.,* p. 106.

13 Within the context of the *Vita di Dante, parlare scientifico* implies the ability to treat any subject whatever. In fact, Bruni takes pain to point out that the *scienza* encompasses all segments of knowledge: "Una spezie adunque di poeti è per interna astrazione ed agitazione di mente; l'altra spezie è per iscienza . . . e di questa seconda spezie fu Dante: perocchè per istudio di filosofia, teologia, astrologia, ed aritmetica, per lezione di storie, per revoluzione di molti e vari libri, vigilando e sudando nelli studi, acquistò la scienza la quale doveva ornare ed esplicare con li suoi versi." *Ibid.,* p. 105.

14 *Vita di Dante,* pp. 106-107. For the text of these remarks, see note 36 to Chap. 7.

15 *Vita di Petrarca,* p. 293.

16 *Vita di Dante,* p. 106.

17 Bruni's telling statement on the potential of the vernacular is made in conjunction with his definition of poetry: "Or questa è la verità certa e assoluta del nome e dell'effetto de' poeti; lo scrivere in istile litterato o vulgare non ha a fare al fatto." *Vita di Dante,* p. 106. Similarly his assessment of Dante's contribution to the legitimacy of the vernacular is limited entirely to Dante's vernacular poetical writing: "apud Dantem poetam;" "certo molte cose sono dette da lui leggiadramente in questa rima volgare;" "che non sarà mai uomo che Dante vantaggi in dire in rima;" "Queste belle cose, con gentilezza di rima esplicate, prendono la mente di ciascuno che legge;" Epistola VI, 10, p. 221 and *Vita di Dante,* pp. 106-107. The only statement by Bruni that would indicate some confidence in the vernacular as an effective instrument for prose writing is the following observation on Boccaccio: "Apparò grammatica da grande, e per questa cagione non ebbe mai la lingua latina molto in sua balia: ma per quel che scrisse in vulgare, si vede che naturalmente egli era eloquentissimo, e aveva ingegno oratorio." *Vita di Boccaccio,* p. 679. However, it should be noted that Boccaccio's vernacular writing was limited entirely to literary subjects; consequently, it would not have satisfied Bruni's criteria of *parlare scientifico,* which, as we have seen above (see note 13 to this chapter), encompasses much more than literature. Moreover, Bruni's reference to Boccaccio's *Vita di Dante* as highly sentimental and purely literary (see note 11 to this chapter) is in a way an acknowledgement of the limitation of Boccaccio's vernacular prose writing.

18 *Vita di Dante,* p. 105.

19 "The Origin and Development of the Language of Italian Prose," in his *Studies in Renaissance Thought and Letters* (Rome, 1956), pp. 473-493.

20 The bulk of Bruni's immense literary production is in Latin. The only works in the vernacular, besides the *Vite di Dante, Petrarca e Boccaccio* are three poems, a novella and some letters and orations written in his capacity of Chancellor of the Republic. See Emilio Santini, "La produzione volgare di Leonardo

Bruni aretino e il suo culto per 'le trè corone fiorentine'," *Giornale storico della letteratura italiana*, 60 (1912), 308. Except, perhaps for the *Vite* whose thought, as we have seen above, he found difficult to express effectively in the vernacular, none of these works can be considered learned in Bruni's strict sense of *parlare scientifico*. As has been noted by Santini, Bruni made use of Latin "per gli alti argomenti storici e filosofici," but relied on the vernacular "per trattare di cose volgari." *Ibid.*, p. 331. Most likely, had Bruni had complete confidence in vernacular prose writing, he would have written at least some of his historical and philosophical works in the vernacular. As it is, he not only wrote them in Latin, but in a Latin that approximates the Ciceronian style.

[21] On Dante see above p. 25.

[22] In the *De Vulgari Eloquentia* Dante notes that the vernacular must be used in both prose and poetry: " . . . ante omnia confitemur latium vulgare illustre tam prosayce quam metrice decere proferri." *DVE*, II, i, 1. Dante makes no specific reference to prose writing in the *Convivio*; however, to the extent that the *Convivio* is a learned work in prose form, the *Convivio* is itself an affirmation of Dante's belief in the viability of vernacular prose writing.

[23] Cf. Baron, *Crisis*, p. 346.

[24] *Ibid.*, pp. 344-345.

[25] *Ibid.*, p. 345.

[26] On the "traditionalist school" and its relationship to Dante, see below pp. 85-88.

CHAPTER FOUR

[1] Biondo became very familiar with Dante's literary production throughout his career. However, his knowledge of Dante at the time of the Florentine debate (the *De Verbis Romanae Locutionis* is Biondo's first work) was probably rather limited. Nevertheless, to the extent that Biondo was reacting to Bruni's argument, which was in turn fueled by Dante's reasoning, Dante's linguistic theories are relevant to Biondo as well. On Biondo's knowledge of Dante see Augusto Campana, "Biondo Flavio," in *ED*, I, 634-635.

[2] On Dante, see above p. 27.

[3] See, among others, Vitale, *La questione*, p. 18 and Fubini, "La coscienza," p. 536.

[4] On this see especially *Roma Triumphans*, p. 1-3. The *Roma Triumphans* together with the *Roma Instaurata, Italia Illustrata*, and the *Decades* constitute Biondo's major works. Their dates of publication are as follows: *Roma Instaurata*, 1446; *Decades* and *Italia Illustrata*, 1453; *Roma Triumphans*, 1459.

[5] For a detailed account of Biondo's notion of the decline of Rome see Mazzocco, "Decline," pp. 249-266.

[6] *Decades*, p. 43. Except for a few orthographic changes, the citations from the 1531 Froben editions of Biondo's works retain the spelling and punctuation of the sixteenth-century texts.

[7] *Ibid.*, p. 163.

[8] On Biondo's assessment of the presence of ancient cultural relics in modern society and of his theory of reclassicizing contemporary Italy see A. Mazzocco, "Rome and the Humanists: The Case of Biondo Flavio," in *Rome in the Renais-*

sance: The City and the Myth, Medieval and Renaissance Texts and Studies, ed. P.A. Ramsey (Binghamton, New York, 1982), pp. 185-195.

[9] See p. 17.

[10] Note, among others, the following observations by Biondo: "Sed illud maxime impellit, quod tanta fuit praeteritorum diu seculorum hominibus studiorum humanitatis ignoratio, ut quum pauca singulis in urbis ipsius aedificiorum partibus, quae olim fuerint, non ab imperita solum multitudine, sed ab his etiam qui doctrina cultiores sunt sciantur, tum multa ac pene omnia falsis et barbaris appellationibus inquinata, vel potius infamata cernamus." *Roma Instaurata*, p. 222. "Mutata itaque navigia, mutata sunt vocabula, et quod maius est, mutata sunt classium loca." *Roma Triumphans* , p. 145. ". . . quamque licet multos interiisse populos, multa excisa oppida, multas delatas urbes non negaverim, plurimas tamen ex ipsis simul cum regionibus, montibus et fluminibus mutasse nomina constat; quo fit ut nec prisca legentes intelligant . . ." *Italia Illustrata*, p. 294.

[11] "Nam Longobardi omnium qui Italiam invaserint externorum superbissimi, Romani imperii et Italiae dignitatem evertere ac omnino delere conati, leges novas quae alicubi in Italia extant condidere; mores, ritus, gentium et rerum vocabula immutavere, ut affirmare audeamus locutionis Romanae latinis verbis, qua nedum Italia, sed Romano quoque imperio subiecti plerique populi utebantur, mutationem factam in vulgarem Italicam nunc appellatam per Longobardorum tempora inchoasse. Idque, icognitum nobis quando opus de locutione Romana ad Leonardum Aretinum dedimus; postea didicimus visis Longobardorum legibus, in quibus de mutatione facta multarum rerum vocabuli tituli tractatusque sunt positi. Quin etiam publicae administrationis et privatim vivendi instituta accuratissime ab eisdem sunt mutata, et eo usque ipsius gentis processit insania ut Romanorum charactere litterarum penitus postposito, novas ipsi et sua ineptia gentis barbariem indicantes cifras pro litteris adinvenerint. E contra vero Ostrogothi aeque ac cives Romani latinis delectati litteris, nullam in illis barbariem offuderunt." *Italia Illustrata*, pp. 374-375.

[12] See note 19 to Chap. 1.

[13] The theory that the fusion of two languages leads to the creation of a third is reinforced by the following remark regarding the formulation of the Bohemian and Polish languages: "Incoluerant autem prius, ut supra diximus, ea loca [in the vicinity of the Danube] Vandali, quos credendum est quando ad Romanorum invadendas provincias sunt profecti, partem gentis in patria reliquisse. Quare Sclavi paulopost supervenientes ita locutiones commiscuere, ut ex utraque tertiam effecerint, quae pro regionis et ducumdiversitate, partim Bohemica, partim Polonica postmodum sit dicta." *Decades*, pp. 115-116.

[14] See below pp. 142-143 and 176.

[15] See pp. 31-32.

[16] Fubini, "La coscienza," p. 534, n. 80. This method of research was fundamental to Biondo and is particularly evident in his antiquarian works: *Roma Instaurata* and *Roma Triumphans*.

[17] See above p. 14.

[18] See above p. 17 and notes 15 and 17 to Chap. 1.

[19] See above p. 15.

[20] Such, I believe, is the implication of the following passages of the *De Verbis Romanae Locutionis*: ". . . quod nostra et patrum nostrorum aetatibus a plerisque factitatum vidimus, de florentini Dantis Comoediis, de luculentis Bocchacii vulgaribus fabulis vel ut ipse appellat novis, quae cum grammaticis astricto

regulis sermone scripta videmus, in latinitatem dicimus esse conversa;" "Nec tamen ideo non latinum vel, quale nostra habent tempora vulgare, omni latinitate carens erat . . . ." *DVRL*, pp. 200 and 203-204.

[21] *Historiarum ab Inclinatione Romanorum Decades*, Biondo's major work, consists of three decades, plus two books of a fourth decade. The first decade covers the period from the sack of Rome in 410 to Pepin the Short's campaign against the Lombards in 752; the second decade extends to the death of Gian Galeazzo Visconti in 1402; and the third decade, leaving a lacuna of ten years, begins with the assassination of Giovanni Maria Visconti in 1412 and ends with the Florentine Council in 1439. The last two books cover the following two years up to the peace of Cavriana and the marriage of Francesco Sforza to Bianca Visconti in 1441.

[22] *Decades*, p. 393.

[23] The deplorable state of modern warfare vis-à-vis its ancient counterpart is one of the recurring themes in Biondo's works. In an analogous statement in the *Italia Illustrata* he notes that ancient Rome was able to assemble large and efficient armies, whereas contemporary Italy could provide only small and ineffectual troops. *Italia Illustrata*, pp. 294-295.

[24] *Decades*, p. 393.

[25] Here Biondo is obviously referring to the stock-battle descriptions exploited by many of his contemporaries.

[26] Much the same could be said of the numerous speeches of the third decade. More often than not these speeches are actual discourses delivered by the potentates of the time. An exception to this realistic rendition of modern events is the description of Francesco Barbaro's defense of Brescia during the siege by Piccinino. *Decades*, pp. 534-540. Out of deference, perhaps, to his friend Barbaro in whose service he began his career, Biondo infuses the account of the battle of Brescia with a dramatic power of epic dimensions.

The discussion on the modernization of classical Latin appears in *Decades*, pp. 393-396. On this passage see also Denys Hay, "Flavio Biondo and the Middle Ages," *Proceedings of the British Academy*, 45 (1959), 113-114, 118-119 and Gary Ianziti "From Flavio Biondo to Lodrisio Crivelli: The Beginnings of Humanistic Historiography in Sforza Milan," *Rinascimento*, 20 (1980), 141-147.

[27] *Ars Poetica*, 58-59.

[28] *Institutio Oratoria* I, v, 58.

[29] *Ibid.*, I, vi, 3. On Quintillian see also below pp. 63-64. In the discussion on the modernization of classical Latin, Biondo seems to suggest that he was the first historian to consider linguistic and stylistic propriety while writing the history of contemporary Italy: "Unde primis et praesenti tempore solis incumbet nobis onus periculum faciundi, quo pacto barbaris et omnino insolitis verborum ineptiis Latinitas possit elegantiave servari." *Decades,* p. 393. However, such matters had also been considered by Lorenzo Valla in his *Gesta Ferdinandi Regis*, which was probably written before Biondo's remarks on the modernization of classical Latin. It is possible, therefore, as Riccardo Fubini suggests (*Umanesimo e secolarizzazione da Petrarca a Valla* [Rome:Bulzoni,1990], p. 15), that Biondo's impetus to modernize Latin came from Valla. On this problem see also Ianziti, "From Flavio Biondo to Lodrisio Crivelli," pp. 143-145 and Ottavio Besomi, "Dai *Gesta Ferdinandi Regis Aragonum* di Valla al *De Orthographia* del Tortelli," *Italia Medioevale e Umanistica*, 9 (1966), 77-85.

[30] See Vittorio Cian, "Contro il volgare," in *Studi letterari e linguistici dedicati a Pio Rajna* (Milan, 1911), pp. 251-297; Rossi, *Il Quattrocento*, pp. 101-110; and Baron, *Crisis*, pp. 338-353.

[31] See especially Paolo Viti, "Umanesimo letterario e primato regionale nell' *Italia Illustrata* di F. Biondo," in *Studi filologici, letterari e storici in memoria di Guido Favati*, eds. Giorgio Veranini and Palmiro Pinagli (Padova: Antenore, 1977), pp. 717-718.

[32] Except for a stinting praise of Boccaccio's vernacular—"Vulgaris potius quam latinae eloquentiae fama clarus" (*Italia Illustrata*, p. 306)—Biondo says precious little about the rich vernacular literature of Duecento and Trecento Florence.

[33] See, among others, Bruni's remarks on the efficacy of the Florentine vernacular, p. 31 above.

[34] On this see Mazzocco, "Decline," pp. 262-263, 266.

[35] *Italia Illustrata*, p. 373.

[36] Giuseppe Toffanin has argued that Biondo's choice of Latin was predicated on the utopian belief that the use of Latin by distinguished intellectuals, such as Biondo himself, would reestablish that language to the preeminence it enjoyed in classical times: "E che altro pensava il Flavio Biondo . . . in quella *Roma Triumphans* (1459) che, se l'ingegno avesse corrisposto al cuore, sarebbe rimasto il poema in prosa di questo idealismo? Nelle *Historiarum ab inclinatione Romanorum decades* egli aveva penosamente approfondita la dimostrazione di quale rullo, 'cum barbarie medii aevi,' fosse passato sulla sostanza politica del retaggio romano: ma egli sapeva con sant'Agostino che 'Roma è morta . . . e Roma non può morire.' La prima Roma aveva unificato il mondo con le guerre fatali e le istituzioni; la seconda l'avrebbe tenuta unita per sempre con il Verbo, in latino." *Storia dell'umanesimo. L'umanesimo italiano* (Bologna, 1964), II, 200.

I believe that this assertion by Toffanin is untenable. Had Biondo believed in the feasibility and necessity of the preeminence of the Latin language, he would certainly have discussed it in the *Roma Triumphans*, the work intended to revive classical culture. Nowhere in the *Roma Triumphans* or in any of his other many works does Biondo address this issue.

[37] For the text of these letters, see Nogara, pp. 210-212.

[38] In the *Italia Illustrata* (p. 350), after stating that Italy had been blessed with a new eloquence from Giovanni da Ravenna and a new system of warfare from Alberico da Barbiano, both of whom were from Romagna, Biondo notes that he hoped that Romagna would give Italy its third glory in the person of Biondo himself, author of three seminal historical works: ". . . eandem quoque Romandiolam per nostras manus tertiam in rebus maximis gloriam Italiae speramus dedisse, qui latentem supra mille annos historiam tanta attingimus diligentia, ut omnem nedum Italiae, sed totius olim Romani imperii provinciarum, regionumque statum, ad quorum vel regum vel principum vel nationum manus pervenerit, clare magis et quam fieri posse videretur diffuse ostenderimus, quum Roma interim instaurata, Italiam quoque abstersa errorum obscuritatum que multa rubigine noverimus illustrare."

[39] *The Civilization of the Renaissance in Italy*, trans. S.G.C. Middlemore (New York-Toronto: The New American Library, 1960), pp. 186-187.

[40] *DVRL*, p. 209.

⁴¹ Biondo believed that the ancient Roman world enjoyed a remarkable linguistic unity: ". . . ut disiunctae mari montibusque et fluminibus separatae gentes, ac linguis literaturaque differentes populi, per Latinae linguae communionem, perque communes omnibus Romanos magistratus una eademque civitas sint effecti." *Roma Triumphans*, p. 2.

⁴² Biondo himself is forced to admit this much while considering Cicero's assessment of classical Latin. See above p. 17. The impact of the *substrata* on classical Latin was understood fully by Poggio. See below p. 62.

⁴³ On the origin and nature of Romance philology see Carlo Tagliavini, *Le origini delle lingue neolatine. Introduzione alla filologia romanza* (Bologna: Pàtron, 1964), pp. 1-53 and B.C. Vidos, *Manuale di linguistica romanza*, trans. G. Francescato (Florence: Olschki, 1959), pp. 3-167.

CHAPTER FIVE

¹ Written about 1460 and modeled on the *Noctes Atticae* of Gellius, the *Politia Literaria* records the convivial gatherings and literary discussions carried out by Guarino's circle at the court of Leonello d'Este. On the *Politia Literaria* and Guarino's circle at Ferrara, see Remigio Sabbadini, *Vita di Guarino Veronese* (Genoa, 1891), pp. 142-148 and John Pearson Perry, "A Fifteenth-Century Dialogue on Literary Taste: Angelo Decembrio's Account of Playwright Ugolino Pisani at the Court of Leonello d'Este," *Renaissance Quarterly*, 39 (1986), 613-643.

² "Opinantur quidam non vernaculam et separatum, uti nunc est, apud antiquos loquendi fuisse consuetudinem, sed unum omnium Italiae civitatum idioma, latini scilicet literatique sermonis. Quod non procedit . . . sequereturque magis nullas unquam puerorum scolas, nullos ludi magistros vel praeceptores apud veteres extitisse, quorum saepenumero mentionem ab iisdem fieri videmus, cum domestico sermone inter plebemque versando id quotidiano usu facile consequi potuisset." *Politia*, p. 227.

³ Though Decembrio shares Bruni's view of the linguistic state of classical antiquity, he does not share Bruni's favorable assessment of the vernacular. Indeed, except for Leonello and some minor vernacular writers, the intellectuals at the court of Ferrara appear to have had nothing but contempt for the vernacular language and literature. Decembrio argues that the numerous works in the vernacular, even the works of such writers as Dante, Petrarch, and Boccaccio, had a decisive popular flavor and were fit only for a plebeian readership: "Caeterum vulgarium auctorum frequentissima sunt opera, Dantis, Petrarchae Boccatiique volumina; sunt et Gallica Hispanaque lingua intra nationem nostram advecta, et pro multitudinis ingenio soluta consonantique ratione composita, sed apud plebem compositionis vocabulo digna." *Politia*, p. 226. The vernacular writers were an uncultivated lot who expressed themselves in a regional jargon: "Cuius ideo generis auctores idiotas nominant, qui illiterati sint, conterraneo tantum usu loquentes." *Ibid.*, p. 226-227. On the issue of Latin vs. vernacular in Quattrocento Ferrara, see Giuseppe Fatini, "Dante presso gli Estensi: contributo allo studio e alla fortuna di Dante nel secolo XV," *Giornale dantesco*, 17 (1909), 126-144.

4 That Guarino would have known of Biondo's *De Verbis Romanae Locutionis*
and that he would have appropriated its reasoning is clear enough, for Guarino
and Biondo were close friends. "Dii boni," Guarino writes in one of his letters,
"qualem virum Flavium nostrum quem Blondum vocant! Quanta morum suavitas,
quanta in homine modestia, quantus litterarum ardor, quantum ingenium! Eius am-
icitiam tanti facio, ut hunc ipsum diem qui me sibi devinxit semper honoratum
solemnemque sim habiturus." *EGV*, I, 306. This strong friendship led to an exchange of ideas and codices (the *Brutus* of Cicero, for example) and to an extensive corrispondence. Guarino's epistolary is replete with letters to Biondo. For
the relationship between Guarino and Biondo, see Nogara, pp. xxxv-lxxxv.

5 " . . . cuius generis lingua maiores nostros usos fuisse iudicemus, cum eos latine locutos dicimus; eane fuerit, quam hac aetate vulgo et ab indoctis usurpari
sentimus, an litteralis et a peritis observata, quam graeco vocabulo recte grammaticam appellamus." *DLLD*, p. 228. As is apparent from this statement, *litteralis*, here, stands for *latinus* (Latin) and *grammatica* for *latina lingua* (Latin language). Note also the following: "Hos grammaticam idest litteralem . . . locutos
contederim . . . ." and " . . . quas omnes latinis et romanis, idest litteralibus, verbis dictas scriptasque cernimus." *Ibid.*, pp. 230-231 and 232. In associating
grammatica with the Latin language and *litteralis* with Latin, Guarino follows a
practice traceable to the Middle Ages and utilized by most of the humanists who
contributed to the Florentine debate. On the binomial *latina lingua/grammatica*,
see Appendix 1. Occasionally, however, Guarino attributes different meanings to
these terms with *grammatica/grammatice* denoting grammar (*ars grammatica*) and
litteralis grammatical regulation. On this, see also notes 11 and 19 to this
chapter.

6 *DLLD*, p. 228.

7 "Latinitatem igitur duobus acceptam modis apud maiores animadverto: uno
quidem pro ea sermocinatione, qua priscos sine ratione sine regulis, urbanos ac
rusticos, uti solitos legimus, cum vox tamen ipsa litteralis esset; altero, qua studio et arte comparata docti posterius usi sunt." *Ibid.*, p. 229.

8 *Ibid.*, p. 230.

9 *Ibid.*

10 Supposedly the episode of Meneneus Agrippa took place in 495 B.C.

11 *Ibid.*, pp. 230-231. *Grammatice* here is used in the context of *ars grammatica* (grammar) rather than Latin language.

12 *Ibid.*, p. 231.

13 "Quarta deinde mixta quaedam emersit seu potius immersit lingua, quam rectius corruptelam linguae quis dixerit." *Ibid.*

14 "Irrumpentibus nanque per varias tempestates gentibus in Italiam, quaedam
sicuti colluvio sordium et polluta barbaries confluxit inquinate loquentium; unde
romani sermonis prophanata est puritas et prior illa maiestas velut e senatu
deiecta degeneravit, infundentibus modo se Gallis nunc Germanis alias Gotthis et
Longobardis, quorum indeleta vestigia luculentum illum romanae suavitatis
splendorem macularunt et instar faecis obscenarunt." *Ibid.*

15 "Latinas autem linguas quattuor esse quidam dixerunt, id est Priscam,
Latinam, Romanam, Mixtam. Prisca est, quam vetustissimi Italiae sub Iano et
Saturno sunt usi, incondita, ut se habent carmina Saliorum. Latina, quam sub
Latino et regibus Tusci et ceteri in Latio sunt locuti, ex qua fuerunt duodecim tabu-
lae scriptae. Romana, quae post reges exactos a populo Romano coepta est, qua
Naevius, Plautus, Ennius, Vergilius poetae, et ex oratoribus Gracchus et Cato et

Cicero vel ceteri effuderunt. Mixta, quae post imperium latius promotum simul cum moribus et hominibus in Romanam civitatem inrupit, integritatem verbi per soloecismos et barbarismos corrumpens," and "Latinas litteras Carmentis nympha prima Italis tradidit. Carmentis autem dicta, quia carminibus futura canebat. Ceterum proprie vocata [est] Nicostrate." *Etymologiae* IX, 1, 6-7, and I, 4, 1.

16 " . . . apparetque sic latinam orationem late per omnes patere solitam, ut etiam illitterati bene latine et loqui et intelligere possent, ut rugire leoni . . . simul cum animabus nasci cernimus." *DLLD*, p. 233.

17 " . . . nullum nisi latinum occurrit, a consuetudine vulgari diversum, qualiter nunc aetatis nostrae viri litterati loquuntur." *Ibid.*, p. 237.

18 "Hi notas quasdam habent ad breviandi usum cum notarii, cum recitarentur ad populum vel exercitum orationes, ad verbum per notas exciperent et exceptas excriberent . . . nisi dicta perciperentur et ad unguem intelligerentur." *Ibid.*

19 *Litteralis* here denotes morphological and syntactical regulation.

20 "Graecam etiam sic litteralem esse et grammaticorum non dicam rationibus sed consuetudine usurpatam esse affirmaverim . . . ." *DLLD*, p. 235.

21 *Ibid.*, p. 236.

22 "Cum variae multiplicesque linguae sint. . . hebraicam graecam et huius filiam latinam . . . ." *Ibid.*, p. 235.

23 "Nuper cum subiratus et excandescens quidam herus in famulum inclamaret, erat autem ex Iberia peregrinus in hoc ferrariensi gymnasio: '*vade,* inquit, *in malas horas cum carnes assadas anseres* et *anserinos* '. Quid latinius fere dici potest? Alter gentis eiusdem dixerat: '*esta civitat habe formosas mulieres*', cum in singulari numero diceret: '*esta e formosa mulier*' et '*dico res honestas*''." *Ibid.*, p. 236.

24 See p. 51 and note 4 to this chapter.

25 "Quibus non omnino falsa dicentibus revehenda est in melius opinio et aperienda est latinae linguae vis differentia ruina sive mutatio." *Ibid.*, p. 228.

26 For Dante's theory on the origin of Latin and the vernacular, see above pp. 27-28.

27*DLLD*, p. 237. Note also the following: "Haec si recte considerentur, haud sane convenire iudicabuntur huic linguae maternae sive plebeiae aut vulgaricae, quam passim effutit haec aetas quamque nequaquam latinam propterea vocabimus . . . ." and " . . . nullum nisi latinum occurrit, a consuetudine vulgari diversum, qualiter nunc aetatis nostrae viri litterati loquuntur." *Ibid.*, pp. 229-230 and 237.

28 These last remarks appear to be directed to those, like Decembrio, who argued that Latin was acquired through formal training. On Decembrio, see above p. 51.

29 "Hanc posteriorem [the *Latinitas* refined with *studio et arte*] sic a Cicerone diffiniri videmus: 'latinitatem esse quae sermonem purum conservat ab omni vitio remotum. Vitia duo sunt in sermone, quo minus is latinus sit: soloecismus et barbarismus.'" *Ibid.*, p. 229. It seems that for Guarino theoretical training implied primarily the acquisition of rhetorical sophistication and lexical elegance.

30 See above pp. 46-47 and note 36 to Chap. 4.

31 " . . . latinam linguam litteralem et grammaticam fuisse ostendam, qua prisci et posteriores usi sint, donec ad hanc non latinam sed latinae corruptricem descensum est." *Ibid.*, p. 236. See also notes 13 and 14 to this chapter.

Guarino's disdain for the vernacular is corroborated by Decembrio's *Politia Literaria*. Decembrio has the character Guarino argue that Dante's *Divine Comedy* is verbose and plebeian in taste and that vernacular literature is useless to men of letters. At best, works in the vernacular could serve as pastime for women and children during a long winter evening. G. Fatini, "Dante presso gli Estensi," *Giornale dantesco*, 17 (1909), 126-128. Moreover, Guarino made practically no use of the vernacular in his writings. In fact, his vernacular writing is limited to a single letter which is stylistically and grammatically very deficient. On this letter, see Remigio Sabbadini, *La scuola e gli studi di Guarino Guarini Veronese* (Catania, 1896), pp. 152 and 224.

[32] "Leonardus Aretinus epistola quam scriptsit ad Flavium Forliviensem probare nititur non fuisse eam linguam omnibus communem, sed aliam popularem, aliam eruditorum virorum extitisse locutionem." And again: "Nam levibus admodum argumentis ostendere [Bruni] nititur 'alium vulgarem, alium literatum', ut suis utar verbis, sermonem extitisse." *DC III*, pp. 239 and 257-258. Poggio notes that he had intended to comment on Bruni's letter when it was first written (indeed Bruni himself had asked him for an assessment of his letter), but other pressing matters had prevented him from doing so earlier. *Ibid.*, p. 240.

[33] On these points by Bruni, see above pp. 18-20.

[34] "Fateor . . . post illam Leonardi epistolam plura ex variis collegisse scriptoribus, quibus facile probatur illos [Bruni and Loschi] non recta sensisse." *DC III*, p. 240.

[35] "Non actam, ut opinatur Leonardus, sed recitatam [Donatus] dixit." *Ibid.*, p. 259.

[36] *Ibid.*, p. 258.

[37] *Ibid.*

[38] "Iuvenalis quoque legistis versum: 'Curritur ad vocem iucundam et carmen amicae Thebaidos'. Si vulgus ad carmen Statii propter versuum suavitatem currebat, illa profecto iucunditas in verbis latinis inerat, non in verbis in alium sermonem translatis. Quae enim suavitas inesset in Vergilii carminibus in nostram linguam traductis?" *Ibid.*, p. 256.

[39] *Ibid.*, p. 239. This last example appears to have been borrowed from Biondo. On Biondo, see above, p. 15.

[40] "Nempe, opinor, illam qua latini populi utebantur, et ab eis ortam, illaque eos fuisse usos qui dicebantur Latini, a quibus et nomen sortita est; quam et Romanis, cum Latini essent et in Latio siti, in usu fuisse communi necesse est. Nam sicut linguam dicimus gallicam, hispanam, germanam, italam, qua Galli, Hispani, Germani, Itali loquuntur . . . eodem modo et latinam linguam eam fuisse oportet, quae in communi erat usu apud Latinos." *Ibid.*, p. 240.

[41] *Ibid.*

[42] "Si enim alius ab hoc sermo extitisset, aliud quoque nomen sortitus esset; sic in nobis est, qui grammaticam, id est latinam linguam, distinguimus a vulgari." *Ibid.* As in Guarino so in Poggio *grammatica* has a double meaning: Latin language and *ars grammatica*. Here it denotes Latin language. For the binomial *latina lingua/grammatica* see also the following: "Diutina me dubitatio tenuit, utrum priscis Romanis latina lingua, quam grammaticam vocamus" and "Quaero a vobis quam linguam appellletis latinam, eam quam grammaticam vocamus." *Ibid.*, p. 239 and p. 240. Cf. Appendix 1. On the correlation *grammatica/ars grammatica* see note 49 to this chapter.

[43] *Ibid.*, pp. 241-242.

44 Due perhaps to Poggio's findings, Biondo, too, came to recognize the Romanian vernacular as a derivative of Latin. In his treatise *Ad Alphonsum Aragonensem Serenissimum Regem de Expeditione in Turchos* written in 1453, three years after Poggio's *Disceptatio Convivalis III*, Biondo notes: "Et qui e regione Danubio item adiacent Ripenses Daci, sive Valachi, originem, quam ad decus prae se ferunt praedicantque Romanam, loquela ostendunt, quos catholice christianos Romam quotannis et Apostolorum limina invisentes aliquando gavisi sumus ita loquentes audire, ut, quae vulgari communique gentis suae more dicunt, rusticam male grammaticam redoleant latinitatem." Nogara, pp. 44-45.

45 Poggio's allusion to these vernaculars' derivation from Latin has earned him the accolade of founder of modern Romance philology. Speaking of this segment of the *Disceptatio Convivalis III*, Ernst Walser notes that here Poggio reveals a novel and modern approach to language study. In fact, Poggio, according to Walser, gathers valuable Latin terms from the Roman, Spanish, and Romanian vernaculars and submits them to an etymological analysis that takes him from the contemporary Romance languages to the Latin language of antiquity. In so far as Poggio reasons a priori from the vulgar speech to the Latin *etyma*, he is engaging in true Romance philology. *Poggius Florentinus, Leben und Werke* (Leipzig, 1914), pp. 260-262. Most Romance philologists have accepted Walser's assessment of Poggio. See, among others, Carlo Tagliavini, *Le origini delle lingue neolatine* (Bologna: Pàtron, 1964), p. 6.
  I do not share Walser's glowing appraisal of Poggio's contribution to Romance philology. It is true that by acknowledging the derivation from Latin of the Roman, Spanish and Romanian vernaculars, Poggio anticipates one of the fundamental discoveries of Romance philology. But such a discovery had already been made by Biondo and Guarino. As to Poggio's study of the Latin *etyma*, I don't believe that this study is as scientific and systematic as suggested by Walser. What concerns Poggio here is not the nature and origin of the vernaculars, but the monolingualism of classical Rome. He thus collects a number of surviving Latin terms (*reliquias*), which help him to prove his thesis. In Fubini's words, Poggio here engages in "una sorta di empirica archeologia lessicale." Fubini, "La coscienza" p. 542 n. 100.

46 " . . . plane patet sermonem maternum fuisse latinum, qui non a magistris, sed usu domestico perciperetur." *DC III*, p. 249. And also: "Non enim verbis utebantur incognitis, sed quae cum nutricum lacte perciperentur." *Ibid.*, p. 241.

47 "Nescio cur non illi ab infantia inflectere nomina, et latinam locutionem usu percipere nequiverint, sicut nos vulgarem." *Ibid.*, p. 259.

48 *Ibid.*, p. 242.

49 *Ibid.*, p. 243. Here *grammatica/grammatice* denote *ars grammatica*.

50 *Ibid.*

51 "His verbis constat eundem fuisse sermonem vulgaris hominis et eloquentis quo ad verborum proprietatem, elocutione differre atque ornatu." *Ibid.*, p. 244.

52 "Etiam in vulgari nostro sermone sunt qui verba selecta proferant, politiusque sunt quam reliqui qui arte quadam componunt orationem, ut multum periti doctique hominis sermo praestat indocto: quod et in latina lingua potuit accidere, ut licet communia essent omnibus verba, tamen eloquentia ac verborum elegantia non item." *Ibid.*, p. 249.

53 See, among others, Decembrio and Valla's arguments p. 51 above and pp. 72-73 below.

54 " . . . qui omnes in urbe recepti, necesse fuit ut suis verbis latinam linguam inquinarent ex frequenti usu . . . hoc pacto et infinita pene vocabula, diutino loquendi usu ab externis recepta immixtaque romanis, latini sermonis sinceritatem puritatemque corripuere." *DC III*, p. 250.

55 It seems that, as for Guarino so for Poggio, the primary objective of formal training in antiquity was the acquisition of linguistic elegance, which was achieved through the elimination of solecisms and barbarisms. On Guarino see note 29 to this chapter.

56 " . . . hi pure, simpliciter, dilucide, incorrupte loquentes, palmam eloquentiae ferebant. Ea causa posuit in Oratore [79] suo Cicero: 'Sermo purus erit et latinus', id est non inquinatus aliorum verborum commixtione." *DC III*, p. 250.

57 " . . . quibus [the classical sources used] probetur latine omnem populum et cuiusque generis homines in urbe et aliis multis in locis fuisse locutos." And again: "Ita multis testibus probatum est priscos Romanos omnes latine fuisse locutos, et latinum sermonem maternum fuisse." *Ibid.*, pp. 244 and 257.

58 Poggio utilizes more sources than either Biondo or Guarino. He makes extensive use of Quintilian, Varro (*De Lingua Latina*), Gellius and the *Scriptores Historiae Augustae*. He also relies on Livy, Sallust, Juvenal and Donatus. His major source, however, as in the case of Biondo and Guarino, is Cicero (*Orator, Brutus, De Oratore, Orationes*).

59 *DC III*, p. 243.

60 "Mitto C. Laelium . . . Scipionem; aetatis illius ista fuit laus tamquam innocentiae sic Latine loquendi—nec omnium tamen, nam illorum aequalis Caecilium et Pacuvium male locutos videmus . . . ." *Brutus*, 258. Laelius and Scipio flourished in the second century B.C.

61 "Quo magis expurgandus est sermo et adhibenda tamquam obrussa ratio, quae mutari non potest, nec utendum pravissima consuetudinis regula." *Ibid.* This passage was well known among the contributors to the Florentine debate. It is cited by Biondo (*DVRL*, pp. 207 and 214) and Guarino (*DLLD*, pp. 232-233). Biondo, like Guarino, subscribed to the linguistic purism of Cicero. However, later on in his career (while writing the *Decades*), Biondo came to appreciate the value of Quintilian's *consuetudo*. On Biondo cf. above, p. 46.

62 See above p. 62 and note 56 to this chapter.

63 "Cum viderem nonnullos in eo versari errore, Laurenti Medices, ut arbitrarentur nihilo prorsus inter se differe sermonem litteralem et latinum, praeterea eadem hac omnes usos vulgari lingua temporibus iis, quibus egregii poetae, tam comici quam tragici, et oratores eloquentissimi floruerunt apud Romanos, qua ipsi nunc utimur . . . " and "Et fieri nulla ratione potuisse Leonardus ait, ut latinitas hominibus indoctis foret cognita, eandemque putat esse latinitatem ac litteraturam . . . ." *FPLM*, pp. 281 and 294. These observations by Filelfo prove further that Bruni believed in a classical bilingualism.

64 Filelfo makes no mention of Guarino in these letters, and he appears to distance himself from Poggio by implying that Poggio's reasoning on the linguistic state of antiquity parallels Bruni's. Nevertheless, his letters reveal a certain conceptual and textual affinity with the treatises of these three humanists.

65 *FPSS*, p. 275.

66 "Nam, si huiusmodi sermone prisci Romani illi essent usi, extarent aliqua eorum scripta, aliqui libri, aut versu aut soluta oratione, qualia videmus hac tempestate volumina plurima perdocte et eleganter scripta ab iis qui proximis temporibus claruere: duobus Guidonibus florentinis, Dante Aldigerio, Francisco

Petrarca, Ioanne Boccacio et Asculano Ciccho aliisque quam plurimis, quorum monimenta nulla unquam memoria obscurabit." *FPLM*, p. 281.

67 "Itaque lingua haec vulgaris qua nunc universa loquitur Italia . . . nihil habet omnino commune cum vetusto illo sermone qui Ciceronis memoria erat in usu." *Ibid.*

68 " . . . quae [the barbaric nations] et linguam ipsam et mores doctrinamque omnem maiestatemque dicendi confuderunt atque inquinarunt." *Ibid.* On this theory by Biondo, see above pp. 40-42.

69 "Caeterum, ut eo redeamus unde divertimus, discutiendum est, et id quidem haud pluribus quam sit opus, idemne sit sermo litteralis et latinus, an diversus omnino. Nec idem est, nec ex omni parte alius." *Ibid.*, p. 282.

70 "Et ut apud Athenienses aliud erat attice loqui, aliud grammatice, eadem quoque differentia fuit apud Romanos, ut alia esset latinitatis ratio, et litteraturae alia, sed ea tamen admodum parva." *Ibid.*, p. 289.

71 *Ibid.*, p. 290.

72 *Ibid.*, p. 286.

73 " . . . quam ipsa [Latinitas] illa quam solet hic idem Cicero forensem populamque appellare." *FPSS*, p. 274.

74 "Latine semper loquendum est, et ab usitata puraque dictione nunquam discendedum." *FPLM*, p. 286.

75 *FPSS*, pp. 275-276.

76 "Et quam aliam appellat Cicero orationem popularem et forensem, praeter eam quae et vulgaris erat et omnibus communis? Hac vero non depravata . . . vocabaturque latina." *FPLM*, p. 287. And also: "Locutio igitur emendata latinaque non erat litteraturae, sed consuetudinis vulgaris." *Ibid.*, p. 284.

77 "Sermo latinus erat doctis indoctisque communis, qui simul cum infantia alebatur . . . ." *Ibid.*, p. 282.

78 "At litteralis sermo rarior erat apud Romanos, et doctis familiaris hominibus, indoctis autem minus notus." *Ibid.* And also: "Num de sermone grammaticorum loquitur Cicero, qui rarissimus erat apud Romanos, nec admodum exquisitus, an de vulgari et omnibus communi?" *Ibid.*, p. 285.

79 " . . . eratque materna ipsa vernaculaque lingua [Latinitas] qualem videmus apud Graecos eam quae ex quinque linguis quas . . . dialectus, vocant . . . coene, hoc est communis, nominatur, quamquam etiam de singulis linguis idem est tenendum . . . ." *Ibid.*, p. 282.

80 "Sed quoniam iam satis ac super mihi videor ostendisse locutionem latinam esse eam, quae non depravata doctis erat indoctisque communis, in qua nec soloecismo foret nec barbarismo locus, quaeque nihil peregrini ineptique sermonis, aut nimis etiam prisci aut inusitati haberet admixtum . . . ." *Ibid.*, p. 293.

81 " Latino inquam sermone, qui et vulgaris erat et omnibus notus, eae comoediae omnes erant scriptae; et non comoediae modo, verumetiam tragoediae quotidiana loquendi consuetudine litterarum monimentis mandabantur." *FPSS*, p. 276.

82 "Nec erat admodum opus litteratura in mera ac pura latinitate, cum et plebiscita et senatusconsulta et decreta et leges ac iurisconsultorum responsa et praetoriae exceptiones, et omnia civitatis iura, instituta, pacta conventaque latine, non grammatice, scriberentur." *FPLM*, p. 283.

83 "Latinus, inquam, sermo et vulgaris erat et omnibus cognitus, litteralis vero non ita prorsus, sed viris peritis ac doctis duntaxat, caeterum talis qui depravatam latinitatem et emendaret et aleret." *Ibid.*, p. 290.

84 "Nec quenquam latinitatis satis excultum putes, qui litteraturam neglexerit, quae bona si fuerit, non solum adiuvat omnen latinitatis rationem, sed etiam regit ac tuetur." *Ibid.*, pp. 295-296.

85 See notes 5, 11 and 19 to this chapter. Cf. also Appendix 1.

CHAPTER SIX

1 On the dating of the *Apologus II*, see Wesseling, "Introduzione," pp. 35-36.

2 " . . . ma assai più interessante è la critica del Valla, fondata non già su di una episodica esemplificazione, ma su di un riesame di concetti e termini." Fubini, "La coscienza," p. 542.

3 "In realtà, ciò che importa principalmente al Valla, e intorno a cui verte tutta la disputa con Bracciolini nell'atto secondo dell'*Apologus*, è la critica a quella che abbiamo indicato come la pregiudiziale identificazione tra 'lingua latina' e 'grammatica', comune tanto a Bruni quanto a Poggio e a Flavio Biondo." Camporeale, *Valla.* p. 187.

4 "Con sua grande sorpresa, Bracciolini si vede ridurre la propria soluzione a quella del Bruni . . . per il Bruni quella differenza [the difference between the speech of the learned and that of the unlearned] era tale da costituire una diversità qualitativa, per il Bracciolini, invece, non arrivava al punto da impedire al volgo di comprendere adeguatamente la lingua dei dotti." *Ibid.*, p. 186.

5 " . . . lo distingue [the acknowledgment of the contemporary vernacular's derivation from the *vulgaris sermo*] dagli umanisti contemporanei per il netto rifiuto di una valutazione negativa del 'vulgaris sermo', quale si trova ad esempio in Flavio Biondo." *Ibid.*, p. 190.

6 "Mi sembra perciò opportuno soffermarmi sulle affermazioni [in *Apologus II*] del Valla, sia perchè sono state spesso fraintese, sia soprattutto perchè alcune di esse sono di sorprendente novità e importanza." "Il latino nell'Umanesimo" in *Letteratura italiana*, ed. Alberto Asor Rosa (Turin: Einaudi, 1986), V, 405.

7 "Non sarà quindi di un caso che proprio il più agguerrito campione del latino . . . cioè Lorenzo Valla, prenda posizione a favore della tesi del Bruni . . . la tesi tradizionale di ascendenza medievale . . . ." *Ibid.*

8 "Nel difendere contro Poggio la tesi del Bruni il Valla vi apporta in realtà alcune modifiche che la trasformano radicalmente. Il Bruni, che, come abbiamo visto, identificava ancora *grammatica* e latino, aveva negato che la lingua parlata dai Romani antichi fosse latina: il Valla, rovesciando i termini della questione, afferma che latina è non solo la lingua parlata dai Romani antichi, ma anche quella parlata dai Romani moderni." *Ibid.*, p. 406. Valla is privileged also by Ari Wesseling (Wesseling, "Introduzione," pp. 25-39), Lucia Cesarini Martinelli ("Note sulla polemica Poggio-Valla e sulla fortuna delle *Elegantiae*," *Interpres*, 3 [1980], 42-43, 59-64), and Richard Waswo. Waswo believes that Valla's fellow humanists, especially Poggio, were outraged by his "refusal to see grammar in the traditional, rationalistic, prescriptive way, and could not comprehend his historical perspective" *Language and Meaning in the Renaissance* (Princeton: Princeton U. Press, 1987), p. 92. Indeed, Valla "develops an alternative conception of the relation of language to meaning, truth, and the phenomenal world." *Ibid.*, p. 94. He reconceives "language as a whole, in all its

uses." *Ibid.*, p. 103. As such "Valla's effort is comparable to that of the most radical reconceiver of language in our time, the later Wittgenstein." *Ibid.*.

[9] Lest my assesment of Valla in this chapter be construed as being too negative, I should note that I concur with contemporary Renaissance scholarship that Valla was a highly original thinker who made a fundamental contribution to Quattrocento intellectual life (though I do not think that he was as radical and modern as Waswo claims; Valla subscribed to the same rationalistic and empirical mode of inquiry peculiar to his fellow humanists). Nevertheless, in *Apologus II*, which is my primary concern here, he resorts to expediency and sophism.

[10] On the appropriateness of the term *oratio* instead of *invectiva* for the invectives of Poggio, see Wesseling, "Introduzione," pp. 36-37.

[11] On the polemic Poggio-Valla, see Camporeale, *Valla*, pp. 180-192; Wesseling, "Introduzione," pp. 25-39; and Lucia Cesarini Martinelli, "Note sulla polemica Poggio-Valla," *Interpres*, 3 (1980), 29-32.

[12] *Apologus II*, pp. 261-262.

[13] *Ibid.*, p. 262.

[14] *Ibid.*

[15] "Aliter istic accipitur vulgaris atque Leonardus intelligit . . . Leonardus sentit de sermone vulgari priscorum, qualis nunc Rome est vulgo loquentium, et si non adeo ut nunc depravato, qui certe sermo latinus non est, sed vulgaris." *Ibid.*, p. 263. In this context, *vulgaris* stands for the modern *volgare*, that is to say, the vernacular spoken in contemporary Italy. On this see also note 18 to this chapter.

[16] *Ibid.*

[17] See p. 60 and note 40 to Chap 5.

[18] "'Vulgarem' tu alicuius gentis appellas sermonem? Afferam tua . . . contra te scripta . . . Si Romani Latini sunt, et a gente nominatur lingua, non ergo lingua Romanorum alia nunc est quam latina, sicut et olim fuit, quemadmodum ab omnibus aliis nationibus appellatur." *Apologus II*, p. 263.

[19] See above p. 60 and note 42 to Chap 5.

[20] "Ecce quem voco 'latinum', hoc est grammaticum: nihil enim interesse volo, 'grammaticum' dixeris an 'latinum'. . . . Ais linguam latinam eandem grammaticam esse . . . ." *Apologus II*, p. 264.

[21] On this, see above pp. 61 and 63-65.

[22] "Quid aliud velit Leonardus, quam omnes Romanos fuisse latine locutos, sed non grammatice?" *Apologus II*, pp. 264-265.

[23] "Nam ea tu non recte accipis, qui ais eum velle emendatius dici grammatice, et doctius, quam latine. Hoc ille non sentit, sed melius esse latine quam grammatice loqui, hoc est ex consuetudine peritorum quam ex artis analogia . . . Ideoque latine loqui inter virtutes rhetorice ponitur, ut grammatica sit locutionis, latinitas elocutionis." *Ibid.*, pp. 265-266. Valla even chides Poggio for having attributed to the genitives *senatus/senati* a meaning not intended by Quintilian: ". . . et quam tu bis falsa ratione conaris probare, inquiens *senatum* quarte dici a doctis, secunde ab indoctis. Nam neque istud, ut tu ais, Quintilianus affirmat, sed plane negat." *Ibid.*, p. 266. On Poggio's interpretation of *senatus/senati* see above p. 63.

[24] "Vides ut latine loqui est oratorum et eruditorum, et plus etiam quam grammatice?" *Ibid.*, p. 265.

[25] "Quo mihi rationem istam, si satis est usus? Quis de lingua gallica, hispana, germanica, florentina, neapolitana, veneta, et item de reliquis, rationem

exigit, et non ipso usu contentus est?" *Ibid.*, pp. 269-270. Following, it seems, Quintilian, ("Rationem praestat praecipue analogia . . . ." *Insitutio* I, vi, 1), Valla equates *ratio* with *analogia*.

26 "Cur dicas 'emendatius', non video . . . si omnium Romanorum sic erat communis lingua latina . . . nunquam animadverti romanum romane . . . alium alio magis loquentem. Unus est modus atque unum genus et una, veluti in suo cuiusque civitatis numismate, figura dicendi. Quod si non loquebantur prisci Romani alius alio latinius, ergo nihil est, quod dicis, emendatius locutos doctos." *Ibid.*, pp. 266-267.

27 "Alius alio ornatius, sublimius, eloquentius, fateor, sed non latinius . . . ." *Ibid.*, p. 266.

28 "Idem, Pogi, modo ais, modo negas: nunc grammaticam esse doctorum et peritorum tantummodo, nunc etiam imperitorum atque infantium." *Ibid.*, p. 267.

29 On this see above p. 61.

30 *Apologus II*, p. 269. On this statement by Poggio, see above p. 61..

31 On these two examples, see above p. 60.

32 *Apologus II*, pp. 267-268.

33 "Ego certe et natus et altus Rome atque in romana, ut vocant, Curia, qui congrue loqueretur cognovi neminem . . . ." *Ibid.*, p. 268.

34 *Ibid.*, p. 270.

35 "Utinam ego recte grammatice loquerer, nec aliquid causarum ac rationum grammatice nossem! . . . Quid ais? Aut ars grammatica est, et ab eruditis, non autem a nutricibus, tradebatur; aut ars non est, quam omnes fatentur esse artem . . . ." *Ibid.*, p. 271.

36 "Quia cum inter se contraria loquaris, idque persepe, non possum facere quin etiam pro te dicam, ut mirum quiddam et prima fronte ridiculum videatur esse altercantes inter se alterum pro altero dicere. Verum hoc inter me atque te interest, quod ego, et si pro te, non tamen contra me dico, tu non magis contra me quam contra te ipsum dicis." *Ibid.*, p. 270.

37 "Dicam igitur non grammaticum vulgi fuisse infantiumque sermonem, sed tanquam grammaticum." *Ibid.*, p. 271.

38 "Hoc ipsum [the difference between the speech of the learned and that of the unlearned], quantum distantie erat, querimus et in controversia est." *Ibid.*

39 "Nolo enim in presentiarum meam promere sententiam, cum non sit id mei propositi, sed ut tue adverser . . . ." *Ibid.*, p. 273.

40 Except for Poggio's *Disceptatio Convivalis III*, *Apologus II* makes no reference to the remaining literature generated by the Florentine debate. Camporeale's claim that "Valla conosceva molto bene la posizione di Guarino, circa il problema in oggetto" (Camporeale,*Valla*, p. 207) is not borne out by the argumentation or the textual evidence of *Apologus II*.

41 Poggio seems to regard the contemporary *volgare* as a fait accompli that needs no justification.

42 Biondo and Guarino argue that classical Rome did not possess two distinct linguistic entitites, Latin and the *volgare*, as suggested by Bruni, because the *volgare* was a recent phenomenon which had come into being with the barbaric invasions.

43 For Poggio, see above p. 60. For Valla, see above p. 71 and note 18 to this chapter.

44 *Apologus II*, p. 262.

45 See pp. 63-65.

⁴⁶ Moreover, by arguing (as he does while criticizing this misreading by Poggio) that for Quintilian, usage and not theory was the guide to good speaking, and that Quintilian's *latine loqui*, the mode of speaking that results from usage, was not a prosaic idiom limited to the unlearned, but a sophisticated language that was very much part of the linguistic patrimony of the learned, Valla broadens our understanding of the linguistic state of antiquity. He demonstrates that the language of the learned was more fluid and less stylized than Biondo, Guarino, and Poggio believed.

⁴⁷ See above pp. 61-62 and note 52 to Chap. 5.

⁴⁸ Biondo, Guarino, and Poggio seem to think that the primary function of theoretical training was the acquisition of rhetorical sophistication and lexical elegance. Cf. notes 29 and 55 to Chap. 5.

⁴⁹ See above p. 73.

⁵⁰ See notes 42 and 49 to Chap. 5.

⁵¹ *Disceptatio Convivalis III*, pp. 239 and 240.

⁵² On the role of this binomial in Dante and the humanists, see Appendix 1.

⁵³ " . . . sed qui fieri potest ut quod nos tanto studio ac labore, instantibus preceptoribus, pedagogis, patribus, in assidua scholarum ac condiscipulorum consuetudine, intra tot annos nequimus assequi—loquor de grammatice fando—id illi infantes inter lusum, nullo instante, intra biennium ex quo ceperant posse verba proloqui, assequerentur, ita ut oratores ac poetas intelligerent, quos vix nos intelligere exacta pueritia possumus? Neque nos tardiori quam illi fuerunt ingenio facias, quoniam quibusdam in artibus nequaquam illis cedimus. Quales si non sumus, sed veteribus pares, unde fit ut vulgus romanum atque adeo italicum, illitteratorum dico, non possit ullo pacto conservare, immo consequi et imitari, sonum litteratarum vocum etiam milies auditarum et quotidie inculcatarum, cuiusmodi sunt ee que a sacerdotibus subinde repetuntur? Et ut de Romanis, de quibus controversia est, potissimum dicam, frequentissime audiunt legentes in Via Appia 'Domine quo vadis?'; at vulgus ait 'domina covata'; de 'Ara Celi' dicit 'arocielo'; de 'Arcus Nerve', 'arcanoè', 'Sancti Petri ad vincula', 'sancto Pietro mencolo', et alia infinita. Adeo nullum litterati soni verbum in ore est vulgi." *Apologus II*, p. 272.

⁵⁴ On the role of the invective in the intellectual life of Quattrocento Italy see C. Nisard, *Les gladiateurs de la Republique des lettres aux XVe, XVIe et XVIIe siècles* (Paris, 1860; rpt. Geneve: Svatkice Reprints, 1970); F. Vismara, *L'invettiva, arma preferita dagli umanisti nelle lotte private, nelle polemiche letterarie, politiche e religiose* (Milan: Allegretti, 1900); and Rossi, *Il Quattrocento*, pp. 147-149.

⁵⁵ I should note that, although he spent most of his professional career outside of Rome, Valla must be acknowledged as one of the founders of Roman humanism. *Romanitas* the root of this humanism was a state of mind that had little to do with one's origin or place of residence. For example, of the three major contributors to Roman humanism, Petrarch, Biondo, and Valla, Petrarch spent all of his life in southern France and northern Italy, Biondo was born in Forlì, northern Italy, but spent much of his adult life in Rome, and Valla grew up in Rome, but was employed by various Italian courts. Yet these three writers have a view of classical Rome and of contemporary Rome's mission that is remarkably alike. They all yearn for a *renovatio* of classical antiquity, and they all insist that this *renovatio* should emanate from contemporary Rome rather than Florence, as the Florentine humanists argued. The difference between the pro-Roman and the

232   NOTES TO PAGES 78-80

Florentine humanists' notion of the trajectory of revival leads to a divergent
assessment of classical civilization. On the divergence between Roman and
Florentine humanism cf. Carlo Dionisotti, *Geografia e storia della letteratura
italiana* (Turin, 1967), pp. 152-154; A. Mazzocco, "The Decline;" and idem,
"Letteratura e letterati nella Roma rinascimentale," *Roma nel Rinascimento.
Bibliografia e note* (1987), pp. 16-20. The Roman humanism of the latter part of
the Quattrocento has been studied effectively by John D'Amico (*Renaissance
Humanism in Papal Rome: Humanism and Churchmen on the Eve of the
Reformation* [Baltimore and London: The Johns Hopkins U. Press, 1983]), but
that of the first part of the Quattrocento remains largely unexplored.

56 See above pp. 52-53.

57 "Siquidem italica lingua, que olim diversa ac multiplex fuit, et mox propter
romanas colonias ac Romanorum consuetudinem in linguam romanam concessit,
idest latinam . . . ." *Apologus II*, p. 263.

58 "Ubinam legit Romanam linguam dici pro latina? . . . Praeterea lingua
Romana est, et ea vulgaris qua sola utuntur Romani . . . At linguam latinam dicere
voluit [Valla] stultissimus barbarus, quae nemini dominatur, sed in usu est et in
precio apud multos." *Oratio I* in *Opera Omnia*, ed. Riccardo Fubini (Turin:
Bottega D'Erasmo, 1964), I, 195. And again: "Latine tunc homines loquebantur,
non Romane. Siquidem Romanam linguam dicimus, qua hodie Romani utuntur
procul a latina. Ita et Florentine Florentini loquuntur, Perusine Perusini. Eodem
modo et reliqui." *Ibid.*, p. 200.

59 "Aut nunc Romana lingua dicetur . . . qua utuntur Romani, ea non dicetur
fuisse lingua Romana qua tunc Romani utebantur?" *Antidotum*, p. 172.

60 "Est itaque et olim fuit Romana lingua Latina et Latina Romana, nisi
dicimus Latinam ut genus, Romanam ut speciem. Ita Romana utique Latina erit,
quod querimus, Latina non protinus et Romana. Latina quidem, quia Latinorum
fuit, unde Romani oriundi sunt; Romana autem, quia propter Romanorum maies-
tatem propagata est et dignitatem accepti, et presertim quod necessarium est linguam civitatis ab ipsa civitate nomen accipere: ut Florentinam a Florentia et
Senensem a Sena et Campanam a Capua, ita Romanam a Roma." *Ibid.*

61 "Certe que nunc lingua in usu Romanis est Latina appellanda est, et si multum degeneravit ab illa prisca. Non enim credibile est aliam quandam nescio unde
venisse linguam et illam veterem e possessione deiecisse et in exilium relegasse
atque in insulas deportasse." *Ibid.* Valla attributes this linguistic degeneration to
the modern learned Latin as well. In fact, the contemporary learned Latin was so
different from its ancient counterpart that Cicero (were he to be revived) would
find it difficult to understand: "cum videamus idem contigisse in lingua grammatice loquentium, quam tu Latinam vocas, que adeo ab illa veteri differt ut vix eam
Cicero si a mortuis redeat queat intelligere." *Ibid.*

62 Though he spent much of his adult life at the Roman Curia, Poggio remained a Florentine at heart.

63 On Bruni's view of the Florentine vernacular cf. p. 31 above.

64 On Biondo, see above pp. 46-47 and Mazzocco, "Decline," pp. 262-263,
266.

65 "Ego certe et natus et altus Rome . . . ." *Apologus II*, p. 268.

66 "Vult [Bruni] Florentiam heredem esse imperii populi Romani, quasi ipsa
Roma extincta sit, eandemque progenitam ab optimis illis Romanis, tamquam
posteriores Romani non ab illis priscis originem ducant." in L. Barozzi and R.
Sabbadini, *Studi sul Panormita e sul Valla* (Florence: 1891), p. 75. Also in

Laurentius Valla, *Opera Omnia*, ed. Eugenio Garin (Turin: Bottega d'Erasmo, 1962), II, 381.

[67] "Vale et hominem levem tua gravitate castiga et somnolentum tuis virgiliis excita et hebetem tuo acumine et pugione confode et prosterne." *Ibid.*

I would argue that the Florentine humanists' characterization of Florence as the new Rome spurred and colored Valla's preface to the first book of the *Elegantiae* (1448). In fact, this preface, a sort of *Laudatio Romanae Urbis*, provides the vindication and rectification Valla had asked of Decembrio. Far from being extinct, Rome continued to dominate the world culturally. This dominance was due to its language, source and vehicle of humankind's greatest civilization: "Amisimus Romam, amisimus regnum atque dominatum; tametsi non nostra sed temporum culpa; verum tamen per hunc splendidiorem dominatum [the Latin language] in magna adhuc orbis parte regnamus. Nostra est Italia, nostra Gallia, nostra Hispania, Germania, Pannonia, Dalmatia, Illyricum, multaeque aliae nationes. Ibi namque romanum imperium est ubicumque romana lingua dominatur." *Elegantiae*, p. 596.

[68] Likewise, Poggio believes that the reconstruction of classical Latin was the responsibility of scholars everywhere. He, thus, rebukes (*Opera Omnia*, ed. Fubini, I, 204-205) what he believes to be Valla's self-appointed role in the *Elegantiae* (*Elegantiae* , p. 600) as sole redeemer of the Latin language.

[69] Dante, among others, characterizes the vernacular and the culture of modern Rome as the worst in modern Italy. See below p. 122.

[70] By insisting on a cultural continuum, Valla deviates not only from the Florentine humanists, but also from Biondo, the other champion of *Romanitas*. In a suggestive passage in the preface of the third book of the *Elegantiae*, Valla notes that Italy and Rome had been repeatedly invaded by the barbarians and that these invasions had had a profound impact on the society and culture of Rome: "Nam postquam hae gentes [Gothi et Vandali] semel iterumque Italiae influentes Romam ceperunt, ut imperium eorum ita linguam quoque, quemadmodum aliqui putant, accepimus, et plurimi forsan ex illis oriundi sumus. Argumento sunt codices gothice scripti, quae magna multitudo est; quae gens, si scripturam romanam depravare potuit, quid de lingua, praesertim relicta sobole, putandum est? Unde post illorum adventum primum alterumque, omnes scriptores nequaquam facundi, ideoque prioribus multo inferiores fuerunt. En quo litteratura romana recidit: veteres admiscebant lingue suae graecam, isti admiscent gothicam." *Elegantiae*, p. 610.

This passage parallels and was most likely influenced by Biondo's assessment of the impact of the barbaric invasions. On Biondo see above pp. 40-42. Like Biondo, Valla sees the barbaric invasions as causing a barbarization of Italy. However, unlike Biondo, Valla does not see this barbarization as engendering a new race and a new language, though it alters profoundly both race ("praesertim relicta sobole") and language ("isti admiscent gothicam"). Cf. Tavoni, pp. 152-154.

[71] The only reference in *Apologus II* which has any bearing on the issue of vernacular language and culture is a denial of Poggio's assertion that the Spanish language possesses relics of Latinity. *Apologus II*, pp. 272-273. On Valla's disregard for the vernacular, cf. Mariangela Regoliosi, "Introduzione," in Lorenzo Valla, *Antidotum in Facium*, ed. M. Regoliosi (Padua: Antenore, 1981), p. lx.

CHAPTER SEVEN

1 Among the several studies of Alberti's proem, the following are the more noteworthy: Mancini, *Alberti*, pp. 197-199; Trabalza, *Storia*, pp. 17-22; Vitale, *La questione*, pp. 19-20; Baron, *Crisis*, pp. 348-350; Achille Tartaro, *Il primo Quattrocento toscano* (Bari: Laterza, 1971), pp. 5-11; Francesco Tateo, *Alberti, Leonardo e la crisi dell'umanesimo* (Bari: Laterza, 1971); Giovanni Ponte, "Lepidus e Libripeta," *Rinascimento*, 12 (1972), 261-265; Dardano, "Alberti," pp. 263-265; but especially Cecil Grayson, "The Humanism of Alberti," *Italian Studies*, 12 (1957), 47-49; idem, "Alberti, Leon Battista," *Dizionario biografico degli italiani*, I (Rome, 1960), 702-709; and idem, "Il prosatore latino e volgare," *Atti del convegno internazionale indetto nel V centenario di Leon Battista Alberti*, Accademia Nazionale dei Lincei, Quaderno 209 (Rome, 1974), pp. 273-286.

2 Guglielmo Gorni, who has edited the *Protesta* and the *Capitolo*, says the following about the *Protesta*: " . . . un documento d'importanza primaria, che spiace non veder quasi mai citato, o utilizzato con la debita attenzione, negli scritti dedicati alle questioni della lingua nel Quattrocento." Gorni, p. 155. The *Capitolo*, according to Gorni, has been equally disregarded. *Ibid.*, pp. 174-175.

3 Proemio, p. 222. On the connotation between the *vostri bellissimi orti* and the Villa del Paradiso, see, among others, F. Tateo, *Alberti, Leonardo e la crisi dell'umanesimo* (Bari: Laterza, 1971), p. 25.

4 "Messere Antonio Alberti, uomo litteratissimo tuo zio, Francesco, quanto nostro padre Lorenzo Alberti a noi spesso referiva, non raro solea co' suoi studiosi amici in que' vostri bellissimi orti passeggiando disputare quale state fosse perdita maggiore; o quella dello antiquo amplissimo nostro imperio, o della antiqua nostra gentilissima lingua latina." Proemio, p. 222.

5 "E forse non era da molto maravigliarsi se le genti tutte da natura cupide di libertà suttrassero sè, e contumace sdegnorono e fuggirono e' ditti nostri e leggi. Ma chi stimasse mai sia stato se non propria nostra infelicità così perdere quello che niun ce lo suttrasse, niun se lo rapì? E pare a me non prima fusse estinto lo splendor del nostro imperio che occecato quasi ogni lume e notizia della lingua e lettere latine." *Ibid.* Valla seems to appropriate this reasoning in the Preface to the first book of the *Elegantiae*. *Elegantiae*, p. 596. On this see also Tavoni, pp. 150-152.

6 "Cosa maravigliosa intanto trovarsi corrotto o mancato quello che per uso si conserva, e a tutti in que' tempi certo era in uso." *Ibid.*, p. 222.

7 On Biondo, see pp. 14-17.

8 Proemio, p. 223.

9 *Ibid.*

10 Epistola VI, 10, pp. 216, 218-219 and 216. On these remarks, see also above pp. 18-20.

11 This same notion is expressed in *La grammatichetta vaticana*, which Cecil Grayson has convincingly attributed to Alberti: "Que' che affermano la lingua latina non essere stata comune a tutti e populi latini, ma solo propria di certi dotti scolastici, come oggi la vediamo in pochi . . . ." *La prima grammatica della lingua volgare. La grammatichetta vaticana*, ed. C. Grayson (Bologna, 1964), p. 39. On Alberti's authorship of *La grammatichetta*, see Grayson's introduction to this work, pp. xvii-xviii.

12 See above pp. 21-22 and note 39 to Chap. 1.

[13] Proemio, p. 224.

[14] See note 4 to this chapter. To my knowledge, all the students of Alberti's proem have missed the cultural and historical implications of this reference.

[15] See above p. 25.

[16] On the Florentines' admiration for Dante in the late Trecento, see A. Mazzocco, "Classicism and Christianity in Salutati: Considerations in Light of Ronald G. Witt's *Hercules at the Crossroads. The Life, Works and Thoughts of Coluccio Salutati*," *Italica*, 65 (1988), 256-261.

[17] The gatherings described in *Il Paradiso degli Alberti* were organized by Antonio Alberti, scion of the Niccolò's branch of the Alberti family. These gatherings seem to have taken place in May of 1389 while the Alberti family was out of power. Giovanni da Prato, then about 30 years old, was one of the participants at these gatherings. His *Paradiso degli Alberti,* therefore, is, to a large degree, a recollection of episodes and discussions that he himself experienced. Wesselofsky, I/1, 47-228 and I/2, 86-109.

Baron has questioned the historical authenticity of *Il Paradiso degli Alberti*. According to Baron, *Il Paradiso* expresses ideas that postdate 1389 by more than a decade. Though some of the ideas of *Il Paradiso* do lack historical authenticity, the work, as even Baron admits, is built around a "core of historical truth." Baron, *Crisis*, p. 81. *Il Paradiso*, therefore, reveals much that is authentic to late Trecento Florence. It is especially accurate in its interpretation of the late Trecento's view of Dante and his vernacular culture, as corroborated by other works written at this time.

[18] Wesselofsky, III, 84. This passage recalls *Convivio*, I, x, 12. On this, see also above p. 25.

[19] "Scusimi ancora l'ardentissima voglia che continuamente mi sprona il . . . edioma materno con ogni possa sapere esaltare e quello nobilitare, come che da tre corone fiorentine principalmente già nobilitato et esaltato si sia." Wesselofsky, II, 2.

[20] Note, among others, the following remarks: "De! guarda e pensa quanto bene in pochi versetti tel dice il nostro Dante divino, d'ogni umana cosa e divina predotto;" "Considera adunque e bene raguarda e sogiugni quanto il nostro miracoloso poeta co' suoi sacri versetti cel mostra;" and "Et bene omai voglio credere quello che io sento del vostro Dante poeta teologo." Wesselofsky, II, 58, 59; III, 84.

[21] The dating of *Liber I* of *Ad Petrum Paulum Histrum Dialogus* has been the subject of much speculation among Bruni's scholars. Baron sets the date at 1401. Baron, *Crisis*, pp. 225-244. In a recent, wide-ranging article, Riccardo Fubini argues that it was published in 1407. "All'uscita della scolastica medievale: Salutati, Bruni, e i *Dialogi ad Petrum Histrum*," to appear in *Archivio storico italiano*, 2-3 (1992) (my thanks to Professor Fubini for a copy of this article). Whether one accepts the later or earlier date, the fact remains that *Liber I* of *Ad Petrum Paulum Histrum Dialogus* is an affirmation of the militant classicism prevalent in Florence at the beginning of the Quattrocento, a classicism shared by Bruni himself. That such classicism did prevail in Florence and that Bruni did take part in it is confirmed by several early-Quattrocento pro-vernacular tracts (the invectives of Rinuccini and Domenico da Prato, for example) which chide the type of argument Bruni expounds in the first book of his *Dialogus*.

22 " . . . certe latinitas defuit. Nos vero non pudebit eum poetam appellare . . .
qui latine loqui non possit?" *Dialogus*, p. 70.

23 "Quamobrem, Coluci, ego istum poetam tuum a concilio litteratorum
seiungam atque eum lanariis, pistoribus atque eiusmodi turbae relinquam. Sic enim
locutus est ut videatur voluisse huic generi hominum esse familiaris." *Ibid*.

24 Giovanni da Prato belonged to the generation of Bruni and Niccoli. Baron,
Crisis, p. 277. Rinuccini, on the other hand, was considerably older (1350-
1417); he, therefore, may very well have taken part in the gatherings at the Villa
del Paradiso.

25 For the dating of this invective, see Baron, *Crisis*, p. 286.

26 *Invettiva*, pp. 310-311.

27 *Ibid.*, p. 311. In this statement we have an echo of Dante: " . . . lo latino
molte cose manifesta concepute ne la mente che lo volgare far non può, sì come
sanno quelli che hanno l'uno e l'altro sermone, più è la vertù sua che quella del
volgare." *Convivio* I, v, 12.

28 *Invettiva*, p. 311.

29 See Baron, *Crisis*, p. 280.

30 *Invettiva*, p. 322.

31 *Ibid.*, pp. 323 and 327.

32 On this, cf. Baron, *Crisis*, pp. 279-285.

33 " . . . correndo una giornata dietro ad una derivazione di vocabolo o ad uno
dittonguzzo." *Invettiva*, p. 327.

34 *Ibid.*, p. 329.

35 See above pp. 33.

36 Compare the following appraisals of Dante by Rinuccini and Bruni respectively: " . . . non dicono che 'l parlar poetico è quello [Dante] che sopra agli altri
come aquila vola, cantando con maravigliosa arte e fatti groliosi degl'ignio-
miniosi uomini e pognendo per nostro ben vivere inanzi agli occhi tutte le storie, mescolando alcuna volta ne' loro poemi sottile filosofia naturale, alcuna
volta la dilettevole astronomia, alcuna volta l'ottima filosofia morale, alcuna
volta e santi comandamenti delle leggi, alcuna volta la vera e santa teologia . . .
niuna invenzione fu più bella, più utile e più sottile che la sua trattando tutte le
storie così moderne come antiche, così de' benfatti come de' mali fatti degli
uomini per nostro essempro con si maravigliosa legiadria, che più tosto è miracoloso che umano . . ." (*Invettiva,* pp. 310-311) and " . . . i quali tutti [the previous vernacular poets] Dante di gran lunga soverchiò di sentenze e di pulitezza, e
d'eleganza e di leggiadria, intanto che è opinione di chi intende, che non sarà mai
uomo che Dante vantaggi in dire in rima. E veramente egli è mirabil cosa la
grandezza e la dolcezza del dire suo prudente sentenzioso e grave, con varietà e
copia mirabile, con scienza di filosofia, con notizia di storie antiche, con tanta
cognizione delle cose moderne, che pare ad ogni atto esser stato presente. Queste
belle cose, con gentilezza di rima esplicate, prendono la mente di ciascuno che
legge, e molto più di quelli che più intendono. La finzione sua fu mirabile, e con
grande ingegno trovata; nella quale concorre descrizione del mondo, descrizione
de' cieli e de' pianeti, descrizione degli uomini, meriti e pene della vita umana, felicità, miseria e mediocrità di vita intra due estremi" (*Vita di Dante*, pp. 106-107).

37 Proemio, p. 224.

38 *Ibid.*, p. 225.

[39] " . . . ma non però veggo in che sia la nostra oggi toscana tanto d'averla in odio, che in essa qualunque benchè ottima cosa scritta ci dispiaccia." *Ibid.*, p. 224.

[40] *Ibid.* Compare with the following statements by Dante: "Tornando dunque al principale proposito, dico che manifestamente si può vedere come lo latino averebbe a pochi dato lo beneficio, ma lo volgare servirà veramente a molti . . . principi, baroni, cavalieri, e molt'altra nobile gente, non solamente maschi ma femmine, che sono molti e molte in questa lingua, volgari e non litterati." *Convivio* I, ix, 4-5.

[41] On this, cf. Giovanni Ponte, "Lepidus e Libripeta," *Rinascimento*, 12 (1972) 237-265, but especially 261-265.

[42] "Nè posso io patire che a molti dispiaccia quello che pur usano, e pur lodino quello che nè intendono, nè in sè curano d'intendere." Proemio, p. 225.

[43] *Ibid.*

[44] "E molto qui a me piacerebbe se chi sa biasimare, ancora altanto sapesse dicendo farsi lodare." *Ibid.*, p. 224.

[45] *Ibid.*, pp. 224-225.

[46] *Ibid.*, p. 225.

[47] *Ibid.*

[48] It seems that Alberti visited Florence for the first time in 1434, and he remained in the Tuscan city with some intervals up to 1443. After this period his contact with Florence is limited to brief visits. See Cecil Grayson, "The Humanism of Alberti," *Italian Studies*, 12 (1957) 37-56.

[49] It should be noted that the prologue of *I libri della famiglia* unfolds a Petrarch-like hymn to Italy and its classical heritage: "E in quanti modi si vide . . . la fortuna contro gli esserciti latini travagliarsi e combattere e in molti modi affaticarsi per opprimere e abbattere l'imperio e la gloria nostra e tutta Italia . . . E tu, Italia nobilissima, capo e arce di tutto l'universo mondo, mentre che tu fusti unita . . . e potesti in tutte l'universe nazioni immettere tue santissime leggi e magistrati . . . a te fu permesso constituire fulgentissimi insigni della tua inestimabile e divina meritata gloria, e per le tue prestantissime virtù, pe' tuoi magnificentissimi, validissimi e fortissimi animi fusti pari agli dii riverita, amata e temuta. Ora poi con tue discordie e civili dissensioni subito incominciasti a cadere di tua antica maiestà . . . le barbare nazioni, le serve remotissime genti, quali soleano al tuo venerando nome, Italia, rimettere ogni superbia, ogni ira, e tremare, subito queste tutte presero audacia di irrumpere in mezzo al tuo seno santissimo, Italia, sino ad incendere el nido e la propria antica sedia dello imperio de tutti li imperii." *Opere volgari*, I, 6-8.

Such reasoning sets Alberti apart from other Florentine humanists, especially Bruni, who had nothing but contempt for the Roman empire and who saw Florence as his only fatherland. On Bruni's contempt for the empire, see Mazzocco, "Decline," pp. 250-254.

[50] Proemio, p. 225. Praise and allegiance to the Alberti family is present also in the prologue of *I libri della famiglia*. *Opere volgari*, I, 10-12.

[51] See note 20 to Chap. 3.

[52] *Theogenius* in *Opere volgari*, II, 56.

[53] On *La grammatichetta*, see note 11 to this chapter.

[54] Gorni, pp. 137-140.

[55] Cf. Gorni, pp. 154, 161-162, 167.

56 *Ibid.*, pp. 167, 179-181. Mancini has compiled a list of the judges of the Certame Coronario. Besides the four noted above, Mancini also lists Carlo Aretino (=Carlo Marsuppini), Giovanni Aurispa, Cristoforo Garatoni, Nikolaus Sekoundinos and George of Trebizond. Mancini, *Alberti*, p. 200. George of Trebizond and Nikolaus Sekoundinos should be excluded from this list, since the former was a *scriptor litterarum apostolicarum* at the time of the Certame and became a papal secretary only in 1444 and the latter was sent to Greece in the summer of 1441. See respectively John Monfasani, *George of Trebizond* (Leiden: E.J. Brill, 1976), p. 53 and P. Mastrodemetris, *Nikolaus Sekoundinos (1402-1464)* (Athens, 1970), p. 49.

57 Gorni, p. 166. Luna's *Capitolo* is published for the first time by Gorni. Gorni, pp. 174-178.

58 *Capitolo*, p. 175.

59 Luna believed that the provinces of pre-Roman Italy, including Tuscany, had flourishing languages of their own, which were eventually overcome by the expanding Roman state and its language: " . . . avevano pello adietro i Toscani la loro lingua propria, et similmente tutte l'altre provincie della Ytalia, le quali lingue tutte furono anichillate et perirono aveniente la lingua latina. Et come molti [et] non mediocre eruditi afermano, quegli che in quel tempo habitavano in Latio avevano, et per loro continuo uso tenevano, la lingua latina, la quale, come apertamente si può giudicare, à recato secho il nome del proprio luogho di Latio, prima i Romani per segnio, et per l'uso dipoi, l'acrebbono et amplificârlla in maggiore parte colla industria e colla exercitatione, acciò che dappoi, per l'universe parti del mondo divulgata e seminata, tutte l'altre lingue avesse oscurate et quasi in maggiore parte annichilate." *Ibid.*, p. 176.

60 " . . . avengha Iddio che lla lingua florentina, pello innanci come apertamente s'è dimostrato, pella latina era obscurata, ora . . . pel presente e pubrico certanime facilmente tutte l'altre avançando, mirificamente sarà amplificata . . . ." *Ibid.*, p. 178.

Luna's thesis of the fall and rise of the Tuscan vernacular would not have been acceptable, of course, to Biondo and his school, including Alberti, who believed that the vernacular was a derivative of Latin. However, this thesis may have been shared by Bruni, who had advanced an analogous argument with regard to the Italian cities. Indeed, I would speculate that Luna's thesis is an offshoot of Bruni's reasoning on the fall and rise of the Italian cities. On Bruni, see Mazzocco, "Decline," pp. 250-251.

61 According to the judges, four of the contestants were deserving of the prize: "Certato ch(e) fu, i giudici disono che 4 erano che lla [the crown] meritauano equalm(en)te . . . ." Appendice III in Gorni, p. 180.

62 Appendice IV in Gorni, p. 181.

63 Mancini, who first published the *Protesta*, speculates that this document was written by the then very young Cristoforo Landino. "Un nuovo documento sul Certame coronario di Firenze del 1441," *Archivio storico italiano*, 9 (1892), 326-346. Mancini's assumption is dismissed by Gorni. Relying on much internal evidence from the *Protesta* and on several vernacular works of Alberti, Gorni concludes that the *Protesta* was written by Alberti himself. Gorni, pp. 155-159. Gorni's argument is, on the whole, quite convincing. However, he fails to take into consideration the rather strong sense of Florentinity peculiar to the *Protesta*, a characteristic absent in Alberti, but common in Landino. See p. 90 above and pp. 97-99 below. At any rate, even if written by Landino, the *Protesta*

can still be taken as a gauge of Alberti's reaction to the outcome of the Certame. Landino was one of Alberti's closest collaborators in the organization of this contest.

Gorni appends (Appendix I) a revised and improved edition of the *Protesta* to his study on the Certame. Gorni, pp. 167-172.

[64] "D'amicizia si disse in santa Maria del Fiore fino a' dì 22 d'ottobre 1441 per molti dicitori . . . Dove avendo a giudicare il dono fatto diecj segretarij di papa Eugienio, e non dando il dono a nesuno, seghuì che uno mandò a' detti quessto scritto dove onesstissimamente gli vitupera, come legiendo si vede." *Protesta*, p. 167.

[65] *Ibid.*, pp. 167-168.

[66] *Ibid.*, p. 169.

[67] *Ibid.*, p. 171.

[68] " . . . quando fra voj più che uno e un altro publichò et affermò essere tra' ciertatorj chi fosse da non posporlo a' primj ottimj passati poeti tosscanj?" *Ibid.*, p. 168.

[69] "Fue di quessto (quello che alchunj maledicj disono) chagione la 'nvidia che vi dolesse vedere in la terra nosstra cittadinj quali, similj a' suoj maggiorj, bem-meritando della sua patria churassero la fama, dignità et ben publico? O ffu pure (chome alchunj credono) che, udendo voj essere alchunj studiosi paratj a produciere in mezzo conmedia, et forse tragiedie, voi deliberasstj proibire quessta ottima principiata consuetudine, per quale la terra nosstra molto ne fosse onestata . . . ." *Ibid.*

[70] *Ibid.*, p. 169. And again "Et fra voj si dicie che tanto premio, degno di coronare e sommj et ottimj poetj, troppo sarebbe indegnio premio a nnoj vul-gari." *Ibid.*, p. 170.

[71] *Ibid.*, pp. 169-170.

[72] "Ma dorremocj se forse voi volessj da quessta nostra età quello non volsero quellj antichi dalla loro, prima che lla lingua latina fosse, quanto ella poj fu, chulta, e ssi stettono contentj a que' primj poetj quali essi aveano forse ingie-gnosi, ma chom poca arte. Così i poeti odiernj potranno dirvj: E nnoj per che ca-gione non vj satisfacciamo, facciendo quando a nnoj fra studio et dottrina?" *Ibid.*, p. 172. Much the same notion is conveyed also by Niccolò di Francesco della Luna: " . . . quanto è questo vostro presente ciertamine, il quale, come voi volete tenere a memoria, fu sempre in tanto honore apresso a' nostri antichissimi padri, che per lungho et assiduo uso infiniti poeti ne furono cielebrati, e la vostra lingua latina ne divenne copiosissima, ornatissima e suavissima . . . ." *Capitolo*, p. 175.

[73] As proved by Biondo (pp. 46-47 above), some papal secretaries came to see the practical value of the vernacular. At the time of the Certame, however, the pa-pal court appears to have been motivated by an uncompromising classicism: "E se pur fusse chi perseverasse vituperandolo [the Certame], il domanderemo se quessto fu usato costume sempre presso agl'antichi, quali voi [the papal secre-taries] tanto proponete et aprovate in ogni fatto et detto, che nulla altro può non dispiaciervj se non quanto e' sente dell'antico." *Protesta*, p. 169. Just how strong this classicism was is demonstrated by Leonardo Dati, one of the contestants of the Certame. Eager to win the support and respect of the high officials of the pa-pal court, after the Certame, Dati downplayed his interest in the vernacular. He eventually limited himself entirely to Latin. See Gorni, pp. 150-154.

[74] See notes 60 and 69 to this chapter.

[75] As an example of this resentment, see Biondo's view of Florentine vernacular and vernacular culture, pp. 46-47 above.

[76] See above p. 16.

[77] For a lucid interpretation of the cultural and linguistic implications of Alberti's Italian grammar, see C. Grayson "Leon Battista Alberti and the Beginning of Italian Grammar," *Proceedings of the British Academy* , 49 (1963), 291-311.

[78] According to Dardano, Alberti's objective is to create a vernacular prose that matches the prestigious Latin. In formulating this prose, Alberti overlooks the great vernacular literature of the Trecento and concentrates instead on classical models, especially Cicero. The result is a prose that blends Latinisms with popular modes of speech: "Su questo sfondo risulta meglio l'originalità della soluzione albertiana, che riesce ad accostare e talvolta a fondere una componente latineggiante e una popolare." Dardano, "Alberti," p. 267.

[79] See note 63 to this chapter. Landino recited the poem submitted by Francesco d'Altobianco Alberti.

[80] For a synthesis of this literature, especially as it regards Landino's stylistic and syntactic tenets, see Mario Santoro, "Cristoforo Landino e il volgare," *Giornale storico della letterature italiana*, 131 (1954), 501-547.

[81] *Orazione*, p. 33.

[82] *Ibid.*, p. 34.

[83] *Ibid.*, p. 35.

[84] *Ibid.*

[85] *Vita*, p. 137. The terms *toscano* and *fiorentino* are used interchangeably by Landino.

[86] " . . . fu el primo che la lingua nostra patria, insino a' suoi tempi roza, inessercitata, e di copia e d'eleganzia molto nobilitò e fecela culta e ornata . . . lui molto la ridusse inverso la perfezione." *Ibid.*

[87] *Ibid.*

[88] *Ibid.*

[89] "E nessuno degl'eloquentissimi negherà trovare in lui non solo espresse ma dipinte molte cose le quali innanzi giudicava essere impossibile dirle con alcuna eleganzia in questa lingua." *Ibid.*, p. 138.

[90] *Orazione*, p. 35.

[91] *Ibid.*, pp. 35-36.

[92] *Vita*, p. 138.

[93] *Orazione*, p. 36. Notwithstanding this glowing praise by Landino, Alberti's brand of vernacular prose (a blend of Latinisms and popular modes of speech) had no followers in Italy. "I trattati dell'Alberti," Dardano notes, "indicano una tradizione che poi non fu seguita . . . ." Dardano, "Alberti," p. 272.

[94] *Orazione*, p. 33.

[95] *Ibid.*, p. 35.

[96] "Ma già fiorisce chi [Lorenzo de' Medici], se 'l mio giudicio vale alcuna cosa, sarà ne' primi tra' rarissimi." *Vita*, p. 138. For Landino's allusion to Lorenzo in the passage, see Solerti, p. 192.

[97] "Ma questi [the successful vernacular writers] sono pochi, e più radi che le porte di Firenze." *Orazione*, pp. 36-37.

[98] " . . . se amate adunque la patria, suvvenitela in questa parte, acciò che, come in molte altre cose tutte le italiche terre avanza, così in questa ottenga il principato." *Ibid.*, p. 38.

[99] *Ibid.*, p. 40.

[100] *Vita*, pp. 139-140.

[101] *Orazione*, p. 38.

[102] "E perchè la nostra lingua non è ancora aveza a molti leggiadri et floridi modi di parlare i quali possono e giocondità e gravità insieme partorire, dobbiamo con buona sicurità in questo imitare e' nostri padri latini . . . ." *Ibid.*, pp 39-40.

[103] *Vita*, p. 139.

[104] On Landino cf. Baron, *Crisis*, pp. 352-353.

[105] "Non niego quanto el naturale ingegno in questo [Lorenzo de' Medici] possa, nientedimeno se da' teneri anni non si fussi con ardentissimo studio dato alle latine lettere e alla oratoria facultà, se a' miei fedelissimi precetti non avessi con somma industria ottemperato, non creda alcuno che la sola forza della natura l'avessi a sì eccelso grado elevato." *Vita*, p. 139. Cf. Rossi, *Il Quattrocento*, pp. 321 and 331. Lorenzo was also very close to Alberti: "Tra Lorenzo e l'Alberti si sviluppò una intima amicizia, come tra padre e figlio; e tali sono i loro rapporti nelle *Disputationes Camaldulenses* del Landino (1475) . . . ." C. Grayson, "Alberti," *Dizionario biografico degli italiani*, I (Rome, 1960), 707.

[106] Also of some value is the epistle accompanying his collection of Tuscan poetry that he sent to Federigo d'Aragona in 1476. This letter can be found in Lorenzo de' Medici, *Opere*, ed. Attilio Simioni, I (Bari: Laterza, 1913), 3-8.

[107] " . . . delle quali [condizioni] una o al più due sieno proprie e vere laudi della lingua, l'altre più tosto dipendino o dalla consuetudine ed oppinione degli uomini o dalla fortuna." *Comento*, p. 307.

[108] *Ibid.*, p. 308.

[109] " . . . pare che più presto reservi la laude nella materia, e che la lingua abbi fatto l'ufficio d'istrumento, il quale è buono o reo secondo il fine." *Ibid.*

[110] *Ibid.*

[111] See above p. 95.

[112] "E però si giudica la lingua greca più perfetta che la latina . . . ." *Comento*, p. 307.

[113] *Ibid.*, p. 308.

[114] "Perchè chi legge la *Commedia* di Dante vi troverrà molte cose teologiche e naturali essere con gran destrezza e facilità espresse; troverrà ancora molto attamente nello scrivere suo quelle tre generazioni di stili che sono dagli oratori laudate, cioè umile, mediocre ed alto; ed in effetto, in uno solo, Dante ha assai perfettamente assoluto quello che in diversi autori, così greci come latini, si truova." *Ibid.*, p. 309. On Dante's characterization and use of these styles, see below pp. 154-157.

[115] *Comento*, p. 309.

[116] *Ibid.*

[117] *Ibid.*, p. 310.

[118] *Ibid.*

[119] "E forse saranno ancora scritte in questa lingua cose sottile ed importanti e degne d'essere lette; massime insino ad ora si può dire essere l'adolescenzia di questa lingua, perchè ognora più si fa elegante e gentile. E potrebbe facilmente nella gioventù ed adulta età sua venire ancora in maggiore perfezione; e tanto più aggiugnendosi qualche prospero successo ed augumento al fiorentino imperio, come si debbe non solamente sperare, ma con tutto l'ingegno e forze per li buoni cittadini aiutare." *Ibid.* In other words, he hopes that the same good fortune

brought about by the expanding Roman state that so benefitted classical Latin will be duplicated in his own day with regard to the Florentine vernacular.

120 *Comento*, p. 311.

121 On Bruni, see above p. 35 and note 20 to Chap. 3.

122 Indeed, Alberti regrets deeply the loss of Latin. See notes 4 and 5 to this chapter.

123 While considering the concept of living language in Renaissance Italy, R. Glynn Faithfull asks: " . . . how and when did Italian first come to be considered as something newly created with its own characteristic form?" Faithfull, p. 284. He adds that the concept of "living language" in Renaissance Italy can be understood only in terms of the Aristotelian principles of *generatio* and *alteratio*: "It is necessary to know that of the four kinds of change recognized by Aristotle in his *De generatione et corruptione* another, besides *generatio*, is relevant, namely *alteratio*. *Generatio* means a change in substance, *alteratio* a change in accidents. Not all corruption therefore leads to the creation of something substantially different." *Ibid.*, p. 285. He thus summarizes the various stages of the concept of "living language" in Renaissance Italy as follows:

(a) An early stage in which the vernacular is seen as the primary, natural language existing *ab initio* with Latin as a secondary, artificial derivative. This stage is represented by Dante's *De vulgari eloquentia*.

(b) Italian and Latin seen as co-existing on different levels *ab antiquo*, the former being spoken by the lower classes. This is the position of Leonardo Bruni.

(c) Italian seen as a derivative of Latin by a process of *alteratio* and considered as a corrupt form of Latin. This stage is represented by the writings in the dispute of 1435 of Flavio Biondo and Leon Battista Alberti.

(d) Italian seen as a new creation by a process of *generatio* out of the corruption of Latin. This is the position of Bembo, Machiavelli, Castiglione and probably most of the other early Cinquecento vernacular philologists.

(e) The elaboration of the *generatio* theory leads to the view of Latin as dead and the newly generated Italian as living. This general conception appears in Tolomei's works but the complementary concepts first appear in a dual formula in Citolini's *Lettera in difesa della lingua volgare. Ibid.*, p. 286.

Faithfull is correct as far as (a), (d) and (e) are concerned, but (b) and (c) need some modification. The notion of Italian "as a new creation" does not begin in the Cinquecento, but is traceable to the Quattrocento. Biondo, Alberti and his school, and even the Bruni of the *Vita di Dante*, subscribe to this notion. Among the contributors to the Florentine debate only Valla and Guarino adhere to the principle of *alteratio*.

124 *Elegantiae*, pp. 595 and 596.

125 On the implications of the polemic *lingua artificialis* vs. *lingua naturalis* in the Florentine debate, see above pp. 30, 39-40. For Dante's use and meaning of these terms, see below p. 122. Cf. Appendix 1.

126 On Lorenzo's appraisal of the vernacular, cf. C. Grayson, "Lorenzo, Machiavelli, and the Italian Language," in *Italian Renaissance Studies: A Tribute to Cecilia M. Ady*, ed. E.F. Jacob (London, 1960), pp. 410-420.

[127] "Latin and Vernacular in Fourteenth- and Fifteenth-Century Italy," *Journal of the Rocky Mountain Medieval and Renaissance Association*, 6 (1985), 116.

[128] On Trissino and Machiavelli see also below pp. 108-109.

[129] A complex problem with numerous linguistic, literary, and political implications, the *questione della lingua* has been the subject of much speculation among contemporary scholars. The following are some of the more valuable studies on this matter: Robert Hall, *The Italian Questione della Lingua: An Interpretative Essay*, University of North Carolina Studies in Romance Languages and Literatures, No. 4 (Chapel Hill: Univ. of North Carolina Press, 1942); Bruno Migliorini, "La questione della lingua," in *Questioni e correnti di storia letteraria*, ed. Attilio Momigliano (Milan: Marzorati, 1949), pp. 1-75; Vitale, *La questione*; and Carlo Dionisotti, *Geografia e storia della letteratura italiana* (Turin, 1967), pp. 75-102.

[130] It seems that the only scholar to continue Biondo's train of thought on the linguistic state of antiquity and its implications in modern time was Paolo Pompilio. In two brief documents, published in about 1485, he treats several of the issues raised by Biondo and his followers. However, Pompilio provides nothing more than a rehashing of the views of his predecessors, being motivated more by a strong sense of *Romanitas* (Pompilio was Roman) than a genuine interest in the linguistic principles expounded by Biondo and his school. On Pompilio cf. Carlo Dionisotti, *Gli umanisti e il volgare fra Quattro e Cinquecento* (Florence, 1968), pp. 34-37 and Tavoni, pp. 182-193. The *De Verbis Romanae Locutionis* itself remained unknown from the Cinquecento on. It was rediscovered only in the late nineteenth-century by Girolamo Mignini, who republished it with an enlightening introduction in the *Propugnatore*, 3 (1890), 135-161.

[131] Proof of Biondo's neglect and of the integration of his discoveries in the culture of sixteenth-century Italy is provided by Francesco Panigarola, a famous preacher and an expert in the area of the *questione della lingua*. Writing in the second half of the sixteenth century, he notes: "Fù la origine della nostra lingua volgare (dice il Bembo) insino da quel tempo, nel quale cominciarono i Barbari ad entrare in Italia, e ad occuparla, e secondo che essi vi dimorarono andò ella crescendo: e il modo fù, che essendo la Romana lingua, e quella de' Barbari fra se lontanissime: Essi a poco a poco hor'une, hor l'altre voci, e questo troncamente, e imperfettamente pigliando, e noi apprendendo similmente delle loro, se ne formò in processo di tempo, e nacquene una nuova lingua." *Il Predicatore di F. Francesco Panigarola Minore Osservante Vescovo d'Asti, overo Parafrase, Commento, e Discorsi intorno al libro dell'Elocutione di Dimitrio Falereo Ove vengono i precetti, e gli essempi del dire . . . ridotti chiaramente alla prattica del ben parlare in prose Italiane . . .* (Venice: Bernardo Giunti, 1609), 15. What Panigarola attributes to Bembo is, in fact, traceable to Biondo and his school.

[132] See p. 50 above.

[133] And we might add Renaissance Europe, since, as noted above (p. 9), the issues raised by this debate influenced several important European students of language.

CHAPTER EIGHT

[1] On the illustrious vernacular, cf. p. 29 above.

[2] For the composition and trajectory of the *De Vulgari Eloquentia*, see P. V. Mengaldo, *"De Vulgari Eloquentia"*, in *ED*, II, 401-402 and 405-407.

[3] *Il Castellano di Giangiorgio Trissino ed Il Cesano di Claudio Tolomei* (Milan: G. Daelli, 1864), p. 53.

[4] *Discorso o dialogo intorno alla nostra lingua*, ed. Bortolo T. Sozzi (Turin: Einaudi, 1976), p. 19.

[5] *Ibid.*, p. 20-21.

[6] *Ibid.*, p. 21.

[7] On the nature and implications of the *questione della lingua* see pp. 104-105 above.

[8] *Il Cesano*, p. 9.

[9] *Opere* (Trieste, 1859), p. 59.

[10] *Dissertazione sopra lo stato presente della lingua italiana* (Milan, 1829), p. 103.

[11] *Nuovi scritti sulla lingua italiana* (Turin, 1868), p. 26.

[12] *Ibid.*, p. 28. On the implications of the *De Vulgari Eloquentia* in the linguistic tradition of Italy from Trissino to Manzoni cf. Claudio Marazzini, "Il *De Vulgari eloquentia* nella tradizione linguistica italiana," in Dante Alighieri, *De Vulgari Eloquentia*, ed. C. Marazzini e C. Del Popolo (Milan: Mondadori, 1990), pp. vii-xxviii.

[13] "Sul trattato *De Vulgari Eloquentia*," in his *Versificazione italiana e arte poetica* (Milan, 1910), p. 548.

[14] *Ibid.*

[15] *Ibid.*, p. 556.

[16] "Il trattato *De Vulgari Eloquentia*," in his *Lectura Dantis. Le opere minori di Dante Alighieri* (Florence, 1906), p. 211.

[17] *Ibid.*, p. 210.

[18] "Il linguaggio," in his *Dante e la cultura medievale. Nuovi saggi di filosofia dantesca* (Bari: Laterza, 1949), p. 239.

[19] *Ibid.*, p. 240.

[20] Marigo, p. lxxiii.

[21] *Ibid.*, p. lxxv.

[22] *Ibid.*, p. lxviii.

[23] *Ibid.*, p. lxxiv.

[24] *Ibid.*

[25] *Ibid.*, p. lxxii.

[26] "Il *De Vulgari Eloquentia*," *Giornale dantesco*, 41 (1940), 76.

[27] For other significant studies on the illustrious vernacular after Marigo, see Di Capua, pp. 279-288; W. Pabst, "Dante und die literarische Viel-sprachigkeit der sudlichen Romania," *Romanistisches Jahrbuch*, 5 (1952), 161-181; Alessandro Passerin d'Entrèves, *Dante politico ed altri saggi* (Turin: Einaudi, 1955), pp. 97-113; Salvatore Santangelo, *Saggi danteschi* (Padova, 1959), pp. 131-142; Dragonetti, pp. 43-52; Alfredo Schiaffini, *Interpretazione del De Vulgari Eloquentia di Dante* (Rome, 1963), pp. 137-148; Cecil Grayson, "Dante e la prosa volgare," *Il Verri*, 9 (1963), 6-8; idem, "'Nobilior est vulgaris': Latin or Vernacular in Dante's Thought," *Centenary Essays on Dante*, Oxford Dante Society (Oxford: Clarendon Press, 1965), pp. 51-65; Ignazio Baldelli, "Sulla teoria linguistica di Dante," *Cultura e scuola*, 13-14 (1965), 705-713; Favati, pp. 151-211; Panvini, pp. 37-42; Corti, pp. 60-76; Marcia Colish, *The Mirror of Language: A Study in the Medieval Theory of Knowledge*, rev. ed. (Lincoln:

University of Nebraska Press, 1983), pp. 177-182; and Ileana Pagani, *La teoria linguistica di Dante* (Naples: Liguori Editore, 1982). Pagani's work, the last, most comprehensive study on Dante's theory of language, is quite valuable as a synthesis of the criticism on Dantean linguistic theories. However, in the area of the illustrious vernacular, she subscribes primarily to Vinay's thesis: "Per quanto riguarda le condizioni della nascita del volgare illustre, esse verranno assunte d'ora in poi secondo la ricostruzione di Vinay, in quanto essa costituisce l'ipotesi più valida . . . ," p. 220.

Recently the illustrious vernacular has been treated also by Albert Russel Ascoli "'Neminem ante nos': Historicity and Authority in the *De vulgari eloquentia*," *Annali d'italianistica*, 8 (1990), pp. 186-231. Unknown to me while formulating the thesis of the illustrious vernacular, Ascoli's piece is engaging and stimulating, but on the whole, rather flawed. Ascoli's problem stems in part from an impressionistic reading of the *De Vulgari Eloquentia*, a reading that leads to fanciful interpretations of concepts and terms. For example, according to Ascoli, the *De Vulgari Eloquentia* is marred by an "opposition between 'vernacular' and 'grammar'" (206); "the 'vulgare illustre' is . . . equated . . with a human author, Dante himself" (211); "the 'vulgare illustre' would be the language of the 'aula' . . . It would also be the language of the 'curia'" (219). In the *De Vulgari Eloquentia* there is no opposition between vernacular and grammar. The *nobilior est vulgaris* (*DVE*, I, i, 4) adduced by Ascoli as indicative of this opposition does not suffice. The vernacular is nobler not because it is linguistically superior to the *gramatica*, as Ascoli suggests, but because it is natural whereas the *gramatica* is artificial. At least in the *De Vulgari Eloquentia*, Dante never negates the greater linguistic efficacy of the *gramatica* (= Latin) he had claimed in the *Convivio*. The *nobilior est vulgaris* is a rhetorical artifice intended to justify the treatment of the vernacular. Ascoli's assumption that Dante saw the *vulgare illustre* as his own creation is equally untenable. There is no question that Dante considered himself a major contributor to the formulation of the illustrious vernacular. Nevertheless, he saw this formulation as an ongoing process that had begun before him and would continue long after his death. On this cf. pp. 125-126, 143 below. In the context of the *De Vulgari Eloquentia, aula* stands for the royal palace whereas *curia* denotes the officialdom of this palace. To say, therefore, as does Ascoli, that the illustrious vernacular was the language of the *aula* and "also" of the *curia* is to misread these two key Dantean terms.

28 Pagliaro, p. 496.
29 *Ibid.*, p. 495.
30 *Ibid.*, p. 497.
31 *Ibid.*
32 *Ibid.*, p. 495.
33 *Ibid.*
34 *Ibid.*, p. 487.
35 Vinay, p. 259.
36 *Ibid.*, p. 261.
37 *Ibid.*, p. 264.
38 *Ibid.*, p. 265.
39 *Ibid.*, p. 268.
40 *Ibid.*, p. 271.
41*Ibid.*
42 *Ibid.*, p. 272.

43 *Ibid.*, pp. 273-74.

44 "Illustre (Il Concetto di Volgare Illustre)" in *ED*, III, 365.

45 Mengaldo, p. 6.

46 "Illustre," p. 365.

47 *Ibid.*, p. 366.

48 *Ibid.*, p. 365.

49 *Ibid.*, p. 366.

50 Mengaldo, *Linguistica*, p. 82.

51 *Ibid.*, pp. 84-85.

52 Dante considers Spaniards (*Yspani*) the inhabitants of Provence and Cataluña.

53 "Cum igitur omnis nostra loquela—preter illam homini primo concreatam a Deo—sit a nostro beneplacito reparata post confusionem illam que nil aliud fuit quam prioris oblivio, et homo sit instabilissimum atque variabilissimum animal, nec durabilis nec continua esse potest, sed sicut alia que nostra sunt, puta mores et habitus, per locorum temporumque distantias variari oportet" (I, ix, 6). On *mores* and *habitus* cf. Corti, pp. 57-58.

54 "Nec dubitandum reor modo in eo quod diximus 'temporum', sed potius opinamur tenendum: nam si alia nostra opera perscrutemur, multo magis discrepare videmus a vetustissimis concivibus nostris quam a coetaneis perlonginquis. Quapropter audacter testamur quod si vetustissimi Papienses nunc resurgerent, sermone vario vel diverso cum modernis Papiensibus loquerentur" (I, ix, 7). The notion of the change of natural languages is present also in Ristoro d'Arezzo, who may have influenced Dante. See Corti, pp. 56-57. Ristoro notes: "E 'mperciò non se trova nulla provincia e nulla città e nulla villa e nullo castello che non abia diversi rigimenti e diversi atti e diverso parlare; e trovaremo li abetatori d'una città e deméno en regimenti e in atti 'e llo parlare èssare svariati, che da l'uno lato de la città parlaranno d'uno modo, e da l'altro parlaranno svariato d'un altro; e so' provinzie che non entende l'uno l'altro. E s'alcuno omo tornasse e lla sua provinzia en meno de mille anni, non conosciarea le sue contradie, ché trovarea travalliati e variati li monti, e li valli, e li rii, e li fiumi, e le fonti, e le città, e le castella, e le ville, e lo parlare de le genti; ché en tale loco lasciò la città che retrovarea lo bosco, e econtra; e en tale loco lasciò lo laco che non li retrovarea, e econtra; e 'n tale loco lasciò lo monte che retrovarea la valle, e econtra; e trovarea la contradia svariata e travalliata in ogne cosa, che non la reconosciarea e non li parrea èssare unquanco suto. E queste casioni non le fanno li elementi, che de loro non pono. E nullo omo fo maio e non sarà maio, e nullo altro animale e nulla planta e nulla follia de planta e nulla altra generazione che s'asomellino ensieme, che non li sia quale che svariamento, o e lla materia o lla forma; e la casione de questo si è che 'l cielo, secondo lo suo movimento e secondo lo suo stato, adopara la generazione sopra la terra." *La composizione del mondo colle sue cascioni*, ed. Alberto Morino (Florence: Accademia della Crusca, 1976), pp. 188-189.

As is apparent from this statement, Ristoro views the change of the natural languages in the context of a universal mutation that involves all terrestrial matters. Dante, however, limits himself to the human/cultural sphere. Natural languages, like all other cultural elements, are changeable because they are the product of man, who is himself extremely changeable.

55 Marigo, p. 81.

56 On this see also Nathaniel Smith, "Arnaut Daniel in the *Purgatorio*: Dante's Ambivalence toward Provençal," *Dante Studies*, 88 (1980), 106-107 and J. Cremona, "Dante's Views on Language," in *The Mind of Dante*, ed. U. Limentani (Cambridge: Cambridge U. Press, 1965) pp. 156-57.

57 To be sure, Dante attributes different expressive capabilities to these three idioms with French being proficient in the area of prose literature and provençal, but especially Italian, in that of lyric poetry. However, he seems to indicate that this expressive difference is due to rhetorical rather than linguistic factors. *DVE*, I, x, 2.

58 The diversification of the Italian vernacular from one (*unum ydioma*) to a multiplicity of idioms (*multa vulgaria*) is rendered quite explicit in Chapters IX, 4-5 an X, 4-7 of Book I.

59 See especially I, ix, 10; xi, 2; xvi, 3.

60 On the *gramatica* , see also pp. 27-28 above, 161 and 165-176 below.

61 On Dante's faith in the potential of the Italian vernacular, see also p. 25 above.

62 It should be noted that the *Convivio* and the *De Vulgari Eloquentia* are interrelated. See, among others, Robert Weiss, "Links between the *Convivio* and the *De Vulgari Eloquentia* ," *The Modern Language Review*, 37 (1942), 156-168.

63 See above p. 25.

64 Such, I believe, is the interpretation of "quod in qualibet redolet civitate nec cubat in ulla" (I, xvi, 4) where *civitas* stands for the regional vernacular.

65 ". . . in omni genere rerum illud est optimum quod est maxime unum, ut Phylosopho placet in hiis que *De simpliciter ente*. Unde fit quod unum esse videtur esse radix eius quod est esse bonum, et multa esse eius quod est esse malum." *Monarchia*, I, xv, 2.

66 ". . . omnia que sunt unius generis reducuntur ad unum, quod est mensura omnium que sub illo genere sunt. . . ." *Ibid.*, III, xi, 1.

67 The *simplicissimum signum* of the *De Vulgari Eloquentia* equates the *optimum est maxime unum* of the *Monarchia*.

68 On this, see also Marigo, pp. 136-137 and Favati, p. 164.

69 *Actiones* here must stand for *species* and not *genera*, for, as Dante makes amply clear in his theory on the *reductio ad unum* (*DVE*, I, xvi, 2-3; *Monarchia*, III, xi, 1-3), the *simplicissimum signum* is the norm of the *species* and not the *genera*. One notes a certain syntactical inaccuracy in this passage. Perhaps a more accurate statement would have been *quibus species latinarum actionum ponderantur et mensurantur*. Such a statement would have been in keeping with ". . . quo [*vulgare illustre*] municipalia vulgaria omnia Latinorum mensurantur et ponderantur et comparantur." *DVE*, I, xvi, 6. This last statement describes the function of the *vulgare illustre*, one of the *simplicissima signa* considered in *DVE*, I, xvi, 2-4.

70 "Potest tamen magis in una quam in alia redolore, sicut simplicissima substantiarum, que Deus est, in homine magis redolet quam in bruto, in animali quam in planta, in hac quam in minera, in hac quam in elemento, in igne quam in terra" (I, xvi, 5).

71 See above pp. 124-126.

72 See especially I, ix, 4-5 and X, 3-7.

73 "Nam sicut quoddam vulgare est invenire quod proprium est Cremone, sic quoddam est invenire quod proprium est Lombardie; et sicut est invenire aliquod quod sit proprium Lombardie, 'sic' est invenire aliquod quod sit totius sinistre

Ytalie proprium; et sicut omnia hec est invenire, sic et illud quod totius Ytalie est. Et sicut illud cremonense ac illud lombardum et tertium semilatium dicitur, sic istud, quod totius Ytalie est, latium vulgare vocatur" (I, xix, 1).

⁷⁴ That *constructionis elatio* and *excellentia vocabulorum* are the major components of the illustrious vernacular is corroborated by *DVE* II, v, 3; v, 8; vi, 8.

⁷⁵ On Dante's notion of the essence of the natural languages see *DVE* I, vi, 4; xiv, 2; xvii, 3; but especially I, i, 4.

⁷⁶ For the *vocabula pexa* Dante cites the following examples: *amore, donna, disio, virtute, donare, letitia, salute, securtate, defesa.* He categorizes the *vocabula yrsuta* in two groups: the necessary and the ornamental. He cites *sì, no, me, te, sè, à, è, ì, ò, ù* for the necessary and *terra, honore, speranza, gravitate, alleviato, impossibilità, impossibilitate, benaventuratissimo, inanimatissimamente, disaventuratissimamente, sovramagnificentissimamente* for the ornamental (II, vii, 5-6). For the orthography of the *vocabula yrsuta* characterized as necessary I have followed Marigo's rendition. Marigo, p. 232.

⁷⁷ "Et pexa vocamus illa que, trisillaba vel vicinissima trisillabitati, sine aspiratione, sine accentu acuto vel circumflexo, sine *z* vel *x* duplicibus, since duarum liquidarum geminatione vel positione inmediate post mutam, dolata quasi, loquentem cum quadam suavitate relinquunt" (II, vii, 5). And again: "Ornativa vero dicimus omnia polisillaba que, mixta cum pexis, pulcram faciunt armoniam compaginis, quamvis asperitatem habeant aspirationis et accentus et duplicium et liquidarum et prolixitatis" (II, vii, 6).

For the meaning of the term *vocabula* in the *De Vulgari Eloquentia* cf. Favati, pp. 188-189.

⁷⁸ See above p. 127.

⁷⁹ Di Capua, p. 326.

⁸⁰ "Dante and the Rhetorical Theory of Sentence Structure," in *Medieval Eloquence. Studies in the Theory and Practice of Medieval Rhetoric,* ed. James J. Murphy (Berkeley: University of California Press, 1978), pp. 254-255.

⁸¹ "Et fortassis utilissimum foret ad illam habituandam regulatos vidisse poetas, Virgilium videlicet, Ovidium Metamorfoseos, Statium atque Lucanum, nec non alios qui usi sunt altissimas prosas, ut Titum Livium, Plinium, Frontinum, Paulum Orosium, et multos alios quos amica sollicitudo nos visitare invitat" (II, vi, 7).

This statement follows eleven vernacular examples by distinguished French, Provençal, and Italian poets, which examples are to serve, according to Dante, as models for the *constructio excelsa.* This emphasis on the exemplariness of the modern vernacular poets has prompted Mengaldo to suggest that here, for the first time in the *De Vulgari Eloquentia,* Dante sees the exemplariness of the classical writers as subordinate to that of their modern counterparts: ". . . sembra l'unico caso del trattato in cui il richiamo ai latini non è primario e perentorio, ma subordinato e faccoltativo." Mengaldo, p. 187. In fact, according to Mengaldo, Dante here attributes a self-sufficiency (*autosufficienza*) to the *auctoritas* of the modern vernacular poets. Mengaldo, *Linguistica,* p. 59 n. 59. Much the same view has been expressed also by Cecil Grayson. "Dante e la prosa volgare," *Il Verri* 9 (1963), 10.

I would argue that this self-sufficiency is only apparent and that even in this passage Dante considers the *auctoritas* of the classical writers primary rather than secondary. Throughout the *De Vulgari Eloquentia,* Dante maintains that close adherence to classical rhetoric constitutes a fundamental factor of great vernacular literature. He, therefore, recommends emulation of classical rhetorical precepts: "Idcirco accidit ut, quantum illos [the classical poets] proximius imitemur, tantum rectius poetemur. Unde . . . doctrinatas eorum poetrias emulari oportet" (II, iv, 3). Hence, the poetry of Guittone d'Arezzo cannot be included among the exemplars of the *constructio excelsa*, because it deviates radically from the style of the classical authors (II, vi, 8).

This being the case, I believe that what Dante is saying in this passage is that the excellent vernacular poetry of the distinguished French, Provençal and Italian poets can serve as a stylistic model for the *constructio excelsa*, because this poetry is imbued with classical rhetorical percepts. However, to the extent that the exemplariness of this poetry is predicated on its being imbued with classical rhetorical percepts, it might be most useful perhaps *(et fortassis utilissimum foret)* if the formulators of the *vulgare illustre* would go directly to classical literature, the actual source of these precepts, and make it an integral part of their cultural background. Even in this passage, then, Dante makes the knowledge and utilization of classical rhetoric imperative rather than optional. After all, the modern vernacular writers have never fully mastered the rhetorical refinement of the classical authors. At best modern literature approximates rather than duplicates the rhetorical excellence of antiquity, as Dante believes is the case with his own poetry and that of Cino da Pistoia: ". . . secundo quia magis videntur initi gramatice [Cino da Pistoia and Dante] que comunis est . . . " (I, x, 2).

82 ". . . quod quidem vere paterfamilias esse videtur. Nonne cotidie extirpat sentosos frutices de ytalia silva? Nonne cotidie vel plantas inserit vel plantaria plantat? Quid aliud agricole sui satagunt nisi ut amoveant et admoveant, ut dictum est?" (I, xviii, 1). Implicit in this statement there is the notion of an illustrious vernacular *in fieri*.

83 "Magistratu quidem sublimatum videtur, cum de tot rudibus Latinorum vocabulis, de tot perplexis constructionibus, de tot defectivis prolationibus, de tot rusticanis accentibus, tam egregium, tam extricatum, tam perfectum et tam urbanum videamus electum ut Cynus Pistoriensis et amicus eius ostendunt in cantionibus suis" (I, xvii, 3).

84 In his assessment of Dante's notion of *discretio*, Di Capua notes: "Egli, pure usando *discretio* in senso di scelta e di prudenza, approfondì e sviluppò il significato teorico, riannodandolo a una concezione filosofica, e su tale più profondo significato innalzò l'edificio del *De v[ulgari] eloquentia*." Di Capua, p. 296. And again: "Poichè la *discretio* è inerente alla natura razionale dell'uomo, essa è un dono divino, è qualche cosa d'innato, non di acquisito. Dante le dà l'appellativo di *ingenua*, affine a *ingenium*, cioè *non-generata*, perciò chi l'ha, l'ha; a chi non l'ha nessun maestro potrebbe procurarla. Il maestro può soltanto dirigerla, affinarla, illuminarla . . . ." *Ibid.*, p. 300. On Dante's notion of *discretio* see also Mengaldo, "Discrezione," in *ED*, II, 490-91.

85 Dante argues that because of its purity and elegance, the illustrious vernacular deserves to be characterized as illustrious *(illustre)*, cardinal *(cardinale)*, royal *(aulicum)*, and courtly *(curiale)*. *DVE*, I, xvii-xviii. On the implications of these four terms in the *De Vulgari Eloquentia*, see Marigo, pp. lxvii-lxxxi and Di Capua, pp. 286-288.

86 See above pp. 126-128.

87 By the same token, the vernacular of Guittone d'Arezzo, according to Dante, lacks *curialitas,* because Guittone never rises to the linguistic *genus* of

the *multa vulgaria* of Italy. Rather he is enslaved by the Tuscan vernacular, which is one of the *species* of this *genus* (I, xiii, 1; II, vi, 8).

[88] I should note that for Dante *curia* implies the officialdom of the royal palace (*aula*), whereas *curialitas* denotes the cultural activities discharged by these officials. Consequently *membra* represent the various groups of the *curia*, whereas *simplicissima signa* constitute the various cultural components of *curialitas*.

[89] See above pp. 126-127.

[90] See p. 122.

[91] ". . . hinc etiam est quod nostrum illustre velut acola peregrinatur et in humilibus hospitatur asilis, cum aula vacemus" (I, xviii, 3). Here *nostrum illustre* stands for the *doctores illustres* of the Italian *locutio*.

[92] See, among others, Frede Jensen, ed. & trans., *The Poetry of the Sicilian School* (New York: Garland Press, 1986), p. xxiv.

[93] An echo of this suffering is apparent also in the *Comedy*:

> Tu proverai sì come sa di sale
> lo pane altrui, e come è duro calle
> lo scendere e'l salir per l'altrui scale.
> *Paradiso* XVII, 58-60

[94] On Dante's contact with Bologna see "Bologna" in *ED*, I, 660-667.

[95] See especially *DVE*, II, iv-vi.

[96] This applies also to such words as *disaventuratissimamente* and *sovramagnificentissimamente* where, as has been rightly observed by Mengaldo, Dante engages in "una sorta di ludismo esemplificatorio." Mengaldo, p. 198. Notwithstanding this "ludismo," however, even in these words the basic terms— *aventurato* and *magnificente*—have a Latin root. On the high frequency of Latinisms in the poetry of the Duecento, see Patrick Boyde, *Dante's Style in His Lyric Poetry* (Cambridge, England, 1971), pp. 91-98.

[97] The poetry of the Sicilian school reached Tuscany in the Tuscan vernacular, having been Tuscanized by the amanuenses who introduced it into this region. On this see, among others, Mengaldo, *Linguistica*, pp. 80-81.

[98] On this, see above pp. 108-110.

[99] For an appreciation of Manzoni's consternation, see Giorgio Petrocchi's illuminating study "Manzoni e il *De Vulgari Eloquentia*," *Forum Italicum*, 19 (1985), 273-283.

[100] See above p. 117.

[101] See p. 27 above.

[102] On these views by Mengaldo, see above p. 117.

[103] See above pp. 129-132.

[104] See above p. 111.

[105] See above p. 125.

[106] See above p. 132.

[107] To my knowledge the only scholars to have alluded to this ascending process are Pagliaro (see above pp. 113-114) and Panvini, pp. 38-40.

[108] See above p. 126.

[109] See especially *Inferno* XVI, 73-78; *Purgatorio* XIV; and *Paradiso* XV-XVI. The very term *novo* is used pejoratively by Dante, unless it implies spiritual re-

newal. See, among others, *Inferno* XVI, 73; *Purgatorio* XVI, 122; and *Paradiso* XVI, 95 and 135.

[110] Dante seems to believe that the formulation of the illustrious vernacular is in a state of becoming. See note 82 to this chapter.

[111] See pp. 27-28 above.

[112] On these views by Mengaldo, see above pp. 117-118.

[113] See above pp. 127-128.

[114] See p. 129.

[115] See *Monarchia* I, v, 3.

[116] Pagliaro, p. 496. Going further than Marigo and Mengaldo, Corti argues that Dante's illustrious vernacular is strictly an abstract phenomenon that is arrived at solely through an a priori method. In fact, in conceptualizing the illustrious vernacular, Dante subscribes to the system and reasoning of speculative grammar: " . . . Dante, subìto il fascino della stupenda costruzione intellettuale modista, si è servito della grammatica speculativa come trampolino verso una originalissima concezione del volgare illustre come *lingua regulata* che, a differenza della grammatica o modello universale astratto, può essere insieme universale e naturale, un linguaggio poetico che in qualche modo ha il felice compito di segnare un ritorno circolare a una situazione da Paradiso Terrestre, nel quale la funzione di Dio passi al dittatore Amore." Corti, p. 70. Indeed, "il volgare poetico del *sì* [the illustrious vernacular] si accosta di più a quell'ideale comune di lingua regolata, costruita organicamente e razionalmente sui *prima principia* o universali linguistici di cui parlano i filosofi." *Ibid.*, p. 63.

The modistic speculation and the a priori method Corti attributes to the illustrious vernacular are negated by the concrete reconstruction I have noted above as well as by the fact that the illustrious vernacular is a regional (the language of the quintessence of the Italian people) rather than a universal language, as is the case with the language of speculative grammar. Moreover, contrary to Corti's view, Dante sees the illustrious vernacular as the language of both prose and poetry, rather than of poetry alone: " . . . ante omnia confitemur latium vulgare illustre tam prosayce quam metrice decere proferri." *DVE*, II, i, 1.

[117] On Dante's empiricism cf. Mark Peterson, "Dante's Physics," *The Divine Comedy and the Encyclopedia of Arts and Sciences*, ed. G. Di Scipio and A. Scaglione (Amsterdam/Philadelphia: John Benjamins, 1988), pp. 163-180.

[118] "Horum aliquos a proprio poetando divertisse audivimus, Thoman videlicet et Ugolinum Bucciolam, Faventinos" (I, xiv, 3); "Inter quos omnes unum audivimus nitentem divertere a materno et ad curiale vulgare intendere, videlicet Ildebrandinum Paduanum" (I, xiv, 7). The absence in these remarks of any high praise for these writers and the use of the term *nitentem* indicates, it seems to me, that Dante sees the language of these poets as an approximation of the illustrious vernacular.

[119] On Cielo d'Alcamo, see also note 141 to this chapter.

[120] Interestingly enough, Dante excludes Giacomo da Lentini from this list. This omission may indicate, as suggested by Marigo, that Dante values the language, but not the style of Giacomo da Lentini. Marigo, pp. 106-107.

[121] "Il nuovo stile della poesia dugentesca secondo Dante," in his *Dante vicino* (Caltanisetta-Roma: Salvatore Sciascia, 1966), pp. 34-35. On Dante's cultural politics and on his disdain for Guittone see also Antonio Enzo Quaglio, *Gli stilnovisti*, in *Lo Stilnovo e la poesia religiosa*, vol. I of *Il Duecento: Dalle Origini a Dante* (Bari: Laterza, 1970), pp. 19-21; Giuseppe Bolognese, "Dante

and Guittone Revisited," *Romanic Review*, 70 (1979), 172-184; but especially Teodolinda Barolini, *Dante's Poets: Textuality and Truth in the Comedy* (Princeton: Princeton U. Press, 1984), pp. 94-112 and 175-187.

[122] In effect this digression constitutes the first phase of what was to become the polemic on the poetics of the sweet new style *(dolce stil novo)*. Indeed, Chapters XI-XV of Book I are closely connected with *Purgatorio* XXIV, 49-62 and XXVI, 92-123, the sections where Dante develops the notion of this style. On this see Appendix 2.

[123] For a fuller account of Vinay and Mengaldo's views on this matter, see above pp. 114-115 and 118.

[124] See pp. 136-137.

[125] See above p. 118.

[126] See above pp. 134-135.

[127] See above p. 137.

[128] See above p. 136.

[129] See above pp. 115-116.

[130] Vinay, p. 263.

[131] See above p. 116.

[132] See above p. 129.

[133] See above p. 121.

[134] See above pp. 137-138. Favati speculates that "prima del febbraio 1305 al massimo, sia accaduto qualcosa che abbia fatto ritenere urgente al poeta comporre un trattato che affermasse e illustrasse l'esistenza di una lingua italiana . . . ." Favati, p. 200.

[135] After all, the emergence of regional vernaculars as literary languages was due not to any deficiency of Latin, but to the widespread ignorance of Latin in contemporary societies. On this, see above pp. 122-123.

[136] On this, cf. Robert Hollander, "Babytalk in Dante's *Commedia*," *Mosaic*, VIII / 4 (1975), 77. Rpt. in his *Studies in Dante* (Ravenna: Longo, 1980), pp. 115-129.

[137] By attributing the low vernacular to the comic style, Dante, in effect, contradicts himself. In the *De Vulgari Eloquentia*, the comic style is seen strictly as a median style. It is possible, therefore, that in the fourth book of the *De Vulgari Eloquentia*, had Dante written it, he would have been forced to rectify this contradiction by recognizing the intermediate vernacular as the sole linguistic medium of the comic style. If the tragic style must make use of the *vulgare illustre* and the elegiac style must rely solely on the low vernacular, why should the comic style make use sometimes of the intermediate and sometimes of the low vernacular?

[138] See above pp. 129-132.

[139] These *inlegitmos et inregulares modos* may have included, as suggested by Marigo, the *discordo*, common to the Provençal and Sicilian poetry, as well as the *lauda* and the *trottola*. Marigo, p. 182.

[140] On this literature and on its influence on Dante see Mengaldo, *Linguistica*, pp. 200-222 and Franz Quadlbauer, *Die Antike Theorie der Genera Dicendi im Lateinischen Mittelalter* (Vienna, 1962), especially pp. 150-152.

[141] Popular love, for example, is the subject matter of Cielo d'Alcamo (I, xii, 6), whose poetry is representative of the comic style, whereas trivial matters prevail in the specimens from the vernaculars of the March of Ancona, Rome,

Lombardy, and the Veneto (I, xi, 2-5; xiv, 6), all of which are representative of the elegiac style.

142 The second book of the *De Vulgari Eloquentia* abounds with statements such as: "optimis conceptionibus optima loquela conveniet" (II, 1, 8); "non omnes versificantes sed tantum excellentissimos illustre uti vulgare debere astruximus . . ." (II, ii, 1); and "Si autem elegiace, solum humile oportet nos sumere" (II, iv, 6).

143 ". . . sicut in isto libro [The *Divine Comedy*] est omnis pars philosophiae," says Benvenuto da Imola, ". . . ita est omnis pars poetriae." Cited in I. Baldelli, "Sulla teoria linguistica di Dante," *Cultura e scuola*, 13-14 (1965), 712. On Dante's use of these three styles, see also Lorenzo's view, p. 100 above. Cf. Amilcare Iannucci, *Forma ed evento nella Divina Commedia* (Rome: Bulzoni, 1984), pp. 15-50.

144 This linguistic richness is apparent already in Dante's later poems, that is to say, in those poems written after the *De Vulgari Eloquentia*. "Dante," Patrick Boyde notes, "deliberately set out to expand his poetic vocabulary in these poems [i.e., the later poems], and in fact more than half the names . . . had not been used in all the earlier groups. . . More important still, he expanded his vocabulary to take in not just new words, but new *classes* of words which had been excluded from the earlier poems. . . This break with the conventions concerning vocabulary which he observed in the earlier poems is one of the major steps towards the lexical richness and variety of the *Comedy*." *Dante's Style in His Lyric Poetry* (Cambridge, England, 1971), p. 99.

145 See Appendix 2.

146 On the stylistic richness of the *Comedy* cf. Margherita Frankel, "Juno among the Counterfeiters: Tragedy vs. Comedy in *Inferno* 30," *Quaderni d'italianistica*, vol. 10, no. 1-2 (1989), 173-197.

CHAPTER NINE

1 Cf. Mengaldo, *Linguistica*, p. 241. While commenting on these tercets, Kevin Brownlee notes that "Adam's description of human linguistic behavior provides the final justification of Dante's *new* illustrious vernacular embodied in the *Paradiso*." "Why the Angels Speak Italian: Dante as Vernacular *Poeta* in *Paradiso* XXV," *Poetics Today*, 5 (1984), 600. "Within the linguistico-theoretical context of the *De vulgari Eloquentia*," Brownlee argues, "this amounts to a radical re-definition of the relationship among all human languages. None—not even that of the prelapsarian Adam—is privileged in terms of God's intervention in human history. Thus, by implication, the ultimate linguistico-poetic enterprise outlined in the *De vulgari Eloquentia* becomes feasible in specifically Christian terms. The conflation of the existential authenticity of the Italian vernacular with the 'systematic' authority of *gramatica*, of *Latinitas*—if successfully achieved—can thus claim to be, by Adamic definition, the ultimate human linguistic vehicle when infused with, inspired by, Faith, Hope, and Charity." *Ibid.*, p.601. This "celestial Italian . . . underscores and illustrates the full linguistic implications of Dante's illustrious, Christian, poetic vernacular." *Ibid.*, p. 609. That in these tercets Dante is thinking in terms of a celestial Italian, Brownlee goes on to argue, is attested to by the vernacularization of Latin sacred

texts in *Paradiso* XXIV-XXVII and by "Dante's self-presentation as a successful vernacular *poeta* at the beginning of *Paradiso* XXV." *Ibid.*, p.602.

These assumptions by Brownlee betray a misinterpretation of the role of the illustrious vernacular in Dante's thought. The illustrious vernacular is not an issue in *Paradiso* XXVI, 124-138. By the time Dante wrote these tercets he had all but abandoned the search for an illustrious vernacular. Moreover, for Dante the illustrious vernacular was not a *gramatica*, as Brownlee suggests. In fact, Dante regarded these two linguistic idioms as fundamentally different: the illustrious vernacular was a natural language limited to Italy whereas the *gramatica* was an artificial one common to much of Europe. As a regional language, the illustrous vernacular would have had nothing in common with a "celestial Italian." What concerns Dante in *Paradiso* XXVI, 124-138 is not a celestial Italian but the instability and the evolution of natural languages, including Adam's. That such is Dante's concern is confirmed by the emphasis on the cause and nature of linguistic mutability. The vernacularizations in *Paradiso* XXIV-XXVII Brownlee considers as proof of the Christian, celestial nature of the Italian vernacular are too few in number and too linguistically limited to verify so far-reaching a concept. Furthermore, by vernacularizing Latin terms, be they from sacred texts or classical authors, Dante subscribes to a practice common to Dante himself as well as to medieval vernacular writers in general. As to "Dante's self-presentation as a successful vernacular *poeta* at the beginning of *Paradiso* XXV," it is true that here Dante acknowledges himself as a supreme vernacular poet, but this does not mean, as Brownlee implies, that prior to this point he had failed to appreciate the full potential of vernacular poets and poetry, believing that the classical authors were the only ones worthy of the attribute *poeta*. The fact is that faith in the efficacy of vernacular poets and poetry is central to *Convivio* I and is implicit in *Vita Nuova* XXV. Contrary to Brownlee's view, *Vita Nuova* XXV does not convey a marginalization of the Italian versifier from the profession of poetry: "The writer of verses in Italian is not—cannot be—called simply *poeta* but must be indicated as *poeta volgare* . . . the term *poeta* excluded the component 'vernacular'." *Ibid.*, pp. 602 and 603. Rather here Dante intends to justify the emergence of a vernacular poetic school. On this, cf. pp. 122-124 above. At any rate, even if we were to accept Brownlee's thesis that in the *Comedy* the Italian vernacular eventually evolves into a celestial, Christian one and that this evolution is realized in *Paradiso* XXIV-XXVII, we are still confronted with the thorny questions: why is the celestial, Christian nature of the Italian vernacular not extended to the whole *Comedy*? Does this mean that the Italian vernacular prior to *Paradiso* XXIV-XXVII lacks the universality and timelessness one associates with a celestial, Christian language?

2 " . . . dicimus certam formam locutionis a Deo cum anima prima concreatam fuisse. Dico autem 'formam' et quantum ad rerum vocabula et quantum vocabulorum constructionem et quantum ad constructionis prolationem." *DVE* I,vi,4. On this statement, see also p. 168 below.

3 See note 24 to this chapter for an interpretation of the term *fabricarunt*.

4 On the *gramatica*, see also pp. 27-28 above.

5 To the extent that mutability was inherent in man's primal language, Dante here seems to suggest that the Babylonian Confusion contributed to the diversification of language, but not to its intrinsic mutability. In the *De Vulgari Eloquentia*, on the other hand, he notes that the Babylonian Confusion engendered both diversification and mutability.

[6] Speaking of the relationship between the *De Civitate Dei* and the *De Vulgari Eloquentia*, Benvenuto Terracini notes: "Non solo . . . Dante ha presente quest'opera *[De Civitate Dei]* nel suo impianto generale, ma nel caso particolare vi è qualche consonanza che ci fa certi della derivazione, o come è più corretto parlando di Dante, dello spunto da cui prendeva le mosse." Terracini, p. 241.

[7] *Genesis* (II, 19-20) says only that Adam named the animals brought to him by God, but makes no reference whatsoever to the creation on the part of God of a full-fledged language, as suggested by Dante.

[8] See, among others, Francesco D'Ovidio, "Dante e la filosofia del linguaggio," in his *Studi sulla Divina Commedia* (Palermo: Sandron, 1901), p. 492 and Rotta, p. 197.

[9] Rotta, pp. 183-233, but especially pp. 192-193.

[10] This same principle was shared also by Thomas Aquinas' disciple, Egidio Romano. Egidio notes: ". . . est naturale homini loqui: habemus enim naturalem impetum et naturalem inclinationem ut loquamur et ut per sermonem manifestemus alteri quod mente concepimus; sed quod loquamur hoc idioma vel aliud, non est naturale, sed ad placitum." *De Regimine Principum Libri III* (Rome: Apud Bartholomeum Zannettum, 1607), p. 518. Indeed, so widespread was the belief in the man-made nature of languages that a saying akin to the Thomist maxim became the motto of medieval students everywhere: "significare conceptus suos est homini naturale, determinare autem signa est ad placitum." Cited in Rotta, p. 187.

[11] Occasionally this distinction was attributed also to such well-established languages as Chaldean and Arabic. Peter Helie, for example, one of John of Salisbury's teachers, included Chaldean among the *gramaticae* of the world: "Est autem gramatica composita in lingua greca, latina, ebrea, et caldea." Cited in Charles Thurot, *Extraits de divers manuscrits latins* (Paris, 1869; rpt. Minerva G.m.b.H. Frankfurt am Main, 1964), p. 127. Roger Bacon, on the other hand, bestows this honor upon Arabic: ". . . non sunt quatuor Latini, qui sciant gramaticam Hebraeorum, et Graecorum, et Arabum." *Opus Tertium* in Roger Bacon, *Opera Quaedam hactenus Inedita*, ed. J. S. Brewer, Rolls Series (London, 1859; rpt. Kraus Reprint Ltd., 1965), I, 33.

[12] Francis J. Carmody, ed., *Li Livres dou Tresor de Brunetto Latini* (Berkeley and Los Angeles: University of California Press, 1948), p. 317. Isidore, Brunetto Latini's source, says the following about the Babylonian Confusion and these three languages: "Linguarum diversitas exorta est in aedificatione turris post dilivium. Nam priusquam superbia turris illius in diversos signorum sonos humanam divideret societatem, una omnium nationum lingua fuit, quae Hebraea vocatur . . . Tres sunt autem linguae sacrae: Hebraea, Graeca, Latina, quae toto orbe maxime excellunt." *Etymologiae* IX, i, 1 and 3.

[13] Alessandro D'Ancona, "Il tesoro di Brunetto Latini versificato," *Atti della Reale Accademia dei Lincei*. classe di scienze morali, storiche e filosofiche, 4, Pt. I (1888), 125.

[14] *Ibid.*, p. 126. The notion of a Latin-speaking world that encompasses all of Europe is apparent also in the fourteenth-century grammarian Henry de Crissey: " . . . et . . . ydiomata multiplicia sunt apud Latinos, quia aliud est apud Gallos, aliud apud Germanos, aliud apud Lombardos seu Ytalicos . . . ." Cited in Thurot, *Extraits de divers manuscrits latins*, p. 131.

[15] "Il tesoro di Brunetto Latini versificato," p. 215.

[16] *Ibid.*

17 *Ibid.*

18 *Ibid.*

19 *De Regimine Principum Libri III* (Rome, 1607), p. 304.

20 See above pp. 27-28 and 161.

21 In *De Vulgari Eloquentia* I, i, 3, speaking of the *gramatica*, Dante notes: "Est et inde alia locutio secundaria nobis, quam Romani gramaticam vocaverunt. Hanc quidem secundariam Greci habent et alii, sed non omnes . . ." I would speculate that Dante's view of Hebrew as a divine language traceable to pre-Babel time prevented him from citing it here, together with Latin and Greek, as an example of *gramatica.*

22 It should be noted that, according to Dante, Adam lived in a state of grace for less than six hours:

> Nel monte che si leva piú da l'onda,
> fu'io, con vita pura e disonesta,
> da la prim'ora a quella che seconda,
> come 'l sol muta quadra, l'ora sesta.
> *Paradiso* XXVI, 139-142

23 See above p. 161.

24 Most contemporary scholars believe that *forma locutionis* here stands for a fully developed language: "Ad ogni modo è ben chiaro che Dante vuol dire che con Adamo Dio ha creato addirittura la struttura del linguaggio, il che è assai più determinato di una semplice facoltà di esprimersi per mezzo della parola." Terracini, p. 242. This being the case, the term *fabricarunt* of *DVE* I, vi, 7 ("quod primi loquentis labia fabricarunt") does not mean that Adam created his language ab ovo, but that he made use of an already existing language: "*fabricarunt:* l'interpretazione del verbo nel senso non di 'creare', ma di 'plasmare', 'manipolare' una materia data e già organizzata . . . ." Mengaldo, p. 56. A dissenting view has been expressed by Corti who argues that *forma locutionis* does not denote "una lingua bell'e fatta," but "la 'causa formale' e il principio generale strutturante della lingua." Consequently *fabricarunt* implies the systematic formulation of a language: "la lingua che Adamo lentamente fabbricherà, vivendo e nominando le cose." Corti, p. 47. I concur with Terracini and Mengaldo. But even if I were to accept Corti's interpretation, my thesis on Dante's reappraisal of the Adamic language in *Paradiso* XXVI would remain essentially unaltered, for, as even Corti admits, in the *De Vulgari Eloquentia* Dante regards Adam's language unchangeable and universal.

25 Terracini, pp. 242-243.

26 Cf. "O fronda mia in che io compiacemmi/pur aspettando, io fui la tua radice." *Paradiso* XV, 88-89.

27 See above pp. 168-169.

28

> Ut silvae foliis pronos mutantur in annos,
> prima cadunt; ita verborum vetus interit aetas,
> et iuvenum ritu florent modo nata vigentque.
> debemur morti nos nostraque: sive receptus
> terra Neptunus classes Aquilonibus arcet,
> regis opus, sterilisve palus diu aptaque remis
> vicinas urbes alit et grave sentit aratrum,

seu cursum mutavit iniquum frugibus amnis
doctus iter melius: mortalia facta peribunt,
nedum sermonum stet honos et gratia vivax.
multa renascentur quae iam cecidere, cadentque
quae nunc sunt in honore vocabula, si volet usus,
quem penes arbitrium est et eius et norma loquendi.
Ars Poetica, 60-72

[29] See especially Marigo, p. 73.

[30] For a synthesis of contemporary scholarship's assessment of *lingua nostra* of *Purgatorio* VII, 17, see Paratore, pp. 146-151 and note 25.

[31] Dante Alighieri, *The Divine Comedy: Purgatorio*, ed. C. Singleton, Pt. 2, Bollingen Series LXXX (Princeton, N.J.: Princeton U. Press, 1982), p. 140.

[32] On this see pp. 165-166 and note 14 to this chapter.

[33] See p. 153.

[34] *Latini* is the *De Vulgari Eloquentia* and *The Divine Comedy's* term for Italians. Dante's characterization of Latin as *lingua nostra* in *Purgatorio* VII, 16-17 may have been influenced also by the bilingualism of contemporary Europe, which he transposes to classical time. Dante seems to believe that as in his own time, so too in antiquity, the peoples of Europe possessed two different linguistic entities: a supernational one (Latin) and a regional one (the local vernacular). That Dante subscribes to this belief is proved by *Inferno* XXVII, 19-21:

... "O tu a cu'io drizzo
la voce e che parlavi mo lombardo,
dicendo 'Istra ten va, piu non t'adizzo' ... "

By having Virgil, the most accomplished author in the Latin language speak a Lombard idiom ("Istra ten va, piu non t'adizzo"), Dante in these verses affirms that Virgil, like Dante himself, indeed like all the leading intellectuals of contemporary Europe, is in possession of two languages: the artificial, supernational Latin and the natural, regional Lombard. On the Lombard nature of the language of this statement, see Dante Alighieri, *La Divina Commedia*, ed. Natalino Sapegno, (Florence, 1965), I, 303-304.

[35] Paratore, p. 150.

[36] *Ibid.*, p. 146.

[37] *Ibid.*, p. 152. A somewhat analogous argument has been made also by Maria Picchio Simonelli. "Per l'esegesi e la critica testuale del *De Vulgari Eloquentia*." *Romance Philology*, 25 (1972), 390-400, but especially 395-396."

Corti advances a thesis diametrically opposed to Paratore's. Following the radical modistic theories of Boethius of Dacia, Dante, according to Corti, conceptualizes a *gramatica* that is philosophical rather than historical in nature and that is arrived at through a deductive rather than an empirical method of investigation. Indeed, for Dante the term *gramatica* does not stand for Latin or Greek, but for the universal language of speculative grammar: " ... (la grammatica è, infatti, presso i modisti, facoltà di rinvenire regole universali, ma anche loro applicazione a una lingua che così diviene *regulata*). Come Boezio Dante parla di latino, greco e altre lingue (Boezio: *de aliis*, Dante: *et alii*), per cui ci appare superflua la problematica della identificazione dei vari commentatori moderni del *De V. E.* (lingua ebraica? ebraica e araba?) in quanto potenzialmente da ogni idioma naturale si può ricavare una grammatica, contenendone ogni idioma i principi generali." Corti, p. 42.

While conceptualizing his *gramatica*, Dante may have born in mind some of the theories of speculative grammar. After all, as a young man writing the *Vita Nuova* (XIII, 4) he had spoken of *nomina sunt consequentia rerum*. But, like the *unum simplicissimum* of the illustrious vernacular (see p. 145 above), the theories of speculative grammar may have served as impetus for an empirical inquiry. Be that as it may, Dante's *gramatica* is much more concrete and less universal than Corti believes. In fact, Dante is not speaking of a *scientia grammatica*, as is Boethius of Dacia, but of a functional, regulated language that would facilitate communication among different peoples and different ages. Contrary to Corti's view, Dante's *gramatica* was to consist not of *principi generali* but of material deduced from the natural languages (*DVE* , X, 1). It is true, as Corti argues (p. 38), that the philosophers *(inventores)* played an important role in the formulation of the Dantean *gramatica*, but it is also true (a fact overlooked by Corti) that the Dantean *gramatica* was reduced to rule by the common consent of many peoples: "Hec . . . de comuni consensu multarum gentium fuerit regulata." *DVE*, I, ix, 11. Because Dante believed that the *gramatica* could be attained only by much time and assiduous study, his *gramatica* is not universal as is Boethius', but is limited to a few cultured peoples, such as the Greeks and the Romans: "Hanc [gramatica] quidem secundariam Greci habent et alii, sed non omnes." *DVE*, I, i, 3. On the flaws of Corti's interpretation of the Dantean *gramatica*, see also Aldo Scaglione, "Dante and the *Ars Gramatica*," in *The Divine Comedy and the Encyclopedia of the Arts*, ed. G. Di Scipio and A. Scaglione (Amsterdam/Philadelphia: John Benjamins, 1988), pp. 27-42, but especially Ileana Pagani, *La teoria linguistica di Dante* (Naples: Liguori, 1982), pp. 253-273.

[38] See above p. 167.

[39] For a more extensive account of Dante's treatment of the origin of the *gramatica*, see above pp. 27-28 and 161.

[40] Paratore, pp. 150 and 151. On the uniformity and timelessness of medieval Latin, see also Erich Auerbach, *Literary Language and Its Public in Late Latin Antiquity and in the Middle Ages*, trans. Ralph Manheim, Pantheon Books, Bollingen Series LXXIV (New York, 1965), pp. 121 and 251-256.

[41] See Chapter 3.

[42] "Quid autem prius vox primi loquentis sonaverit, viro sane mentis in promptu esse non titubo ipsum fuisse quod 'Deus' est, scilicet *El*, vel per modum interrogationis vel per modum responsionis." *DVE* I, iv, 4.

[43] "Il nome adamitico di Dio," in his *Di alcuni versi dotti della Divina Commedia* (Città di Castello, 1908), pp. 112-113. Other significant studies on *Paradiso* XXVI, 133-136 are: A.D. Austin, "Gleanings from 'Dante's Latin Dictionary,'" *Italica*, 12 (1935), 89-90; Nardi, "Il linguaggio," pp. 241-246; Terracini, pp. 238-243; Philip Damon, "Adam on the Primal Language: *Paradiso* 26. 124," *Italica*, 38 (1961), 60-62; Claus Riessner, *Die Magnae Derivationes des Uguccione da Pisa* (Rome: Edizione di Storia e Letteratura, 1965), pp. 85-102, and P. V. Mengaldo, "Adamo: La lingua di Adamo," in *ED*, I, 47-48.

[44] "Il nome adamitico di Dio," p. 113.

[45] On this, see above pp. 127-128 and 142-143.

[46] The remaining nine names, according to Isidore are: Eloi, Eloe, Sabaoth, Elion, Eie, Adonai, Ia, Tetragrammaton, and Saddai. *Etymologiae* VII, i, 4-17.

⁴⁷ This reasoning must have been reinforced by Uguccione's rendition of the Hebrew names for God (the source most likely used by Dante) where the first four names indicate a definite genetic relationship and phonological mutation: "El et eli et eloi et eloe nomina sunt Dei apud Ebreos." *Magnae Derivationes,* lemma El. On Dante's use of Uguccione, see C. Reissner, *Die Magnae Derivationes des Uguccione da Pisa* (Rome,1965), pp. 93-102.

⁴⁸ Dragonetti, pp. 85 and 88.

⁴⁹ It is logical that *I,* the most slender of all five vowels in both form and sound, should evolve into *E,* the second most slender of the vowels. The slenderness of the *I* was acknowledged, among others, by Isidore: ". . . ut puta I et O, quarum uni sicut exilis sonus, ita tenuis virgula, alterius pinguis sonus, sicut et plena figura." *Etymologiae* I, iv, 17.

APPENDIX ONE

¹ The binomial *latinus/litteralis* is also present in Egidio Romano: " . . . quod dicitur latinum, vel idioma literale." *De Regimine Principum Libri III* (Rome, 1607), p. 304.

² *DVRL,* p. 198.

³ *Ibid.,* p. 208.

⁴ *Vita di Boccaccio,* p. 679.

⁵ Epistola VI, 10, p. 219.

⁶ *Ibid.,* pp. 216 and 219.

⁷ *Vita di Dante,* p. 106 and *Vita di Petrarca,* p. 290.

⁸ See p. 76 above.

⁹ *DLLD,* pp. 228 and 230-231.

APPENDIX TWO

¹ See above pp. 148-149 and note 122 to Chap. 8.

² On this, cf. pp. 125 and 137-138 above.

³ " 'Noi ti preghiamo che tu ne dichi ove sta questa tua beatitudine'. Ed io, rispondendo lei dissi cotanto: 'In quelle parole che lodano la donna mia'."*Vita Nuova* XVIII, 6.

⁴ We must assume, therefore, that for Dante only a few of those writers characterized as *doctores illustres* in the *De Vulgari Eloquentia* were worthy of the sweet new style school.

⁵ On the relationship between the *De Vulgari Eloquentia* and *Purgatorio* XXIV, 42-62 and XXVI, 92-193 cf. Teodolinda Barolini, *Dante's Poets: Textuality and Truth in the Comedy* (Princeton: Princeton U. Press, 1984), pp. 85-94 and 112-132.

APPENDIX THREE

1 "Atque latina lingua a vulgari in multis differt, plurimum tamen termina-
tione, inflexione, significatione, constructione et accentu, de quibus omnibus
simul dicamus." Epistola VI, 10, p. 219.

2 On Biondo's reference to the *medius modus*, cf. above p. 15.

3 Tavoni adopts this term from Charles Ferguson, who defines it as follows:
"Diglossia is a relatively stable language situation in which, in addition to the
primary dialects of the language (which may include a standard or regional standards), there is a very divergent, highly codified (often grammatically more complex) superposed variety, the vehicle of a large and respected body of written literature, either of an earlier period or in another speech community, which is
learned largely by formal education and is used for most written and formal spoken purposes but is not used by any sector of the community for ordinary conver-
sation." "Diglossia," *Word*, XV (1959), 336.

4 On this document, see above pp. 91-92.

5 *DLLD*, p. 229. See pp. 52-54 for my interpretation of these statements.

6 On Poggio's use of these terms by Quintilian, see above pp. 63-65.

7 See p. 77 above for my interpretation of these remarks by Valla.

8 See above pp. 84-85.

9 On Filelfo cf. pp. 66-68 above.

10 *FPLM*, p. 294.

11 Cf. the bitter Poggio-Valla polemic, p. 70 above.

12 See pp, 70-81 above.

13 On Tavoni's use of Schuchardt, see p. 197 above. On Schuchardt's reference to the Florentine debate, see pp. 30-31 above and note 4 to Chap. 3.

14 " . . . il Biondo può svincolarsi dalla rigidezza dottrinale, e porsi nuova-
mente sul terreno dei fatti: gli oratori, egli suppone, dovettero usare abitualmente
un linguaggio 'medio', non definibile come tale in base alla classificazione re-
torica dei tre stili, ma in rapporto alla capacità di comunicazione col pubblico,
che per il comune lessico poteva ben afferrare il senso dei discorsi, anche se ig-
naro delle ragioni tecniche dell'arte: così come si può intendere una lingua che
pur non si sappia correttamente parlare." Fubini, "La coscienza," p. 534.

15 On this, see above p. 22.

16 See quotation from the *Vita di Petrarca* on p. 34 above.

17 Epistola VI, 10, p. 219. The *latina lingua* of the letter to Biondo stands for
Latin in general rather than the scholarly Latin of modern time, as Tavoni contends, " . . . che col suo presente acronico introduce la perentoria argomentazione
su come in assoluto al volgare si contrapponga il latino: affermazione data come
valida anche per l'età antica, ma evidentemente pensata sulla base empirica della
situazione moderna" (29-30). To the extent that, as I have argued above, Bruni
believed that the vernacular had coexisted with Latin since antiquity, the present
(*differt*) of this statement denotes the relationship of Latin with the vernacular
through the ages.

18 On this see also Appendix 1.

19 On this misconstruction by Valla, see pp. 76-77 above. For the implications of the binomial *latina lingua/grammatica* in Dante and the humanists, see
Appendix 1.

20 On the correlation between Biondo and Guarino, see pp. 51, 55-56 above
and note 4 to Chap. 5.

21 " . . . quo loquendi more duodecim tabularum leges anno ab urbe condita tercentesimo scriptae creduntur." *DLLD*, 230.

22 For Guarino's interpretation of this term, see notes 5, 11, and 19 to Chap. 5 and Appendix 1.

23 On the meaning of this statement in the context of Guarino's treatise, cf. p. 52 above.

24 On Guarino's contempt for the contemporary vernacular, see p. 57 and note 31 to Chap. 5.

25 On Bruni's assessment of the vernacular and on his link to Alberti, see pp. 32-36 and 88-89 above.

26 On Bruni's assessment of the *Divine Comedy* and its language, see note 36 to Chap. 7.

27 On this, see pp. 86-88, 92-94 and notes 70 and 73 to Chap. 7.

28 See Gorni, p. 159.

29 Forced reading of the sources mars much of Tavoni's criticism. Another glaring example is his reading of Valla's remarks regarding the ease with which the children of antiquity learned grammatical Latin. See pp. 198-199 above. Tavoni interprets these remarks as the logical sequence to Valla's ongoing ridicule of Poggio, when in fact, a close reading of *Apologus II* reveals clearly that these remarks constitute a contradiction in Valla's argument. Cf. my interpretation of these remarks, p. 77 above.

30 Much of my criticism of Tavoni is corroborated by Riccardo Fubini. In a recent study prompted by Tavoni's book, Fubini argues that Tavoni's reconstruction of the humanists' literature on language is disconnected, specialized and sophistic: "È per l'appunto questo tessuto connettivo culturale e ideologico che non ritrovo nell'esposizione del Tavoni. Il suo punto di partenza non era stato un rappresentante o momento della cultura umanistica, ma una trattazione eccentrica teologico-linguistica . . . il punto di vista specialistico, quello di un linguista . . . Non sempre tuttavia, come ho premesso, so tradurre una tale indagine nei termini a me familiari di un discorso storico-culturale, parendomi anzi talora che l'eccesso di sottilizzazione si riveli una spia di manchevolezze del ragionamento e della documentazione, quando non addirittura di impostazione errata." "La coscienza del latino: postscriptum," in his *Umanesimo e secolarizzazione da Petrarca a Valla* (Rome, Bulzoni, 1990), pp. 56-57. And again: "Confeso che non so seguire il Tavoni nelle sottigliezze spinte fino al sofisma con cui s'ingegna di difendere la sua tesi." *Ibid.*, p. 71.

INDEX

Adam, 120, 159-160, 162, 164-165, 168, 169-171, 177-179, 253, 254-256

Adamic language, 8, 158, 160, 162-165, 168, 169, 171-172, 176, 179, 256; seen as a natural language, 169-170; and the phenomenon of creation, 170-171

Alberico da Barbiano, 220

Alberti, Antonio, 83, 85-86, 234-235

Alberti family, 50, 90, 235, 237

Alberti, Francesco d'Altobianco, 83, 91, 240

Alberti, Leon Battista, 5, 7, 18, 82-85, 89-92, 94, 96-99, 101-104, 183, 189, 193-194, 197, 200-201, 206-209, 213-214, 234-242, 261; on classical monolingualism, 83-85; and the Dantean vernacular tradition, 85-89; organizer of the Certame Coronario, 91; and Landino, 98-99; author (?) of the *Protesta,* 238-239 n. 63; *La grammatichetta vaticana (La prima grammatica della lingua volgare),* 234, 237; *Libri della famiglia,* 82-83, 85, 91, 93, 237; *Theogenius,* 237. *See also* Certame Coronario

Aldobrandino dei Mezzabati, 147

Amaseo, Romolo, 104

Aquinas, Thomas, 163, 164, 255; *Summa Theologica,* 164

Arabic language, 255

Aristotle, 142, 145, 178, 242

artificial language (in Dante), 27, 57, 84, 143, 161, 165-166, 173, 175-176, 182. *See also gramatica* (= *latina lingua*)

Ascoli, Albert Russell, 245

Athens, 67, 167

Auerbach, Erich, 258

Augustine, Saint, 163-164, 168; *De Civitate Dei* 163, 255

aula (the royal palace), 115, 137, 138, 250

Aurispa, Giovanni, 93-94, 238

Auruncians, 52

Austin, A.D., 258

Babylonian Confusion, 39, 57, 139, 142, 153, 160, 163-166, 175, 178, 254-255. *See also* Tower of Babel

Bacon, Roger, 255

Baldelli, Ignazio, 244

barbaric invasions, 4-5, 17, 39-41, 49, 54, 56, 66, 70, 83, 91, 230, 233

barbarisms, 49, 52, 54, 67, 226-227. *See also* solecisms

Barbaro, Francesco, 219

Barolini, Teodolinda, 252, 259

Baron, Hans, 8, 31, 36-37, 193, 206, 210, 213, 215, 217, 220, 234-236, 241

Barozzi, Luciano, 232

Bembo, Pietro, 104, 243

Benvenuto da Imola, 253

bilingualism (classical), 4, 8, 21-23, 30, 32, 39, 40, 42, 51, 60, 63, 65, 74, 85, 192, 199-200, 203, 213, 226, 257; in Bruni, 21-23, 30, 32, 51, 60, 63, 65, 74, 85; in Dante, 4, 8, 85, 199-200. *See also* monolingualism

Biondo Flavio, 4-6, 9, 13-23, 31-33, 39-51, 55-58, 61, 66, 68-70, 74-

258; (in Ristoro d'Arezzo), 246
n. 54. *See also* vernacular
Navarrete, Ignacio, 209
Nebrija, Antonio de, 9, 209
Niccoli, Niccolò, 86-89, 236
Nicostrata, 52, 195, 205
Nimrod, 162, 164
Nisard, C., 231
Nogara, Bartolomeo, 209, 220, 222, 225
Ostrogoths, 41
Ovid, 53
Pabst, W., 244
Padoan, Giorgio, 214
Pagani, Ileana, 245, 258
Pagliaro, Antonino, 113-114, 117, 119, 145, 245, 250-251
Palmieri, Matteo, 96
Panigarola, Francesco, 243
Panvini, Bruno, 213, 244, 250
Paratore, Ettore, 8, 174-176, 257-258
Pelasgians, 52
Pellegrini, Silvio, 213
Pepin the Short, 219
Perry, John Pearson, 221
Peterson, Mark, 251
Petrarch, Francesco, 32, 34, 47, 66, 87-88, 94, 96, 98, 100, 102, 193, 208, 215, 221, 231
Petrocchi, Giorgio, 250
Piacenza, 121
Piccinino, Jacopo, 219
Pirondoli, Niccolò, 51
Plautus, 18, 54, 222
Poggio, 5, 7, 9, 13-14, 18, 54, 58-66, 68-80, 82, 85, 91, 93, 183, 189, 196, 197-199, 201-205, 213, 221, 224- 226, 228-233, 260-261; disagreement with Bruni on the linguistic state of antiquity, 58-61; on the monolingualism of ancient Rome, 60-61, 63; on the Roman, Spanish, and Romanian vernaculars' derivation from Latin, 61, 225 n. 45; misinterpretation of Quintilian's *Institutio Oratoria* (I, vi, 27), 63-65; polemic with Valla, 79, 232-233; *Disceptatio Con-*

vivalis III (Tertiae Convivalis Historiae Disceptatio), 58, 62, 69-71, 74-76, 78, 189, 197-198, 225, 230, 231; *Oratio I*, 70, 79, 232. *See also grammatice loqui; latine loqui; ratio*
Polish language, 218
Pompilio, Paolo, 189, 199, 243
Ponte, Giovanni, 234, 237
Protesta, 82, 92, 93, 101, 234, 238, 239; cultural politics of (the vernacular vs. Latin), 92-94
Quadlbauer, Franz, 252
Quaglio, Antonio Enzo, 251
questione della lingua, 5, 7, 36, 94, 104, 109-110, 112, 140, 243-244
Quintilian, 46, 49, 59, 61, 63-65, 71-72, 75-76, 196-197, 210, 226, 229-231, 260; on linguistic usage, 64; *Institutio Oratoria*, 59, 61, 63. *See also consuetudo; ratio*
Rajna, Pio, 111, 119, 140, 220
ratio (theory), 63, 65; as *analogia* in Valla 72; *grammaticorum ratio* in Guarino, 55; *lumen rationis* in Dante, 116, 151
reductio ad unum, 6, 29, 116, 126, 128, 134-135, 145, 151-152, 247
Renaudet, Augustin, 209
Rhetorica ad Herennium, 52
Riessner, Claus, 258
Rinaldo d'Aquino, 146
Rinuccini, Cino, 37, 87-89, 90, 98, 235-236; *Invettiva*, 236
Ristoro d'Arezzo, 246
Rizzo, Silvia, 70
Romagna, 47, 48, 121, 220
romana lingua (in Valla; = *latina lingua*), 79, 232-233
Roman Curia, 60, 73, 76, 232
Roman Empire, 41, 60, 95, 100, 237
"Romance" idioms (in Dante), 28, 30, 173-175; *oc* (Spanish/Provençal), 25, 27, 119-121, 123, 175; *oil* (French) 27, 119-121, 175; *sì* (Italian) 27, 28, 119, 120, 121, 123, 127, 175, 251

BRILL'S STUDIES
IN
INTELLECTUAL HISTORY

1. POPKIN, R.H. *Isaac la Peyrère (1596-1676)*. His Life, Work and Influence. 1987. ISBN 90 04 08157 7
2. THOMSON, A. *Barbary and Enlightenment*. European Attitudes towards the Maghreb in the 18th Century. 1987. ISBN 90 04 08273 5
3. DUHEM, P. *Prémices Philosophiques*. With an Introduction in English by S.L. Jaki. 1987. ISBN 90 04 08117 8
4. OUDEMANS, TH.C.W. & A.P.M.H. LARDINOIS. *Tragic ambiguity*. Anthropology, Philosophy and Sophocles' *Antigone*. 1987. ISBN 90 04 08417 7
5. FRIEDMAN, J.B. (ed.). *John de Foxton's Liber Cosmographiae* (1408). An Edition and Codicological Study. 1988. ISBN 90 04 08528 9
6. AKKERMAN, F. & A.J. VANDERJAGT (eds.). *Rodolphus Agricola Phrisius, 1444-1485*. Proceedings of the International Conference at the University of Groningen, 28-30 October 1985. 1988. ISBN 90 04 08599 8
7. CRAIG, W.L. *The Problem of Divine Foreknowledge and Future Contingents from Aristotle to Suarez*. 1988. ISBN 90 04 08516 5
8. STROLL, M. *The Jewish Pope*. Ideology and Politics in the Papal Schism of 1130. 1987. ISBN 90 04 08590 4
9. STANESCO, M. *Jeux d'errance du chevalier médiéval*. Aspects ludiques de la fonction guerrière dans la littérature du Moyen Age flamboyant. 1988. ISBN 90 04 08684 6
10. KATZ, D. *Sabbath and Sectarianism in Seventeenth-Century England*. 1988. ISBN 90 04 08754 0
11. LERMOND, L. *The Form of Man*. Human Essence in Spinoza's *Ethic*. 1988. ISBN 90 04 08829 6
12. JONG, M. DE. *In Samuel's Image*. Early Medieval Child Oblation. (in preparation)
13. PYENSON, L. *Empire of Reason*. Exact Sciences in Indonesia, 1840-1940. 1989. ISBN 90 04 08984 5
14. CURLEY, E. & P.-F. MOREAU (eds.). *Spinoza. Issues and Directions*. The Proceedings of the Chicago Spinoza Conference. 1990. ISBN 90 04 09334 6
15. KAPLAN, Y., H. MÉCHOULAN & R.H. POPKIN (eds.). *Menasseh Ben Israel and His World*. 1989. ISBN 90 04 09114 9
16. BOS, A.P. *Cosmic and Meta-Cosmic Theology in Aristotle's Lost Dialogues*. 1989. ISBN 90 04 09155 6
17. KATZ, D.S. & J.I. ISRAEL (eds.) *Sceptics, Millenarians and Jews*. 1990. ISBN 90 04 09160 2
18. DALES, R.C. *Medieval Discussions of the Eternity of the World*. 1990. ISBN 90 04 09215 3
19. CRAIG, W.L. *Divine Foreknowledge and Human Freedom*. The Coherence of Theism: Omniscience. 1991. ISBN 90 04 09250 1
20. OTTEN, W. *The Anthropology of Johannes Scottus Eriugena*. 1991. ISBN 90 04 09302 8
21. ÅKERMAN, S. *Queen Christina of Sweden and Her Circle*. The Transformation of a Seventeenth-Century Philosophical Libertine. 1991. ISBN 90 04 09310 9
22. POPKIN, R.H. *The Third Force in Seventeenth-Century Thought*. 1992. ISBN 90 04 09324 0
23. DALES, R.C. & O. ARGERAMI (eds.). *Medieval Latin Texts on the Eternity of the World*. 1990. ISBN 90 04 09376 1
24. STROLL, M. *Symbols as Power*. The Papacy Following the Investiture Contest. 1991. ISBN 90 04 09374 5

25. FARAGO, C.J. *Leonardo da Vinci's 'Paragone'*. A Critical Interpretation with a New Edition of the Text in the *Codex Urbinas*. 1992. ISBN 90 04 09415 6
26. JONES, R. *Learning Arabic in Renaissance Europe*. 1992. ISBN 90 04 09451 2
27. DRIJVERS, J.W. *Helena Augusta*. The Mother of Constantine the Great and the Legend of Her Finding of the True Cross. 1992. ISBN 90 04 09435 0
28. BOUCHER, W.I. *Spinoza in English*. A Bibliography from the Seventeenth-Century to the Present. 1991. ISBN 90 04 09499 7
29. McINTOSH, C. *The Rose Cross and the Age of Reason*. Eighteenth-Century Rosicrucianism in Central Europe and its Relationship to the Enlightenment. 1992. ISBN 90 04 09502 0
30. CRAVEN, K. *Jonathan Swift and the Millennium of Madness*. The Information Age in Swift's *A Tale of a Tub*. 1992. ISBN 90 04 09524 1
31. BERKVENS-STEVELINCK, C., H. BOTS, P.G. HOFTIJZER & O.S. LANKHORST (eds.). *Le Magasin de l'Univers*. *The Dutch Republic as the Centre of the European Book Trade*. Papers Presented at the International Colloquium, held at Wassenaar, 5-7 July 1990. 1992. ISBN 90 04 09493 8
32. GRIFFIN, JR., M.I.J. *Latitudinarianism in the Seventeenth-Century Church of England*. Annotated by R.H. Popkin. Edited by L. Freedman. 1992. ISBN 90 04 09653 1
33. WES, M.A. *Classics in Russia 1700-1855*. Between Two Bronze Horsemen. 1992. ISBN 90 04 09664 7
34. BULHOF, I.N. *The Language of Science*. A Study of the Relationship between Literature and Science in the Perspective of a Hermeneutical Ontology. With a Case Study of Darwin's *The Origin of Species*. 1992. ISBN 90 04 09644 2
35. LAURSEN, J.C. *The Politics of Skepticism in the Ancients, Montaigne, Hume, and Kant*. 1992. ISBN 90 04 09459 8
36. COHEN, E. *The Crossroads of Justice*. Law and Culture in Late Medieval France. 1993. ISBN 90 04 09569 1
37. POPKIN, R.H. & A.J. VANDERJAGT (eds.). *Scepticism and Irreligion in the Seventeenth and Eighteenth Centuries*. 1993. ISBN 90 04 09596 9
38. MAZZOCCO, A. *Linguistic Theories in Dante and the Humanists*. Studies of Language and Intellectual History in Late Medieval and Early Renaissance Italy. 1993. ISBN 90 04 09702 3
39. KROOK, D. *John Sergeant and His Circle*. A Study of Three Seventeenth-Century English Aristotelians. Edited with an Introduction by B.C. Southgate. 1993. ISBN 90 04 09756 2
40. AKKERMAN, F., G.C. HUISMAN & A.J. VANDERJAGT (eds.). *Wessel Gansfort (1419-1489) and Northern Humanism*. 1993. ISBN 90 04 09857 7
41. COLISH, M.L. *Peter Lombard*. 2 vols. 1993. ISBN 90 04 09861 5 (set)